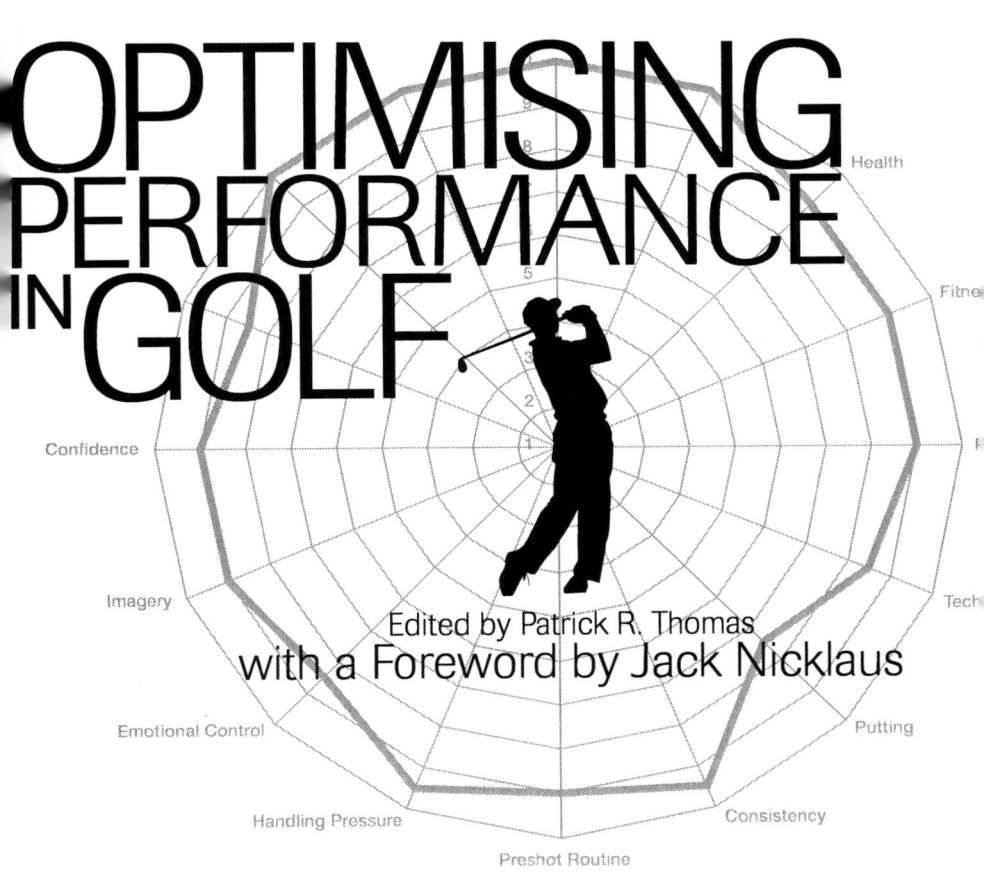

OPTIMISING PERFORMANCE IN GOLF

Edited by Patrick R. Thomas

with a Foreword by Jack Nicklaus

First published in 2001 by Australian Academic Press Pty. Ltd., Brisbane, from a completed manuscript presented to the publishers by the Editor.

The Publisher, Editor and Authors disclaim responsibility for any adverse effects or consequences from the misapplication or injudicious use of the information contained within this text.

© 2001, Griffith University and the authors of each chapter.

All rights reserved. No part of this publication may be reproduced, stored in a retrieval system, transmitted in any form or by any means, electronic, mechanical, photocopying, recording or otherwise, without the prior written permission of the publisher.

Optimising Performance in Golf.

Bibliography.
Includes index.
ISBN 1 875378 37 5.

1. Golf. 2. Sports sciences. 3. Golf — Physiological aspects. 4. Golf — Psychological aspects. 5. Golf — Training. I. Thomas, Patrick R. (Patrick Robert).

796.352

Typeset in Adobe Garamond by Australian Academic Press.
www.australianacademicpress.com.au

FOREWORD

I have always maintained that the game of golf is a "work in progress" for the ambitious player. You never reach the point at which you have mastered the game, because the knowledge and skills it demands are virtually limitless. However, when a golfer has honed a golf swing based solidly on the fundamentals of the game and has developed an understanding of course management, the challenge that remains is to learn how to *win*.

Obviously there are certain innate traits which contribute to the ability to win: desire, self-confidence, self-discipline, being hungry for victory and unafraid of failure — or success.

However, these qualities alone do not guarantee a winner; and it is possible to have these traits as well as a fundamentally superb golf game and still not know the inside of the winner's circle. I maintain there are four vital keys:

1) You must learn to think clearly under pressure so that you can focus on the tasks and challenges of playing the game under competitive demands. I think this ability alone has had the greatest influence on my success.

2) You must train yourself to remain patient so that you do not succumb to judgment errors and hasty decisions that can undermine your skill and derail your competitive ability.

3) You must be self-focused so that you devote your energies entirely to optimizing your own performance rather than being distracted by the competition.

4) You must constantly rededicate yourself to mastering these skills — even more so when you are playing poorly than when you are playing well.

I am sure you will be presented with many interesting and valuable techniques for optimizing performance in golf. I suspect that you may hear these four points mentioned again. In any case, I hope you acquire a valuable perspective on methods that produce successful results.

Good Golfing,

Jack Nicklaus
September 2000

CONTENTS

Foreword   iii

Preface   vii

COACHING AND LEARNING

CHAPTER 1   The Path to Expert Golf Performance: Insights from the Masters on How to Improve Performance by Deliberate Practice   1
K. Anders Ericsson

CHAPTER 2   The Development of Expertise by Senior PGA Tour Players   58
Leonard Zaichkowsky and Kevin Morris

CHAPTER 3   The First Tee: Teaching Youth to Succeed in Golf and Life   67
Steven J. Danish

CHAPTER 4   The Role of Amateur Golf Coaches in Australia   75
Dominic Wall

CHAPTER 5   Golf Professional Training and Professional Development Programs: An Australian Perspective   82
Phil Ayres

CHAPTER 6   The Influence of Video and Verbal Information on Learning the Golf Swing   94
Mark A. Guadagnoli, Al McDaniels, Jimmie Bullard, Richard D. Tandy, and William R. Holcomb

CHAPTER 7   A Laser-Based Evaluation of Two Different Alignment Strategies Used in Golf Putting   104
Albert D. Potts and Neil K. Roach

CHAPTER 8   Periodisation for Golf   112
Peter W. Knight

CHAPTER 9   A Performance History of International Golfers in the US Masters   121
Raymond J. Leigh

EXERCISE SCIENCE AND SPORTS MEDICINE

CHAPTER 10   The Physiology of Optimising Golf Performance in Hot Environments   127
Tom M. McLellan

CHAPTER 11	Golf: Exercise for Health and Longevity *Gi Broman*	149
CHAPTER 12	Aerobic Fitness and Psychophysiological Stress Responses to Competition Golf *John S. Carlson, Jennifer M. McKay, Steve E. Selig, and Tony Morris*	164
CHAPTER 13	How Has Research Influenced Golf Teaching and Equipment? *Robert J. Neal, Eric J. Sprigings, and Michael J. Dalgleish*	175
CHAPTER 14	The Importance of Stretching the "X-Factor" in the Downswing of Golf: The "X-Factor Stretch" *Phillip J. Cheetham, Philip E. Martin, Robert E. Mottram, and Bryan F. St. Laurent*	192
CHAPTER 15	Swing Technique Change and Adjunctive Exercises in the Treatment of Wrist Pain in a Golfer: A Case Report *Michael J. Dalgleish, Bill Vicenzino, and Robert J. Neal*	200
CHAPTER 16	Strength and Conditioning for Golf *David K. Chettle and Robert J. Neal*	207
CHAPTER 17	The Rhetoric and Reality of Warm-up Activity Among Junior Golfers *Raymond J. Leigh*	224
CHAPTER 18	An Integrated Approach to the Golfer's Physical and Technical Development *Ramsay McMaster, Ross Herbert, Sandy Jamieson, and Patrick R. Thomas*	231

SPORT PSYCHOLOGY

CHAPTER 19	Performance Under Pressure: A Little Knowledge is a Dangerous Thing? *Lew Hardy and Richard Mullen*	245
CHAPTER 20	Preperformance Routine Training Using Holistic Process Goals *Kieran M. Kingston and Lew Hardy*	264
CHAPTER 21	The Preshot Routine: A Prerequisite for Successful Performance? *Robin C. Jackson*	279
CHAPTER 22	How Do We Define Success? Differences in the Goal Orientations of Higher and Lower Ability Golfers *Kieran M. Kingston and Lew Hardy*	289

CHAPTER 23 Self-Efficacy, Confidence Judgments,
and Self-Monitoring in Golfers — 300
Gerard J. Fogarty, Chris Graham, and David Else

CHAPTER 24 The Role of Imagery Ability in the Learning
and Performance of Golf Skills — 311
J. Robert Grove, Vicki de Prazer, Robert S. Weinberg, and Russell Pitcher

CHAPTER 25 Preperformance Mood and Elite Golf Performance:
What are the Optimal Mood Factors Before Competition? — 327
John F. Mathers and Richard L. Cox

CHAPTER 26 Cognitions, Emotions and Golf Performance — 337
Patrick R. Thomas

About the Editor — 355

List of Authors — 357

Index — 361

PREFACE

Golf Science 2000, an interim conference of the World Scientific Congress of Golf, was scheduled on Australia's Gold Coast in the week preceding the Sydney Olympics. Researchers, practitioners, coaches and players were invited to share insights on the theme, Optimising Performance in Golf, from the multidisciplinary perspectives of sport psychology, exercise science and sports medicine, coaching and learning.

Despite the superb location and what was expected to be ideal timing, there were insufficient papers for a 3-day scientific program. Many of those who wanted to participate were prevented from doing so because of their professional responsibilities with athletes preparing for the Games or because of teaching commitments — in some cases calendars were rearranged to accommodate the Games and their participants.

This book contains the three outstanding keynote presentations prepared for the conference and many other excellent chapters that together demonstrate the depth of knowledge about golf performance within each discipline; the significant benefits to be derived from multidisciplinary perspectives; and the value of a sound research base for professional practice aimed at optimising performance in golf. The decision to publish an edited book rather than a monograph of conference proceedings meant chapters could be updated, modified and strengthened. It also permitted the inclusion of important work being done by some authors who would not have been able to attend the conference.

Jack Nicklaus kindly agreed to write a letter of welcome to delegates that could be reproduced as a Foreword for this book. We are indeed privileged to share the insights of such an outstanding player. Like Karrie Webb and a number of other outstanding golfers from the state of Queensland, Greg Norman's willingness to support the conference is also acknowledged with gratitude.

All of the authors responded enthusiastically to the invitation to prepare chapters, and those who originally submitted their work for conference presentation are thanked for their loyalty and patience. We are all indebted to the external peer reviewers who must remain anonymous, for their incisive and helpful comments on each of the manuscripts.

Other members of the World Scientific Congress of Golf Steering Committee and all associated with the Trust are thanked for their encouragement and support, particularly Martin Farrally and Eric Thain. Staff at Griffith University supported the Centre for Movement Education and Research's bid to host the conference. Roger Hunter, Marilyn McMeniman and Neil Dempster allowed me to pursue these goals, and Pamela Steele helped turn them into reality. Colleagues who served on the conference Organising Committee: Laurence Chalip, Rod Edwards, Greg Gass, Ian Robilliard, Dwight Zakus, and particularly Dick Roebuck, the Conference Manager, are thanked for their encouragement and advice. Christine Clarke provided graphic design support, and Chris Thomas developed and managed an excellent web site. Ray Over and Gerry Fogarty's highly valued advice is also acknowledged with much gratitude.

Finally, Stephen May and his staff at Australian Academic Press provided the expertise needed to publish this book. Stephen offered the flexibility we needed when originally planning to publish conference proceedings. He remained very supportive when these plans changed and has always displayed a commitment to excellence in publishing standards that is highly commendable.

When Professor Struther Arnott, Principal, University of St Andrews, opened the Third World Scientific Congress of Golf in 1998, he commented that if delegates gained just one good idea from the work presented, then their attendance at the congress would have been well worthwhile. There are many excellent ideas throughout this book. My hope is that these ideas contribute significantly to the development of golf science research and practice, and help all of us optimise our performance in golf.

GRIFFITH UNIVERSITY

The Path to Expert Golf Performance: Insights from the Masters on How to Improve Performance by Deliberate Practice

K. Anders Ericsson

Most people interested in a sport can recall, often with surprising clarity, amazing achievements by outstanding athletes. The performance of these athletes sometimes seems to transcend the humanly possible, allowing us to glimpse the extraordinary. These experiences are filled with such strong and complex feelings that most people are reluctant to analyse these magical phenomena. It is therefore reasonable to assume that these individuals have characteristics that make them qualitatively different. These characteristics allow outstanding athletes to perform repeatedly at the level far superior to that of amateurs and less accomplished athletes in the same domain. It is tempting to explain these amazing and consistently superior performances by inborn differences and innate talents. This interpretation is particularly common for sports such as golf, archery, rifle shooting and darts, where most individuals reach a stable level of performance after months or years of active participation when the actions are elicited seemingly automatically. It is difficult for individuals who have reached this modest level of stable performance to conceive of any alternative account for large individual differences in achievement.

In this chapter I will propose a very different framework for explaining the path to expert performance in a wide range of domains such as chess, medicine, music, and sports, including, of course, golf. The central idea is that expert performance has a complex structure and is gradually acquired by deliberate practice over years and even decades of focused training. When we observe athletes and other experts perform, we are unaware of the many years of training, the thousands of hours that were necessary for these individuals to reach their current level of performance. Expert performance is similar to an iceberg, where only one tenth of the iceberg is visible above the surface of the water, and the other nine tenths are hidden below it. When fans observe an elite athlete perform at a competition lasting a few hours they may not be aware of the over 10,000 hours of practice that preceded this display of elite performance. The fans can only see less than a thousandth of the activity that was necessary to produce that performance.

I will show that the necessity for relevant experience and practice applies to everyone attaining superior expert performance — even the most "talented." In the words of the golfer voted the best player of the 20th century, Jack Nicklaus (1974, p. 204, italics in original) agrees:

> Nobody — but *nobody* — has ever become really proficient at golf without practice, without doing a lot of thinking and then hitting a lot of shots. It isn't so much a lack of talent; it's a lack of being able to repeat good shots consistently that frustrates most players. And the only answer to that is practice.

Most individuals active in a domain believe that performance increases with experience and practice but after the attained performance reaches a stable level within months or a year it becomes automatic and thus seemingly impossible to control consciously. According to this popular view, the stable level of attainable performance is limited by basic innate capacities and anatomical differences which cannot be changed by training and practice. Later in this chapter I will show that these beliefs are incorrect for most aspects of expert performance.

Drawing on accounts from masters and data from scientific research, I will describe types of practice that allow future expert performers to keep improving and increasing control over their performance during years and even decades of sustained practice. This type of practice is quite distinct from the types typically engaged in by amateurs. I will discuss how individuals can acquire mechanisms to control performance even when it is rapid and seemingly automatic, such as hitting by baseball players, rapid movement sequences by pianists, and even the golfer's swing. Unfortunately, some discussion of golf performance will be speculative because the necessary scientific studies have not been published, at least not to my knowledge.

To what extent do individuals' anatomy and basic capacities constrain the level of performance that they can attain? Scientists often try to explain the human body by drawing analogies to machines, such as the explanation of blood circulation by the heart working as a pump and the explanation of movements by coordinated contractions by muscles akin to puppets on strings and mechanical robots. The brain is even compared to a computer where it is easy to modify the computer programs (software) but impossible to change the electronic hardware that executes the programs. Unlike machines, however, the human body consists of living biological systems that can change in response to external events. We all know that the body — unlike machines — can heal itself after an injury, such as after a cut or a broken bone, and that the body becomes more efficient with extensive use, rather than wears out as machines tend to do. The human body's remarkable capacity to respond to emergencies reveals the potential for adaptation and change that might be induced by extended periods of intense practice.

Before outlining the main topic of my chapter, namely the study of expert performance, I want to convince you that humans of all ages, even adults, can alter seemingly basic characteristics and follow the path to expert performance. I have selected examples of large improvements in the performance of rather basic functions, such as memory and motor performance, to show how performance of adults assumed to reflect basic functions can be changed by the acquisition of complex mechanisms that circumvent basic constraints or alter physiological functions.

Scientific Analysis of Large Improvements in Basic Functions

Anytime one argues against rigid limits on performance and the possibility of improvement, it is essential to distinguish the scientifically-based argument for flexible limits from the largely unscientific claims that "anything is possible if one believes in oneself and works hard enough." Scientific reviews of the claims for the self-made man have found virtually no rigorous evidence for self-generated fundamental change and attained success among large representative groups (Ericsson, Krampe, & Heizmann, 1993). The difficulty of changing abilities and performance, especially among adults, has led to the popular view that adults' abilities and performance are determined by fixed innate capacities.

My personal search for evidence of plasticity in adult abilities led to a study with Bill Chase that was eventually published in *Science* (Ericsson, Chase, & Faloon, 1980). Bill Chase and I were interested in whether one could improve the capacity of short-term memory. One of the key discoveries in cognitive psychology is that adults have a very limited ability to remember unrelated pieces of information, especially when they are presented briefly. George Miller (1956) found that the number of unrelated items that could be recalled was surprisingly invariant with the same limit of around seven items for many types of materials, such as letters, colors and numbers — the equivalent of most seven-digit phone numbers. Figure 1 shows the digit memory performance of four randomly selected college students, whose initial recall was limited to around seven digits. All of the participants increased their memory by 200%, to over 20 digits, after around 50 hours of practice on this task and two of them by more than 1000%, to over 80 digits, after 200–400 hours. Analysis revealed that their performance was mediated by acquired knowledge and skills which closely matched the demands of the trained task (Chase & Ericsson, 1982; Ericsson, 1985, 1988). In other words, their acquired abilities tended to be task specific. In spite of the large improvement in their memory for digits, their memory performance for other material, such as letters, remained at their original unexceptional level.

Research shows that the effects of practice are far greater on the specifically trained activity than most people believe possible. The examples from motor performance are particularly striking. A musician recently broke the record for sustaining a continuous tone on a wind instrument. An amateur musician might be able to sustain a note for about a minute. Saxophonist, Kenny G, played a continuous note for over 45 minutes. This performance is easily explained by the acquired method of circular breathing, where the musician is able to breathe through the nose while the mouth exhales air at a constant stream. Just one other example: How many push-ups can a college student in a Physical Education class complete in a row? Around 20, plus or minus 12, that is between 8 and 32. How many are possible after special

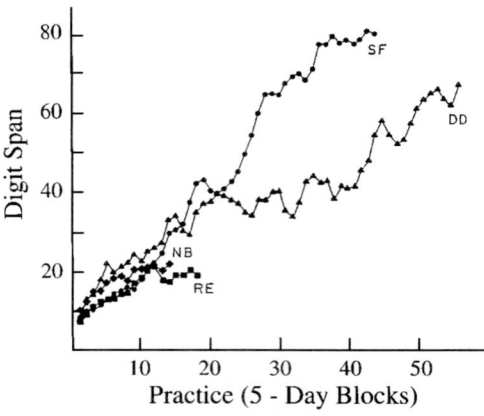

Figure 1

The average digit span for four college students (SF, DD, RE, and NB) as a function of number of practice sessions.

practice? In 1966, the record was almost 7,000, but that has been broken and currently is over 20,000. Even more impressively, the Guinness-book record for one-arm pushups is now almost 9,000 in a row!

The changes in performance on tasks originally designed to measure stable capacities of short-term memory and anaerobic fitness are dramatic. These demonstrations of improvements by 1000% to 10,000% wouldn't be possible if these functions were tightly constrained by unmodifiable genetic factors. Even more compelling is the nature of the mechanisms that mediate these large improvements in performance. The untrained original performance can either be fundamentally changed, as is the case in push-ups, or circumvented by acquired specific skills and adaptations, as it is in short-term memory for digits and continuous playing of notes. It is important to note that these large improvements are very specific adaptations to particular tasks and situations. They do not lead to superior memory for all materials or strength to perform any physical activity.

Outline of Chapter

It is only possible to study expert performance with scientific methods when we can specify an observable empirical phenomenon. Scientific methods, such as analysis and experimentation, require that the phenomenon is reproducible. My colleagues and I therefore limit our investigation to those aspects of expert performance that can be consistently reproduced at a superior level by individuals in competition and practice. In the first section on general characteristics of expert performance, I will first argue that once we define superior achievement in domains of expertise as valid reproducible performance, we can capture that performance under standardised conditions. When we constrain our claims to this type of reproducibly superior performance then an interpretable picture of findings emerges. For example, I will show that even the performance of the most skilled practitioners develops gradually and, with rare exception, takes at least 10 years of active involvement within a domain to reach an international level (Ericsson, 1996, 1997, 1998; Ericsson & Charness, 1994; Ericsson, Krampe, & Tesch-Römer, 1993; Ericsson & Lehmann, 1996). However, the vast majority of amateurs active in domains of expertise such as golf and tennis show minimal performance improvements even after decades of participation. The first section will be concluded with a discussion of the difference between mere participation in domain-related activities and activities designed to improve performance — deliberate practice. In the second section of my chapter I will for the first time apply the expert performance framework to capture expert performance in golf and discuss how it might be acquired through training. The final section of the chapter will integrate the new findings from golf with more extensively studied domains of expertise and discuss the development of golf performance in a life-span perspective and the cognitive mechanisms mediating deliberate practice.

The Scientific Study of Expert Performance

Many of the most amazing accomplishments, such as those by the famous musician, Paganini, and the famous mathematician, Gauss, refer to events that cannot be independently verified and are likely to reflect distortions and misunderstandings (Ericsson, 1996, 1997, 1998). Outstanding sports achievements are often performed in front of large audiences and their authenticity is not in question. However, would these athletes be able to reproduce their exceptional achievement repeatedly? For example, would a golfer be able to sink a decisive 40-foot putt in the championship again and again, if given the opportunity to make the same putt several times? Only those aspects that can be reliably regenerated can be explained by stable attributes of the expert performer. To study exceptional achievement scientifically, it is necessary that we distinguish astonishing anecdotes and singular successes from empirical evidence reflecting stable phenomena that can be independently verified and reproduced under controlled circumstances. Reviews (Ericsson & Lehmann, 1996; Ericsson & Smith, 1991) show that restricting research to this clearly defined empirical evidence yields an orderly and consistent body of knowledge.

In most domains of expertise, individuals have been interested in assessing the level of reproducible performance under fair and controlled circumstances. Most competitions in sports are highly standardised and even approach the level of rigorous control of laboratory studies of performance. In a similar manner, musicians, dancers, and chess players perform under controlled conditions during competitions and tournaments. Individuals who display superior performance from competition to competition meet the standards of reproducible superior performance. In golf, the number of strokes necessary to complete one or more rounds of an 18-hole golf course differs reliably between golf players. This measure of golf ability is related to aspects of components of golf playing in tournaments, such as the average accuracy and distance of drives and average number of putts for amateurs (Reddy, 1990; Riccio, 1990; Thomas & Over, 1994a) and professionals (Belkin et al., 1994; Rotella & Boutcher, 1990).

Is it reasonable to extend the concept of expertise to any domain of activity where individuals become increasingly experienced and knowledgeable, as the pioneering researchers of expertise (Chase & Simon, 1973; Glaser & Chi, 1988) had proposed? As a first step to identify reproducible performance, Ericsson and Smith (1991) discussed how various types of professional expertise could be measured by performance under comparable conditions. Recent reviews show that only experts in certain domains perform at a consistently superior level to less experienced individuals (Ericsson & Lehmann, 1996). For example, highly experienced psychotherapists are not more successful in treatment of patients than novice therapists (Dawes, 1994) and stock-market experts and bankers were not able to forecast stock prices better than university teachers and students (Stael von Holstein, 1972). If we are interested in understanding the structure and acquisition of excellence in the representative activities that define expertise in a given domain, we need to restrict ourselves to domains in which experts exhibit objectively superior performance.

If expert performers can reliably reproduce their performance in public, it is likely that they could do the same during training, and even under laboratory conditions, a finding confirmed by recent research (Ericsson & Lehmann, 1996). Unfortunately, the conditions of naturally occurring expert performance are quite complex and frequently differ markedly across domains. For example, musicians are allowed to select their own pieces of music for their performance, the sequence of moves that chess players make in a game is never the same and the exact sequence of shots required by different golfers playing the same course in a tournament will differ considerably.

Capturing Expert Performance under Standardised Controlled Conditions

Is it possible to present all performers with the same set of tasks or situations so their performance can be directly compared? Ericsson and Smith (1991) proposed that the naturally occurring performance should first be analysed to identify critical activities that capture expertise in the domain. Next, representative situations should be identified and performers be instructed to perform the associated tasks. Once the tasks that represent typical demands in the domain are recognised, it should be possible to reproduce expert performance under controlled laboratory conditions so that investigators can identify the responsible mediating mechanisms.

Figure 2 illustrates three types of tasks believed to capture the essence of expertise, where the measured performance is closely related to the level of naturally occurring performance. First, when studying chess expertise, players at different skill levels are asked to find the best move for chess positions that have been selected from chess games between masters but would still be unfamiliar to the tested players. Any chess player who can select consistently better chess moves than other chess players for virtually any chess position would almost by definition have to be a superior chess player. Secondly, given that expertise in typing should generalise to any type of material, we can simply give all typists the same text material and ask them to type it accurately as fast as possible. Lastly, when studying music expertise, we need to confront the problem that the expert musicians typically perform pieces of music that are too difficult for less accomplished musicians to master. It is possible to instruct all musicians to play familiar or unfamiliar pieces of lower difficulty, then ask them to repeat their performance. When musicians are instructed to repeat their original performance, experts can do it with much less deviation than less skilled musicians, thus exhibiting greater control over their performance.

When capturing golf expertise, it should be possible to present golfers of different ability with a series of the same ball placements on a course and ask them to execute each of these shots several times. In each of these tasks the golfer has to decide how and where to hit the golf ball before actually striking it, a task which relies on both cognitive and perceptual-motor abilities. Golfers differ in where they aim the golf ball as well as in their execution of the actual shot. Consequently, if we want to assess golfers' control over their shots, we should assess their variability and control over specified shots. For example, Hill, Ericsson, and Watson (1999) asked golf players to perform an even simpler task, namely reproducing the same putting stroke many times, and found that expert golfers were much less variable than golfers with higher handicaps. To determine some of the cognitive factors mediating the

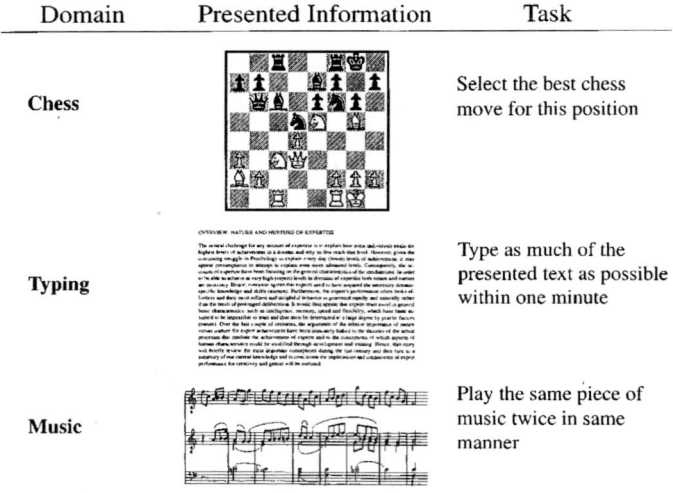

Figure 2

Three examples of laboratory tasks that capture the consistently superior performance of domain experts in chess, typing and music. (From "Expertise," by K. A. Ericsson & Andreas C. Lehmann, 1999, *Encyclopedia of Creativity*. Copyright by Academic Press.)

preparation of a specific shot, we might also ask the golfers to indicate where they are aiming the golf ball and its projected trajectory toward the intended target (Hill et al., 1999).

When we consider only the superior reproducible performance of experts, it is possible to identify several claims about expertise that generalise across domains. Next, I will show that expert performance is primarily acquired, and that extensive domain-related experience is necessary but not sufficient for its development.

The Necessity of Domain-Specific Experience and Practice

Recent reviews of the development of expert performance in a wide range of domains of expertise (Ericsson, 1996; Ericsson & Lehmann, 1996) show that extended engagement in domain-related activities is necessary to attain expert performance in that domain. There are several types of evidence for the necessity of domain-specific experience. First, when performance is measured under the same test conditions over years and decades, performance is found to improve gradually, as illustrated in Figure 3. There is no evidence for abrupt changes in the reproducible performance from one time to the next. Even the performance of child prodigies in music and chess, whose performance is vastly superior to that of their peers, shows gradual, steady improvement over time when measured by adult standards.

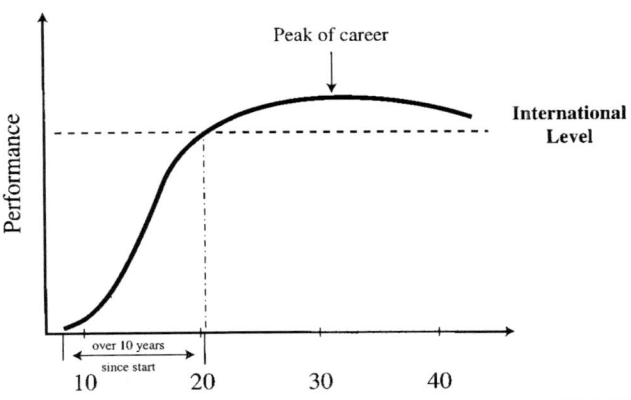

Figure 3
An illustration of the gradual increases in expert performance as a function of age, in domains such as chess. The international level, which is attained after more than around 10 years of involvement in the domain, is indicated by the horizontal dashed line. (From "Expertise," by K. A. Ericsson & Andreas C. Lehmann, 1999, *Encyclopedia of Creativity*. Copyright by Academic Press.)

Similarly, outstanding, "talented" swimmers, tennis players, musicians, and chess players frequently start at very young ages. Parents often encourage their children to begin practice in some domains as early as 3 or 4 years of age, with average starting ages for the most elite performers of around 6 years of age (Ericsson, Krampe, & Tesch-Römer, 1993). An analysis of the top nine golf players voted the best of the 20th century (based on the average ages given in Barkow & Barrett, 1998, and Goodner, 1978) gave a mean starting age of 8.8 years. When young elite performers from all these domains first participate in competitions with adult standards as adolescents, their high level of initial achievement must, at least in large part, reflect the results of many years of intense involvement and practice. Later in this chapter I will discuss evidence suggesting that early experience and practice in domains, especially those involving perceptual-motor activities, might induce physiological and anatomical changes that will facilitate the level of performance that can be attained in adulthood.

If elite performance were limited primarily by the functional capacity of the body and brain, one would expect performance to peak around the age of physical maturation — the late teens in industrialised countries. However, experts' best performances are often observed many years, or even decades, later, as illustrated in Figure 3. The age at which performers typically reach their highest level of performance in many vigorous sports is the mid- to late 20s; for fine-motor athletic activities and the arts and science, it is a decade later, in the 30s and 40s (Lehman, 1953; Schulz & Curnow, 1988). It is generally assumed that skilled aspects of performance improve with experience until these benefits are offset by inevitable decrements in the physiological capacities due to increased age (Schulz, Musa, Staszewski, & Siegler, 1994). The peak performance of elite golfers is generally observed when they are in their 30s (Schulz & Curnow, 1988). However, the age-related decrements in performance of elite athletes, especially professional golfers, are remarkably small (Ericsson, 1990; Spirduso, 1995).[1] When the golf performance of the top 10 players from the PGA and Senior PGA tour, respectively, were compared, the differences in all categories, including driving and percent greens in regulation, were found to be remarkably small (Spirduso, 1995). In fact, at the age of 50, Raymond Floyd won the Doral Ryder Open tournament in 1992. More recent laboratory studies of performers with maintained expert performance, such as expert pianists in their 60s (Krampe & Ericsson, 1996), have raised doubt about the explanations based on inevitable aging decrements, which I will return to later in my chapter.

Finally, the most compelling evidence for the role of vast experience in expertise is that even the most "talented" need around 10 years of intense involvement before they reach an international level, and for most individuals it takes considerably longer. Simon and Chase (1973) originally proposed the 10-year rule, showing that no modern chess master had reached the international level in less than approximately 10 years of playing. Subsequent reviews show that the 10-year rule extends to music composition, as well as to sports, science, and the arts (Ericsson, Krampe, & Tesch-Römer, 1993). An informal analysis of the top nine golfers of the 20th century (Barkow & Barrett, 1998) showed that they won their first international competition at around 25 years of age, which, on the average, was almost 16 years after they started golfing. Gary Player was the only player in this group to achieve international success in less than 10 years — it took him 7 years. However, Gary Player started playing golf unusually late, at age 15 (Barkow & Barrett, 1998). It is likely that his early involvement in "cricket, rugby, soccer, track, swimming, and diving" (Barkow & Barrett, 1998, p. 147) contributed significantly to his unusually rapid acquisition of golf performance. In sum, the fact that prolonged engagement in specific, domain-related activities is necessary to acquiring expertise is well established. Most importantly, given that very few individuals sustain a full commitment toward reaching one's highest level of performance in a sport for more than a few months, much less years, the rest of us will never know the upper limit of our performance.

Extensive domain experience is clearly a prerequisite for the select group of elite individuals who reach very high levels. On the other hand, extensive experience is necessary but not sufficient. For example, once the necessary training has been completed the length of professional experience has often been found to be a weak predictor of performance in representative professional activities, such as medical diagnosis (Norman, Coblentz, Brooks, & Babcook, 1992; Schmidt, Norman, & Boshuizen, 1990), auditing (Bedard & Chi, 1993; Bonner & Pennington, 1991), text editing (Rosson, 1985), and judgment and decision making (Camerer & Johnson, 1991; Shanteau & Stewart, 1992). Furthermore, consider the stability of the modest performance of recreational golfers, tennis players and skiers even after decades of active involvement in the domain. A more detailed study of the differences in the development of elite and amateur performers reveals differences in the particular types of domain-related activities they engage in.

Bloom's (1985) retrospective interviews of international-level performers in many domains show that elite performers are typically introduced to their future domain in a playful manner. As soon as they enjoy the activity and show promise compared to their peers in the local school or neighborhood, they are encouraged to seek out a teacher and initiate regular practice. Bloom and his colleagues have shown the importance of access to the best training environments and the most qualified teachers. The parents of the future elite performers spent large sums of money for teachers and equipment, and devote considerable time to escorting their child to training and weekend competitions. In some cases, the performer and their family even relocate to be closer to the teacher and the training facilities. Bloom (1985) has argued that access to the best training resources was necessary to reach the highest levels, but obviously not sufficient.

Given the limited opportunities available to work with the best teachers and training resources, only the individuals perceived to have the most promise for success are admitted at each stage. Could it be that superior training resources do not really enhance the rate of improvement, and that highly selected individuals would improve just as well by themselves? The best single source of evidence for the value of current training methods comes from historical comparisons (Ericsson, Krampe, & Tesch-Römer, 1993; Lehmann & Ericsson, 1998). The most dramatic improvements in the level of performance over historical time are found in sports. In some events there have been only very minor changes in rules and equipment over time, which allows us to infer that increases in performance reflect genuine increase in the elite performers' ability and skill. For example, in the marathon and swimming events, many serious amateurs of today could easily beat the gold medal winners of the early Olympic games. Furthermore, after the IVth Olympic Games in 1908, they almost prohibited the double somersault in dives because they believed that these dives were so dangerous that no human would ever be able to control them. Similarly, some music compositions deemed nearly impossible to play in the 19th century have become part of the standard repertoire today. In golf, large increases in elite performance have also been documented. During the last 100 years the number of strokes in the British Open have been reduced by almost 10 strokes per round (Hale & Hale, 1999). Changes in golf clubs, balls, and course management may explain part of these changes but much of the improvements in golf performance are clearly due to other sources, such as training and practice. In sum, large improvements in performance over the last centuries imply that expert performers do not automatically reach their highest level. Furthermore, large increases in performance that cannot be attributed to improved equipment implicate better and more extensive training.

If the best individuals in a discipline already differ from other individuals at the start of training with master teachers and coaches, how can we explain these differences in performance prior to this advanced level? To determine which activities could improve performance development prior to advanced training, we should first consider which conditions facilitate effective learning and performance improvement. A century of laboratory research has revealed that learning is most effective when it includes explicit goals, such as improving a specific aspect of performance; feedback that compares the actual to the desired performance; and opportunities for repetition, so the desired level of performance can be achieved.

In an attempt to assess the role of practice in attaining very high levels of performance my colleagues and I (Ericsson, Krampe, & Tesch-Römer, 1993) searched for a domain where the techniques for training outstanding performers have been refined over a long period of time. We selected the domain of music because historically music training of expert musicians has started at relatively young ages (often around 5 to 7 years), and has for many centuries been conducted by professional teachers who developed training methods and improved pedagogy. Based on interviews with expert violinists at the music academy in Berlin, we identified activities for which we could trace the duration of the music students' engagement during the period prior to their entry in the music academy. We were particularly interested in those activities that had been specifically designed to improve performance. When individuals engage in these activities with full concentration we call these activities deliberate practice. A good opportunity for deliberate practice is the music students' solitary practice in which they can work to master specific goals determined by their music teacher at weekly lessons. We were able to compare the time use among several groups of musicians differing in their level of music performance, based on daily diaries and retrospective estimates. Even among these expert groups we were able to find that the most accomplished musicians had spent more time in activities offering opportunities for deliberate practice during their development (see Figure 4) and that these differences were reliably observable before their admittance to the academy at around age 18. By the age of 20, the best musicians had spent over 10,000 hours practising, which is 2,500 and 5,000 hours more than two less accomplished groups of expert musicians, respectively, and 8,000 hours more than amateur pianists of the same age (Krampe & Ericsson, 1996).

Several studies and reviews have found a consistent relation between performance level and the amount of activities offering opportunities for deliberate practice in chess (Charness, Krampe, & Mayr, 1996), sports (Helsen, Starkes, & Hodges, 1998; Hodges & Starkes, 1996; Starkes et al., 1996) and music (Krampe & Ericsson, 1996; Lehmann & Ericsson, 1996; Sloboda, 1996). The concept of deliberate practice also accounts for many earlier findings in other domains (Ericsson & Lehmann, 1996), as well as for the results from the rare longitudinal studies of elite performers (Schneider, 1993).

The Distinctive Characteristics of Deliberate Practice

Many people find it difficult to believe that expert performance can result from practice, because of their conceptions of practice which differs

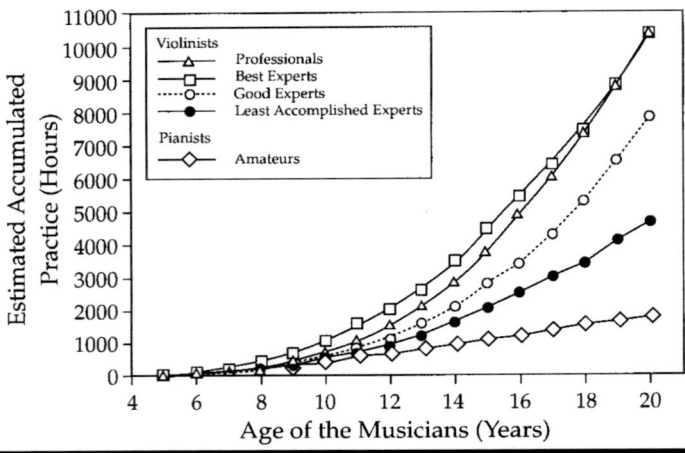

Figure 4
Estimated amount of time for solitary practice as a function of age for the middle-aged *professional* violinists (triangles), the *best* expert violinists (squares), the *good* expert violinists (empty circles), the *least accomplished* expert violinists (filled circles) and *amateur* pianists (diamonds). (From "The role of deliberate practice in the acquisition of expert performance," by K. A. Ericsson, R. Th. Krampe & C. Tesch-Römer, 1993, *Psychological Review, 100*(3), p. 379 and p. 384. Copyright 1993 by American Psychological Association. Adapted with permission.)

markedly from our definition of deliberate practice. When most people imagine a child practising the piano, they tend to think of someone mindlessly repeating the same short piece, while the sound remains unmusical, aversive, and without any noticeable improvement. Nobody could seriously argue that poor or mediocre piano students could become outstanding musicians merely by spending more time on this type of mechanical practice. Mindless repetition is the direct opposite of deliberate practice, when individuals concentrate on actively trying to go beyond their current abilities. Consistent with the mental demands of problem solving and other types of learning, deliberate practice is done in limited periods of intense concentration. Diaries of the expert musicians revealed that they only engaged in practice without rest for around an hour and they preferred to practise early in the morning when their minds were fresh (Ericsson, Krampe, & Tesch-Römer, 1993). Even more interesting, the best expert musicians were found to practise, on the average, the same amount every day, including weekends, and the amount of practice never consistently exceeded 4 to 5 hours per day. The experts told us during interviews that it was primarily their ability to sustain the concentration necessary for deliberate practice that limited their hours of practice. And their diaries reveal that the more the experts practised, the more time they spent resting and sleeping — the increased sleep was primarily in the form of afternoon naps. Our review of other research (Ericsson, Krampe, & Tesch-Römer, 1993) showed that deliberate practice or similarly demanding activities by elite performers was limited to 4–5 hours per day for a wide range of domains of expertise. For instance, famous authors restricted the amount of daily writing to around four hours in the morning and they spent the rest of the day recuperating. Furthermore, unless the daily levels of practice were restricted, such that subsequent rest and nighttime sleep allowed the individual to restore their equilibrium, individuals would encounter overtraining injuries, and eventually incapacitating "burnout" (Ericsson, Krampe, & Tesch-Römer, 1993).

Do the best performers in a domain also need deliberate practice to perfect their skills, or are they fundamentally different? Do they make better — and different — use of the same training activities than their less "talented" peers? Fortunately, many of the famous musicians and acclaimed music teachers have been interviewed about the structure of their practice, so we have the perspective gained from their experience. Their answers are remarkably consistent (Ericsson, in press) and are eloquently summarised by one of the best-known violin teachers and virtuosi, Emil Sauer (1913, p. 238):

> One hour of concentrated practice with the mind fresh and the body rested is better than four hours of dissipated practice with the mind stale and the body tired.... I find in my own daily practice that it is best for me to practise two hours in the morning and then two hours later in the day. When I am finished with two hours of hard study I am exhausted from close concentration. I have also noted that any time over this period is wasted.

It is clear that the need for specific types of practice, such as etudes and scales, diminishes for musicians who have already attained technical mastery, but not the need for deliberate practice in mastering new pieces: "With the limited time I have practice nowadays, I apply myself immediately to works that I am preparing" (Katims, 1972, p. 238). Many elite musicians are able to engage in mental practice: "I have a favorite silent study that I do all of the time, I do it before I start practising. I do it on the train during my travel, and before I come out on the platform. I do it constantly" (Primrose, 1972, p. 248).

Remarkably similar statements are made by coaches and outstanding athletes in domains involving fine-motor skills, such as billiards, darts, bowling and golf. Jack Nicklaus (1974) said that even in his mid 30s he maintained a regular level of play during the whole year, but that his overall amount of practice was reduced from his early career as he mastered the basics of his swing and as his practice became more efficient (p. 197):

> whenever I do go out with a bag of balls I have a very specific objective in mind and, once I've achieved it, I quit. All my life I've tried to hit practice shots with great care. I try to have a clear-cut purpose in mind on every swing. I always practise as I intend to play. And I learned long ago that there is a limit to the number of shots you can hit effectively before losing your concentration on your basic objectives.

When professional golfers keep practising too much, Nicklaus (1974, p. 197) suggested that "they often weaken their games by letting their practice become pointless through sheer monotony or fatigue." The famous golf coach Jim McLean (1999, p. 127) recommends that "Practise only as long as you can concentrate. Stop when you're not having fun or if you lose focus. Short, focused practice sessions are often the most productive."

After reading many books on the development of elite performance in music, golf and many other fine-motor activities, I find it interesting how often individual differences among young performers who practise similar amounts of time are attributed to differences in the quality of their practice. The famous violin teacher Ivan Galamian (1972, p. 351) argued:

> If we analyse the development of the well-known artists, we see that in almost every case the success of their entire career was dependent upon the quality of their practising. In practically each case, the practising was constantly supervised either by the teacher or an assistant to the teacher. The lesson is not all. Children do not know how to work alone. The teacher must constantly teach the child how to practise.

Kroen (1999, p. 53) similarly explained the lack of improvement of golfers' swings, despite much practice:

> Many players confuse hitting balls with practice. If you watch golfers at a crowded driving range you will see many who are hitting ball after ball with the same club (usually a driver) without ever checking their grip, stance or alignment. Every shot in practice should be hit at a target with concentration on the fundamentals and an evaluation of the result.

Sam Snead (1989, p. 159), who was voted the 4th best golfer in the 20th century, also emphasised the difference between the enjoyment of mastered movements and the demanding process of improvement:

> It is only human nature to want to practise what you can already do well, since it's a hell of a lot less work and a hell of a lot more fun. Sad to say, though, it doesn't do a lot to lower your handicap. ... I know it's a lot more fun to stand out on the practice tee and rip drivers than it is to chip and pitch, or practise sand shots with sand flying back in your face, but it all comes back to the question of how much you're willing to pay for success.

An essential prerequisite for deliberate practice is sustained concentration, but even concentration appears to be subject to practice. For example, Ben Hogan (1948, p. 172) claimed that:

> While I am practising I am also trying to develop my powers of concentration. I never just walk up and hit the ball. I decide in advance how I want to hit and where I want it to go. ... Adopt the habit of concentrating to the exclusion of everything else while you

are at the practice tee and you will find that you are automatically following the same routine while playing a round in competition.

More generally, Starkes et al. (1996) showed that the duration of daily training given future expert performers was very similar across several domains, such as music and sports. During the first year, the daily level of practice was around 15–30 minutes, on average, with steady increases for each additional year, reaching 4–5 hours after around a decade. Starkes et al. found an intriguing similarity between increases in the amount of practice for sports when the athletes started practice around age 12, and music, when start of practice is closer to 6–7 years of age. If this pattern of results is found consistently across all domains, it would suggest that the level of increased training may require a slow physiological adaptation to increased demands of habitual practice. This slow adaptation may be relatively insensitive to chronological age.

The attainment of expert performance requires an extended period of high-level deliberate practice, where the duration of practice is limited by the ability to sustain concentration, a capacity which appears to increase as a function of years of practice in the domain. Consequently, a certain amount of deliberate practice may be necessary to reach the highest performance levels, and individual differences, even among experts, may reflect primarily differences in the amount and quality of practice. However, most people would argue that there are distinct limits to the influence of practice, and that inborn capacities and innate talent will play a very important role in determining performance, especially at the highest levels within a domain. Sternberg (1996) has even proposed that individuals with more innate talent would be more successful during practice, and thus more willing to engage in practice — possibly explaining at least part of the relation between amount of deliberate practice and performance.

In the next section of this chapter, I will propose that expert performance can be viewed as the end product of an extended series of psychological modifications and physiological adaptations. Furthermore, I will explain how expert performance is mediated by complex memory mechanisms and representations which have been acquired as a result of practice, and how these mechanisms are critical to continued performance improvement. There are many general characteristics of acquiring expert performance that appear to be invariant across domains. However, an analysis of how expert performance is acquired in a particular domain, such as golf, through deliberate practice, must explain the acquisition of the unique characteristics of expert golf and thus be specific to that domain. In the next section I will develop an expert-performance framework for golf, where the reproducible performance of expert golfers is first captured, then analysed and finally the acquisition of its mediating mechanisms and representations is related to deliberate practice reported by the golf masters. The development of this framework has been a challenge for me, because I didn't know hardly anything about golf until a couple of years ago. During my subsequent reading of a large number of books on golf, I have been searching for quotes by eminent golfers that would express my own ideas on expert performance, as well as disagree with them. In the following section I have included quotes by expert golfers to support critical points, which shows that several of the most knowledgeable individuals about the acquisition of expert performance in golf share these ideas on expert performance and deliberate practice.

The Structure and Acquisition of Expert Performance in Golf

The popular conception of how everyday skills are acquired has little in common with our view that expert performance is acquired through deliberate practice. In contrast to the rapid automatisation of everyday skills, such as preparing food or driving a car, and the emergence of a stable level of performance, expert performance continues to improve as a function of increased experience and deliberate practice, as illustrated in Figure 5. The key challenge for aspiring experts is avoiding the arrested development associated with generalised automaticity of performance and acquiring the cognitive skills that support continued learning and improvement. Expert performers achieve this by deliberately acquiring and refining cognitive mechanisms to enhance their control and monitoring of performance. For example, they deliberately construct training situations that induce discrepancies between their actual and desired performance. By comparing their performance to that of more proficient individuals in their domain of expertise, they can identify differences and gradually reduce them through extended deliberate practice. Given that expert performance is an adaptation to the task constraints of the representative domain activities, we need to study those constraints in order to understand the mechanisms underlying expertise and the associated deliberate practice activities.

The Essence of Golf: Capturing Expert Golf Performance

When we examine the structure of expert golf performance it becomes clear that there are no magical techniques for hitting the ball or shortcuts to attaining elite performance. To hit a golf ball to an exact location is more than difficult. It is impossible even for the best golf players to do so consistently — at least for shots and putts traveling more than a few feet. The belief that a player would be able to control the motion of the ball so completely that it would always reach its exact desired destination is fundamentally incorrect. The motion of the golfers' limbs and clubs and the induced path of a golf ball

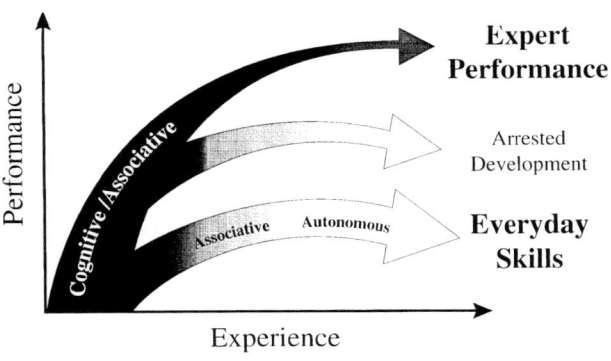

Figure 5
An illustration of the qualitative difference between the course of improvement of expert performance and of everyday activities. The goal for everyday activities is to reach as rapidly as possible a satisfactory level that is fixed and "autonomous." After individuals pass through the "cognitive" and "associative" phases they can generate their performance with a minimal amount of effort (see the gray/white plateau at the bottom of the graph). In contrast, expert performers counteract automaticity by developing increasingly complex mental representations to attain higher levels of control of their performance and will therefore remain within the "cognitive" and "associative" phases. Some experts do not continue to seek improvement through deliberate practice and thus their performance will be automated prematurely. (Adapted from "The scientific study of expert levels of performance: General implications for optimal learning and creativity" by K. A. Ericsson in *High Ability Studies, 9*, p. 90. Copyright 1998 by European Council for High Ability.)

will always be to some degree unpredictable. Furthermore, the motion of a golf ball rolling on grass is also influenced by many uncontrollable factors. The essence of expertise in golf is, thus, to increase the players' level of control and reduce the unpredictability of their shots.

To what degree are shots and putts controllable? It is difficult to assess how much control an expert golfer has while playing. When a golfer drives the ball off the tee on longer holes, an observer cannot tell if the ball has landed exactly where it was aimed, as long as it reaches the fairway — after all, few golfers intentionally aim for the rough! However, when the expert golfer is close enough to reach the hole either by a single shot or a putt and it is reasonable "to go for the flag," we can infer that any deviation between the resting place of the ball and the hole was unintended, and thus is reflecting uncontrollable factors. Analyses of the putting performance by professionals (Cochran & Stobbs, 1968; Diaz, 1989; Tierney & Coop, 1999) show them to be rather inaccurate, especially at the longer distances, as is illustrated in Figure 6. Most interestingly, when 20 pros were asked to guess the probability of sinking a 6-

foot putt on the PGA Tour (Diaz, 1989), they predicted the probability to be over 70% — well above the Tour average of around 55%. "The only player who guessed lower than the Tour average was the acknowledged best putter among the pros, Ben Crenshaw" (Diaz, 1989, p. 77).

In order to assess the maximal level of putting performance, Cochran and Stobbs (1968) built a putting machine and found that on "perfect greens" this machine could sink 97% of 6-foot putts, only 50% of the 20-foot putts, and a mere 20% of the 60-foot putts. Similar estimates have been obtained by other mechanical putting devices (Hill et al., 1999; Pelz, 1989, 1994). Consistent findings are found for other types of shots when the variability of human and mechanical devices have been compared (Olsavsky, 1994).

To understand the development of expert performance in golf it is necessary to realise that golf shots and putts are relatively uncontrollable events. Someone might contest this claim by pointing to golf players' amazing accuracy when they are "hot" during competitions. However, scientific studies of elite basketball players suggest that "hot" streaks are not reliable effects. These streaks of outstanding performance can be explained by a series of chance occurrences (Gilovich, Vallone, & Tversky, 1985). For example, even a putting machine, such as the one developed by Pelz (1989, 1994) or Hill et al. (1999), would exhibit streaks of successful putts just by chance. During my reading I have found claims even by professionals that seem too good to be true. For example, even the analytical Tom Watson

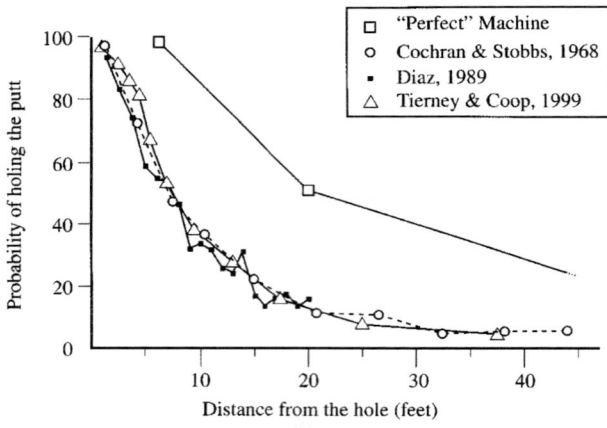

Figure 6
The relation between successful putting and the putts' distance from the hole for three samples of professional golfers and Cochran and Stobbs' (1968) mechanical putting device operating under "perfect green conditions."

(1983, p. 43) says "When I am putting well, I can place two balls 40 feet from the hole, putt the first ball and then putt the second ball without looking up — and hit the first ball with the second." Based on the earlier reviewed evidence with mechanical putting devices, I believe this feat might have been due to chance, that Tom Watson would not be able to consistently putt that accurately even on days when he is "putting well." It is reasonable to assume that a golfer would not be able to putt better than, or even as well as, the mechanical putting devices operating under "perfect green conditions" (Cochran & Stobbs, 1968).

Elite golfers sometimes comment on the unpredictability of shots. Cohn (1994, p. 19) quotes David Edwards as saying: "You can hit a great shot and end up 10 to 15 feet from the hole, or you can hit a lousy shot and it goes in the hole, and that's just the nature of golf." During play in tournaments there is no way to tell if a better shot could have been produced consistently because only a single shot is allowed. When elite players discuss differences between good and bad rounds they appear to disregard the possibility that chance factors (outside their control) played an important role (Kirschenbaum, O'Connor, & Owens, 1999) and often attribute their performance to poor concentration, tenseness, and poor imagination and feel (McCaffrey & Orlick, 1989). However, some elite golfers do seem to accept limits to control. McLean (1999, p. 96) cites Jackie Burke as claiming that:

> golf is basically a game of hitting circles. The first circle is the area in which you're trying to drive the ball. ...When you are on the green, you're trying to hit the ball into roughly a 3-foot circle around the cup. Once you get into that 3-foot circle, you putt to the ultimate and smallest circle, the cup.

Ben Hogan (1957, p. 113, italics added) claimed that he gained a dramatic increase in confidence when:

> I had stopped trying to do a great many difficult things *perfectly* because it had become clear in my mind that *this ambitious overthoroughness was neither possible nor advisable*, or even necessary. All you needed to groove were the fundamental movements — and there weren't so many of them. Moreover, they were movements that were basically controllable and so could be executed fairly well whether you happened to be sharp or not so sharp that morning.

In conclusion, the fact that many elite golfers seem to have difficulty determining the limits of their control and accepting the role of chance factors is important for a couple of reasons. First, if the elite golfers generate methods to control what are inherently chance factors, these methods will be neither valid nor reliable. The role of "superstition" has been well documented in golf (Melvin & Grealy, 1999) and other sports, such as baseball (Ciborowski, 1997). The possible use of spurious methods means that it is necessary to carefully evaluate reports by elite golfers to distinguish those based on consistent, controllable elements and observations from those that are not. Second, even when misses are due solely to uncontrollable chance factors, they will have emotional effects which in turn may influence subsequent performance (Kirschenbaum et al., 1999). However, the complex issues regarding control of negative emotions and cognitions are outside the scope of this chapter and the reader is referred to other chapters, reviews by Rotella and Lerner (1993) and Zaichkowsky and Takenaka (1993), and some recent intriguing proposals for ironic control processes by Janelle (1999; Hall, Hardy, & Gammage, 1999; Taylor, 1999).

The challenge of controlling golf shots. When one observes elite golfers, their swings and putts look effortless and natural. However, when one tries to build a mechanical device to generate the same types of shots or to instruct a novice golfer to duplicate them, the difficulties become apparent. Based on extensive tests under controlled conditions, Cochran and Stobbs (1968, p. 144) found that the club head of a driver moves with a speed of 100 miles per hour at the time of contact with the golf ball. After about 0.0005 seconds, the ball springs clear of the club head and moves with speed of around 135 miles per hour. For a perfect shot, the driver head has to make contact with the ball exactly at the "sweet spot" (p. 120) — deviation of less than half an inch will noticeably reduce the length of the drive. The orientation of the driver has to be correct to avoid hooking or slicing the shot, and even one to three degrees of deviation may send the ball into the rough (p. 124). Similarly during putting, the time of contact between the club and ball is only 0.0006 seconds. These extremely short periods of contact between club and ball make adjustments during that time completely impossible.

How are golf shots controlled? Extensive research (see Ericsson & Lehmann, 1996, for a brief overview and references) shows that any type of rapid movements must be prepared well in advance of their execution. Highly skilled athletes are able to anticipate situations before they actually happen and thus start preparing their overall movements well in advance. For example, someone who catches a ball has prepared the catching movements before the last 0.2 seconds prior to contact and can complete the action even if an experimenter turns off the lights during that period. Cochran and Stobbs (1968) found that golfers were able to complete their swings normally in the laboratory even if the lights were turned out during the downswing. In fact, the participants could not even tell when the lights were turned out; "if the lights went out at the beginning of the downswing, most thought it went out at about impact" (p. 102). Even more intriguing they found that "If the light was switched off at the very beginning of the back swing, when the club head was only a few inches away from the ball, nearly all the players were able, in total darkness, to carry on to the top of the swing, and come down and through the ball in a perfectly normal way" (p. 102). The stroke has to be preprogrammed and aimed and if the light was switched off even *before* the backswing had been initiated, that is *before* "the club head was drawn away from the ball, very few could hit the shot consistently" (pp. 102–103). However, seeing the ball prior to initiating the stroke cannot be absolutely necessary because blind golfers have been able to acquire the skill to strike balls in a consistent manner. Later in this chapter I will discuss how expert golf players are able to hit shots to accommodate wind and overhanging branches and other obstacles. To attain a desired ball trajectory the expert golfer must sometimes vary the shots systematically to create fades and draws to accommodate lie and direction. Regardless, in order to aim and program the stroke in advance for an accurate trajectory, the striking action must be predictable and highly reproducible. However, not even athletes can make major adjustments within the last 0.2 seconds, which is the shortest possible reaction time for visual stimuli. For example, cricket players cannot catch a ball that bounces unpredictably on a rough surface (McLeod, 1987).

The requirement that expert golfers' drives and putts have to be reproducible has strong implications for deliberate practice and how to develop optimal conditions for competitive play. During play in a golf tournament golfers are allowed only a single chance to hit the ball without penalty, so it is virtually impossible to assess the reproducibility of a given shot. However, under practice conditions a golfer can attempt to hit the same shot many times on the same or even different days to assess the distribution of outcomes. Unless golfers have swings and shots that remain reasonably reproducible across golf competitions and seasons, it is difficult to see how gradual improvements could occur.

Characteristics of Expert Performance in Golf

The key measure of golf performance is the number of strokes per round or series of rounds of a tournament. However, professional golfers engage in many types of activities during a tournament besides playing their rounds, some of the activities aimed to improve performance are illustrated in Figure 7. The performance during a round (see Figure 7) is the sum of the strokes required for each of the 18 holes. Among expert golfers who can control their emotions and are in good physical condition, one would predict that performance on different holes would be independent of each other and reflect stable characteristics of the golfer. However, the strokes taken to complete a given hole are not independent, because each shot will influence the nature of the following stroke. Consequently, it is necessary to consider the sequential relationship between strokes and how experts might improve their performance by planning the sequence of potential shots for a hole to reduce the total number of strokes.

Before discussing planning for sequences of shots I will discuss the characteristics involved in preparation and execution of individual shots, as is illustrated in Figure 7. I will begin by discussing the issues surrounding reproducibility of shots and discuss the challenges involved in attaining the high degree of motor control which is ultimately responsible for making the club hit the golf ball (see the final element in Figure 7). I will continue my discussion by commenting on potential procedures that can be executed before individual shots to increase the reproducibility of the intended shot. Then I will describe processes involved in aiming shots and deciding on the intended force at impact, before concluding with a brief discussion about planning. This review will be selective and focus on those characteristics that are consistent with reports by elite players and coaches, and are supported by empirical data from golf and related domains of expertise.

The acquisition of reproducible shots. When older children and adults start playing golf they do not learn the shot from scratch but rely on previously acquired similar movements. An important problem for beginning golfers is that they try to hit the golf ball with the rigid club, as though it were a sledge hammer, rather than swinging the club as though it was a sling. Harry Vardon (1914, p. 5) observed the typical problems with driving results when:

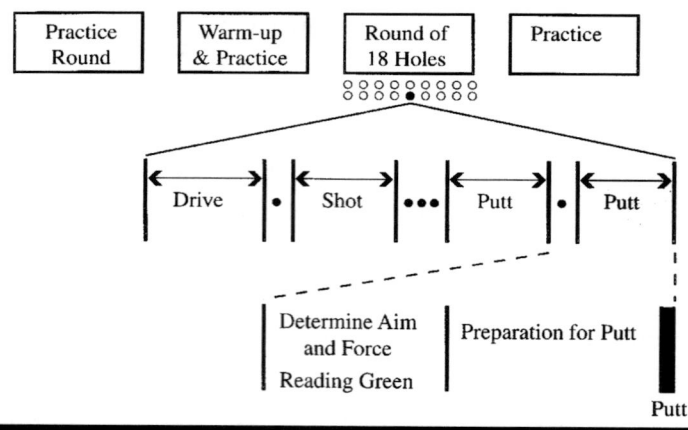

Figure 7

A description of some of the activities preceding and following a round of tournament golf. At a more detailed level the playing of each of the 18 holes can be viewed as a sequence of shots which in turn can be broken down into stages involved in the preparation and execution of a particular stroke.

> The player induces such a state of rigidity in his resolve to hit with desperate force that he simply cannot swing the club freely. ...What he usually does — unwittingly, but none the less surely — is to begin to stop the club before it reaches the ball. His arms are not sufficiently free to allow the driver to do the work for him.

Expert golfers know that "You can strike it harder with a swinging action than you can in any other way with the power at your command" (Jones & Brown, 1937, p. 51). However:

> A swinging action must begin smoothly and rhythmically, and the force producing it must be applied gradually. There can be no quick jerky movement at any stage of the procedure. ...Steadiness, not speed, is the keynote (Jones & Brown, 1937, p. 51).

Consistent with our discussion of the difficulty of actively controlling the swing once it is initiated, Jones and Brown (1937) discouraged such attempts and recommended that the swing be allowed to run its course. After extended practice, the swing becomes more controllable and predictable.

For a long time it was believed that there was an ideal natural swing that "talented" individuals would find through extensive repetition. However, after analysing the swings of the best golfers, it is clear that there is no single superior swing, there are many varieties of effective swings (McLean, 1999; Price, 1999). Adlington (1996, p. 10) even claimed that "Golf swings are unique; they are like fingerprints. Because no two are alike, it is risky to assume that what works for one will work for another."

The primary characteristic that distinguishes expert from less accomplished golfers appears to be that their putts and swings are more consistent. To grasp the most basic elements underlying consistency in golf shots, let us first consider some of the issues in building a mechanical device that will generate shots as reliably as possible, before turning to the complexities of human performance. The mechanism should be simple with few sources of variability, such as a pendulum, and constructed so the club could be firmly attached in a specific position. The frame should be rigid with firm grounding so it wouldn't shake during the set-up or initiation of the movement of the pendulum toward the ball. These attributes are easily observable in the putting device designed by Cochran and Stobbs (1968).

What are the physical elements of expert golfers' effective shots? Most introductory golf books start by describing the importance of selecting a grip that can be repeatedly reproduced. The preferred grip should reduce the degrees of freedom and facilitate the reproduction of the movements involved in the shot. According to Hogan (1957), one should practise the grip for 30 minutes daily for at least a week to make the subsequent learning easier. Similarly the stance and posture are designed to support the necessary movements and to maintain adequate balance during their execution.

Furthermore, extraneous movements should be reduced to make each shot very consistent. For example, Cochran and Stobbs (1968) reported that the foot placement of expert golfers was more similar when asked to make the same shot on several different occasions than was the foot placement of less accomplished golfers.

Hogan (1957, p. 38) claimed that it is necessary to acquire "a correct, powerful, repeating swing ... It really boils down to learning and practising a few fundamentals until performing them becomes as instinctive as walking." Like many golf coaches, he recommended that players acquire a few fundamental strokes, where the distance of putts and chip shots are regulated by the length of the downswing. In support of this claim, Delay, Nougier, Orliaguet, and Coello (1997) showed that experts have the same fundamental movement for putts of 1, 2, 3, and 4 m with only the length of the takeaway varying as a function of the distance. In contrast, amateur golfers rely on different movements for each of the distances. Analyses of variability in movement patterns during the swings with the driver and irons show a similar pattern. Expert golfers showed less movement of their shoes and less variability of the force pattern than less skilled players (Koening, Tamres, & Mann, 1994) suggesting greater stability and body control. Expert golfers were found to be less variable in the temporal and spatial characteristics of their swings than were novices (Neal, Abernethy, Moran, & Parker, 1990, p. 11): "Clearly as skill develops the player is able to refine the control of the swing so that trial-to-trial variability and deviations from an optimal swing pattern are minimised." At the same time, efforts to identify generalisable characteristics of the swing that mediate strokes with different clubs and for different distances have been relatively unsuccessful. However, golfers clearly view their swing as a stable and generalisable action pattern. When they make adjustments to play balls lying in difficult and variable locations on the golf course, they alter their stance (Nelson, 1946; Player, 1980) and avoid changing the fundamental swing.

In a recent review on the biomechanics of the golf swing, Dillman and Lange (1994) discussed the challenge of controlling and coordinating a very large number of motor units during the execution of the swing. In contrast to the simple mechanical devices with a few sources of variability, the human golfers' movements are influenced by a large number of dynamic interactions, such as the level of activity in the many parts of the motor system. Abernethy, Neal, and Moran (1990) found indirect support for these interactions and higher level invariances by failing to find any simple sequential pattern of activation of the muscles involved.

There are two important ways that human golfers control reproducibility by indirect means. First, there is considerable evidence that the downswing is "automatic" in the sense that it cannot be improved by intentional corrections. However, there is emerging evidence that experts acquire skilled movements where the motor system can make implicit adjustments even during ballistic movements, such as hitting a ball in table tennis (Bootsma & van Wieringen, 1990) and other racquet sports (Abernethy & Burgess-Limerick, 1992). In these cases the variability of the hitting movement for experts is greater at the initiation of the ballistic movement than it is at the critical time of subsequent contact with the ball — the ballistic movement execution serves as a funnel. Cochran and Stobbs (1968) reported comparisons between expert golfers and amateurs showing that the initial variability of experts' swings was reduced as the contact with the ball approached, unlike that of the amateurs.

Second, the motor system is highly complex and makes "automatic" adjustments for a wide range of factors, even muscle tension induced by anxiety. To generate the same action repeatedly with a high degree of consistency it is important to reproduce the same mental and physiological state on each occasion. Laboratory research shows that skilled golfers are more able to reduce the respiratory movements and associated EMG activity during the swing than less skilled golfers (Kawashima, Takeshita, Zaitsu, & Meshizuka, 1994). Barclay and McIlroy (1990) and Abernethy et al. (1990) found less variability in relevant and extraneous muscles by skilled compared to less skilled golfers. More generally, expert golfers follow a relatively set routine after they have decided on a preferred ball trajectory, as documented in the interviews by McCaffrey and Orlick (1989). The purpose of this routine is to induce a specific state of mind and body prior to executing the shot. During this routine and execution of the shot, the player is fully concentrated to minimise the disturbance from external and irrelevant stimuli.

A complementary method used consistently by expert golfers (Hogan, 1948; McCaffrey & Orlick, 1989) is to warm up and take shots on the driving range and putting green prior to the competition, as illustrated in Figure 7. Ben Hogan (1948, p. 171) described his extended warm up that "seldom varies. I start with the short clubs, usually a nine iron and hit the ball easily" and goes through playing each club ending up with the driver, to make certain that he can "hit each shot exactly where I want it to go." Although this process has the function of making the muscles more limber, it may also be beneficial in rehearsing and calibrating each shot before the round of competition.

In sum, expert golfers have acquired highly reproducible swings that differ among the experts. The execution of the downswings, once initiated, cannot be intentionally controlled, leading the golfer to focus on controlling the preparation and the initiating conditions. Jack Nicklaus (1974, p. 77) pointed to the set-up as "the single most important maneuver in golf. It is the only aspect of the swing over which you have 100 percent conscious control." Experts have uncovered methods to increase their indirect control over their shots by influencing their mental and physical states prior to initiating their swing and putts.

Aiming and shot selection. An individual or a mechanical device that could execute all types of shots with great consistency would still require additional skill and mechanisms for aiming the shots. Virtually all shots in golf follow complex trajectories. For example, the ball path of a drive might be influenced by wind, and more importantly, the ball will not stop exactly where it lands but it will bounce and roll until it reaches its end state. Similarly, the ball path of a putt will not be completely straight. Its path will be influenced by the undulations and slopes of the green. An expert golfer needs to be able to predict the likely ball paths associated with different types of shots. In addition, shot selection and aim will be influenced by strategic factors, such as optimising the circumstances for the subsequent shots.

Beginning golfers are likely to aim in an unsophisticated way and through experience make corrections to their natural aim. It is likely that their natural aim will reflect prior adjustments based on idiosyncratic striking motions and deviations from hitting the ball with a straight club. For example, most putts would have to be aimed to adjust for their "break" where a straight putt toward the hole will break away from its original path in a curvilinear manner on slanted surfaces, especially as the ball slows. For many amateur golfers, these adjustments become essentially automatic so that they don't have to figure out the ball trajectory, especially when they play on the familiar greens. Having misjudged a break on one putt, they may try to make a large break adjustment next time they encounter similar circumstances. Given the large number of factors that might influence ball trajectories, including weather, it is clear that golfers who make frequent corrections in response to misses are unlikely to gradually refine their mechanisms for accurately aiming shots.

A very different approach is advocated by elite golfers, such as Jack Nicklaus (1974, p. 79), who insisted that:

> I never hit a shot, even in practice, without having a very sharp, in-focus picture of it in my head. It is like a color movie. First I 'see' the ball where I want it to finish, nice and white and sitting up high on the bright green grass. Then the scene quickly changes and I 'see' the ball going there; its path, trajectory, and shape, even its behavior on landing.

But he acknowledged that less accomplished golfers are likely unable to "go to the movies." Nicklaus (1974, p. 78) argued that to produce this mental simulation of the intended shot he needs to be very deliberate in his assessment of the situation and "that's why setting up takes me so long." In particular he emphasised his preparation for "a putt that I'm trying to make. Then I need time to concentrate on all the factors of speed and line and grain involved" (p. 78).

The ability to generate similar types of "movies" or mental anticipations of outcomes is well documented in other areas of expertise and it is very plausible that these abilities can be empirically validated in golf. Tiger Woods' father (Woods, 1997, pp. 62-63) described how mental images of a putting situation were deliberately developed by having Tiger alternate looking at the hole and the ball as many times as necessary to "see the picture of the hole" without looking at it. Tiger was asked to "Putt to the picture." This ability to mentally represent the green is developed gradually over time by making the distance to the hole longer and trying it under more challenging conditions, such as slow, wet greens. Eventually golfers are able to build an elaborate representation of the situation during set-up that includes judgments about how much the ball will break, leading them to aim

> at a corresponding distance to that side of the hole. This permits the golfer to focus on distance rather than direction because distance control is more important than direction control. By putting to the picture and allowing the human computer to function, the golfer is free *to concentrate only on stroking the ball to the picture*. (p. 63, italics added)

In a recent study Hill et al. (1999) examined the mental representations of situations involving putting for expert (less than 5 handicap) and novice (over 25 handicap) golfers. In this experiment we tried to assess golfers' ability to report aspects of the set-up for putts and learn whether golfers knew what kinds of adjustments would be necessary under hypothetical changes in putting conditions. We found that the experts reported a reliably larger number of factors, such as wetness, length of grass and physical contour that they would consider during set-up than the novices. We also found that when we asked the participants questions after they had determined how to aim a putt in a given putting situation, such as "How, if at all, would the line that you have chosen for this putt change if the green was wet with dew?" (Hill, 1999, p. 52). The experts were reliably better at reporting appropriate adjustments to putting conditions than the novices.

We also analysed the putting lines reported by experts and novices for 10 actual putting situations to assess the amount of predicted break. To evaluate the accuracy of their prediction we derived the "true" putting line by a putting device that we designed without knowledge of Pelz's (1989, 1994) work with his "true roller." Overall, we didn't find any statistically reliable advantage of the experts over the novices in their respective putting lines. However, when we restricted the analysis to the longest putts with more than a single break, the experts' initial line was reliably superior to those reported by the novices. Our results were consistent with those of Pelz (1989, 1994), who found a small average advantage for the best golfers, without reporting if the differences were statistically reliable. In sum, our studies provide support for the expert golfers' development of advanced representations that allow them to respond to changes in conditions and generate putting lines in complex putting situations. At the same time, we found that both experts' and novices' putting lines indicated consistently less break than our putting device, thus replicating Pelz's (1989, 1994) earlier pioneering results. In several ongoing studies we are trying to understand the factors that might explain these large discrepancies between the true and estimated putting lines and relate them to documented deviations in visual alignments for both expert and amateur golfers (Coffey et al., 1990; McGlynn, Jones, & Kerwin, 1990), as well as other potential differences between the putts by our device and human golfers.

Planning and strategic processes during course management. Expert golf performance involves sequential planning that goes beyond aiming and hitting individual shots. It requires the ability to examine the challenges of a hole and come up with a plan for how to reach the green in a reliable and efficient manner. Tom Watson (1993, p. 57) wrote "Good pool players are thinking not only one shot ahead but several shots ahead. That's how you make a run. The essence of laying up in golf is the same: Plan ahead to leave yourself in good position for the next shot, whether you're laying up short of trouble off the tee or on your subsequent shots on up to the green." Prior to playing in a competition at an unfamiliar golf course, professional players conduct "a practice round to formulate your game plan." (p. 85). During the practice round Watson (1993, p. 85) explained that " I want to learn where I can and cannot miss a shot. If I do miss a shot I want to be sure I can recover and not incur a big score on the hole." Based on the expert golfers' understanding of the accuracy of their respective shots, the prevailing weather conditions, and the structure of the golf course, they select shots that will lay up for the next shot. "A consistent golfer gives himself the percentage play most times. He isn't afraid to lay up" (Watson, 1993, p. 58).

Expert golfers avoid risky carries and deliberately plan to increase the likelihood that they can approach the hole up the slope of the green with a full shot with their favorite club from a flat lie. Unfortunately, I don't know of any systematic studies confirming that realistic planning is related to performance among expert golfers. In recent studies with regular golfers (average handicaps around 20), Kirschenbaum et al. (1999) found that around 80% of the players generated overly optimistic plans for their shots given their accuracy and length of their drives. Kirschenbaum et al. (1999) were able to influence an experimental group to use more appropriate club selection with a better outcome for a particular shot, but disappointingly, the total number of strokes for the corresponding hole was not reliably improved.

In sum, a number of complex interacting characteristics distinguish expert from novice level golf performance. Expert golfers have attained control over their shots and can reproduce the same stroke consistently with more predictable outcomes. They have acquired more knowledge about the external factors influencing ball trajectories and can reason out methods of play in hypothetical situations better than less skilled players. Finally, there are suggestions that expert players have developed complex procedures to prepare for competitions. All distinguishing characteristics of expert golf performance depend on the predictability and control of shots. Without a thorough understanding of the variables that can affect a shot, planning the appropriate approach for a given hole would be difficult. It would be impossible to project potential ball trajectories without being able to accurately read the conditions of each situation. Given the central importance of executing consistent shots, I will focus the next part on the acquisition of that skill.

The Acquisition of Superior Shots through Deliberate Practice

In this part I will discuss the golf masters' insights into the hallmark of expert golf performance, namely the ability to strike the ball so it ends up closer to its intended target than amateur players. The primary distinguishing feature of experts' swings was their reproducibility. Many of these swings look so natural that one might believe that they were just discovered suddenly one day and then effortlessly retained. This is not so, however. The available evidence suggests that the swing should be viewed as a feat of skilled mastery resulting from supervised training and extended deliberate effort in acquiring other expert motor skills, as is the case for dancing ballet and playing the violin. To quote one of the elite golfers, Nick Price (1999, p. 41, italics added), "An efficient golf swing incorporates the fewest moving parts while producing maximum results in terms of direction, distance and ball flight. These factors add up to control, and to me *the ultimate art of golf is in controlling the ball.* It is an attribute common to all the top ball-strikers." The demand for control may seem a little puzzling for many people because they associate high consistency with a machine that reproduces the same action repeatedly and expect that consistent human action would also be automatic and devoid of control. I will first briefly discuss some differences between how amateurs seem to acquire their swing and how expert coaches recommend that it should be acquired. I will then turn to a discussion about how the experts can increase their control of the swing and thereby reduce its variability from time to time.

In one of the earliest books on "Advanced Golf," Baird (1908, p. 173) criticised the average golfer for having "no definite system," when "Playing one tee shot he will have the open stance, and the next one it may be almost square; while in one case the ball may be brought opposite the left toe, and in the other it may be back again much nearer the right." Baird (p. 173) recommended "serious practice — that is to say, practise alone, and with one club or a few. It is such practice as this that makes the quickest and surest improvements in a player." Expert golfers and golf coaches generally agree that stroke consistency is critical for improvement in golf performance as long as the elements of the stroke are fundamentally sound. Most of the books on golf instruction break the swing into its basic elements. They nearly always recommend a sequence of mastery akin to the instructional sequences for mastery of the violin. The instruction starts with the acquisition of a consistent grip, the adoption of an appropriate stance and posture, then the backswing and the downswing. Most instructional schemes recommend mastering the iron clubs and then end up with the driver.

Few individuals who begin playing golf as adults are patient enough to follow the recommended sequence of successive mastery and want to drive the ball as far as possible as soon as possible. On the other hand, if beginning golfers followed these instructions and mastered the corresponding elements, shouldn't the only remaining step be to entrench and automate the sequence of steps? Many researchers studying golf draw on Fitts and Posner's (1967) theoretical framework for understanding skill acquisition in golf. According to their framework mastery of skilled activities is mediated by a sequence of stages, in which a task and its associated goals are first understood and then suitable procedures are developed — which roughly corresponds to understanding the sequential steps of the swing, then the elements are mastered and coordinated. During the final stage these procedures are automated in a manner consistent with the influential work by Shiffrin and Schneider (1977; Schneider & Shiffrin, 1977). As I explained when discussing Figure 5, my problem does not refer to the application of this theoretical account for amateur golfers who reach a stable level of performance within months or a year or two. My disagreement concerns the hypothesis that expert golf performance can be explained as a mere extension of continued practice.

The theory of automaticity proposed by Shiffrin and Schneider (1977; Schneider & Shiffrin, 1977) and its application to the final stage of skill acquisition (Anderson, 1982) explains well how performance can become faster when automated, but not how a variable motor action can become more consistent. Let us consider how a sequential procedure would be automated through practice. For example, when children learn to add digits they typically start by counting out each added element, such as "three plus three" is "three, four, five, six," where "six" is the answer. This type of process can be automated by eliminating intermediate steps in the original sequence of steps by directly retrieving the answer "six" in response to "three plus three." It is important to notice that the accuracy of the generated answer remains high throughout practice and it is primarily the speed of retrieving the answers that increases. For these types of cognitive activities, the initial mental states, such as "three plus three" remain roughly the same before and after the automation. In contrast, during motor activities such as a golf swing, the mental states cannot contain a description of all relevant aspects of the motor activity. A very large number of muscle fibres and joints are simultaneously engaged in interactions to maintain balance and posture any time a human merely stands. Given the limitations of our attention and cognitive systems, it is clearly impossible to control all, or even a large number, of the basic elements. The key message is that control over the motor system is never perfect and is typically attained by indirect means and in gradual increments. My argument with respect to the gradual improvement of expert golf performance is that it is not a process of automating its procedures but rather an extended quest for increased control.

Once the problem is posed in terms of controlling a highly complex interactive motor system, it is easy to see how "simple activities," such as generating a consistent grip and assuming a reproducible stance, can be executed more consistently. It becomes clear that for every motor act there is variability and differences and that it is essential for players to develop their ability to perceive those differences and acquire the appropriate "feel." Improvements in control will thus require an interaction between the development of systems for monitoring (perception) and for control (action). Let me support my somewhat speculative argument with a few examples along with some supporting quotes by elite golfers.

In an earlier section I reviewed evidence showing that concurrent intentional control is impossible during the downswing. How can expert golfers then improve the reproducibility of their downswing? Expert golfers seem to agree that beneficial intentional corrections during the downswing are not possible, which would explain why less skilled golfers experience difficulty when trying to make corrections during the downswing (Moore & Stevenson, 1991, 1994). The intentional control of the downswing has to be completed during set-up and prior to the initiation of the downswing. Before Nicklaus (1974, p. 99) hits a shot in competition he spends considerable time setting up and getting ready for the shot:

I must stress, however, that no matter how many things you think about at address, you are, so to speak, merely programming the computer. Once you throw the switch, the computer must take over. The golf swing happens far too fast for you consciously to direct your muscles. Frequently I can make very minor adjustments in midswing, but they are always instinctive, never conscious.

Nick Price (1999, p. 46) pretty much agreed:

The secret in golf is to have a backswing so sound that on the course you don't have to think about the downswing. ... The correct backswing will set up the conditions that make it much more likely that the right things will happen later.

The most important method for controlling the motor system is developing techniques for controlling those aspects that can be monitored and controlled during set-up. In addition, it may be possible to attain indirect (unintentional) rapid adjustments to the motor system by acquiring representations that encode and monitor the intended goal or "feel" of the swing, as discussed earlier.

How are the representations acquired that allow expert golfers to distinguish differences in the states during set-up and address prior to the swing? The representations do not appear to emerge automatically as a function of mere playing, but do require the expert golfers' intentional efforts to attain deliberate control over their set-up and associated shots during practice. Ben Hogan (1957, pp. 37–38) wrote:

Golf also seems to bring out the scientist in a person. He soon discovers that unless he goes about observing and testing with an orderly method, he is simply complicating his problems. In this general connection, I have found out that it helps me immensely to bring along a notebook and pencil to the practice tee and to write down after each session just what it was I had been working on, exactly how it was coming, and precisely where it was that I should resume my testing the next time I went out to practice.

Price (1999) even published excerpts of his own diary on the observations during practice. Elite golfers are not satisfied with a single straight shot and acquire a range of variations of shots that require controlled adjustments of the set-up. Jack Nicklaus (1974, p. 203) said that during practice he often intentionally varies his shots and

in a session where I'm basically trying to fade the ball. I'll intentionally hit two or three draws out of every twenty shots. It's challenging to 'work' the ball, and it's also highly instructive to learn just what causes what results.

Nicklaus (1974, p. 99) discusses a number of different aspects that he might attend to during the address of his swing, such as "keeping my head in a certain position on the backswing; keeping my hands low going back." The number of things that Nicklaus feels that he can focus on at address (prior to the initiation of the downswing) is often "only one or two swing keys." Bobby Jones (1966, p. 203) is even more adamant:

> It has never been possible for me to think of more than two or three details of the swing and still hit the ball correctly. If more than that number have to be handled, I simply must play badly until by patient work and practice I can reduce the parts that have to be controlled. The two or three are not always the same, sometime a man's swing will be functioning so well he need worry about nothing; then, of course, on those rare occasions, the game is a simple thing.

The practice techniques that elite golfers recommend provide another source of evidence that underscores the importance of deliberate development of representations for perceiving and control action. Many of these exercises do not have any simple relation to the actual execution of shots during tournament play. For example, Gary Player (1980) recommended exercises involving shots made by a single arm, especially the left arm, to improve control for right-handed golfers. He also recommended that players hit shots while balancing on a single foot as a means to attain a higher level of balance and control. With respect to improving feel, Price (1999) recommended practice in the dark and practice with a baseball bat. Future case studies and designed field experiments with observed performance would be desirable to assess the benefits of associated exercises and evaluate whether they result in refined representations and mechanisms of improved control for expert golfers.

A golf swing requires frequent tune-ups as well as continued maintenance with adjustments throughout a golf season and a career of golf playing.

> The golf swing is not a static entity. It changes as the knowledge changes, as the body changes, as the particular desired shot pattern changes. My swing probably has changed every year, and it looks a lot different today than it did 20 years ago, or even two years ago. For me it has been a series of steps forward and steps back and steps forward again. (Kite & Dennis, 1990, p. 37).

Acquired representations play an important role in maintaining the execution of shots as noted by Bobby Jones (1966, p. 211):

> It is of great value to have a clear understanding of the successive movements making up a correct golf swing; this much is needed in order to enable one to recognise and correct faults as they appear. But no human is able to think through and at the same time execute the entire sequence of correct movements. The player himself must seek for a conception, or fix upon one or two movements concentration on which will enable him to hit the ball.

Nicklaus (1974) reported that he is able to deal with most changes during "the normal day-to-day fine tuning," but sometimes he has developed more complex flaws that require "major surgery." For this purpose Nicklaus recorded all television broadcasts of his golf playing to help him analyse his performance and to identify unintentional changes that eventually lead to performance problems.

Finally, it is necessary for expert golfers to acquire general skills for setting up shots under all types of conditions on the course, because only putting and driving are done under relatively standardised conditions. Most approach shots have to be executed in varied situations where the area with the ball is not level, thus requiring the golfers to adjust their stance and posture. There may be obstacles in front of the ball that require directing the path of the ball toward the left or the right or making it flatter or steeper. There may be obstacles behind or near the ball that will constrain the normal swing path. Consequently, expert golfers need to acquire representations and skills that would allow them to set up a shot during a tournament without any opportunities for test shots. To acquire refined representations to deal with varied conditions on the golf course should be the most challenging and difficult even for elite golfers. In support of that hypothesis, Cochran and Stobbs (1968) found that these types of varied approach shots revealed the largest differences between the most and least successful British professional golfers that they studied. To improve these representations and the associated performance the golfers may need to engage in "on-course practice" of the type recommended by Sam Snead (1989) where the player plays two or three balls from each ball position. Snead (1989, p. 160) recommends that you play

> your next shot from where the worst ball lies. Not only will this improve your short game, but it will also help you develop the shots you need to scramble out of trouble, as well as teach you just how much you can realistically afford to gamble when in a jam.

More generally, there is remarkable consensus among experts and coaches about the methods for gradually attaining increased control over golf strokes. Even the reports by elite athletes that during peak performance "skill execution felt automatic and required minimal conscious effort or attention" (Moore & Stevenson, 1991, p. 281) can be reinterpreted as stating that no additional conscious control seemed necessary during highly successful performance. Even if athletes were quite able to control and adjust their swings prior to the initiation of the downswing it is unclear why anything should be changed as long as it works very well. Moore and Stevenson's (1994; Ravizza & Osborne, 1991) recommendations to release control during the actual execution and "let it go" is consistent with the proposed idea of limiting control to the events prior to initiation of the downswing, although the theoretical rationale differs. From my reading, I found ample evidence for deliberate efforts to acquire and refine representations to monitor and adjust those aspects of the set-up and the address that can be controlled, in line with the pattern predicted in Figure 5. Unfortunately, there are no laboratory studies that provide objective evidence for the performance benefits of these types of representations. In my concluding remarks I will review some experimental evidence from other domains of expertise involving perceptual-motor performance, which makes the proposed mechanisms mediating expert performance in golf more plausible. Before discussing those issues I will briefly comment on the relevance of expert golf performance for amateur golfers.

Implications of the Acquisition of Expert Golf Performance for Amateur Golfers

Our analysis of the acquisition of expert and novice golf performance illustrated in Figure 5 presents a bleak picture for anyone who wants to discover some simple and easy method for improving amateur performance.[2] There is no known shortcut to skilled performance. The requirement for gradual development of reproducible shots is inconsistent with the beliefs and conceptions of most amateurs. This was recognised by Ouimet (1914, pp. 109–110) at the start of the 20th century:

> It is hard to understand how a golfer can try one style of putting, to-day, another tomorrow and a third the day following and hope to improve that important department of his game. The trouble with him, as a rule, is that every time he sees another golfer get first-class results with a style of putting dissimilar to that which he most recently adopted, he either consciously or unconsciously adopts that new style. Or, he sees one golfer do exceptionally well with a style of putter that is different from his own and immediately jumps mentally to the conclusion that it is not his putting style, after all, that is at fault, but his style of putter.

Some expert golfers, such as Ray Floyd (1989, p. 166), have explicitly rejected the idea of short-cuts and dramatic improvements: "I said early in this book that you can enjoy golf without playing it particularly well, without improving. That's the beauty of it. If you are satisfied at that point, bless you and have fun. But if you want to lower your score, you'll have to make an effort." He summarises "I don't know any other way to improve, whether you are building your game or trying to get out of a slump. And it works, not always immediately, but eventually" (p. 166).

According to the framework outlined in Figure 5, amateur golf performance typically improves most rapidly within the first couple of years before reaching a stable level that is maintained as long as the player keeps playing. As the middle curve illustrates, it is possible to maintain systematic practice for longer periods and thus reach a higher level performance before stabilising or automating performance at that level. It would be possible for golfers to play in a relaxed and "automatic" manner even at very high levels. Nicklaus (1974, p. 77) claimed that "In a casual round of golf with friends I can walk up to the ball, put the club down, draw back, and pop it in no time flat" but the results would not be good enough for tournament golf. This account by Nicklaus is consistent with the general framework outlined in Figure 5, where even experts have to refine and maintain their representations to have the level of control necessary to achieve their best performance.

Very little was known about psychomotor skills of amateur golfers and their relation to practice and other performance enhancing activities until

Thomas and Over (1994a, 1994b) developed their questionnaire where they asked amateur golfers to rate their agreement with a large number of statements related to psychological and psychomotor skills in golf. There are now several studies that have examined the relations between these ratings and reported golf performance in golfers below the age of 20 (Ellis, Filyer, & Wilson, 1999) and above the age of 20 (Thomas & Over, 1994a, 1994b). Over and Thomas (1995) focused on analyses of older golfers, which I will discuss further in my concluding remarks.

Given the focus of my chapter on expert performance I will limit my discussion to Thomas and Over's (1994a, 1994b) and Ellis et al.'s (1999) findings relevant to their factor analyses of statements relevant to psychomotor skills. Both studies uncovered three similar factors for both samples of golfers of different ages. The factor most closely related to golf performance (self-reported handicap) consisted of statements describing driving and the reliability of shots and was defined by a negative loading on items, such as "Lose more than one ball per round" and "Drives depend on luck and chance." Thomas and Over (1994a, 1994b) called this factor "automaticity," because other statements loading on the factor emphasised the consistency, but in a subsequent study of ten-pin bowling Thomas, Schlinker, and Over (1996) used the label "consistency" to refer to a similar factor in close agreement with our general framework. In the study of teenaged golfers Ellis et al. (1999) found a similar factor that loaded highly on the statements cited above, but they emphasised the variability induced by striving for distance and called it "grip it and rip it" — the more variability the worse the golf performance. Both studies identified a second factor related to putting skill, which was not reliably related to golf performance.

The third factor related to practice and other activities associated with efforts by golfers to improve and would be of particular interest to our framework. Ellis et al. (1999) found that "practice" for teenaged golfers could be measured by high agreement for items like "Lessons with a golf professional" and "Hit practice balls before a round." Agreement with these items was reliably related to better golf performance. For older golfers (over age 20), Thomas and Over (1994a, 1994b) found a factor that loaded on the above "practice" items along with statements about other improvement-related activities, such as "Learn by watching professionals play," "Changed clubs to improve performance," and "Watched golf instructional video." However, this "practice" factor was not reliably related to better golf performance for the older golfers (Thomas & Over, 1994a, 1994b). In sum, the reliable correlation between self-reported consistency of the swing and handicap for both samples of amateur golfers ($0.4 < r < 0.5$) is remarkable for a questionnaire study using rated agreement with statements and is consistent with our framework. Furthermore, the reliable role of practice for the younger sample (Ellis et al., 1999) but not for the adult sample (Thomas & Over, 1994a, 1994b) is, at least, consistent with our framework. We know that amateurs increase their performance most when they are first introduced to golf and it is during this period that attitudes toward practice and instruction would be likely to have greatest benefits. When golf performance has reached a stable level during adulthood, which kinds of practice activities are known to improve older amateurs' performance?

Within the framework of deliberate practice many enjoyable activities believed relevant to improvement, such as watching elite golfers play, watching instructional videos, and imaging their best performance, can be used to improve performance within the context of deliberate practice. However, Ray Floyd (1989, p. 166) argues "Reading an instruction book or watching a videotape can give you knowledge, but it won't give you feel. To really learn a swing or a shot or a putt, to build the muscle memory that will let you repeat it consistently on the course, you have to practise it." Without deliberate practice to translate this knowledge and implement reproducible changes to performance, these imaging and observational activities may have limited benefits for performance. Furthermore, amateur golfers may need to increase their level of weekly deliberate practice to gradually refine performance and to maintain changes. It seems highly unlikely that a couple of hours of practice by themselves could lead to stable increases in consistent shot-making, which is consistent with the difficulties of many experimental studies to demonstrate immediate improvement of golf performance, especially among experienced golfers. Studies with successful interventions (Cohn, Rotella, & Lloyd, 1990; Thomas & Fogarty, 1997) typically involve long-term interventions or follow-ups where changes in practice behavior become possible or even likely mediating factors. In my final and concluding section I will argue that the necessary level of deliberate practice for reliable sustained improvement in experienced golfers may be higher than generally assumed.

Toward an Integrated Perspective for the Acquisition of Expert Performance

Following the path to expertise in golf is not easy, even for the most "talented." The path is hard to follow even when we can study the routes taken by elite golfers who have completed the journey, and these golfers don't seem to have uncovered any shortcuts to excellence. In this final section, I will summarise our knowledge about how expert performance is acquired and maintained in domains that have been studied more intensively than golf and propose potential parallels between those findings and phenomena in golf. Once one realises the long and specialised preparation that is necessary, even for the most "talented," to reach elite golf performance then it doesn't seem necessary or appropriate to explain this elite level of performance by natural ability.

Deliberate Practice across the Life Span

Attaining expert performance in many domains takes the entire healthy life span. The most successful performers start at young ages and remain active as long as they can, until their 60s, 70s, or even 80s, for many musicians and scientists. Why does the acquisition process tend to start so early and how are some of these individuals able to sustain remarkable levels of performance into advanced age?

Practice during the early years. In my introductory remarks, I showed that early practice in a domain appears to increase the chance of reaching elite levels and that this is particularly true for domains involving perceptual-motor activities, such as music, dance, and most sports. There appear to be distinct benefits to an early start as long as children are not pushed into premature "burn out." First, starting practice early provides children with a head start in acquiring necessary skills. Given that virtually all competitions for children involve competing against children in the same age group, a child who has studied music or practised golf for several years will perform much better than a child of the same age with only a single year of training. This initial advantage is particularly important in domains where teachers and coaches search for children with "innate talent" to admit them to programs for talent development. Children with extensive prior practice and training will perform at a higher level, seem more "talented," and are thus likely to gain access to the best teachers and coaches and their superior training environments.

Second, when children learn their first motor skills, or even their first language, there appear to be some benefits to learning essentially from scratch. Subsequent, related learning will often be more efficient because that learning can draw on earlier acquired skills. When skills are adapted from other activities, the transfer is inexact, because these skills don't match the fundamentals of the target domain. Adaptation and relearning will be necessary. When children's initial learning is closely monitored by an expert coach or teacher the children have the opportunity to acquire the correct fundamentals from the beginning of training. Early supervised learning by highly skilled teachers has been documented for nearly all of the outstanding musicians (Lehmann, 1997; Lehmann & Ericsson, 1996) and some outstanding golf players, such as Tiger Woods (Woods, 1997).

Third, when the practice activity imposes mental and physical strain on the body and the nervous system (Ericsson, 1998, in press), the body and the nervous system will eventually adapt to perform the desired activity more efficiently. The types of anatomical and physiological adaptations observed depend on the stage of development of the individual as well as the domain requirements. For example, there appears to be a narrow window in the development of children between the ages of 3 and 5 years when any normal child seems able to acquire perfect pitch — the ability to recognise tones when presented one by one (Ericsson, 1996; Takeuchi & Hulse, 1993). Early intense training in music has also been correlated with changes in the structure and organisation of the brain that facilitates the execution of demanding perceptual and motor activities (Elbert et al., 1995). As the bones become calcified during development, the range of the joints becomes fixed. Intense training prior to this fixation is correlated with range of motion allowing ballet dancers to exhibit "turn out" and baseball pitchers to extend their throwing arm far behind their head (Ericsson & Lehmann, 1996). More generally, training during particular periods in childhood and adolescence is known to result in irreversible physiological changes that may give these individuals an acquired advantage in certain activities (Ericsson, 1996). Though I have not found firm evidence for irreversible changes in the domain of golf, I am confident that such differences will soon be discovered.

Fourth, children who start practice and build a daily schedule around their practice and competition have already attained a high level of daily deliberate practice. Not only do they have the advantage of previously acquired skills, these individuals are learning a practice regimen that will help them continue to improve at a higher rate, as the increase in the daily amount of deliberate practice develops gradually over a long time (Starkes et al., 1996).

Finally, when children start with an activity at very young ages their initial performance is very unimpressive when evaluated with standards used for older children and adults. However, adults often feel that they are able to see future potential of some "talented" children by observing their raw and untrained behaviour and spotting signs of talent. However, there is no scientific evidence to support those beliefs and recent reviews of the evidence for early signs of talent show that early talent does not accurately predict the level of performance attained after training (Ericsson & Lehmann, 1996; Howe, Davidson, & Sloboda, 1998). In fact some of the evidence from sports shows that coaches who search for talent then confuse it with age-related variability in size and physical maturation. When soccer players start playing together at around 6–8 years of age children are grouped according to age with birth dates ranging from August 1st in one year to July 31st of the next year (Helsen, Starkes, & van Winckel, 1998). Hence, the age difference between the oldest and youngest can be close to a year. Research has found that the soccer players with the highest relative age are far more likely to succeed, giving rise to a higher proportion of professional soccer players having birth dates in the most favorable months. These findings (Helsen, Starkes, & van Winckel, 1998) are consistent with a confusion of "talent" and relative age of young soccer players that leads to differential development of their soccer performance. Similar findings have been reported for ice-hockey players from Canada where the relative-age effects appear to be even greater (Boucher & Mutimer, 1994). It is interesting to note that the relative-age effects on professional performance appear to be most consistent and pronounced in domains of sports where the search for "talented" children has been developed to its most advanced level, such as ice hockey in Canada and soccer in the Netherlands. In sum, these findings show that the identification of "perceived talent," even in the absence of objective correlates, will influence motivational support and access to training opportunities that are known to facilitate development of expert performance (Ericsson, 1996).

Reaching and maintaining peak levels of reproducible performance. It is well-known that sustained regular involvement in aerobic exercise or other comparable forms of intense physical activity are necessary to maintain high levels of aerobic fitness (Shephard, 1994). Similarly, regular training is necessary to maintain endurance and strength. Even in activities such as piano and violin performance, and non-vigorous sports, high-level performers engage in practice on basically a daily basis. Many of you are familiar with the famous quote by music virtuoso Ignacy Jan Paderewski (Crofton & Fraser, 1985, p. 118): "If I don't practise for one day, I know it. If I don't practise for two days, the critics know it. If I don't practise for three days, the audience knows it." Famous golfers, such as Sam Snead (1997), claim to "practise every day" and those golfers who do not practise regularly are rare and controversial exceptions.

Is it necessary to keep up this daily practice to maintain expert performance? If so, why would that be? Most people's acquired skills, such as swimming, bicycling, and typing, appear to be maintained virtually indefinitely, seemingly without practice. Those experiences are not inconsistent because the expert performers do not forget how to swing or to play the violin within a few days. The difference in performance after days or weeks without practice is a matter of degree. The loss of "feel" and refined control of performance might not be relevant to amateurs, but it may well be a critical difference between performers at the highest levels.

Research on swimmers and other athletes in vigorous sports shows that muscle fibres involved in particular activities, such as swimming, are closely attuned to the metabolic demands of daily practice, and within days after termination of regular practice, large changes have been observed in them. After weeks, months, and years without practice, additional changes take place. The distinctive physiological characteristics of athletic expertise are gradually lost (see Ericsson, 1990; Ericsson, Krampe, & Tesch-Römer, 1993; Ericsson & Lehmann, 1996; Robergs & Roberts, 1997, for reviews).

These changes in the adaptation of muscle fibres and other cells in the body will have implications even for skilled activities, such as music and golf. By executing the fundamental movements during practice, the components of the motor system can be adjusted to produce a coordinated action. Given that the critical motor activities in golf and music require movements that are not part of daily living, they will be lost without specialised practice. Without appropriate practice, coordination will decrease over time with associated decrements in performance. Changes in muscles will reduce the successful coordination of the muscle groups into precision movements. These human physiological changes over time are analogous to the more familiar changes observed in some music instruments, such as violins and pianos. After a period of disuse the strings of the instrument have to be tuned before each performance to produce the desired sound. In sum, continued practice appears to be necessary to maintain the adaptation of individual cells and to sustain the coordination of muscles that are critical to precision activities.

The reciprocal relationship between practice and high level of performance in golf and music potentially explains several phenomena. It accounts for why expert performers maintain regular practice and avoid long periods without any relevant activity. After long periods of disuse due to injury, individuals need to gradually reestablish the lost adaptations and coordinated actions before they can regain their old level of performance. Many adaptations require extensive intense practice to be attained, but once acquired they can be maintained with less, though still regular, practice with maintained intensity (Shephard, 1994).

The need to maintain high levels of practice may explain some performance decrements attributed to age. In domains which require physical precision, it is well known that some older individuals in their 50s and 60s are competitive with younger experts, and occasionally win national championships. At age 85 Sam Snead (1997, p. xv) claimed that "I can still shoot even par when my putting cooperates." Older musicians, such as Horowitz and Ravi Shankar, are famous for their remarkable ability to perform at the international level. In a recent study, Ralf Krampe and I (Krampe &

Ericsson, 1996) studied both amateur and expert pianists in their 20s and in their 60s to understand the effects of aging on speeded precision movements in piano-related tasks. Interestingly, we found that only the older amateurs exhibited the typical decreases in speeded performance. In contrast, the older expert pianists who maintained sufficient deliberate practice (around 10 hours per week) matched the performance of younger expert pianists when tested on representative tasks for piano playing. It appears possible for pianists to maintain expertise into their 60s, with regular deliberate practice. Reduced levels of performance in older individuals may reflect, to a large degree, reduced levels of practice. Comparisons between the amount and intensity of practice among young athletes and older master athletes suggest that much of the age-related difference in performance can be attributed to differences in practice (see, Ericsson, 1990, for a brief review). The finding that experts tend to peak at certain ages may be, at least in part, a result of motivational factors. It is difficult for individuals to focus completely on their practice and career development for years and decades as well as to gradually regain earlier levels of elite performance after disuse due to injury. For older golf professionals there are alternative careers in golf that may be better paid and less demanding than professional play in golf tournaments. On the other hand, the recent establishment of competitive events for master athletes grouped by their ages have led to large increases in the top level of performance for older athletes, especially among athletes in their 70s and 80s.

Research on the relationship between aging and golf performance shows a reasonably consistent picture. The performance of older elite golfers on the senior tour is surprisingly close to that of younger players on the regular PGA tour (Spirduso, 1995; Wiseman, Chatterjee, Wiseman, & Chatterjee, 1994),[1] and thus remains superior to the vast majority of young players. Analyses of all currently active amateur golfers' performance handicaps has shown remarkable performance stability from the 40s to the early 70s (Lockwood, 1999). In a retrospective longitudinal study, Over and Thomas (1995) found that the decrement in reported performance over a 10-year period for golfers in their 60s was statistically reliable. However, Over and Thomas (1995) did not find a uniform decrement in golf performance of the older golfers' performance, and for around half of them the performance had remained stable, or even improved. Further research is necessary to assess the factors that influence age-related decrements in golf performance and to what extent these factors are mediated by changes in the quantity, quality, and intensity of practice.

In sum, the acquisition and maintenance of expert performance in golf appears to follow a pattern similar to that found in many other domains involving perceptual-motor skill. Once we view the future and current expert performers as biological systems, many requirements for acquiring and maintaining expert performance become apparent. The bodies and brains of the expert performer are complex systems that adapt to the demands of daily activities, such as extended deliberate practice. The future expert performers need to gradually increase their level of practice over years of involvement in the domain and then maintain high levels of practice to sustain the current level of adaptation. When expert performers decrease the amount and intensity of their daily practice then the body will change resulting in a new level of adaptation typically with reduced functionality. The reduction in performance of older performers and golfers appears to be in large part the result of reduced levels of practice and physical activity.

The Path to Increased Control

One of the most important insights about the game of golf for me, as a non-golfer, is how difficult it is to hit correct shots in a reproducible manner. Even the best mechanical devices, designed for the sole purpose of driving or putting golf balls cannot produce completely consistent shots. And neither can the best players! All golfers need to accept that there is inherent variability in golf that is outside human control, just as there is in playing the roulette, tossing a coin, or throwing a pair of dice. They must also accept that humans are all-purpose organisms that are constantly changing and adapting to a wide range of regular activities and demands. In light of this unavoidable variability, the task of acquiring expertise in perceptual-motor domains means acquiring the mechanisms to reduce variability by monitoring and controlling one's performance, striving for consistence, and gaining knowledge of one's variability, in order to produce the most effective performance under specified conditions.

The focus on acquiring mechanisms that reduce variability makes the search for quick fixes or sudden insights in golf seem unrealistic. It is hard to imagine any chance discovery that could elevate the level of consistent performance of a recreational golfer to the level of expert golfers. Furthermore, it is obvious why improved golf performance is attained only by gradually reducing sources of variability over years or even decades. The consistency of golf shots can be increased by designing practice activities that allow repeated opportunities to get feedback on shots that are the same or intentionally varied by the golfer. Increased consistency of shots will facilitate the development of representations for predicting ball trajectories and of strategies for planning one's shots for particular holes on golf courses.

In a more speculative vein, I propose that attaining and maintaining high levels of performance in golf require the acquisition of representations that allow individuals to monitor and control aspects of their swing and putting. According to this argument, expert performance cannot be fully automated because it requires continued adjustment and control (Ericsson, 1996, 1998). Let me illustrate my argument by discussing another exceptional motor activity that has been studied experimentally, namely juggling. Jugglers monitor the trajectories of the juggled objects at the summit of their arch — the rest of the visual field can be occluded without decrements in performance (Beek, 1989). After assessing any deviations from the preferred path of an object at the summit, the juggler adjusts the throwing action a fraction of second later when that object reaches the juggler's hand. Control of rapid movement appears to be attained by anticipatory processing where an expert performer is able to predict necessary adjustments to allow programming of the ballistic motor action in advance.

This general type of anticipatory adjustment of rapid movements has been demonstrated in many sports, such as, baseball, hockey, volleyball, and tennis (Abernethy, 1991). For example, expert racquet players are able to predict the ball trajectory of a tennis serve better than novice players — in fact, they are able to predict the ball path better than chance *even before* the serving tennis player has made contact between the ball and racquet by reading the preparatory movements that set up the serve. This form of anticipatory processing allows experts to prepare their motor actions well in advance of the brief impact between ball and club/racquet — "programming the computer" to use Nicklaus' (1974) phrase. It is probable that expert golfers engage in this type of preparation before a shot, when they plan and image the desired trajectory clearly, and then proceed to align and set up and making potential adjustments before they initiate the downswing to hit the ball with their club.

Our current knowledge about the representations that allow expert golfers to control their performance better is limited. In the absence of experimental evidence from expert performance in golf, I will base my discussion on the existing knowledge from other domains of expertise, such as music and chess. Research on music expertise (Ericsson, 1997, 1998; Lehmann & Ericsson, 1997a) has revealed evidence for the development of three general types of interacting representations illustrated in Figure 8. One type of representation allows the expert performer to create an image of the desired goal, such as the sound of the music performance. In the case of golf, this would correspond to the desired ball trajectory for a shot where the terrain, weather conditions, and consistency of the required shot are taken into account. Another type of representation allows the expert to translate the goal into an appropriate sequence of motor actions, where the musicians generate the speed and loudness necessary to produce the desired sound.

Because musicians must sometimes perform music without prior opportunity to prepare and rehearse their interpretation, called sight reading, they have to be able to plan mentally how their fingers will strike the keys during their music performance (Lehmann & Ericsson, 1993, 1996). Expert pianists retain control over their motor performance even after a piece has been memorised and they have been shown to be able to perform the piece without additional practice under changed conditions, such as in a different key or at a slower tempo (Lehmann & Ericsson, 1995, 1997b). Similarly, during tournament play the golfer has to generate the appropriate stance, alignment and other adjustments, such as producing a fade, to achieve the intended shot without the opportunity to try out various shots in advance.

The third and final type of representation allows the expert to monitor and compare their concurrent performance with their desired goal, such as the intended musical sound or the intended sequence of a pianist's finger movements. In some recent studies Woody, Lehmann, and Ericsson (1998) documented this ability of expert musicians by observing them reproduce several different versions of an expert's prerecorded interpretations of pieces of music. Furthermore, expert pianists can rapidly identify their incorrect

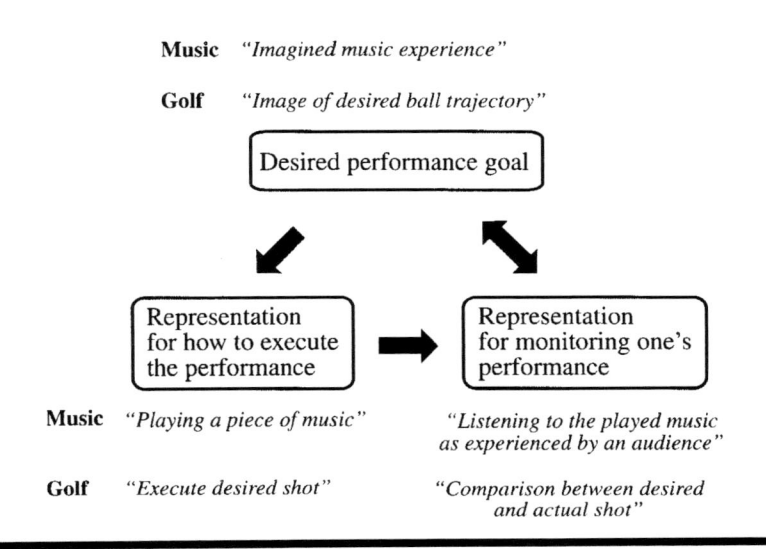

Music *"Imagined music experience"*

Golf *"Image of desired ball trajectory"*

Desired performance goal

Representation for how to execute the performance → Representation for monitoring one's performance

Music *"Playing a piece of music"* — *"Listening to the played music as experienced by an audience"*

Golf *"Execute desired shot"* — *"Comparison between desired and actual shot"*

Figure 8
Three types of internal representations that mediate expert music and golf performance and its continued improvement during practice. (Adapted from "The scientific study of expert levels of performance: General implications for optimal learning and creativity" by K. A. Ericsson in *High Ability Studies*, 9, p. 92. Copyright 1998 by European Council for High Ability.)

keystrokes on the piano and "hide" their mistakes by modifying their subsequent playing. A similar type of representation should allow a golfer to identify missed putts based on very early cues — well before the ball comes to a stop. This assessment should allow them to distinguish misdirected shots and incorrect reading of greens from normal variability of ball trajectories that would not require adjustments. Ideally, the expert golfer should not only be able to identify the error, but also localise the source of the miss, which would allow them to make adjustments or at least be able to assess the component that requires correction during subsequent practice. In accord with these speculations, expert golfers report that they engage in practice after competitive rounds to correct faults and errors (Jones, 1966; Nicklaus, 1974). Furthermore, expert minigolfers exhibit better memory for their performance during a round than less accomplished players and they can better recall the types of strokes made during the round (Bäckman & Molander, 1986).

How are these representations acquired? Many expert golfers report seeing visual images of the desired ball trajectories when they play and also when they reflect back on events during a competition. It is tempting to believe that novices might benefit from engaging in similar visual imagery as well as watching experts perform. However, from extensive research in many other domains of expertise, such as music and chess, we know that these representations do not result from mere experience or even passive observation of experts' performance. For example, a music student is not likely to attain the performance of a virtuoso violinist by merely observing video recordings or even trying to recall images of those performances. In order to benefit from rehearsing visual memory images, the memory image should correspond to the perceived events and situations.

A vast body of research on memory has shown that in many domains there is close correspondence between level of expertise and the ability to reproduce representative stimuli after a brief exposure (Chase & Simon, 1973; Ericsson & Kintsch, 1995; Ericsson & Lehmann, 1996; Ericsson, Patel, & Kintsch, 2000). For example, the memory for briefly presented chess positions increases slowly as the performers' chess skill increases and associated representations develop and become increasingly refined. Expert chess players have been shown to collect books and magazines with the recorded games of chess masters (Charness et al., 1996). They can play through the games to see if their selected moves correspond to those originally selected by the masters. If the chess master's move differed from their own, it would imply that they must have missed something in their planning and evaluation. Through careful, extended analysis, the chess expert is generally able to discover the reasons for the chess master's move. Similarly, the chess player can read published analyses of various opening combinations and supplement their own knowledge by examining the consequences of new variations of these openings. Serious chess players spend as much as four hours every day engaged in this type of deliberate practice (Charness et al., 1996; Ericsson, Krampe, & Tesch-Römer, 1993). The memory of chess players improves gradually and when they reach the level of chess master they are able to play games under blindfold conditions without any perceptually available chessboards. However, this memory is not visual or photographic, because if the same pieces from a chess position are scrambled before they are blindfolded, the chess masters' memory is reduced to virtually the level of beginner.

In a manner similar to chess, one would predict that golfers would need to deliberately acquire valid mental representations by engaging in the type of practice activities described earlier, where the expert golfers systematically explored the consequences of different types of variations in the shots. As the acuity and validity of the representations increase, the expert golfer can benefit from engaging in mental practice akin to the chess player thinking about chess problems and the musician thinking about musical interpretations. They will also be able to benefit from studying their own performance and other expert performance on video recordings. However, it is less clear that watching tournament events will by itself improve their performance, though it might give golfers some ideas that would be implemented later over many practice sessions (Floyd, 1989).

In sum, many people think of golf and other sports, such as archery and darts, as simple where there seem to be restricted room for improvements through practice. However, once we start focusing on consistency of shots and efforts to exert increased control over our bodies and the motor system then the complexity of elite golf performance becomes apparent. The expert golfers' ability to perceive minute differences and exert control of the ball trajectories did not emerge naturally but through the process of acquiring refined representations for perceiving, monitoring and controlling the motor system. The beginning golfers cannot easily find the long and difficult path to the successful acquisition of the fundamental strokes in golf. Beginning golfers need a guide in the form of a teacher or a golf professional who can support their development of the required representations for monitoring and control. They need to understand that expert golf performance is based on consistency and control of shot-making and that these aspects of performance are the results of extended deliberate practice where golfers seek out training activities that provide reliable feedback and opportunities for repetition. As the causal link between training and improvements of golf performance is better explicated I believe that an increasing proportion of young aspiring golfers will be motivated to engage in regular deliberate practice and will seek guidance of golf coaches. These potential developments would bring golf closer to other domains of expertise, such as music and dance, where the technical proficiency of elite performers provides motivation to beginners, especially children and adolescents, to seek the guidance of a qualified teacher to find the extended and challenging path to expert performance.

As our scientific analysis of the highest levels of performance produces new insights into the complexity of skilled performance that is attainable after many thousands of hours of deliberate efforts to improve, I believe that we will uncover a deeper understanding of how effective learning and specialised practice methods can be used to target particular training goals. Instead of celebrating signs of innate talent and natural gifts, I would recommend that we marvel at the discipline and the monumental effort that go into mastering a domain.

Acknowledgments

This research was supported by the FSCW/Conradi Endowment Fund of Florida State University Foundation. The author wants to thank Jeff Feddon, Len Hill, Elizabeth Kirk, Chris Meissner and Gershon Tenenbaum for their very valuable comments on earlier drafts of this manuscript.

Footnotes

1. Given that senior PGA is not played under exactly the same course conditions as the regular PGA, it is not appropriate to infer that a comparable number of strokes for the two groups of players implies the absence of differences in performance. It is generally assumed that the preparation of courses for the regular PGA differs from that for senior PGA events. During regular PGA events the course is designed to be more difficult with a narrower fairway and more difficult placement of the hole on the greens.
2. In my chapter I am only concerned with efforts to increase the consistency of performance of amateurs beyond previously attained levels. It is clear that when the performance of amateurs decreases due to the sudden emergence of a problem, such as performance anxiety or inability to concentrate, then there may be short-term effective methods to restore the original performance.

References

Abernethy, B. (1991). Visual search strategies and decision-making in sport. *International Journal of Sport Psychology, 22,* 189–210.

Abernethy, B., & Burgess-Limerick, R. (1992). Visual information for the timing of skilled movements: A review. In J. J. Summers (Ed.), *Approaches to the study of motor control and learning* (pp. 343–384). Amsterdam: Elsevier.

Abernethy, B., Neal, R. J., & Moran, M. J. (1990). Expert-novice differences in muscle activity during the golf swing. In A. J. Cochran (Ed.), *Science and golf: Proceedings of the First World Scientific Congress of Golf* (pp. 54–60). London: E & FN Spon.

Adlington, G. S. (1996). Proper swing technique and biomechanics of golf. *Clinics in Sports Medicine, 15,* 9–26.

Anderson, J. R. (1982). Acquisition of cognitive skill. *Psychological Review, 89,* 369–406.

Bäckman, L., & Molander, B. (1986). Effects of adult age and level of skill on the ability to cope with high-stress conditions in a precision sport. *Psychology of Aging, 1,* 334–336.

Baird, J. (1908). *Advanced golf or hints and instruction for progressive players.* London: Methuen & Co.

Barclay, J. K., & McIlroy, W. E. (1990). Effect of skill level on muscle activity in neck and forearm muscles during the golf swing. In A. J. Cochran (Ed.), *Science and golf: Proceedings of the First World Scientific Congress of Golf* (pp. 49–53). London: E & FN Spon.

Barkow, A., & Barrett, D. (1998). *Golf legends of all time.* Lincolnwood, IL: Publications International.

Bédard, J., & Chi, M. T. H. (1993). Expertise in auditing. *Auditing, 12,* (Suppl.), 1–25.

Beek, P. J. (1989). *Juggling dynamics.* Amsterdam, Netherlands: Free University Press.

Belkin, D. S., Gansneder, B., Pickens, M., Rotella, R. J., & Striegel, D. (1994). Predictability and stability of Professional Golf Association tour statistics. *Perceptual and Motor Skills, 78,* 1275–1280.

Bloom, B. S. (1985). Generalizations about talent development. In B. S. Bloom (Ed.), *Developing talent in young people* (pp. 507–549). New York: Ballantine Books.

Bonner, S. E., & Pennington, N. (1991). Cognitive processes and knowledge as determinants of auditor expertise. *Journal of Accounting Literature, 10,* 1–50.

Bootsma, R. J., & van Wieringen, P. C. W. (1990). Timing of an attacking forehand drive in table tennis. *Journal of Experimental Psychology: Human Perception and Performance, 16,* 21–29.

Boucher, J. L., & Mutimer, B. T. P. (1994). The relative age phenomenon in sport: A replication and extension with ice-hockey players. *Research Quarterly for Exercise and Sport, 65,* 377–381.

Camerer, C. F., & Johnson, E. J. (1991). The process-performance paradox in expert judgment: How can the experts know so much and predict so badly? In K. A. Ericsson & J. Smith (Eds.), *Towards a general theory of expertise: Prospects and limits* (pp. 195–217). Cambridge: Cambridge University Press.

Charness, N., Krampe, R. Th., & Mayr, U. (1996). The role of practice and coaching in entrepreneurial skill domains: An international comparison of life-span chess skill acquisition. In K. A. Ericsson (Ed.), *The road to excellence: The acquisition of expert performance in the arts and sciences, sports, and games* (pp. 51–80). Mahwah, NJ: Erlbaum.

Chase, W. G., & Ericsson, K. A. (1982). Skill and working memory. In G. H. Bower (Ed.), *The psychology of learning and motivation* (Vol. 16, pp. 1–58). New York: Academic Press.

Chase, W. G., & Simon, H. A. (1973). The mind's eye in chess. In W. G. Chase (Ed.), *Visual information processing* (pp. 215–281). New York: Academic Press.

Ciborowski, T. (1997). "Superstition" in the collegiate baseball player. *The Sport Psychologist, 11,* 305–317.

Cochran, A., & Stobbs, J. (1968). *The search for the perfect swing.* Philadephia, PA: J. B. Lippincott Co.

Coffey, B., Mathison, T., Viker, M., Reichow, A., Hogan, C., & Pelz, D. (1990). Visual alignment considerations in golf putting consistency. In A. J. Cochran (Ed.), *Science and golf: Proceedings of the First World Scientific Congress of Golf* (pp. 76–80). London: E & FN Spon.

Cohn, P. J. (1994). *The mental game of golf: A guide to peak performance.* South Bend, In: Diamond Communications.

Cohn, P. J., Rotella, R. J., & Lloyd, J. W. (1990). Effects of a cognitive-behavioral intervention on the preshot routine and performance in golf. *The Sport Psychologist, 4,* 33–47.

Crofton, I., & Fraser, D. (1985). *A dictionary of music quotations.* New York: Schirmer Books.

Dawes, R. M. (1994). *House of cards: Psychology and psychotherapy built on myth.* New York: Free Press.

Delay, D., Nougier, V., Orliaguet, J.-P., & Coello, Y. (1997). Movement control in golf putting. *Human Movement Science, 16*, 597–619.

Diaz, J. (1989). Perils of putting. *Sports Illustrated, 70*, 76–79.

Dillman, C. J., & Lange, G. W. (1994). How has biomechanics contributed to the understanding of the golf swing? In A. J. Cochran & M. R. Farrally (Eds.), *Science and golf II: Proceedings of the 1994 World Scientific Congress of Golf* (pp. 3–13). London: E & FN Spon.

Elbert, T., Pantev, C., Wienbruch, C., Rockstroh, & Taub, E. (1995). Increased cortical representation of fingers of the left hand in string players. *Science, 270*, 305–307.

Ellis, W. H., Filyer, R., & Wilson, D. (1999) Psychological and psychomotor approach to the development of junior golfers. In M. R. Farrally & A. J. Cochran (Eds.), *Science and golf III: Proceedings of the 1998 World Scientific Congress of Golf* (pp. 254–260). Champaign, IL: Human Kinetics.

Ericsson, K. A. (1985). Memory skill. *Canadian Journal of Psychology, 39*, 188–231.

Ericsson, K. A. (1988). Analysis of memory performance in terms of memory skill. In R. J. Sternberg (Ed.), *Advances in the psychology of human intelligence*, (Vol. 4, pp. 137–179). Hillsdale, NJ: Erlbaum.

Ericsson, K. A. (1990). Peak performance and age: An examination of peak performance in sports. In P. B. Baltes & M. M. Baltes (Eds.), *Successful aging: Perspectives from the behavioral sciences* (pp. 164–195). New York: Cambridge University Press.

Ericsson, K. A. (1996). The acquisition of expert performance: An introduction to some of the issues. In K. A. Ericsson (Ed.), *The road to excellence: The acquisition of expert performance in the arts and sciences, sports, and games* (pp. 1–50). Mahwah, NJ: Erlbaum.

Ericsson, K. A. (1997). Deliberate practice and the acquisition of expert performance: An overview. In H. Jorgensen & A. C. Lehmann (Eds.), *Does practice make perfect? Current theory and research on instrumental music practice*. NMH-publikasjoner 1997:1. Oslo, Norway: Norges musikkhögskole.

Ericsson, K. A. (1998). The scientific study of expert levels of performance: General implications for optimal learning and creativity. *High Ability Studies, 9*, 75–100.

Ericsson, K. A. (in press). Attaining excellence through deliberate practice: Insights from the study of expert performance. In M. Ferrari (Ed.), *The pursuit of excellence in education*. Hillsdale, NJ: Erlbaum.

Ericsson, K. A., & Charness, N. (1994). Expert performance: Its structure and acquisition. *American Psychologist, 49*, 725–747.

Ericsson, K. A., Chase, W. G., & Faloon, S. (1980). Acquisition of a memory skill. *Science, 208*, 1181–1182.

Ericsson, K. A., & Kintsch, W. (1995). Long-term working memory. *Psychological Review, 102*, 211–245.

Ericsson, K. A., Krampe, R. Th., & Heizmann, S. (1993). Can we create gifted people? In CIBA Foundation Symposium 178 *The origin and development of high ability* (pp. 222–249). Chichester, UK: Wiley.

Ericsson, K. A., Krampe, R. Th., & Tesch-Römer, C. (1993). The role of deliberate practice in the acquisition of expert performance. *Psychological Review, 100*, 363–406.

Ericsson, K. A., & Lehmann, A. C. (1996). Expert and exceptional performance: Evidence on maximal adaptations on task constraints. *Annual Review of Psychology, 47*, 273–305.

Ericsson, K. A., & Lehmann, A. C. (1999). Expertise. In M. A. Runco & S. Pritzer (Eds.), *Encyclopedia of creativity*, Vol. 1 (pp. 695–707). San Diego, CA: Academic Press.

Ericsson, K. A., Patel, V. L., & Kintsch, W. (2000). How experts' adaptations to representative task demands account for the expertise effect in memory recall: Comment on Vicente and Wang (1998). *Psychological Review, 107*, 578–592.

Ericsson, K. A., & Smith, J. (1991). Prospects and limits in the empirical study of expertise: An introduction. In K. A. Ericsson & J. Smith (Eds.), *Toward a general theory of expertise: Prospects and limits* (pp. 1–38). Cambridge: Cambridge University Press.

Fitts, P., & Posner, M. I. (1967). *Human performance.* Belmont, CA: Brooks/Cole.

Floyd, R. (with Dennis, L.). (1989). *From 60 yards in.* New York: Harper Collins.

Galamian, I. (1972). Ivan Galamian. In S. Applebaum & S. Applebaum (Eds.), *The way they play, Book I* (pp. 240–351). Neptune City, NJ: Paganiniana Publications.

Gilovich, T., Vallone, R., & Tversky, A. (1985). The hot hand in basketball: On the misperception of random sequences. *Cognitive Psychology, 17,* 295–314.

Glaser, R., & Chi, M. T. H. (1988). Overview. In M. T. H. Chi, R. Glaser, & M. J. Farr (Eds.), *The nature of expertise* (pp. xv–xxxvi). Hillsdale, NJ: Erlbaum.

Goodner, R. (1978). *Golf's greatest: The legendary world golf hall of famers.* Norwalk, CT: Golf Digest.

Hale, T., & Hale, G. T. (1999). Analysis of performance in the Open championship 1892–1997. In M. R. Farrally & A. J. Cochran (Eds.), *Science and golf III: Proceedings of the 1998 World Scientific Congress of Golf* (pp. 394–403). Champaign, IL: Human Kinetics.

Hall, C. R., Hardy, J., & Gammage, K. L. (1999). About hitting golf balls in the water: Comments on Janelle's (1999) article on ironic processes. *The Sport Psychologist, 13,* 221–224.

Helsen, W. F., Starkes, J. L., & Hodges, N. J. (1998). Team sports and the theory of deliberate practice. *Journal of Sport and Exercise Psychology, 20,* 12–34.

Helsen, W. F., Starkes, J. L., & van Winckel, J. (1998). The influence of relative age on success and dropout in male soccer players. *American Journal of Human Biology, 10,* 791–798.

Hill, L. (1999). *Mental representations in skilled golf putting.* Masters thesis, Department of Psychology, Florida State University, Florida, USA.

Hill. L. A., Ericsson, K. A., & Watson, J. C. (1999, November). *Expert golf putting: Better prediction and higher consistency of ball trajectories.* Poster presented at the 40th annual meeting of the Psychonomic Society, Los Angeles, CA.

Hodges, N. J., & Starkes, J. L. (1996). Wrestling with the nature of expertise: A sport specific test of Ericsson, Krampe and Tesch-Römer's (1993) theory of "Deliberate Practice". *International Journal of Sport Psychology, 27,* 1–25.

Hogan, B. (1948). *Power golf.* New York: Pocket Books.

Hogan, B. (with Warren, H.). (1957). *Five lessons: The modern fundamentals of golf.* New York: Simon & Schuster.

Howe, M.J.A., Davidson, J.W., & Sloboda, J.A. (1998). Innate talents: Reality or myth? *Behavioral and Brain Sciences, 21,* 399–442.

Janelle, C. M. (1999). Ironic mental processes in sport: Implications for sport psychologists. *The Sport Psychologist, 13,* 201–220.

Jones, E., & Brown, I. (1937). *Swinging into golf.* New York: McGraw-Hill.

Jones, R. T. (1966). *Bobby Jones on golf.* New York: Doubleday.

Katims, M. (1972). Milton Katims. In S. Applebaum & S. Applebaum (Eds.), *The way they play, Book I* (pp. 233–242). Neptune City, NJ: Paganiniana Publications.

Kawashima, K., Takeshita, S., Zaitsu, H., & Meshizuka, T. (1994). A biomechanical analysis of respiratory pattern during the golf swing. In A. J. Cochran & M. R. Farrally (Eds.), *Science and golf II: Proceedings of the 1994 World Scientific Congress of Golf* (pp. 46–49). London: E & FN Spon.

Kirschenbaum, D. S., O'Connor, E. A., & Owens, D. (1999). Positive illusions in golf: Empirical and conceptual analyses. *Journal of Applied Sport Psychology, 11,* 1–27.

Kite, T., & Dennis, L. (1990). *How to play consistent golf.* New York: Golf Digest.

Koening, G., Tamres, M., & Mann, R. W. (1994). The biomechanics of the shoe-ground interaction in golf. In A. J. Cochran & M. R. Farrally (Eds.), *Science and golf II: Proceedings of the 1994 World Scientific Congress of Golf* (pp. 40–45). London: E & FN Spon.

Krampe, R. Th., & Ericsson, K. A. (1996). Maintaining excellence: Deliberate practice and elite performance in young and older pianists. *Journal of Experimental Psychology: General, 125*, 331–359.

Kroen, W. C. (1999). *The new why book of golf.* New York: Barnes & Noble Books.

Lehman, H. C. (1953). *Age and achievement.* Princeton, NJ: Princeton University Press.

Lehmann, A. C. (1997). Acquisition of expertise in music: Efficiency of deliberate practice as a moderating variable in accounting for sub-expert performance. In I. Deliege & J. A. Sloboda (Eds.), *Perception and cognition of music* (pp. 165–191). Hillsdale, NJ: Erlbaum.

Lehmann, A. C., & Ericsson, K. A. (1993). Sight-reading ability of expert pianists in the context of piano accompanying, *Psychomusicology, 12,* 182–195.

Lehmann, A. C., & Ericsson, K. A. (1995, November). *Expert pianists' mental representation of memorized music.* Poster presented at the 36th annual meeting of the Psychonomic Society, Los Angeles, CA.

Lehmann, A. C., & Ericsson, K. A. (1996). Music performance without preparation: Structure and acquisition of expert sight-reading. *Psychomusicology, 15,* 1–29.

Lehmann, A. C., & Ericsson K. A. (1997a). Research on expert performance and deliberate practice: Some implications for the education of amateur musicians and music students. *Psychomusicology, 16,* 40–58.

Lehmann, A. C., & Ericsson K. A. (1997b). Expert pianists' mental representations: Evidence from successful adaptation to unexpected performance demands. *Proceedings of the Third Triennial ESCOM Conference* (pp. 165–169). Uppsala, Sweden: SLU Service/Reproenheten.

Lehmann, A. C., & Ericsson K. A. (1998). The historical development of domains of expertise: Performance standards and innovations in music. In A. Steptoe (Ed.), *Genius and the mind* (pp. 67–94). Oxford, UK: Oxford University Press.

Lockwood, J. (1999). A small-scale local survey of age-related male golfing ability. In M. R. Farrally & A. J. Cochran (Eds.), *Science and golf III: Proceedings of the 1998 World Scientific Congress of Golf* (pp. 112–119). Champaign, IL: Human Kinetics.

McCaffrey, N., & Orlick, T. (1989). Mental factors related to excellence among top professional golfers. *International Journal of Sport Psychology, 20,* 256–278.

McGlynn, F. G., Jones, R., & Kerwin, D. G. (1990). A laser based putting alignment test. In A. J. Cochran (Ed.), *Science and golf: Proceedings of the First World Scientific Congress of Golf* (pp. 70–75). London: E & FN Spon.

McLean, J. (1999). *Golf school: The tuition-free tee-to-green curriculum for golf's finest high-end academy.* New York: Doubleday.

McLeod, P. (1987). Visual reaction time and high-speed ball games. *Perception, 16,* 49–59.

Melvin, V. C., & Grealy, M. A. (1999). Superstitious and routine behaviours in male and female golfers of varying levels of ability. In M. R. Farrally & A. J. Cochran (Eds.), *Science and golf III: Proceedings of the 1998 World Scientific Congress of Golf* (pp. 213–219). Champaign, IL: Human Kinetics.

Miller, G. A. (1956). The magical number seven, plus or minus two: Some limits of our capacity for processing information. *Psychological Review, 63,* 81–97.

Moore, W. E., & Stevenson, J. R. (1991). Understanding trust in the performance of complex automatic sport skills. *The Sport Psychologist, 5,* 281–289.

Moore, W. E., & Stevenson, J. R. (1994). Training for trust in sport skills. *The Sport Psychologist, 8,* 1–12.

Neal, R. J., Abernethy, B., Moran, M. J., & Parker, A. W. (1990). The influence of club length and shot distances on the temporal characteristics of the swings of expert and novice golfers.

In A. J. Cochran (Ed.), *Science and golf: Proceedings of the First World Scientific Congress of Golf* (pp. 36–42). London: E & FN Spon.

Nelson, B. (1946). *Winning golf.* New York: A. S. Barnes.

Nicklaus, J. (with Bowden, K.). (1974). *Golf my way.* New York: Simon & Schuster.

Norman, D. A., Coblentz, C. L., Brooks, L. R., & Babcook, C. J. (1992). Expertise in visual diagnosis: A review of the literature. *Academic Medicine, 67*(10), S78–S83.

Olsavsky, T. (1994). The effects of driver head size on performance. In A. J. Cochran & M. R. Farrally (Eds.), *Science and golf II: Proceedings of the 1994 World Scientific Congress of Golf* (pp. 321–326). London: E & FN Spon.

Ouimet, F. (1914). Suggestions for putting. In H. Vardon, A. Herd, G. Duncan, W. Reid, & F. Ouimet (Eds.), *Success at golf* (pp. 103–116). Boston: Little, Brown, & Company.

Over, R., & Thomas, P. R. (1995). Age and skilled psychomotor performance: A comparison of young and older golfers. *International Journal of Aging and Human Development, 41,* 1–12.

Pelz, D. (1989). *Putt like the pros.* New York: Harper & Row.

Pelz, D. (1994). A study of golfers' abilities to read greens. In A. J. Cochran & M. R. Farrally (Eds.), *Science and golf II: Proceedings of the 1994 World Scientific Congress of Golf* (pp. 180–185). London: E & FN Spon.

Player, G. (1980). *Gary Player's golf book for young people.* Norwalk, CT: Golf Digest.

Price, N. (with Rubenstein, L.). (1999). *The swing: Mastering the principles of the game.* New York: Alfred A. Knopf.

Primrose, W. (1972). William Primrose. In S. Applebaum & S. Applebaum (Eds.), *The way they play, Book I* (pp. 243–261). Neptune City, NJ: Paganiniana Publications.

Ravizza, K., & Osborne, T. (1991). Nebraska's 3 R's: One-play-at-a-time preperformance routine for collegiate football. *The Sport Psychologist, 5,* 256–265.

Reddy, A. P. (1990). Relationships among technical skills and physical fitness of amateur golf players in India. In A. J. Cochran (Ed.), *Science and golf: Proceedings of the First World Scientific Congress of Golf* (pp. 64–69). London: E & FN Spon.

Riccio, L. J. (1990). Statistical analysis of the average golfer. In A. J. Cochran (Ed.), *Science and golf: Proceedings of the First World Scientific Congress of Golf* (pp. 153–158). London: E & FN Spon.

Robergs, R. A., & Roberts, S. O. (1997). *Exercise physiology: Exercise, performance, and clinical applications.* St. Louis, MO: Mosby-Year Book.

Rosson, M. B. (1985). The role of experience in editing. *Proceedings of INTERACT '84 IFIP Conference on Human-Computer Interaction* (pp. 45–50). New York: Elsevier.

Rotella, R. J., & Boutcher, S. H. (1990). A closer look at the role of the mind in golf. In A. J. Cochran (Ed.), *Science and golf: Proceedings of the First World Scientific Congress of Golf* (pp. 93–97). London: E & FN Spon.

Rotella, R. J., & Lerner, J. D. (1993). Responding to competitive pressure. In R. N Singer, M. Murphey, & L. K. Tennant (Eds.), *Handbook of research on sport psychology* (pp. 528–541). London/New York: Macmillan.

Sauer, E. (1913). The training of the virtuoso. In J. F. Cooke (Ed.), *Great pianists on piano playing: Study talks with foremost virtuosos* (pp. 236–250). Philadelphia, PA: Theo Presser.

Schmidt, H. G., Norman, G. R., & Boshuizen, H. P. A. (1990). A cognitive perspective on medical expertise: Theory and implications. *Academic Medicine, 65,* 611–621.

Schneider, W. (1993). Acquiring expertise: Determinants of exceptional performance. In K. A. Heller, J. Mönks, & H. Passow (Eds.), *International handbook of research and development of giftedness and talent* (pp. 311–324). Oxford, UK: Pergamon Press.

Schneider, W., & Shiffrin, R. M. (1977). Controlled and automatic human information processing: I. Detection, search, and attention. *Psychological Review, 84,* 1–66.

Schulz, R., & Curnow, C. (1988). Peak performance and age among superathletes: Track and field, swimming, baseball, tennis and golf. *Journal of Gerontology: Psychological Sciences, 43,* 113–120.

Schulz, R., Musa, D., Staszewski, J., & Siegler, R. S. (1994). The relationship between age and major league baseball performance: Implications for development. *Psychology and Aging, 9,* 274–286.

Shanteau, J., & Stewart, T. R. (1992). Why study expert decision making? Some historical perspectives and comments. *Organizational Behaviour and Human Decision Processes, 53,* 95–106.

Shephard, R. J. (1994). *Aerobic fitness and health.* Champaign, IL: Human Kinetics.

Shiffrin, R. M., & Schneider, W. (1977). Controlled and automatic human information processing: II. Perceptual learning, automatic attending and a general theory. *Psychological Review, 84,* 127–189.

Simon, H. A., & Chase, W. G. (1973). Skill in chess. *American Scientist, 61,* 394–403.

Sloboda, J. A. (1996). The acquisition of musical performance expertise: Deconstructing the "talent" account of individual differences in musical expressivity. In K. A. Ericsson (Ed.), *The road to excellence: The acquisition of expert performance in the arts and sciences, sports, and games* (pp. 107–126). Mahwah, NJ: Erlbaum.

Snead, S. (with Wade, D.). (1989). *Better golf the Sam Snead way.* Chicago, IL: Contemporary Books.

Snead, S. (with Pirozzolo, F.). (1997). *The game I love.* New York: Ballentine Books.

Spirduso, W. W. (1995). *Physical dimensions of aging.* Champaign, IL: Human Kinetics.

Stael von Holstein, C.-A. S. (1972). Probabilistic forecasting: An experiment related to the stock market. *Organizational Behavior and Human Performance, 8,* 139–158.

Starkes, J. L., Deakin, J., Allard, F., Hodges, N. J., & Hayes, A. (1996). Deliberate practice in sports: What is it anyway? In K. A. Ericsson (Ed.), *The road to excellence: The acquisition of expert performance in the arts and sciences, sports, and games* (pp. 81–106). Mahwah, NJ: Erlbaum.

Sternberg. R. J. (1996). Costs of expertise. In K. A. Ericsson (Ed.), *The road to excellence: The acquisition of expert performance in the arts and sciences, sports, and games* (pp. 347–354). Mahwah, NJ: Erlbaum.

Takeuchi, A. H., & Hulse, S. H. (1993). Absolute pitch. *Psychological Bulletin, 113,* 345–361.

Taylor, J. (1999). Isn't it ironic? Or irony is in the unconscious eye of the beholder. *The Sport Psychologist, 13,* 225–230.

Thomas, P. R., & Fogarty, G. J. (1997). Psychological skills training in golf: The role of individual differences in cognitive preferences. *The Sport Psychologist, 11,* 86–106.

Thomas, P. R., & Over, R. (1994a). Contributions of psychological, psychomotor, and shot-making skills to prowess at golf. In A. J. Cochran & M. R. Farrally (Eds.), *Science and golf II: Proceedings of the 1994 World Scientific Congress of Golf* (pp. 138–143). London: E & FN Spon.

Thomas, P. R., & Over, R. (1994b). Psychological and psychomotor skills associated with performance in golf. *The Sport Psychologist, 8,* 73–86.

Thomas, P. R., Schlinker, P. J., & Over, R. (1996). Psychological and psychomotor skills associated with prowess at ten-pin bowling. *Journal of Sports Sciences, 14,* 255–268.

Tierney, D. E., & Coop, R. (1999). A bivariate probability model for putting efficiency. In M. R. Farrally & A. J. Cochran (Eds.), *Science and golf III: Proceedings of the 1998 World Scientific Congress of Golf* (pp. 385–394). Champaign, IL: Human Kinetics.

Vardon, H. (1914). The art of driving. In H. Vardon, A. Herd, G. Duncan, W. Reid, & F. Quimet (Eds.), *Success at golf* (pp. 3–18). Boston: Little, Brown, & Company.

Watson, T. (with Seitz, N.). (1983). *Getting up and down: How to save strokes from forty yards and in.* New York: Random House.

Watson, T. (with Seitz, N.). (1993). *Tom Watson's strategic golf.* New York: Pocket Books.

Wiseman, F., Chatterjee, S., Wiseman, D., & Chatterjee, N. S. (1994). An analysis of the 1992 performance statistics for players on the US PGA, Senior PGA and LPGA tours. In A. J. Cochran & M. R. Farrally (Eds.), *Science and golf II: Proceedings of the 1994 World Scientific Congress of Golf* (pp. 199–204). London: E & FN Spon.

Woods, E. (with McDaniel, P.). (1997). *Training a tiger.* New York: Harper Collins.

Woody, R. H., Lehmann, A. C., & Ericsson K. A. (1998). Evidence for mental representations mediating expert musicians' expressive performance. (Abstract). *Abstracts of the Psychonomic Society, 3,* 49.

Zaichkowsky, L., & Takenaka, K. (1993). Optimizing arousal level. In R. N Singer, M. Murphey, & L. K. Tennant (Eds.), *Handbook of research on sport psychology* (pp. 511–527). London/New York: Macmillan.

CHAPTER 2

The Development of Expertise by Senior PGA Tour Players

Leonard Zaichkowsky and Kevin Morris

Although interest in the characteristics of outstanding achievers in sport, literature, science, and the arts has likely existed since the beginning of mankind, it is only recently that academics have addressed the question seriously. In sport we commonly refer to outstanding performers as *champions*, however other domains will use related terms such as *excellence, exceptional, talented,* and *skilled.* Although a variety of terms have been used to describe exceptionality, the recent literature typically uses the term "expert" to describe this phenomenon (see for instance, Ericsson, 1996). Webster's new dictionary would confirm use of this term, "(someone) experienced, taught by use of practice; skillful; dexterous; adroit; having a facility of operation or performance from practice. A skillful or practiced person" (Webster, 1965). What we do not know unequivocally is whether expertise is acquired primarily through experience and practice (nurture) or if expertise is genetically endowed (nature). In golf the annual father/son challenge matches remind us of this age-old question: "Did the son benefit from being in a golf environment and hence learned to be an expert, or did he acquire golf genes from his father?"

The current study was prompted by and informed by a number of developments. David Hemery, Olympic hurdling champion and outstanding track and field coach at Boston University asked the first author this question, "what makes a champion in sports?" Since I had opinions but no definitive answer for David, I challenged him to pursue this question for his doctoral dissertation at Boston University. The dissertation was also published as a book, *The Pursuit of Sporting Excellence* (Hemery, 1986). Since that time I have followed with interest, journalistic accounts as well as scholarly writings on the topic.

The scholarly theoretical writing that has been most influential is that of Bloom (1985); Csikszentmihalyi, Rathunde, and Whalen (1993); Ericsson, Krampe, and Tesch-Romer (1993); and Ericsson's (1996) excellent edited text. John Salmela and his graduate students at the University of Ottawa have also written strong review and empirical papers on expertise (Cote, 1999; Durand-Bush & Salmela, 1996; Young & Salmela, in press). Howe, Davidson, and Sloboda (1998) published an extensive review of the arguments in support of hereditary accounts of expertise and environmental explanations in *Behavioral and Brain Sciences*. The April-June, 1999 issue of the *International Journal of Sport Psychology* was entirely devoted to examining the issue of nature versus nurture in the development of sport expertise, however, the Singer and Janelle (1999) review provided the most cogent summary of the current knowledge about sport expertise.

Although the above scholarly papers keep posing questions about expertise that need to be answered, it was the book, *Training a Tiger*, by Earl Woods (1997) that prompted this initial study with exceptional golfers. In this book, Mr. Woods details how he coached his son, Tiger, to become the foremost golfer in the world. Because much of what he described regarding the development of practice habits was consistent with what was written by Bloom (1985), Hemery (1986), and Ericsson (1996), we were interested in knowing whether current Senior PGA players developed their high levels of skill by following a training pattern that might be similar to that used by Tiger Woods. Secondly, we were interested in their philosophy and practice in developing the golf expertise of their own children.

Before describing the methodology and results of this study it is important that we describe the current state of knowledge regarding sport expertise. Hemery started his quest to learn what factors contributed to outstanding sport performance in the early 1980s and published his findings in 1986 (Hemery, 1986). He interviewed 63 champion calibre athletes from 12 countries representing 22 individual and team sports. Hemery established strong criteria for defining champion athletes including repeated Olympic, world, or national (e.g., National Football League, National Basketball Association, and National Hockey League) championships in their sport. One championship season was not sufficient for being included in the study.

Questions focused on physical factors related to training, social relationships, psychological factors including coping strategies, and moral factors. Although Hemery did not specifically examine possible genetic influences in high-level performance, results showed that 100% of the athletes reported total commitment to quality, intense training; and 89% believed they had control of their own destiny. The vast majority had a stable childhood and very supportive, but not pushing, parents.

About the same time Hemery was doing his research, Bloom (1985) conducted a 4-year study of talented athletes, musicians, artists, and scientists. Bloom identified three distinct stages of talent development which he labeled the early years, middle years, and later years. The early years were characterised as a period where the child was introduced to the sport (swimming, tennis) and the emphasis by teachers, coaches, and parents was on fun, playful activities. During the middle years the child got "hooked" on the sport. Their practice became more serious and they were more concerned with commitment and achievement. It was during the later years that the athletes became totally immersed in their sport and became experts. Bloom concluded that children are likely to have initial predispositions for excellence in a particular sport, however, "unless there is a long and intensive process of encouragement, nurturance, education, and training, the individuals will not attain extreme levels of capability in these particular fields" (p. 3).

Despite Bloom's conclusions, some people inside and outside of sport believed that excellence in performance could best be explained genetically (for a review see Bouchard, Malina, & Perusse, 1997). The most extreme and provocative position in favour of biology and genetics is taken by Entine (2000) who claims black athletes have an advantage in sports and this superiority (if it exists) can be explained genetically. However, a paper by Anders Ericsson and his colleagues (Ericsson, Krampe, & Tesch-Romer, 1993) challenged this position. Ericsson et al. (1993) presented evidence showing that many human anatomical and physiological characteristics such as size of heart, number of capillaries supplying blood to muscles, and metabolic properties of fast and slow twitch muscles are modifiable with intense practice. After examining human performance across a number of domains, Ericsson and Lehmann (1996) concluded that, "the influence of innate, domain-specific capacities on expert performance is small, possibly even negligible" (p. 281). Ericsson proposed that expert performance is achieved through what he called "deliberate" practice that was carried out for a minimum of 10 years or 10,000 hours.

Csikszentmihalyi and his colleagues (Csikszentmihalyi, Rathunde, & Whalen, 1993) were also interested in the development of expertise of youth during Bloom's middle years. Their theoretical approach was, however, different from that of Ericsson. Csikszentmihalyi believed that the development of talent across a variety of domains requires a peculiar mind-set, based on habits cultivated in one's early environment that eventually become so ingrained that they end up forming something like a personality trait. They called this the "flow model of optimal experience." According to Csikszentmihalyi, flow was the result of concentration on the task, merging of action and awareness, clear goals and feedback, the paradox of control, loss of self-consciousness, transformation of time, and a challenging activity that requires skill. Individuals seek new challenges to avoid boredom, and perfect new skills in order to avoid anxiety. Like Ericsson, Csikszentmihalyi believed quality practice and intense involvement was essential for skill development. But they differed in that Ericsson did not believe deliberate practice to be enjoyable, whereas Csikszentmihalyi believed practice needed to be fun and enjoyable.

In her presentation at the 1998 World Scientific Congress of Golf, Donnelly (1999) drew from the literature in educational psychology to argue for a reasoned approach to teaching and motivating children for the sport of golf. She emphasised the development of life skills such as self-esteem, self-discipline, and motivation. She concluded with this statement, "In this highly technological age of sophisticated equipment and complex analysis, it is critical to find the fun, the simplicity, the joy of golf. In this manner, young players will enjoy the game for a lifetime" (p. 252).

The purpose of our study was to obtain information about the influences on male professional golfers when they were learning the game, particularly their father's influence in cultivating their enthusiasm for and skill level in the game. Would they report training habits similar to those described by Hemery, and the gradual development via mentoring identified by Bloom? Would there be a strong emphasis on deliberate practice as proposed by Ericsson and embraced by Tiger Woods? The other purpose was to investigate the players' attitudes toward introducing their children to the game, and whether they would encourage them to become elite players.

Method
Instrument
The methodology of the study was to prepare a quick-answer, two-page, anonymous questionnaire. The survey was designed to cover the two distinct topic areas: family influences and parenting attitudes. Part 1 consisted of eight questions providing information about the influences on a participant when he was learning the game, particularly his father's influence. Part 2 contained five questions providing information about the participants'

attitudes as parents — how they would/have approached introducing their child/children to the game.

Participants

The questionnaire, including informed consent, was distributed to professional golfers aged 50 or more who were members of the Senior PGA Tour in the United States. The questionnaire was delivered to 80 players, the full field of one tour event. Players were asked to return the survey to a box in the players' locker room. Completed surveys were received from 20 players.

Results

The players' responses to questions on family influences are summarised in Table 1.

Table 2 summarises the players' responses regarding their own parenting patterns.

Finally, players were asked to provide comments about how to raise elite golfers. From these open-ended responses we discovered three themes.

Learning Environment

Here players discussed the need for an appropriate learning environment, not necessarily for learning the mechanics of the game but the "culture" of high performance golf. "Discuss all aspects of the game," said one player.

Table 1

Senior PGA Tour Players' Perceptions of Family Influences on their Development

TOPIC	FINDING
Father's influence	75% of the respondents indicated that their father played the game during their childhood.
Father's skill level	70% of the respondents' fathers who played the game had a handicap of 12 or better, with one respondent having a father who was a professional player.
Father's attitude	70% of the respondents said they were encouraged and received positive support from their father; 30% indicated a negative experience; 10% indicated that their father was "overbearing".
Perceived influence of father	Asked to describe the degree of influence from *insignificant* to *incredible*, 60% of the respondents described their father's influence as *strong* or *incredible*.
Golf club membership and access	75% of the respondents were either members of a club themselves when they were young, or their families were members; 75% also had unlimited access to golf.
Age when first started playing golf	The average age when participants began playing golf was 10 years (range 4–15, median = 10).
Amount of practice in youth	80% of the respondents played on a daily basis or 3–4 times per week, had lessons, and said they were able to achieve "quality practice"; 20% played only occasionally and did occasional work on the range.

Table 2
Senior PGA Tour Players' Parenting Attitudes

TOPIC	FINDING
Instruction to children	85% of the respondents provided instruction for their children, with just 10% choosing not to provide any instruction (one respondent has no children).
Attitude toward child's golf development	40% of the respondents did not push their children to participate in golf in any form, whereas 25% encouraged their children to play to the best of their ability and to compete well.
Encouragement to pursue a professional golf career	50% of the respondents indicated that they would encourage their children to pursue a career in professional golf provided they showed an interest.

"Help them understand the sacrifices they'll make to reach the top." "Help them understand that it's a game." Some respondents believed that by the teen years their desire to perform at a high level needs to be cultivated. "Encourage them to strive for excellence as they reach adolescence." Several mentioned the importance of finding a coach who is a good match for the child on a social level. "Find someone who can relate to your child. Someone who will become a respected friend. This is the best thing you can do."

Freedom

Players were conscious of accepting their children's career choices and playing ability. "Encourage, don't push, and accept the result," wrote one player. "Enjoy your children and let them live their own lives," said another. "Let them have fun, learn to love the game."

Opportunity

Players were consistently in support of providing opportunities to their children for playing golf and other sports. "Make the game available to them," said one player. They also believed that a varied sports experience is preferable: "Encourage all ball sports, as they teach hand/eye coordination."

Discussion

Although the sample size is small and the response rate relatively low, the results of this study are remarkably consistent with findings reported by Bloom (1985), Hemery (1986), Cote (1999), and the expertise framework provided by Ericsson et al. (1993). The father's influence was powerful in most cases. The father helped socialise the golfers to the sport in part because the father played the sport and was competent at it (low handicap).

The father also provided instruction, and strong encouragement to pursue the game of golf. Hemery (1986) reported the vast majority of athletes in his study to have a close relationship with parents. Arnold Palmer, the sole golf participant in Hemery's study, reported a strong father influence on his game. Earl Woods (1997) by his own accounts had a remarkable influence on his son, Tiger. Bloom (1985) also reported it was parents who initially introduced the child to a particular sport during what he called the early years. Cote (1999) called this period the "sampling years" (6–13 years) where children merely played for fun and parents provided support. The senior golfers in this study reported they started playing the game between 4 and 15 years of age, with the average age being 10 years.

Golfers in this study reported strong access to the game and opportunities. Seventy-five percent of the golfers had unlimited access to the game in their youth and 80% said they practised (with quality) 3–4 times per week which is consistent with Ericsson's notion behind the development of expertise. Ericsson (1993, 1996) claimed that in order for an individual to engage in 10 years or 10,000 hours of deliberate practice, resources needed to be accessible. By resources he meant time, energy, access to teachers, and training facilities. Other researchers point out that the amount and the quality of support that is provided by parents, teachers, and coaches is critical to the development of talent (Bloom, 1985; Cote, 1999; Naylor, 2000; Zaichkowsky & Haberl, 1999).

Of particular interest in this study were the golfers' remarks about "raising their own children." They emphasised providing good coaching and a supportive environment. They wanted their children to have fun, enjoy the game, and learn lessons about life from the game of golf. The comments made by the golfers in this study are also very similar to those reported by "stars of the game," published in *Golf Science International* (1999, June). Lee Janzen had this to say:

> If I had to advise young golfers, I would say enjoy playing and if you want to pursue a career professionally, don't worry too much about instruction until you are about 16 plus, unless you are already fully grown. I would practise the short game a lot. I tell them to write down some goals and map out like a little story of what you think you have to do to reach those goals (p. 3).

Colin Montgomerie said, "I came into golf late and I must admit you need encouragement in your teenage years. You need competition and you need to win the odd competition to keep it all going along" (p. 3).

The data from this study of talented senior golfers essentially confirm what Bloom (1985), Csikszentmihalyi et al. (1993), Hemery (1986), and Ericsson et al. (1993) propose regarding the development of expertise. Several events or stages appear to occur (Naylor, 2000). First they are socialised into the sport by their parents, in particular their father. Next the father assists them with instruction, and provides encouragement so that skill is developed. A talent or "gift" begins to be present in the young golfer. Expert instruction is then provided to further develop skill level. At this stage the young golfer develops a "focused striving" or a desire to be the best. This striving for excellence continues while these golfers are on the regular PGA professional tour and in fact to the Senior PGA Tour. Hale Irwin believes his current play is better now than it ever was on the PGA tour (personal communication, August 23, 1998).

So how do players on the Senior Golf Tour become "experts"? Firstly, we need to acknowledge the limitations of our initial study on this topic. We have data from a small, perhaps non-representative sample of Senior PGA Tour players on issues that warrant further research in more depth and on a wider scale. Nevertheless, on the basis of our findings and those of other researchers, we would have to concur with the conclusions arrived at by Howe et al. (1998). After their extensive review of high achievers across a number of domains they wrote, "An analysis of positive and negative evidence and arguments suggests that differences in early experiences, preferences, opportunities, habits, training, and practice are the real determinants of excellence" (p. 399).

References

Bloom, B.S. (Ed.). (1985). *Developing talent in young people.* New York: Ballantine.

Bouchard, C., Malina, R.M., & Perusse, L. (1997). *Genetics of fitness and physical performance.* Champaign, IL: Human Kinetics.

Cote, J. (1999). The influence of the family in the development of talent in sport. *The Sport Psychologist, 13,* 395–417.

Csikszentmihalyi, M., Rathunde, K., & Whalen, S. (1993). *Talented teenagers. The roots of success and failure.* New York: Cambridge University Press.

Donnelly, P.M. (1999). Teaching and sustaining the child player. In M.R. Farrally & A.J. Cochran (Eds.), *Science and golf III: Proceedings of the 1998 World Scientific Congress of Golf* (pp. 242–253). Champaign, IL: Human Kinetics.

Donnelly, P.M. (1999, June). Training your tiger. *Golf Science International,* p. 3.

Durand-Bush, N., & Salmela, J.H. (1996). Nurture over nature: A new twist to the development of expertise. *Avante, 2*(2), 87–109.

Entine, J. (2000). *Taboo: Why black athletes dominate sports and why we're afraid to talk about it.* New York: Public Affairs.

Ericsson, K.A. (Ed.). (1996). *The road to excellence: The acquisition of expert performance in the arts and sciences, sports, and games.* Mahwah, NJ: Lawrence Erlbaum.

Ericsson, K.A., Krampe, R.T., & Tesch-Romer, C. (1993). The role of deliberate practice in the acquisition of expert performance. *Psychological Review, 100,* 363–406.

Ericsson, K.A., & Lehman, A.C. (1996). Expert and exceptional performance: Evidence of maximal adaptation to task constraints. *Annual Review of Psychology, 47,* 273–305.

Hemery, D. (1986). *The pursuit of sporting excellence: A study of sport's highest achievers.* London: Willow Books.

Howe, M.J.A., Davidson, J.W., & Sloboda, J.A. (1998). Innate talents: Reality or myth? *Behavioral and Brain Sciences, 21*, 399–422.

Naylor, A. (2000). *The developmental environment of elite athletics: An evolving system.* Unpublished paper, Boston University.

Singer, R.N., & Janelle, C.M. (1999). Determining sport expertise: From genes to supremes. *International Journal of Sport Psychology, 30*, 117–150.

Webster dictionary of the English language (1965). Chicago: Processing and Books.

Woods, E. (1997). *Training a Tiger: Raising a winner in golf and life.* New York: Harper.

Young, B., & Salmela, J. (in press). Diary analysis of practice and recovery activities for elite and intermediate middle distance runners. *International Journal of Sport Psychology.*

Zaichkowsky, L.D., & Haberl, P. (1999). Cross-domain implications of motor development. In R.L. Mosher, D.J. Youngman, & J.M. Day (Eds.), *Human development across the life span: Educational and psychological applications* (pp. 9–21). Westport, CT: Praeger.

CHAPTER 3

The First Tee: Teaching Youth to Succeed in Golf and Life

Steven J. Danish

The First Tee is a national initiative started in November of 1997 with a mission to impact the lives of young people by creating affordable and accessible golf facilities for those who have traditionally not had access to the game. Youth in general, but especially those who are underserved such as minorities or those from low-income families, lack accessibility to the game. The single most significant obstacle to youth participation is the scarcity of facilities where youth can learn golf and are welcome to play at affordable prices.

The United States' leading golf organisations, The PGA Tour, The PGA of America, The USGA, The LPGA, and Augusta National Golf Club were determined to change that and The First Tee was born. These organisations became The First Tee's Oversight Committee. Their vision was to enable youth from every walk of life to have a place to learn to play golf and to enrich their lives by learning the lessons taught through golf. Implementation of this concept began in earnest in 1998. By the end of 2001, the Oversight Committee's goal is to have 100 local sites open, including some international sites. About 50 sites are presently open and the Committee now expects to exceed their original goal.

The First Tee has supported the creation of not-for-profit chapters that are generally the result of public-private partnerships as a means of developing local sites. The national organisation's role has been to provide local chapters with capital grants and to arrange supplier discounts in the form of architectural services, building materials, draining and irrigation systems, fertilizer and grass seed, and golf course equipment. The specifics of site design, operations, fundraising and organisational issues have been left to the chapters. The result is that some First Tee courses are nine holes, others are 18 holes, and some are even three holes and a driving range with a nearby non-First Tee golf course available to play. Staff selection is also left up to the site. However, each site must have at least one PGA or LPGA professional to direct the golf instruction.

In the development of sites, several principles were adopted. First, sites should be low-cost and easily accessible. They should be built near the population they are to serve. Second, the sites should be available to use when youth have free time such as after school and during the summer. Third, the facilities should be safe, structured environments for youth, a safe haven from some of the dangers of the neighbourhoods in which youth live. The target group chosen by the Oversight Committee was young people from 8 to 18.

A national teaching and certification program has been developed for all youth participants. Initially, the areas of teaching and assessment were on golf skills, golf rules and golf etiquette. It was believed that by playing the game and learning rules and etiquette, some of the valuable lessons golf teaches would be learned by participating youth. However, some members of the Oversight Committee felt that there should be a specific focus on life skills as well. Thus, participants are tested in golf skills, golf rules and etiquette, and life skills. Upon becoming certified, participants receive a First Tee card that rewards them with reduced fees for golf and other benefits. In contrast, then, to some other programs, it is possible to keep track of each participant's progress and to document the number of youth involved.

The Life Skill Center was invited to develop the life skills component for The First Tee. The Center was also asked to work with the organisation to train staff how to implement the life skills and to help evaluate this component. In this chapter, the development of the life skills component, implementation strategies and an initial program evaluation will be described.

Developing a Life Skills Component for The First Tee

In developing a life skills component, the vision of the Center was threefold: (1) to grow both the game of golf and the youth who play it; (2) to enable participants to understand that the life skills they learn in golf can be applied in other life domains; and (3) to teach golf as a lifetime game in which participants can set their own goals and achieve their own personal par. In other words, by building an effective golf and life skills instructional program — one that would propel participating youth on a successful life trajectory — they would have an activity for a lifetime and be able to apply the values and skills learned to other areas of their lives. Hence the term *life skills*.

Life skills enable individuals to succeed in the environments in which they live. Examples of these environments include families, schools, workplaces, neighbourhoods, and communities. Life skills are both behavioural (e.g., effective communication with peers and adults) and cognitive (e.g., effective decision making). As individuals age, the number of environments in which they must be successful increases. Environments vary from individual to individual, just as the definition of what it means to succeed differs across individuals and across environments.

Individuals in the same environment are likely to be dissimilar from each other as a result of the life skills they have already mastered, their other resources, and their opportunities, real or perceived. For this reason, those who teach life skills must be sensitive to developmental, environmental, and individual differences and the possibility that the needed life skills may not be the same for individuals of different ages, ethnic and/or racial groups, or economic status (Danish, 1995).

Although it is necessary to be sensitive to individual differences, it is also important to recognise that individuals can often effectively apply life skills learned in one environment to other environments. Sport is a particularly appropriate environment to learn skills that can be transferred to other environments. First, physical skills are similar to life skills in the way they are learned, through demonstration and practice (Danish, Nellen, & Owens, 1996). Second, many of the skills learned in sport have been found to be applicable to other life domains (Danish, 1983; Danish, Kleiber, & Hall, 1987).

In developing the life skills component, one of the first decisions Center staff made was to design a curriculum that could be integrated into the golf instruction. Since the age range of The First Tee extended from 8–18, it was necessary to develop two separate components, what were eventually called flights, to be responsive to the developmental differences that exist between the youngest and oldest participants. For the younger group, who were developmentally not able to understand how to do *consequence analysis thinking*, the focus was to help them understand what life skills were, to have some experience in learning and applying several of the skills, and to begin to develop an understanding that skills learned in one context can be generalised to other areas of life. The older group members were taught specific life skills, both as applied to golf and to other life areas simultaneously. As with the golf instruction, the life skills program was divided into three skill levels: par, birdie, and eagle. Participants were taught increasingly more advanced skills as they progressed through these skill levels and were expected to pass a certification test for each level.

Children and adolescents are active individuals. They learn best by doing rather than by talking. They have become accustomed to being "coached" and expect concrete suggestions, feedback and tasks on how to improve. Skills, regardless of whether they are golf or life skills, are taught differently than knowledge, attitudes or values. Just as learning to drive a car or dance cannot occur solely through listening to a tape or reading a book, sport skills or skills for living cannot be taught in a passive manner. When learning any new skill, the skill is first named and described and a rationale for its use is given. The skill is demonstrated so that the individual can observe correct and incorrect use of the skill. Finally, there is extensive supervised practice of the skill with continuous feedback (Danish & Hale, 1981).

Choosing the Life Skills for The First Tee

The first skills taught are the basics of interpersonal communication such as how to introduce oneself and carry on a conversation with adults. The next skill taught is to help participants, especially the older group, to distinguish between the physical and mental aspects of sport and to make them aware of the contribution mental skills has to performance, both on and off the course. Following the introduction to the importance of mental skills, the process of setting and attaining goals is taught (Danish, 1997). It begins with having participants choose both a golf and non-golf dream and then learn the distinction between dreams and goals (goals are dreams that one works hard to reach). Participants then learn how to set a reachable goal (one that is positively-stated, specific, important to the goal setter and under the goal setter's control). As part of this process, participants learn the difference between a goal (something they control) and a result (an outcome such as a specific score or winning a tournament or match, that is only partially under their control). They are then taught how to develop a plan or a goal ladder for reaching the goal. Finally, as part of the goal-setting skills, participants are taught how to identify and overcome roadblocks and then to set both a golf and non-golf goal to work on over the next 6 to 8 weeks.

Teaching how to set individual goals provides an opportunity to teach the concept of "personal par." First, the concept of par is an unusual one for children and adolescents. In most sporting activities, they usually compete against others. Golf provides a very different opportunity — to compete against the course and its par. However, the established par represents a difficult, if not impossible, challenge for most young golfers. Therefore, participants are taught how to compete against themselves. Their present level of performance — for example, the number of 5-foot putts they can make out of 10 chances — is their present personal par. Developing a personal par enables participants to learn to compete against their own potential rather than their opponent, or even the established par on the course. One's personal par will likely change with age and practice. Competing against one's potential is an important but often ignored concept. For example, the Swedish National Golf Team under the direction of their head coach, Pia Nilsson, has developed a *54 vision* which means birdying every hole on a par-72 course (Nilsson, 1998). Developing such a vision enables Swedish golfers to consistently focus on their potential and trying to reach it.

Among the other skills taught are how to "stay cool" by using self-talk to manage one's emotions, to develop a personal support team to help reach one's goals and to develop self-confidence and self-awareness. At the eagle level, especially for the older participants, skills such as how to appreciate differences among people, develop a healthy mind and body, engage in career planning and learn how to be a peer mentor and a coach to younger participants are taught.

Designing the Life Skills Implementation Process

As The First Tee and Life Skills Center staff began to discuss the most effective process of implementing the life skills component, it became evident that the golf professional might not be the individual responsible for this activity. The golf professional might be too busy or feel uncomfortable about teaching this component effectively. In some sites, the life skills instructor might be another staff member or an adult mentor; in other sites, it might be an older peer mentor (Danish, 1997). Regardless of who was responsible for implementation, it was critical that it be taught easily and effectively.

To make the implementation process easier a number of steps were taken. First, an Operations Manual was developed for First Tee sites with guidelines for implementing the life skills component. Second, an Instructor's Manual containing the par, birdie and eagle programs for both flights was developed with specific instructions to the leader, teacher or mentor about what to say and do. The format for this manual was, in part, based on the manuals developed for the Going for the Goal Program (Danish, 1997) and the SUPER Program (Danish & Nellen, 1997; Danish, Nellen, & Owens, 1996).

Third, in designing the skill modules, a format was used that contained a number of characteristics found to be useful in similar kinds of training programs (Danish, 2000). The program was developed to be: (a) *modular* — a number of components that could be used independently; (b) *flexible* —

the modules could be adapted and customised to the particular participants; (c) *cost and time efficient* — each module was about 15 to 20 minutes in length; (d) *multi-media* — a "yardage book" was developed for the participants with the essential information included and space for them to write notes; (e) *portable* — the modules were able to be used either on or off the golf course and separate from or integrated into the golf instruction; and (f) *evaluate-able* — changes or progress were able to be assessed and some of the assessment mechanisms were embedded in the program. Fourth, the Life Skills Center staff sought to identify a cadre of sport psychologists and/or their graduate students who live and work in close proximity to the local sites and who could serve as life skill supervisors.

Finally, a number of training workshops were conducted to prepare life skill instructors for the task of teaching the program. These workshops followed the skill development format described above. Instructors reviewed the skills to better understand them, applied the skills to themselves, taught them to each other and received feedback on their teaching, and where possible, taught them to youth at the workshop site and received feedback. When evaluating the effectiveness of a program, determining the fidelity of the implementation is a critical factor (Dane & Schneider, 1998). In other words, was the program implemented the way it was designed to be taught?

An Initial Evaluation

During the summer of 2000, a First Tee National Youth Golf and Leadership Academy was held at Kansas State University. The purpose of the Academy was threefold: (1) to help participants incorporate life skills into their own lives, on and off the golf course; (2) to improve their golf skills; and (3) to prepare them to teach and model life skills to younger First Tee participants at their respective sites. A total of 119 youth, ages 14–17, from 22 states attended. During this week-long experience, the developers of the Academy hoped to impact the personal values (e.g., concern with the welfare of others), emotional intelligence (e.g., empathy, effective interpersonal skills), and leadership ability (e.g., helping others set goals and develop plans to reach these goals) of participants. Each participant completed a pre- and post-survey to measure the amount of change that occurred on a number of instruments.

The Academy seemed to have a positive impact on the participants. Many of the changes were associated with the specific leadership and life skills that the participants formally learned and practised during the week. They felt more competent to lead others and to set and achieve their goals. However, there were also changes in some of the values and attitudes measures which was surprising as attitudes and values are more resistant to change and more likely evolve over time and through experience. For example, they felt more concern for others, felt that they better understood the importance of effective communications and felt more able to act responsibly. Although these results were very preliminary, it does appear that teaching life skills through golf may be an effective primer for continued growth, both in skills and values.

Implications for the Future of Golf

Golf has been viewed by many who play as an activity that teaches values and character. Although golf might provide a clear picture of the values and character of those who do play, the game itself does not teach values, character or even life skills. There is nothing about a golf club, golf ball or golf course that teaches someone how to live successfully or by what values to live. Teaching values or life skills must be an integral part of the design of a program. In other words, to teach golf skills and life skills, the focus of instruction should be both on how to play the game well and on how the game should be played. Teaching the former will not result in teaching the latter any more than the reverse is true. Moreover, one should have no expectation that any life skills or values learned on the golf course automatically will be able to be applied to other life areas. For transfer of learning to take place, it must be specifically planned. As Weiss (1995) has noted, if "... the physical, psychological, and social benefits available though sport are to occur, they must be purposely planned, structured, and taught as well as positively reinforced" (p. 40).

It is the hope of The First Tee that youth who have heretofore lacked access to the game of golf will have an opportunity to play. Moreover, by adding a life skill component, The First Tee hopes to teach a generation of young golfers a set of mental skills that will enhance their performance on the golf course as well as in school, in their homes and neighbourhoods, and in the workplace. In short, The First Tee has undertaken the task of producing better citizens.

Acknowledgments

The author would like to thank Drs. Al Petitpas and Linda Petlichkoff for their help in developing The First Tee life skills program; John Brunelle, Rob Fazio and Chris Hogan for their involvement in the implementation and evaluation of the life skills program; and Dedric Holmes for his overall leadership of The First Tee program development.

References

Dane, A.V., & Schneider, B.H. (1998). Program integrity in primary and early secondary prevention: Are implementation effects out of control? *Clinical Psychology Review, 18,* 23–45.

Danish, S. (1983). Musing about personal competence: The contributions of sport, health, and fitness. *American Journal of Community Psychology, 11*(3), 221–240.

Danish, S. (1995). Reflections on the status and future of community psychology. *Community Psychologist, 28*, 16–18.

Danish, S. (1997). Going for the Goal: A life skills program for adolescents. In T. Gullotta & G. Albee (Eds.), *Primary prevention works* (pp. 291–312). Newbury Park: Sage.

Danish, S. (2000). Youth and community development: How after-school programming can make a difference. In S. Danish & T. Gullotta (Eds.), *Developing competent youth and strong communities through after-school programming*. Washington, DC: Child Welfare League of America.

Danish, S.J., & Hale, B.D. (1981). Toward an understanding of the practice of sport psychology. *Journal of Sport Psychology, 3*, 90–99.

Danish, S., Kleiber, D., & Hall, H. (1987). Developmental intervention and motivation enhancement in the context of sport. In M. Maehr & D. Kleiber (Eds.), *Advances in motivation and achievement: Enhancing motivation* (Vol. 5, pp. 211–238). Greenwich, CT: JAI Press.

Danish, S.J., & Nellen, V.C. (1997). New roles for sport psychologists: Teaching life skills through sport to at-risk youth. *Quest, 49*(1), 100–113.

Danish, S., Nellen, V., & Owens, S. (1996). Community-based life skills programs: Using sports to teach life skills to adolescents. In J. Van Raalte & B. Brewer (Eds.), *Exploring sport and exercise psychology* (pp. 205–225). Washington: APA Books.

Nilsson, P. (1998). *Swedish national golf team*. Danderyd, Sweden: Swedish Golf Federation.

Weiss, M. R. (1995). Children in sport: An educational model. In S. M. Murphy (Ed.), *Sport psychology interventions* (pp. 39–69). Champaign, IL: Human Kinetics.

CHAPTER 4

The Role of Amateur Golf Coaches in Australia

Dominic Wall

This chapter outlines the amateur golf coaching program operating in Australia. The Australian Golf Union has developed a comprehensive coach education system with courses at three levels aimed at assisting amateur golfers gain coaching skills. The system makes a significant contribution to the development of golf in Australia and has educated many amateur golfers in the field of golf instruction. Intrinsic to this system is an integrated approach with the professional golfers. The courses are not designed to replace the role of professional golf coaches but are aimed at broadening the base of qualified and competent personnel able to develop golf.

Level 0 and Level 1 Golf Coaching Courses have been in operation since mid-1992. The Australian Coaching Council (ACC) approved both these courses and they have made a considerable impact over the last 8 years. The Level 0 orientation to coaching course is based on the Wilson Go-Go Golf program, whereas the Level 1 course is the first level of the National Coaching Accreditation Scheme (NCAS). There are currently more than 2,000 Level 0 instructors and 700 Level 1 coaches.

The Level 2 Golf Coaching Course was approved by the ACC in June 1999. It is a more comprehensive coaching course and was developed in partnership between the Australian Golf Union (AGU), Australian Ladies'

Professional Golf (ALPG), and Women's Golf Australia (WGA). This course was developed to target specific problems in golf, in particular lack of female coaches and lack of coaches in country areas.

Level 0

The Level 0 Course is aimed at preparing personnel to conduct the Wilson Go-Go Golf program, a modified golf program designed for children aged 9–15 years. Level 0 is a coaching orientation program, not a formal coaching qualification or part of the National Coaching Accreditation Scheme. The course is, however, approved by the Australian Coaching Council. Level 0 is delivered by State golf associations based on guidelines developed by the AGU. The course takes 6.5 hours to complete and covers the topics shown in Table 1.

After completion of the course, personnel are awarded a Level 0 certificate and referred to as a Go-Go Golf Instructor. They are able to deliver the basic skills of Go-Go Golf, organise games and activities and get children involved in golf in a fun and safe environment. There is no formal examination, however 100% attendance is required.

Level 1

The Level 1 Golf Coordinator Course is the first level of the National Coaching Accreditation Scheme. This course is designed for beginner coaches. The target group includes school teachers, golf club personnel interested in developing junior golf, parents, late secondary and tertiary students and competent golfers of a handicap 20 or better. The aims of the course are to:

1. Prepare coordinators to introduce junior players to basic technical and playing aspects of the game.
2. Ensure a minimum standard of preparation for coordinators.

Table 1
Topics and Time Allocations in the Level 0 Golf Coaching Course

TOPIC	TIME (HOURS)
Introduction	0.5
Safety and warm-up	0.5
Organisation	1.0
Go-Go Golf skills	2.5
Games and activities	1.0
Basic rules and etiquette	0.5
Resources and evaluation	0.5
Total	6.5

3. Provide an understanding of the general principles of coaching junior players.
4. Provide knowledge and understanding of the technical essentials for coaching basic aspects of the game of golf to junior players.
5. Ensure coordinators are able to provide a safe and fun environment.

The Level 1 course has two core requirements: 22.5 hours of coursework and 25 hours of practical coaching experience. The coursework, including general principles of coaching and golf-specific information, covers the units shown in Table 2.

In addition to the coursework, candidates must complete 25 hours of structured practical coaching. This may involve assisting a professional golfer or current Level 1 coordinator or a variety of other supervised coaching activities.

Once an accreditation is awarded it is valid for 4 years. During this period coordinators are required to undertake a number of activities to maintain their current status. This ensures that they are up-to-date with any new issues or techniques and are active in golf. If a coordinator maintains their updating requirements they will be re-accredited after 4 years.

Since 1992 approximately 1,300 Level 1 coordinators have been accredited (there are 700 current accreditations). These personnel have made a significant contribution to the development of golf across Australia and have

Table 2
Units and Time Allocations in the Level 1 Golf Coordinator Course

UNIT	TIME (HOURS)
Role of the coach	1.0
Developing the athlete	2.5
Coach in action	1.0
Sports safety	1.0
Equipment and dress	1.0
Grip	1.0
Set-up	1.0
The swing	3.0
The short game	2.0
Putting	1.0
Playing the game	1.0
Planning a golf program	1.5
Mental game	1.0
Golf rules	0.5
Golf etiquette	0.5
Role of the golf coordinator	0.5
Peer coaching assessment	1.0
Review assignment	2.0
Total	22.5

encouraged many new golfers into the sport. Previous to the establishment of this scheme there was no voluntary coaching system in golf. This contrasted dramatically with most other sports in Australia where there is a strong reliance on voluntary coaches.

Level 2

The Australian Golf Union, Australian Ladies' Professional Golf and Women's Golf Australia have jointly developed the Level 2 Coaching Course and it was included in the National Coaching Accreditation Scheme in June 1999. To date three Level 2 courses have been held.

The expansion into Level 2 initially created a number of concerns with the Professional Golfers' Association (PGA) of Australia. There was a feeling that amateurs were encroaching into their field of expertise and would be taking business from professional coaches. To address these concerns, strict guidelines are in operation concerning the role of Level 2 amateur coaches.

A number of issues brought about the development of the Level 2 coaching course and these will now be discussed in some detail.

Deregulation of the National Coaching Accreditation Scheme

In late 1997 the Australian Coaching Council decided to deregulate the NCAS. This meant that providers other than National Sporting Organisations (NSO) could, under ACC conditions, run courses with NCAS endorsement. In effect, this opened the NCAS to various organisations, including commercial operators, who could run courses in direct opposition to NSOs. Both the AGU and PGA, along with a number of other NSOs, opposed this move. We were concerned with a number of issues related to deregulation including the potential for a lowering of standards in golf coaching and a loss of quality control of courses. Unfortunately, however, the ACC proceeded with deregulation.

We therefore felt it important to develop an integrated model that catered for both professionals and amateurs. This meant we control who can attend courses and have a disciplinary procedure in place if there is a breach of amateur status rules. If we did not expand into Level 2 the door would be open for an external provider to deliver courses; but we would have no control on the quality and potential actions of their coaches. Our move does not prevent external providers. However, by offering high-quality courses, conducted on a cost-recovery basis and linked to the national bodies, we will be one step ahead.

Lack of Female Coaches

Both the ALPG and WGA have identified a lack of female golf coaches and feel the new Level 2 course addresses this situation. In mid-1999, for instance, there were only 33 female PGA Level 2 coaches in Australia. It is pleasing to note that over 60% of attendees at our first three courses have been female.

Lack of Coaches in Country Areas

Another area of concern was the lack of qualified coaches in country areas. Many of our country clubs in Australia do not have a PGA member and some have not had a visit from a professional coach in many years. There are, however, a number of very keen amateur golfers willing to assist at their club. These personnel are able to attend a course and thereafter offer sound coaching where previously none was available. Again it is interesting to note that the rural towns of Gayndah and Roma in Queensland were represented at the inaugural course.

Increasing the Number of Qualified Coaches

Golf is the largest participant sport in Australia with more than 600,000 affiliated members of 1,600 clubs and an additional 1.2 million regular social golfers. (Recent Australian Bureau of Statistics figures independently confirm golf's number one position). In 1999 when our Level 2 course was first approved there were fewer than 2,000 PGA members with only 443 Level 2 PGA coaches. There is, however, a demand for more coaches across Australia to keep up with the growth of the sport. Australian Football, for example, has more than 450,000 registered players and over 12,500 NCAS coaches.

There is also a need to generate a greater coaching ethos in golf and encourage more golfers to receive regular coaching. Amateur coaches can therefore assist in this process and ultimately act as a feeding system for the more qualified PGA coaches.

Listed above are a number of reasons why the Level 2 course was developed. An overview of the course and the requirements for accreditation are now presented. The course has three prerequisites: amateurs must hold a handicap of 12 or better (A-Grade golfer), have been a Level 1 Golf Coordinator for a minimum of 1 year, and have reached their 19th birthday. Three aspects of the Level 2 course must be completed before an accreditation is awarded: a golf-specific course covering the topics shown in Table 3 (31 hours); a general principles of coaching course (30 hours); and practical coaching experience after the golf-specific course (60 hours).

The general principles of coaching course takes 30 hours to complete and is offered across Australia. It covers the coaching principles applicable to advanced-level coaches and is offered in a variety of formats including correspondence.

Those enrolled in the Level 2 course must attend all course sessions. They need to successfully complete an 80-question review exam and their practical coaching assessment. Amateur candidates cannot, therefore, attend

Table 3
Topics Covered in the Golf-specific Level 2 Coaching Course

TOPIC	DESCRIPTION
Role of the coach	Roles, duties and responsibilities of the coach; assessor training
Physical development	Functional anatomy and body types; golf fitness; injury prevention and stretching; other issues: drugs, nutrition and travel
Psychological development	Routines for golf; anxiety and relaxation skills; visualisation and rehearsal
The swing	Laws, principles and preferences; preshot fundamentals: grip, aim, set-up; in-swing fundamentals
The short game and specialist shots	Putting; chipping and pitching; bunker play; specialist shots and unusual conditions
Teaching golf skills	Terminology for teachers of golf; practice drills and teaching aids; how to give lessons and error correction; teaching groups, clinics and schools
Other relevant topics	Teaching special populations: women, aged, challenged, children; rules and etiquette

the 31-hour golf-specific course to gain NCAS accreditation. They must be a Level 1 coordinator for at least 1 year, which means they have attended a course requiring 47.5 hours (22.5 hours coursework and 25 hours practical coaching). They must then meet the course prerequisites and complete the three components outlined above. This may take considerable time to achieve and means they must achieve a high level of competency.

Amateur Status

Being an amateur golf coach (Level 1 or Level 2) does not mean the coach can receive payment for coaching. The rules governing amateur status are very clear on this matter and a breach will incur significant penalties. The Royal and Ancient Golf Club of St Andrews have recently said amateurs can receive reimbursement of actual expenses (i.e., accommodation and travel costs) for coaching at a program approved by the national governing body but not an actual coaching fee. One of the sessions at the Level 2 course outlines these rules and also addresses the roles and responsibilities of amateur coaches, particularly when working in clubs and with PGA members. Amateur coaches must also follow protocols when coaching at a club with a PGA member.

Conclusion

Golf is but one of many activities and recreations competing in the marketplace for participants. We, as a sport, must ensure that the product on offer is of the highest possible standard and that 'newcomers' are attracted by a positive initial experience. It is therefore essential that the personnel introducing the sport are well trained and competent. It is also important that beginners, whether at schools, clubs or in the general community, are able to readily access good coaching. Limiting the availability of coaching to just professional golfers will therefore not adequately address the demand for coaches.

The system and role of amateur golf coaches outlined above is part of an overall golf development system operating in Australia. Amateur coaches are an important link in bringing many new people into the sport and encouraging them to take up club memberships and seek out more advanced-level coaching. The relationship of amateur and professional bodies is of particular importance in this process as is the acknowledgement of the roles of both groups. The amateur golf coaching system in Australia is based on high quality courses that produce good coaches. The role of these coaches in developing the sport is becoming increasingly important and will mean that golf continues as the number one participant sport in Australia.

CHAPTER 5

Golf Professional Training and Professional Development Programs: An Australian Perspective

Phil Ayres

The Professional Golfers' Association of Australia (APGA) has as its mission statement to: *Maintain the Traditions of Excellence in the Promotion of Golf.* In so doing, the APGA seeks to promote the game of golf and provide opportunities for its members to benefit from an involvement in this unique game.

In addition to conducting over 430 professional tournaments each year, the APGA stages many major corporate and grassroots events through its extensive member network. All of these activities are aimed at growing the game and thereby creating further opportunities for both APGA members and the greater industry in general. Many of these events and programs are aimed at the amateur playing base where promotion of the game ensures growth in participation and in turn growth of the industry.

An underpinning philosophy to the successful promotion of the game is the APGA conducting industry best practice coach and retail/business education programs. These education initiatives ensure excellence in the delivery of programs and services to the golfing public by the member professional.

Education has become a key currency in business, and the APGA has sought throughout its history, from inception in 1911 to the present, to place education as a cornerstone of its operation. The Trainee Professional Program (TPP) and the Professional Development Program (PDP) for APGA members have grown and become recognised, both within the golf industry and also by external government bodies, as leading sport education programs.

Australian PGA Membership Profile

The APGA membership comprises all Australian professional golfers ranging from tournament professionals, to club professionals, assistant professionals, teaching professionals, seniors and trainees. At present there are approximately 1,600 Full Members, and an additional 320 trainees (apprentice professionals). The APGA's members service the Australian golfing community and accordingly this sees member professionals dealing directly with over 1.2 million people who regularly participate in golf within Australia. A geographic breakdown of APGA membership is shown in Figure 1.

Links with Other World PGAs and Amateur Bodies

The APGA sees its role in the South Pacific Rim as one of great importance. As the second-oldest world PGA, the APGA has seen the remote and isolated nature of Australia as a motivation to ensure that it provides programs and initiatives the equal of the larger PGAs such as the US PGA and the British PGA. The APGA at all times endeavours to match or better the delivery of programs and benefits to its members as compared to these larger organisations.

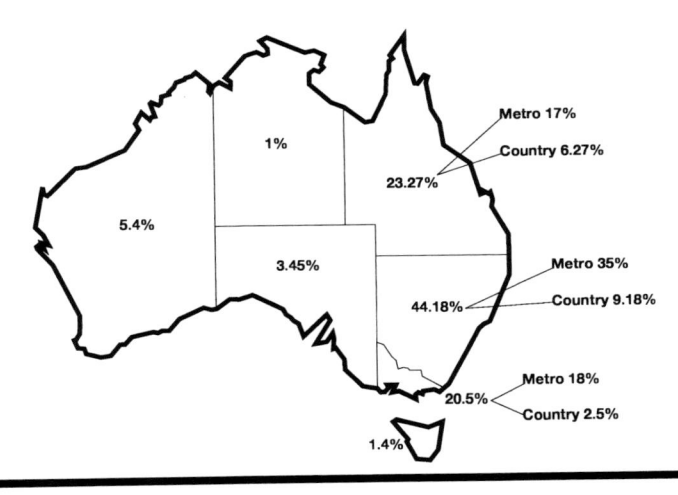

Figure 1
Breakdown of Professional Golfers' Association of Australia membership.

The APGA has positioned itself as a leader in the region, and has for several years been involved in the NZ PGA's education programs in a consultative role. This has helped to ensure that the NZ PGA standards of education are the equal to those of Australian PGA members, and thus in turn allow them to have access to the Australasian industry through their equivalent level of credentials.

There are a number of organisations that are involved in the governance of golf within Australia. They include the PGA of Australia (golf professionals — men and women), the PGA Tour of Australasia (tour professionals only), the Australian Golf Union (amateur men only) and Women's Golf Australia (amateur women only).

Golf instruction was traditionally undertaken only by APGA members, and credentialling/registration for these golf professional members was undertaken only by the APGA. However, in recent years the amateur bodies have sought to credential amateur golf instructors in roles assisting with juniors and players in country areas where APGA members are not employed. As discussed later, the APGA has viewed this move with caution because the golfing public, who have traditionally received high standards of service from APGA members who undertake extensive training and updating programs, may not be in receipt of such quality instruction from amateur coaches.

The performance of Australian players on the world circuit, especially in recent years, is often lauded as the result of the extensive institute and junior programs undertaken by the amateur bodies in this country. Although these are well-developed and successful programs, what makes them so is the guidance the APGA member provides. This is in addition to the strength of the individual programs conducted by APGA members in each golf club and facility around the country. The APGA sees the TPP and PDP structures as having created a framework for the dissemination of information and development of skills, which allow the PGA members the opportunity to work effectively at their individual facilities. Norman Von Nida (1999) states that it is the club professional working with his/her members on a daily basis which has provided a great base of talent which the elite programs of the country have been able to draw upon, and it is the local PGA member who is responsible for the success of Australian players on the world circuit.

The purpose of this chapter, therefore, is to outline the underlying principles behind the APGA's education and training programs and to overview the scope of operation of these programs, in particular the Professional Development Program. These programs have given APGA members the tools with which to operate in a best practice sense and provide leading standards of service in all areas of the game, both as a sport and as a business.

Coach Education Accreditation in Australia: An Historical Perspective

Historically, education programs for those seeking to service the sport industry in Australia have centred on the coach education pathway. The Australian Government in the 1980s formalised coach education programs conducted by various National Sporting Organisations (NSOs) through what has been known as the National Coach Accreditation Scheme (NCAS). This was administered by the Australian Coaching Council and provides a framework for coaching levels from 1–3 (this division of the Australian Sports Commission has recently merged with other departments to become known as the Sport Education Unit). A fundamental key behind these programs was the issue of ensuring the coaching which players, particularly children, received was of a standard which ensured that they were being instructed in a correct, safe and ethical environment.

These coach education programs require formalised training of the prospective coaches, either by the relevant NSO itself or in partnership with other groups assisting in the delivery. The programs focused only on coaching and coaching-related areas in response to the large target market that was primarily amateur coaches. In Australia, it is now a requirement of most NSOs that any coach at any level must be trained and must be currently registered through the NCAS system. Interestingly, coach education has now been deregulated, meaning proponents other than the sport's governing NSO can seek to credential coaches.

Following initial training, the ACC requires coaches to be actively coaching in addition to participating in a variety of coach-updating programs and courses. This cycle of currency is maintained for a 4-year period, by which time coaches are required to demonstrate they have achieved a satisfactory level of updating in order to retain their registration with the NSO and the ACC.

The Australian PGA

Since inception the APGA has had the training of future members of the Association as a cornerstone to its operation. In the first meeting of the Association at Royal Sydney Golf Club in 1911, it was moved that the By Laws of the Association state that one key purpose of its formation was to ensure the training of future members, or apprentices as they were then known. This training was inclusive of all areas of the profession including retail services, club manufacturing, repair and fitting, coaching and teaching, and small business operation; and was undertaken in the format of on-the-job apprenticeships under the indenture and tutelage of a Full Member of the Australian PGA (de Groot & Webster, 1991).

Initially this training was set for a 2-year period and was extended in the 1960s to a 3-year period. All instruction was provided by the indenturing Professional, with written and practical examinations being undertaken prior to graduation. In the 1980s the PGA looked to further formalise training of apprentices, now known as trainees, and formed the PGA Academy of Golf. This dedicated department within the PGA administration set and formalised a curriculum for trainee professionals and requirements of the indenturing member. At this time correspondence and face-to-face training at dedicated training schools was introduced in addition to the on-the-job training received at the workplace from the indenturing member. Such a program was set to ensure the underpinning academic standard of the prospective PGA member was at a consistently high level, commensurate with the requirements of operating successfully within an ever-changing industry. It ensured the standards of education and operational standards of members were continually improved.

Although the PGA has always managed and developed its own training programs, the advent of the ACC and the NCAS saw the PGA align its training programs and protocols with this system. This ensured that PGA members were recognised both within and outside of the golf industry as the leading providers of coaching in golf, through what had become the only recognised system of credentialling across all sports in Australia.

The Australian National Training Reform Agenda

The APGA has always seen it as vital to the prospective professional golfer that an education in golf is made available to ensure that they can continue to work in the industry should they not be in a position to maintain a playing career. Other sports have, in recent years, taken a similar approach with many team sports in Australia having training academies to develop their young players' skills across a variety of areas which would see them remaining in the industry when their playing careers were over or did not eventuate.

Linked with this philosophy of vocational training for persons in the sport industry was the advent of the Australian Training Reform Agenda initiated by the Federal Government in the 1980s. The premise of this reform agenda was the recognition of on-the-job skills which were achieved at sub-University level across all industries. This now sees the Australian Qualifications Framework (AQF) applied to the sport and recreation industry, and unlike the NCAS, recognises skills in the various sport industries as broader than just coaching and teaching.

As this framework better represents the competencies which the APGA Professional possesses, the APGA has recently aligned with the AQF through the relevant government statutory authorities, ANTA (Australian National Training Authority) and VETAB (Vocational Education Training Accreditation Board — independent in each state), in addition to maintaining registration of its members through the NCAS framework. What the APGA seeks to achieve at all times is excellence in its programs, and in turn excellence in the standards of its members. As such, it seeks to align with training and recognition frameworks which recognise this standard of training and currency of qualifications.

The APGA's training and education programs for both the TPP and PDP are therefore structured to reflect these frameworks and are continually developed to ensure the specific nature of the golf industry and ethos of the APGA are reflected in their operation. Figure 2 provides a diagrammatic representation of the qualifications and registration frameworks as they apply to golf in Australia.

Philosophies Underpinning Formulation of the TPP and PDP

The recent work by Paul Schempp and colleagues clearly states that the antecedents to expert golf instruction include high standards of education and training, well-structured professional development activities, high standards of playing ability/experience, student-centred teaching approaches and on-the-job teaching experience (Schempp, You, & Clark, 1999). The APGA's TPP and PDP both require trainees/members to have achieved high levels of performance in a number of the areas identified by Schempp. Further, these programs create a framework for the ongoing development of these indicators by virtue of their format and structure. In addition, the framework ensures that there are opportunities for professional golf coaches in Australia to obtain and maintain a standard of golf instruction commensurate with that of the experts identified by Schempp. His studies clearly support the underlying philosophies of the programs, their structure and format. The principles guiding the operation of these programs ensure excellence in delivery, create opportunities for discussion and debate, allow for the dissemination of information amongst the membership, and ensure high standards of achievement prior to certification from the TPP and PDP programs.

As noted earlier, the APGA is cautious of the existence of amateur coaches and their credentialling and recognition through the NCAS system. The APGA sees that there is a potential for the possible dilution in the quality of golf instruction should there be a proliferation in proponents who are "amateur coaches." This is very much the case where these proponents do

Level	Authority / Description	AQF Level	Golf Coaching Credentials as applied against ANTA and ASC	NCAS Level	Australian Sports Commission (ASC) / NSO Description
FEDERAL LEVEL	**Australian National Training Authority (ANTA)** — Determines competency requirements for all industries and the qualification level they represent on the Australian Qualifications Framework (AQF).				**Australian Sports Commission (ASC)** — The National Coaching Accreditation Scheme (NCAS) is overseen by the department within the Sports Commission known as the Sport Education Unit (previously known as the Coaching Council). It oversees coach education against a 4-stage framework.
STATE LEVEL	**Vocational Education Training Accreditation Board (VETAB)** — Sets and administers the operating guidelines of Registered Training Operators (RTOs) and ensures compliance to the delivery of training packages as set by ANTA.				
INDIVIDUAL TRAINING PROVIDERS	**Registered Training Operators** — These organisations have been audited by their state VETAB and have been approved as operating under the requirements of VETAB and ANTA. The RTO is authorised to train and assess candidates and award qualifications on the AQF. The PGA is authorised to award the Diploma in Sport Coaching (Professional Golf) Level V from the Sport Training Package. Persons who train trainees must be recognised as having current qualifications. Update training over a 4-year period is considered current by VETAB.	Advanced Diploma — Highest level available just below Degree status	Proposed PGA High Performance Coaching Course	Level 4 — Highest level available	**National Sport Organisations or Private Providers** — The NSO or private provider is authorised by the ASC to conduct courses and credential graduates. Qualifications are a government initiative that gives standards of delivery to Coaching within Australia both at amateur and professional level.
		Diploma	AAA / AA PGA Members	Level 3	Qualifications are only given for 4-year periods of currency. The accredited coach is required through their NSO to demonstrate the currency of their qualification by way of completion of courses, seminars and other programs.
		Certificate IV	Amateur Coaches only recognised through the NCAS system Level 1 & 2	Level 2	When this is demonstrated the NSO is permitted to re-accredit the coach for a further 4-year period.
		Certificate I - III		Level 1	The "current competencies" are programmed into the PDP cycle for renewal every 4 years.

Figure 2
Golf qualifications in Australia.

not have access to, nor are required to work within, a framework conducive to the identified indicators of expert golf instruction. As such the APGA has sought to work with the AGU and WGA to ensure that these coaches work with the APGA member who services their facility, so they augment the APGA member's services rather than work in opposition to him or her. The APGA would see that there is a clear role for these amateur coaches to work with APGA members to assist in promoting and growing the game, particularly in the area of junior development programs in schools.

Whereas Schempp's work is centred on golf instruction, the APGA would argue that there are similar antecedents and Key Performance Indicators (KPIs) of expert retail service and business management skills in servicing the golf business. The TPP and PDP therefore reflect the same principles in the area of Golf Operations and Management.

The PGA of Australia's PDP Program

The APGA's Professional Development Program has been evolving since its formal implementation in July 1993. Part of that development is for the program structure, seminars and education pathways to continue to be reviewed while meeting the demands of the membership and an ever-changing industry. The implementation of that review process has addressed the need to establish minimum requirements in relation to the stipulations of the ACC in regard to updating and registration, and the requirements of ANTA which oversees the AQF.

As the NCAS requirements pertained only to coaching, the APGA sought to ensure that the PDP program operated across both this competency category and that of Golf Operations and Management to represent an accurate cross-section of the competencies or KPIs required of a golf professional. The operation of the PDP is therefore replicated for both categories of Coaching and Golf Operations and Management, using the NCAS requirements as a basis.

In addition to the NCAS requirements, the APGA moved to recognise members' currency of training through membership classifications based on activity in updating training programs. These classifications are A, AA, and AAA. The base-level AA classification is reached when NCAS Level III re-accreditation is achieved (i.e., 100 points are accumulated). The same minimum number of points must be earned for the category of Golf Operations and Management, although these activities are not recognised for re-accreditation within the NCAS coach registration system. Figure 3 shows how each category is divided into three areas for point accumulation.

AAA membership is obtained on accumulating 150 points in each category during the 4-year cycle of currency. A further membership classifica-

	COACHING		GOLF OPERATIONS AND MANAGEMENT
(i)	Seminar Attendance	(i)	Seminar Attendance
(iia)	Coaching (Max 20%)	(iib)	Membership Service (Max 20%)
(iii)	Self-Study Courses (Max 30%)	(iii)	Self-Study Courses (Max 30%)

Figure 3
Categories for point accumulation in the Professional Development Program.

tion is to be introduced, that of Master Professional. This classification will be reserved for PGA members who have demonstrated outstanding levels of achievement, have remained current through the PDP, and have achieved a minimum of 30 years experience in the industry as PGA members.

Point Allocation

(i) Seminar Attendance. Points are allocated on the basis of hours per session and category of operation. The category of operation refers to whether the seminar is Divisional, National or International. Figure 4 shows how points are allocated for seminar attendance. The PGA conducts approximately five national seminar programs each year. Here speakers/facilitators from Australia and overseas undertake 1-day workshop/seminar programs across a variety of topics determined via feedback and surveys. An example of such programs is the Biannual Coaching Summit which in the past has had a high-profile coach from the United States as a keynote, supported by Australian coaches conducting specialist workshops. National seminars are augmented by half-day workshop programs undertaken on a regional basis. Where possible the concepts developed at the "formal" national programs are dealt with by facilitators in a practical workshop format.

A maximum of 20 points can be accumulated over the 4-year period for this section. This represents a possible 20% contribution to the total 100-point target.

(iia) Coaching. Members wishing to apply for this 20% contribution must send to the Academy a declaration and reconciliation form indicating the average hours per week spent on the teaching tee over the 12 months between January to December. The form must be independently verified as a true and accurate record.

(iib) Membership Services. Members wishing to apply for this 20% contribution must send to the Academy a declaration and reconciliation form

EXAMPLE	DIVISIONAL/ REGIONAL	NATIONAL	INTERNATIONAL
Point Allocation (per hour)	1	2	3
(a) 1-Day Seminar	8 hours	8 hours	8 hours
TOTAL POINTS	**8**	**16**	**24**
(b) 2-Day Seminar	16 hours	16 hours	16 hours
TOTAL POINTS	**16**	**32**	**48**
(c) 3-Day Seminar	24 hours	24 hours	24 hours
TOTAL POINTS	**24**	**48**	**72**

Note. Members are able to accumulate the 100-point target from seminar attendance alone if they so choose.

Figure 4
Point allocation for seminar attendance in the Professional Development Program.

indicating attendance at various PGA-operated events. Some examples include National and Divisional AGMs, Tournaments (Pro-Ams, Foundation, National, International Events), Annual Merchandise Show, International Golf Show, Industry and Trade Days.

(iii) Self-Study Courses. A maximum of 30 points can be accumulated over the 4-year period for this section. This represents a possible 30% contribution to the total 100-point target. Members who undertake self-study courses must seek PDP approval for the courses if they wish to apply the course to their accreditation statement. The PGA Academy currently recognises a number of courses and service providers who hold PDP approval. Members who attend these courses must provide a statement of attendance and a brief overview, and the points will be applied accordingly. Some examples include the State offices of the Australian Coaching Council, and Institutions of Higher Education such as Griffith University.

The 2000 PDP Schedule
Figure 5 provides an example of the programs and self-study formats offered in the Professional Development Program in 2000.

Future Directions
It is the intention of the Board of PGA Australia, through the National Education Committee, to ensure the members of the APGA have access to a world-class education and training system. The APGA sees the future directions of both the TPP and PDP involving continual refinement and devel-

Seminar Programs

2000 Tommy Armour Coaching Summit
Keynote *Other sessions*
Jimmy Ballard Curriculum for Australian golf
 Teaching and club fitting
 Left- and right-sided player instruction
 Is it technical, is it physiological?
 Periodisation for golf
 Developing teaching programs that work

2000 Merchandise Show Education Convention
Making junior programs work
Building a winning team - Management techniques for staff success
Marketing strategies for your business
The Internet and retail – Friend or foe?
Wealth creation through financial planning
Small business into the new millennium – An Australian perspective
Future trends in the golf industry – A US perspective
Merchandising makes money!
What's hot and what's not - Equipment trends into 2000 and beyond

National Programs
Fitness screening - A practical workshop
Visualisation methods for golf
Retail service training
Financial analysis for small business success

Video Library
Extensive video library of all national seminar speakers since 1996
– 30 titles available

Self-Study Programs
Study modules in Coaching – 10 titles available
Griffith University Certificate in Golf Management Foundations
– 6 modules available

Figure 5
An overview of Professional Development Program activities in 2000.

opment as opposed to any wholesale changes in their direction and operations. Such controlled development is indicative of long-term strategies providing a clearly defined pathway for the operation of these programs.

This stability allows the participant, the APGA member or trainee, the confidence to undertake programs while understanding the long-term requirements to maintain the currency of their qualifications. Clearly the underpinning philosophies of the programs are supported by the research previously noted in this chapter. In the absence of research conflicting with these underpinning principles of professional development, there is no reason to operate under an altered philosophy.

As with most industries at present, the issue of technology and the World Wide Web is one which does allow the APGA's programs to become more user friendly and accessible. Australia's vast size is a continual challenge for the delivery of education and training programs. The APGA's ability to harness these new technologies and ensure its members are utilising them allows for another dimension in the field of training and professional development.

As for the training topics and areas of study to be pursued, the APGA will continue to provide programs which address changes to the industry as they occur. Further, where possible the APGA will align programs with relevant institutions which will allow for further credentialling of members who undertake these courses or programs. The course content will at all times seek to bring new relevant researched theory to the attention of PGA members. This will be done in a format that engenders discussion and allows for the implementation of these researched theories in a practical and real way for PGA members working with the golfing public at the "rock face."

Programs will continue to be formatted in such a manner as to provide the Professionals in the field with strategies, methods and tools which can assist them in the delivery of quality service to the industry, particularly their client base. By each individual APGA member providing industry best practice in Coaching and Golf Operations and Management, the consumer and the potential golfing public are better serviced and the whole industry grows in a positive fashion.

The Australian PGA will at all times seek to ensure that the high standing of its members in the golf community is maintained, and that they are seen as the pre-eminent deliverer of coaching and retail services to the golf market. Continual development of programs in training and education, and their recognition as industry-leading programs, are the cornerstones to this philosophy. This will allow the Australian PGA member to: *Maintain the Traditions of Excellence in the Promotion of Golf.*

References

de Groot, C., & Webster, J. (1991). *Pro golf: Out of the rough.* Crows Nest, Australia: Professional Golfers' Association of Australia.

Schempp, P.G., You, J.A., & Clark, B. (1999). The antecedents of expertise in golf instruction. In M.R. Farrally & A.J. Cochran (Eds.), *Science and golf III: Proceedings of the 1998 World Scientific Congress of Golf* (pp. 282–294). Champaign, IL: Human Kinetics.

Von Nida, N., & Robertson, B. (1999). *The Von: Stories and suggestions from Australian golf's little master.* Brisbane, Australia: University of Queensland Press.

CHAPTER 6

The Influence of Video and Verbal Information on Learning the Golf Swing

Mark A. Guadagnoli, Al McDaniels, Jimmie Bullard, Richard D. Tandy, and William R. Holcomb

A common question among motor learning theorists and practitioners is the degree to which various practice protocols enhance learning (Schmidt & Bjork, 1992). That is, "how can one make practice more efficient?" One such debate exists in regard to the appropriateness of various feedback methods for different levels of learners (Guadagnoli, Dornier, & Tandy, 1996). In research circles, this feedback is known as knowledge of results (KR) and is often defined as augmented, post-response error information about the movement outcome (Schmidt & Lee, 1999). Basically, this means that KR is information given to the learner by a teacher, coach, video camera, and so on, about that learner's performance. A PGA professional telling a student that the swing plane was too steep is an example of using KR in a golf setting. The importance of KR to the learning of motor skills has been documented by many studies in recent decades (see KR reviews of Adams, 1987; Salmoni, Schmidt, & Walter, 1984). It is rather ironic then that KR has rarely been applied to the game of golf. The current study was designed to remedy this gap in the literature by creating a bridge between laboratory research regarding KR and its application to the game of golf. Specifically, the current study was designed to investigate the effects of verbal and video feedback in learning a basic golf stroke.

Background

One of the main roles of KR is to provide information for the user (Adams, 1987; Guadagnoli, 2000; Schmidt & Lee, 1999). Such information is needed because many performers cannot adequately evaluate errors on their own. Anyone who remembers learning the golf swing will remember miss-hitting a ball, but why the ball was miss-hit was a mystery. Likewise, the novice will occasionally hit the ball well and be equally dumbfounded as to why. The point is that until one has developed a mental representation of a skill, a model must be provided for them. This model often comes in the form of KR. One logical question is how much KR is best, and in what form?

There have been several studies that have examined the most appropriate KR frequency and schedule. For example, Schmidt, Lange, and Young (1990) found that optimal KR was task specific. That is, the more complex the task, the more immediate KR should be given. Guadagnoli et al. (1996) extended this line of thinking by investigating the relationship between KR, task complexity, and performer experience. They found that optimal KR depends on the level of the performer and the complexity of the task. For a complex task, or a novice performer, KR should be given more immediately than for a simple task or experienced performer. That is, Guadagnoli et al. suggested that optimal KR is dependent on the relative task difficulty. Relative task difficulty is defined as the difficulty of the task relative to the skill of the person performing it. For example, a novice golfer trying to make a 4-foot putt on the practice green may find that task very difficult. A PGA professional attempting the same putt may find it quite easy. In this example, the relative task difficulty for the professional is much lower than for the novice. On the other hand, a 4-foot putt for a novice may have the same relative difficulty as a 20-foot putt for the professional. In short, KR should be matched to the relative task difficulty.

To get a fuller picture of KR one would need to understand the relationship between relative task difficulty and KR frequency, KR precision (the preciseness of the information), and KR timing (immediate or delayed). One must also understand the relationship between KR type and relative task difficulty. For example, is it more appropriate to teach the golf swing using video or verbal information as KR? Although this is an important question in this age of technology, there is little research investigating the most appropriate type of KR one should receive in learning the golf swing. Therefore, this question is the focus of the current study.

On the one hand, it could be argued that verbal KR is best for teaching the golf swing. Since the novice golfer knows little about the swing, simple verbal cues (e.g., keep your head steady) could be very useful. Clearly, verbal information is the most frequent form of KR from the golf professional, and has the advantage of being inexpensive from both a monetary perspective and time perspective. Additionally, in comparing verbal to video feedback, one could make the argument that verbal feedback would be better because the novice golfer would not know how to interpret video information. Verbal feedback could be interpreted as being more precise for the novice golfer, and to some extent, studies have found more precise feedback to lead to greater learning (e.g., Bennett & Simmons, 1984; Magill & Wood, 1986; Reeve, Dornier, & Weeks, 1990). However, counters to these arguments could be levied as well.

Just as likely as the superiority of verbal feedback, it could be argued that video feedback would be more useful for the novice performer because the novice performer would not know how to interpret verbal information, nor would they be able to translate the words into actions. For example, telling a novice that they are "moving past parallel" may not mean much to them. Even if they do understand that this means that the backswing is going too far, they may not know how to translate this information into a more appropriate action. That is, the novice may not have a mental representation of parallel. A video would provide such information. The obvious disadvantage for video feedback is that it is costly, both from a time and monetary perspective. However, if it is demonstrated that video feedback is better for the novice performer, perhaps the cost could be justified.

Finally, one may ask about the advantage of combining both verbal and video feedback. Obviously there is a cost associated with it, as mentioned above. However, the combination of verbal and video information could remedy the problems associated with each individually. Therefore, the current study was designed to examine the extent to which verbal feedback, video feedback, and video + verbal feedback affect learning of the golf swing. The results of the study have both practical and theoretical implications. From a practical perspective, the results could help improve the golf instructor's effectiveness and hence improve the golfer's game and enjoyment. From a theoretical perspective, the results could help shed light on a fuller understanding of the role and appropriateness of KR.

Logic for the Study

There were three treatment groups in the current study: verbal, video, and video+verbal. The verbal group received verbal feedback only. The video group received video feedback only, and the video + verbal group received both verbal and video feedback. All groups completed a pretest, practised under their respective feedback condition, and then completed a posttest.

The most appropriate feedback method for enhancing learning of the golf swing was determined by examining the group differences on the posttest.

Method

Participants

Participants were 45 undergraduate volunteers recruited from Kinesiology and Physical Education courses ranging in age from 21–36 years. All participants were informed as to the task and the specific experimental protocol, but were naive to the theoretical nature of the experiment. Informed consent was obtained from each participant prior to data collection and each participant was debriefed after data collection.

Experimental Design

The study was a 3 (group [verbal, video, video+verbal]) x 2 (test [pretest, posttest]) mixed design. Group was a between-subjects factor and test was a within-subjects factor. The dependent measure of interest was accuracy distance relative to a predefined target (as explained in the Procedure section).

Apparatus and Task

The apparatus consisted of a video analysis system capable of analysing a golf swing with a high-speed video camera (Neat Vision Video Capture). Apparatus also included a standard 7-iron provided by the participant or the experimenter, an artificial turf mat, 100 golf balls, and a golf net. The golf mat, club, balls, and net were used for practice. Training was conducted both in a laboratory (approximately 8 m x 8 m isolated room), and the pre- and posttests were conducted in an open field. Because participants were hitting into a net during practice, they received little feedback concerning distance and accuracy. The focus of their practice was using proper mechanics and making good ball contact.

Procedure

Prior to data acquisition, participants were asked to complete a questionnaire about their golf experience. Each individual also performed a pretest in which they were required to strike 15 golf balls for distance and accuracy with a 7-iron. The pretest was conducted on an artificial turf mat in an open field (100 m x 250 m). The target was a white chalk line running from the tee to 200 m away from the tee. Two distance estimations were used to calculate the distance the ball travelled relative to the target (Figure 1). First, the landing point for each ball was determined. Then a perpendicular line was drawn from this point to the target line. The distance from the tee to where this line crossed the target line was labelled *target distance* (TD). The perpendicular distance from the landing point to the target line was also calculated and labelled *error distance* (ED). The participant's *accuracy distance* (AD) relative to the target was then determined by subtracting ED from TD (Figure 1). The calculations were based on all 15 balls and the AD scores were reported in metres.

Immediately following the pretest, all participants watched a 20-minute instructional video on the golf swing. The video overviewed the grip, stance, and swing. Based on the questionnaire and the pretest, participants were randomly assigned to one of the three feedback conditions (video, verbal, and video + verbal).

The day following the pretest, participants in all groups reported to the testing centre for training. The training began with each participant warming up for 5 minutes. During this time the participants followed a predefined protocol to lessen the chance of injury. After the warm-up on all days, participants were asked to strike 10 balls, one at a time, at a pace that was comfortable to the participant. In all cases the balls were to be struck with a 7-iron in the direction of the centre of the target net. After 10 trials, participants were given feedback about those 10 trials. This process was repeated four times per day for a total of 40 practice swings and 40 KR trials per day.

Participants in the video group were shown a video recording of their last 10 attempts but given no verbal feedback. Participants in the verbal group

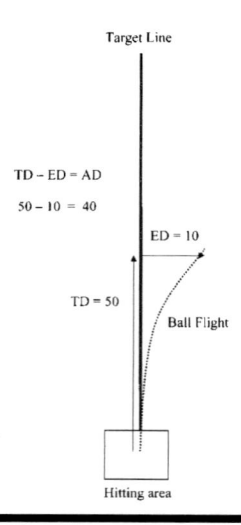

Figure 1

Graphic demonstration of dependent measure calculations.

were given verbal feedback about their last 10 attempts by a PGA professional but received no video feedback. Participants in the video + verbal group were given verbal feedback in a similar fashion while they watched the video of their swing.

Each training session lasted approximately 30 minutes. There were four training sessions with each session being separated by one day. Participants were asked not to practise golf other than during the training session. Twenty-four hours after the last training session, participants were posttested. The posttest was identical to the pretest.

Results

Mean accuracy distance (AD) data were analysed using a 3 (group [verbal, video, video+verbal]) x 2 (test [pretest, posttest]) analysis of variance (ANOVA) procedure with repeated measures on the last factor. It is worth noting that the accuracy distances are low, however, this should make sense considering that the reported numbers are the target distance (TD) minus the error distance (ED). The analysis revealed a significant main effect for group, $F(2, 42) = 23.57$, $p < .001$, with means being 62.5 m, 72.5 m, and 76.5 m for the verbal, video, and video + verbal groups, respectively. The analysis also revealed a significant main effect for test, $F(1, 42) = 283.98$, $p < .001$, with means being 63 m and 78.3 m for the pre- and posttests, respectively. Most importantly, the analysis revealed a Group x Test interaction, $F(2, 42) = 43.04$, $p < .001$ (Figure 2). Follow-up analyses revealed that the groups were not reliably different from each other on the pretest. However, on the posttest the video and video + verbal groups were significantly better than the verbal group.

Finally, the data may be further partitioned into component parts of target distance (TD), error distance (ED), and accuracy distance (AD) (Figure 3). Notice that the relative magnitudes for TD and AD are nearly identical across treatment groups, whereas ED is not different between groups. This suggests that whereas target distance hit changed from pre- to posttests, relative accuracy did not. This can be interpreted to suggest that when learning a golf swing, the distance hit changes first followed by enhanced accuracy. The difference between the video groups and verbal groups in this regard is shown graphically in Figure 4.

Discussion

The current study was designed to examine the extent to which verbal feedback, video feedback, and video + verbal feedback, affect learning of the golf swing. The logic of the study was that if the treatment groups did not differ before training but did differ after training, one could determine

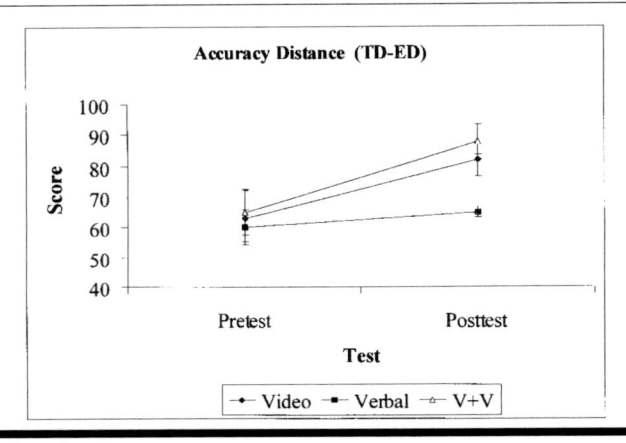

Figure 2
Feedback x Test interaction for the accuracy distance measure. Numbers represented in metres.

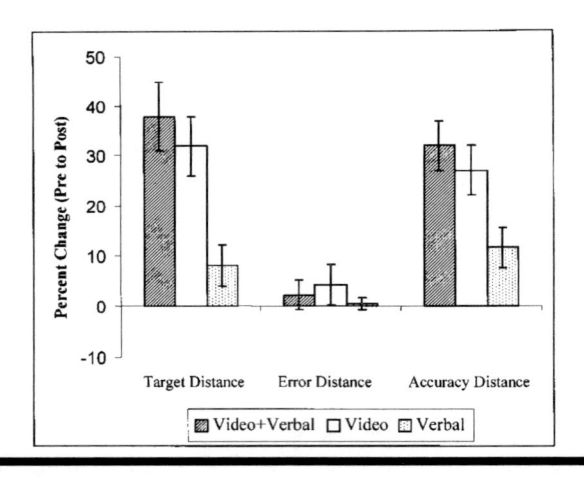

Figure 3
Graphic representation of dependent measures partitioned for the conditions. Graph represents the percentage change from pre- to post-test.

which type of feedback method was most appropriate for learning the golf swing. The results of this study demonstrated that the video group, and the video + verbal group, performed superior to the verbal group on retention. Additionally, the results demonstrated that the video group and the video + verbal group did not perform differently from each other. That is to say, the video groups learned more than the verbal group.

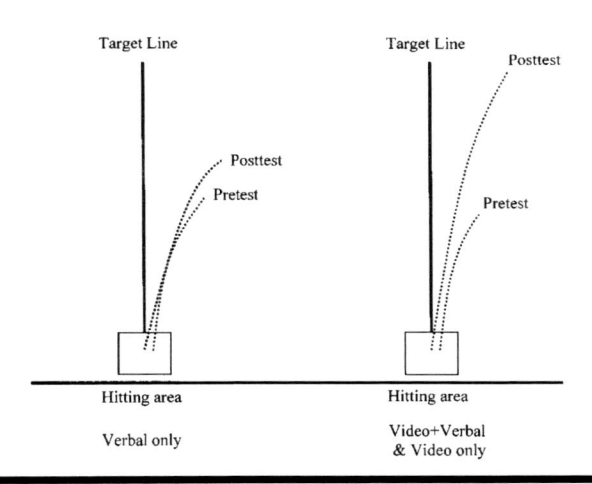

Figure 4
Graphic representation of typical differences in data from pre- to posttest.

Although it may seem counterintuitive, it was suggested in the introduction of this chapter that one could argue that video feedback could be more useful than verbal feedback for the novice performer. The logic consistent with this statement was that the novice performer may not know how to interpret verbal information, nor would they be able to translate the words into actions. The example given was that telling a novice that they are "moving past parallel" might convey little useful information. Even if the novice does understand that this means the backswing is going too far, they may not know how to translate this information into a more appropriate action. That is, the novice may not have a mental representation or kinesthetic awareness of parallel. A video may provide such information. Consistent with this logic, it has been found that the greater the precision of KR, the greater the learning, to a point (Newell, 1985). Perhaps the verbal feedback for the novice was too precise.

One obvious question is why was there no difference between the video and the video+verbal groups? First, it should be noted that the means differed but this difference was not statistically reliable. This is perhaps due to variability in the data. However, with this concession, there are several potential reasons for these findings. For example, earlier in this chapter it was suggested that the novice performer needs KR because their ability to detect and correct errors is rather poor. Video may be a more appropriate source of information for the novice because vision is a gross form of feedback; meaning that visual information can provide very general information in a form that is readily usable by the performer. The addition of verbal information may overwhelm the performer's ability to process information. Whereas the video provides usable information, the verbal KR may provide information that is redundant to the more dominant visual information. Therefore, only the visual information is used, and hence the addition of verbal information does not significantly improve learning. Additionally, interpreting the verbal information may exceed the ability of the novice with or without the addition of visual information. That is, novice performers may not be capable of making sense of the words as efficiently as they can make sense of the pictures.

The results of this study have both practical and theoretical implications. From a practical perspective, the results can help improve the golf instructor's effectiveness and hence improve the golfer's game and enjoyment. The results should not be interpreted to suggest that verbal feedback is not good for learning. Rather, under the current circumstances, verbal feedback was not as efficient as video. However, there are many forms of verbal feedback, and it may be how the verbal KR is couched that will impact its effectiveness. From a theoretical perspective, the results can help shed light on a fuller understanding of the role and appropriateness of KR. Finally, it should be noted strongly that although these results may be readily applied to a novice golfer, it would be imprudent to apply them to an experienced golfer. It is clearly logical that the most efficient means by which novices learn may not be the most efficient means for experts (Guadagnoli et al., 1996; Lee & Maraj, 1994).

Acknowledgments

The authors would like to thank Morgan Kearney for his assistance with data collection and Jeff Wells for his assistance with facilities. This project was sponsored by the College of Extended Studies at the University of Nevada, Las Vegas.

References

Adams, J. A. (1987). Historical review and appraisal of research on the learning, retention, and transfer of human motor skills. *Psychological Bulletin, 101*, 41–74.

Bennett, D.M., & Simmons, R.W. (1984). Effects of precision of knowledge of results on acquisition and retention of simple motor skills. *Perceptual and Motor Skills, 58*, 785–786.

Guadagnoli, M.A. (2000). Motor behavior. In S.P. Brown (Ed.), *Introduction to exercise science* (pp. 334–358). Baltimore: Lippincott, Williams and Wilkins.

Guadagnoli, M.A., Dornier, L.A., & Tandy, R. (1996). Optimal length for summary of results: The influence of task related experience and complexity. *Research Quarterly for Exercise and Sport, 67*, 239–348.

Lee, T.D., & Maraj, B.K.V. (1994). Effects of bandwidth goals and bandwidth knowledge of results on motor learning. *Research Quarterly for Exercise and Sport, 65*, 244–249.

Magill, R.A., & Wood, C.A. (1986). Knowledge of results precision as a learning variable in motor skill acquisition. *Research Quarterly for Exercise and Sport, 57*, 170–173.

Newell, K.M. (1985). Skill learning. In D.H. Holding (Ed.), *Human skills* (pp. 203–226). New York: Wiley.

Reeve, T.G., Dornier, L.A., & Weeks, D.J. (1990). Precision of knowledge of results: Consideration of the accuracy requirements imposed by the task. *Research Quarterly for Exercise and Sport, 61,* 284–290.

Salmoni, A.W., Schmidt, R.A., & Walter, C.B. (1984). Knowledge of results and motor learning: A review and critical reappraisal. *Psychological Review, 82,* 225–260.

Schmidt, R.A., & Bjork, R.A. (1992). New conceptualizations of practice: Common principles in three paradigms suggest new concepts for training. *Psychological Science, 3,* 207–217.

Schmidt, R.A., Lange, C., & Young, D.E. (1990). Optimizing summary knowledge of results for skill learning. *Human Movement Studies, 9,* 325–348.

Schmidt, R.A., & Lee, T.D. (1999). *Motor control and learning: A behavioral emphasis.* Champaign, IL: Human Kinetics.

CHAPTER 7

A Laser-Based Evaluation of Two Different Alignment Strategies Used in Golf Putting

Albert D. Potts and Neil K. Roach

The simplistic scoring system of strokes taken to complete a given 18-hole course belies a great complexity and an almost infinite variety of possible outcomes in the game of golf. A multifaceted sport, golf has attracted the attention of scholars and participants alike for many years (MacCulloch, 1892). Unfortunately, although it is fair to say that golf generates a full range of observational comment, it is also true that much of what is discussed tends to be based on anecdotal evidence and personal experience. Indeed until recent years and the development of human movement science, little of what could be seen or heard around the practice areas of the world had been derived from empirical study.

To date there have been a number of studies which have specifically investigated putting performance and subsequently compared success rates of novice, competent and expert golfers (Beauchamp et al., 1994; Delay et al., 1997; Gott & McGown, 1988; Gwyn et al., 1996). However, many such studies have tended to focus on putting outcomes and not the separate components of putting skill which ultimately define the observed outcome. Certainly if one wished to understand the causes of error or inaccuracy in putting then it would seem reasonable to consider the skill in terms of its component parts. Indeed, more than 30 years ago Neale and Anderson

(1966) made the observation that putting inaccuracies in previous studies could not be categorically attributed to errors either in aiming or stroke generation. Yet still no great emphasis has been placed on the investigation of the separate components of putting. One notable exception here was a study by McGlynn et al. (1990) which described putting in terms of three elemental components (i) the ability to assess the correct target line (reading the green), (ii) the ability to align the putter face at the intended target, and (iii) the ability to stroke the ball along the intended target line with appropriate pace to drop into the hole.

Within the context of this discussion it is intended to focus on the second of these components, the ability to align the putter with the intended target. Specifically the rationale behind this study, as with many studies, stems from observed behaviours on the golf course. Perhaps as a result of studying the golfing partnership of Nick Faldo and his caddie Fanny Sunnesson in recent years, there has been noticeable interest in the use of a caddie or partner assisting in the alignment of putts by standing directly behind the line of putt and offering prestroke alignment advice. It is the intention of this study to attempt to quantify putting alignment skills, in isolation from other components of putting, and to compare the effectiveness of a conventional alignment strategy with alignments made from the perspective of a caddie or playing partner.

Methods

Thirty participants (25 male, 5 female; Mean age = 31.4 years; SD = 15.1) gave written, informed consent and were recruited to this study. For the purpose of subsequent data analysis each participant was classified into one of three groups based on their performance standard and previous golf experience: 2–11 handicap (n = 10), 12–24 handicap (n = 10), novice golfers (n = 10).

The experimental data collection instrumentation was designed to be portable and allowed testing of participants in a variety of locations. In order to ensure consistency, all putting alignments were carried out on a plain green putting carpet (4 m x 1 m). The straight edges of the carpet were covered with a ruckered cotton sheet which prevented participants from gaining peripheral alignment cues.

Participants were required to undertake two different putting alignment techniques (conventional and horizontal) aiming to a target 3.66 m (12 feet) distant. Conventional alignment reflected an alignment procedure where the person aligns the putter by looking vertically down onto the top of the putter head. The horizontal alignment technique was intended to mimic the action of a caddie or playing partner who may assist the golfer with prestroke alignment feedback. Here the participants positioned themselves behind the putter, directly in line with the intended target.

Putting alignment was measured using a novel arrangement (see Figure 1) whereby a laser diode module (1 mW, 670 nm; RS Components U.K.) was embedded into the heel of a putter (Challenge, Slazenger Golf, U.K.). The recess into which the laser unit was sunk was machined such that the laser source projected precisely at right angles to the face of the putter. A 3-volt battery power source for the laser was located within the shaft of the putter and was activated using a fine wire and switch arrangement which exited the putter through the top of the putter grip. Alignment was quantified when the activated laser light source impinged onto a graduated scoreboard located behind the intended target. The default setting for the laser light source was the *off* position, and only when the switching mechanism was depressed did the laser indicate the direction of alignment. To facilitate accuracy of measurement, the graduated scoreboard was videotaped continuously throughout, ensuring a permanent record of the alignment scores.

The positions of the putter head and the graduated scoreboard were fixed 5.49 m apart. The alignment target was a steel disc placed on an imaginary centre line between the putter head and the graduated scoreboard at a distance of 3.66 m from the putter head. The diameter of the steel disc was 0.108 m which corresponds to the dimensions of a golf hole. The putter itself

Figure 1
Golf putter showing location of laser light source.

was held in position on the putting carpet by means of a steel pin which projected from beneath the carpet to insert into a hole bored into the base of the putter. The arrangement ensured that the frame of reference for the laser light source was always the same, yet allowed the participant to freely rotate the putter head whilst undertaking the task of correct alignment.

Each participant was required to undertake 10 separate alignments, for each of the two alignment techniques. In collecting data using the conventional vertical alignment technique, participants were asked to rotate the putter head on its retaining pin until they believed the putter was correctly aligned. At this point participants gave a verbal command to the tester, who then depressed the laser switching mechanism and activated the laser light source so illuminating the graduated scoreboard. In the case of the horizontal alignment technique, it was the tester who held the putter on its retaining pin, while the participant was positioned directly behind the putter, in line with the intended target. Each of the participants issued instructions to the tester detailing how to align the putter with the intended target. Again when the participant believed the putter to be correctly aligned, a verbal command was given and the laser light source activated.

The order of each set of 10 alignments was randomised and precautions were taken to ensure that participants were not able to receive any knowledge of results until after all data were collected. Following each separate alignment, the putter head was twisted through 90 degrees such that the previous alignment would not form a foundation for any subsequent alignment.

On completion of data collection, the videotape used to monitor the graduated scoreboard was played back in a frame-by-frame mode allowing alignment scores to be quantified. After taking into account the offset of the laser light source from the centre of the putter, calculations of angular deviations could be made. Subsequently the derived data were expressed in two ways *(i) Mean Alignment Error* — where the alignment deviations were presented as an absolute angular deviation from the centre of the target, and *(ii) Percentage Success Rate* — where each individual alignment was categorised as to whether or not the measured alignment deviation fell within the bandwidth of a standard golf hole (0.108 m). Alignments which fell into this bandwidth were deemed to be successful alignments.

Paired *t* tests were used to test for differences between the conventional and horizontal alignment techniques.

Results
Mean Alignment Error

The results presented in Figure 2 clearly show that experienced golfers, from either handicap category, are unable to match their conventional vertical putting alignment technique when using the horizontal alignment technique. Mean horizontal alignment errors of 1.64° ± 0.26 (SEM) for 2–11 handicap golfers, and 1.29° ± 0.13 (SEM) for 12–24 handicap golfers, were significantly different from those values obtained during the conventional vertical alignment procedure: 0.90° ± 0.15 (SEM) ($p < .03$) and 0.92° ± 0.16 (SEM) ($p < .04$) respectively.

In contrast to the findings relating to experienced golfers, it is interesting to note that novice golfers demonstrated a mean horizontal alignment error of 1.16° ± 0.15 (SEM) which compared favourably with their conventional vertical alignment scores of 1.31° ± 0.21 (SEM). The two values were not significantly different ($p > .05$).

Percentage Success Rate

Table 1 summarises alignment data presented as a percentage success rate in terms of the number of alignments which fell within the bandwidth of a standard golf hole. Again the use of a horizontal alignment technique appears to compromise the performance of experienced golfers whilst novice golfers seem able to improve their alignment scores.

Discussion

On first inspection the magnitude of the measured error in conventionally aligned putts may offer some reassurance to the typical club golfer. For instance, a 1° error in alignment from the centre of the target would still mean that the alignment would be within a standard hole width from a putting distance of 2.86 m. Unfortunately when this error is added to other

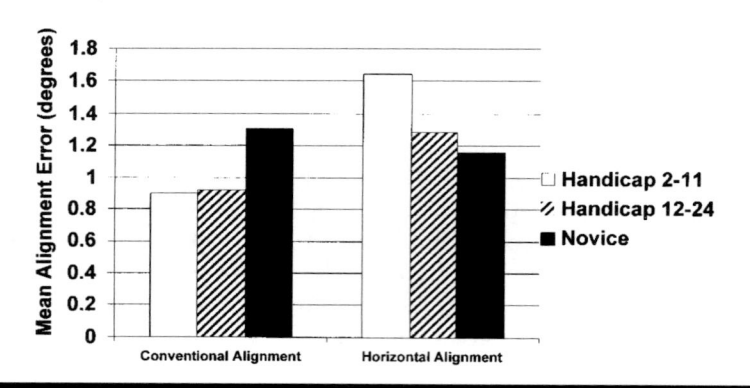

Figure 2
Angular deviations of putting alignments for golfers of different skill levels aiming to a target 3.66 m distant.

Table 1
Percentage Success Rates for Conventional and Horizontal Alignment Strategies

	HANDICAP GROUP		
	2–11	12–24	NOVICE
Conventional	51%	57%	35%
Horizontal	29%	38%	45%

sources of error in putting, such as reading the green (Pelz, 1994), control of the putting stroke (Delay et al., 1997), and trueness of roll on the actual putting surface (Koslow & Wenos, 1998), then it is perhaps not surprising that even the best golfers in the world occasionally miss short putts.

As a specific aim of this study, the comparison of conventional and horizontal alignment techniques in putting produced some interesting results. The finding that the two groups of experienced golfers were unable to match their conventional vertical alignment scores when using a horizontal alignment technique has immediate implications. Not least of these is the perceived value of allowing a caddie or playing partner to offer prestroke assistance in the alignment of putts from directly behind the ball. In contrast, investigation of the alignment errors of novice golfers shows there to be a potential improvement in performance when alignments were carried out using the horizontal technique as compared to the conventional vertical alignment technique.

In terms of an explanation of these results, one is inclined to consider the tasks set as falling somewhere along the *novel* to *well-drilled* practice continuum. Clearly for a group of novice golfers, both the conventional vertical alignment technique and the horizontal alignment technique were novel tasks. In this context it is perhaps not unreasonable to suggest, as did Neale and Anderson (1966), that a person who faces the hole during the alignment process may be in a better position to evaluate the actual alignment of the putter head in relation to the target. Indeed an improvement in alignment success rate from 35% to 45% is likely to lead to an overall improvement in putting performance.

However, when considering experienced golfers, this is not the case. Where players have previously executed the task of putting alignment using a conventional vertical alignment strategy, then the novel task scenario disappears. In such a case one is effectively comparing the results of a previously learned task (conventional alignment) with a novel task (horizontal alignment). Hence it is perhaps not surprising that performance in the novel task cannot match performance in the learned task. A decrease in alignment success rate to less than 30%, even before the ball has been struck, suggests that overall putting performance would be severely inhibited. Here the implication is clear: experienced players who allow an untrained party to assist in the alignment of their putts are unlikely to reduce the alignment errors in putting. Even if the player only uses the advice of a caddie to confirm a proposed alignment, then the results presented here would suggest that such a confirmation would be based on a potentially flawed observation. Furthermore if the player relied entirely on the advice of the caddie, then the alignment errors observed may well be exacerbated.

The word *untrained* in the paragraph above is used deliberately and raises a number of issues. If it is accepted that a horizontal alignment technique is a relatively novel task to most experienced golfers, then perhaps there is a case for the training of caddies in the use of the horizontal alignment technique, such that it is no longer a novel task. Certainly from the preliminary data presented here (novice golfers performing better using horizontal alignment compared to conventional vertical alignment), there seems to be a suggestion that standing directly behind the line of a putt may offer the opportunity to enhance alignment performance. To continue this line of study it might be proposed that a caddie who is actively trained to use the horizontal alignment technique may well be able to offer their playing partner a useful advantage. Further research would provide valuable information here.

Conclusions

Actual errors in conventional putter alignment are relatively small and in experienced golfers are of a lower magnitude compared to errors associated with horizontal alignment. Any assistance in alignment gained from an untrained caddie or playing partner standing directly in line with the ball and the target may well exacerbate errors in putting alignment. There may be a case for the instrumentation, described here, to be used as a training device to improve alignment skills in putting.

References

Beauchamp, P.H., Landsberger, L.M., Halliwell, W.R., Koestner, R., & Ford, M.E. (1994). Toward putting performance enhancement: A methodology using quantitative feedback. In A.J. Cochran & M.R. Farrally (Eds.), *Science and golf II: Proceedings of the 1994 World Scientific Congress of Golf* (pp. 174–179). London: E & FN Spon.

Delay, D., Nougier, V., Orliaguet, J.P., & Coello, Y. (1997). Movement control in golf putting. *Human Movement Science, 16,* 597–619.

Gott, E., & McGown, C. (1988). Effects of a combination of stances and points of aim on putting accuracy. *Perceptual and Motor Skills, 66,* 139–143.

Gwyn, R.G., Ormond, F., & Patch, C.E. (1996). Comparing putters with a conventional blade and a cylindrically shaped clubhead. *Perceptual and Motor Skills, 82,* 31–34.

Koslow, R., & Wenos, D. (1998). Realistic expectations on the putting green: Within and between days trueness of roll. *Perceptual and Motor Skills, 87,* 1441–1442.

MacCulloch, J. (1892). *Golf in the year 2000, or, What we are coming to? By J.A.C.K [i.e. J. MacCulloch].* London: T. Fisher Unwin.

McGlynn, F.G., Jones, R., & Kerwin, D.G. (1990). A laser-based putting alignment test. In A.J. Cochran (Ed.), *Science and golf: Proceedings of the First World Scientific Congress of Golf* (pp. 70–75). London: E & FN Spon.

Neale, D.C., & Anderson, B.D. (1966). Accuracy of aim with conventional and croquet-style golf putters. *The Research Quarterly, 37,* 89–94.

Pelz, D. (1994). A study of golfers' abilities to read greens. In A.J. Cochran & M.R. Farrally (Eds.), *Science and golf II: Proceedings of the 1994 World Scientific Congress of Golf* (pp 180–185). London: E & FN Spon.

CHAPTER 8

Periodisation for Golf

Peter W. Knight

The term periodisation has been used with most Olympic sports for a number of years. Its application to golf has been virtually non-existent. Or has it?

Periodisation is a process of dividing the annual plan into small phases of training in order to allow a program to be set into more manageable segments and to ensure correct peaking for the main competition(s) of the year (Bompa, 1983). These phases are called: general preparation, specific preparation, precompetition, competition and transition.

A simple plan would have one competition period per year with all preparation geared toward that period. For most competitive golfers there is only one competitive period per year. It lasts 12 months! So what then is the best format for golf when the competition period is not clearly defined?

The sample plan shown in Figure 1 will be used to explain the way an annual plan for golf is devised. This plan is for an elite male amateur golfer competing in Australia. While this player is close to national standard, there are still many areas where improvements need to occur. Later in the chapter, case study information is presented to illustrate how the annual plan is implemented.

Annual Plan for Golf

The coach should start by plotting the main competitions for the year. A judgment needs to be made as to how the year is to be broken up into general preparation, specific preparation, precompetition, competition and transition periods. Assuming developmental work needs to be carried out, the year cannot be one long competitive period. In any case the player is not able to sustain a peak for the entire year. The timing of these periods may be fine tuned as more data are obtained for the plan.

Preliminary work in establishing the plan means determining what the player wants to achieve for the year. It is worth considering that this annual plan forms part of a longer term plan, perhaps a 5-year plan. The player's goals for the year must be considered in terms of what has happened in the past 12 months to ensure the aims are realistic.

Baseline performance data come from round analyses taken during competition and skills testing. The more comprehensive these are the better, although a compromise needs to be struck. If the player is asked to collect too much information the data collection will only be spasmodic. In the section of the plan headed *objectives*, the highest numbers are in the April–July columns. This is because work to improve these statistics will only begin after the main competitive period has ended.

Strength, medical and musculo-skeletal testing will be carried out in early April but will not be acted upon substantially until after the competitive period. Strength-testing results have shown explained instances where a coach may not have been able to achieve a technique change for physiological reasons. Musculo-skeletal screenings have shown that long-term practising and playing golf produces the same problems in nearly all golfers (Chim & McMaster, 1994). Following the screenings the player will have goals for development in those areas.

Further strength and musculo-skeletal screenings are carried out in August to ensure the player is progressing physically, as planned. This is at the end of the general preparation period where any major changes should have already occurred. If there is a need for the player to continue to do significant physical training then it would be wise to schedule another testing date.

Preparation

There are four areas of preparation to be considered: physical, mental, technical and tactical. For the sake of simplicity we will consider that any facet of preparation will fall into one of these four categories.

MONTH	June				July				August					Sept				Oct				
WEEK BEGINNING	7	14	21	28	5	12	19	26	2	9	16	23	30	6	13	20	27	4	11	18	25	1
COMPETITIONS													Interstate Series									
club/state																						
national																						
PERIODISATION			GP						SP					PC	C	T			SP			
MACROCYCLES	1								2					3	4	5	6					
physical		strength, fitness & flexibility development																	maintenance:			
mental		goals, relaxation positive self talk							preshot, precompetition, preevent routines focus/refocus, visualisation, concentration												
technical		full swing & short game development							high intensity competition drills						T	tech dev't if required			fine high int		
tactical		gather baseline practice data																	formulate monitor			
microcycles	1	2	3	4	5	6	7	8	9	10	11	12	13	14	15	16	17	18	19	20	21	22	23
TESTING																						
- strength																						
- medical																						
- musculo-skeletal																						
- biomechanical																						
OBJECTIVES																						
Score v par	+2								+1.8									+1.4				
Putts	32.5								32									31.5				
Putts / green in reg	1.83								1.82									1.81				
% Fairways hit	54								60									65				
% Greens hit	65								66									67				
% Chipping convert	62								63									64				
% Sand convert	48								50									52				

GP - general preparation   SP - specific preparation   PC - precompetition

Figure 1
An annual plan for an elite amateur golfer in Australia.

Physical

General fitness, resistance to fatigue, ability to practise for longer periods, resistance to injury and muscular balance can all be improved through physical training. The fitness trailer on the US PGA Tour is at every tournament site and is used by a large percentage of the players. This indicates the acceptance of the importance of strength and fitness training by some of the best players in the world. The period mid-June to mid-August is chosen as

PERIODISATION FOR GOLF

	Nov				Dec				Jan				Feb				Mar				Apr				May		
25	1	8	15	22	29	6	13	20	27	4	11	18	25	1	8	15	22	1	8	15	22	29	5	12	19	26	3	10	17
							Australian Open						Lake Macquarie					Tasmanian Open	Riversdale Cup	Australian Amateur	NSW Amateur		Mandurah				QLD Amateur		

P		PC	C	T		SP		PC	C	PC					C			T	
		7	8	9	10		11	12	13	14								15	

tenance: flexibility, Swiss ball®, Theraband®, light weights, core stability

utines	evaluate and refine mental skills
ration	stress management, regeneration
fine tune	T	maintain high intensity, competitive drills	T
high intensity		event focus	

formulate game plans according to own strengths and weakneses
monitor performance data and adapt game plans accordingly

21	22	23	24	25	26	27	28	29	30	31	32	33	34	35	36	37	38	39	40	41	42	43	44	45	46	47	48	49	50

+1.4	+1.2	+0.8	+0.6
31.5	31	30.5	30
1.81	1.80	1.80	1.80
65	65	68	70
67	68	68	70
64	65	66	66
52	55	57	57

npetition   C - competition   T - transition

Figure 1 Continued
An annual plan for an elite amateur golfer in Australia.

the best time to do concentrated strength and fitness work as it is the quietest time of the year in terms of competitions. It won't matter then if there is a slight performance decline as the body gets used to the different type of training.

After this period of intense physical training, the rest of the year is given to a maintenance program. Ideally this should include continued weight training where possible. When the player is competing there should still be some form of resistance training as it will serve to maintain the player's strength levels and help ward off injury. This can be achieved using Theraband®, light weights or Swiss balls®. Flexibility work is probably the most important element of physical preparation as it assists in recovery and maintenance of joint range of movement.

Mental

The same approach needs to be taken for mental skills as for physical skills. Make an assessment of the players current mental skills; develop the basics in a non-threatening environment; further train those skills in practice and low-level competition; and refine them in major competition. All the time, monitor progress and make adjustments to the program where required (Bacon, 1989).

Assessment of mental skills is available through a range of different types of questionnaires. While there is debate as to the accuracy of these tests, they will still give a good indication of a player's areas of mental weakness. Athletes should first learn the basic mental skills such as relaxation (in a darkened quiet room) and learn progressively to be able to apply that skill in a game situation — for example, using progressive relaxation before a game, taking centring breaths on the field and shaking out the arms before swinging (Bacon, 1989).

The mental skills training must also be compatible with other modes of training. Failure to provide mental training programs that are consistent with the ups and downs of training cycles and the competitive season can lower motivation and self-confidence, increase anxiety and possibly lower athletic performance (Bacon, 1989). For this reason a logical progression would be to learn mental skills in the following order: relaxation, positive self-talk, energisation, visualisation and concentration.

Technical

The majority of coaching in golf is technical. This is partly because most players see technical improvement as being the answer to their performance problems. Even where this is the case, planning technical changes still needs to take into account the playing schedule of the golfer, especially the elite player. It may well be that a player is willing to sacrifice performance short-term as swing improvements or new shots are learned. It is better, however, to only make minor adjustments except during the general preparation periods.

Assessment can be via video, swing computers and the coach's eye. A plan for technique development should be established and monitored with further video analysis as the changes are being created. During this period of change the player is likely to hit a lot of shots. It is best at this stage to limit the variety so as not to put too much pressure on the new movements.

As the player moves into the specific preparation period, much more variety is added to the practice. The total volume may fall as the player is working to constantly change targets and clubs during practice (especially with short-game development). More time is spent in skills testing and competitive practice. The player must learn how well the changes are likely to stand up under increasing pressure.

During the precompetition period the player should spend time practising the types of shots likely to be played on the tournament courses, as well as continuing a base level of practice. Practice sessions need to be intense and challenging: competing against another player, more time spent on the course instead of the range, playing mental games in practice, and so on.

If the lead-up work has been performed according to plan then there will only need to be a maintenance level of practice during the competitive period. This will allow the player to avoid the possibility of fatigue in competition that has occurred because of heavy practice sessions.

Tactical

Tactics involve knowing oneself, the course, and in some cases the opponent. Assessment will be tied closely to that for mental skills but can include questions such as: what are the carry distances for each club? how wide are realistic target areas for each club? what are the conversion rates with chipping versus pitching or sand shots? Historic information from round analyses, skills testing, and observation of others during competition all contribute to this assessment.

Low-level tactical development during general preparation can include recognising one's own strengths and weaknesses and monitoring improvements. Here preshot, preround and precompetition routines need to be developed or refined.

Specific preparation includes applying knowledge of one's carry distances to courses for which yardages are available. Competitive games such as *Aussie Rules* golf can be played to develop awareness of one's strengths — for example, driver versus three wood, fade versus draw, and so on (Crampton, 1986). These games should involve using the preshot routine and competing against others where applicable.

Precompetition preparation includes getting to know the course, and working to an established preround and precompetition routine. Game plans need to be developed for the competition site. The more thorough the plan the better the player will know the course and the more options the player is likely to recognise in any given situation.

Case Study
Background

Allan's low fitness levels showed through during testing which involved among other tests, a shuttle run (Level 6 Stage 3) and sit-and-reach test –6 cm. During multiround tournaments there was a pattern of performance levels dropping in the latter rounds. Allan attributed this to technical errors in his swing, the outcome of which was a drop in confidence levels which was to become chronic.

Recommendations

Technique errors did manifest themselves through what empirically appeared to be a combination of state of mind and fitness levels. A combination of work to develop all three areas was most desirable.

The Plan

Allan was given a list of specific stretches to complete each day. These stretches addressed the entire body and focused specifically on the hips and hamstrings. Allan chose to complete these each evening while watching television.

Running was included as the preferred method of increasing fitness. The plan commenced with slow running three times per week beginning with a 15-minute run and gradually increasing the amount of time to 30 minutes after 4 weeks. Weeks 5 to 12 included variety in the running program. One session was a long slow run, another was a series of 400-metre runs where each was to be completed in a specific time. The third was a hill run.

The confidence levels were addressed by first having Allan gain an understanding of confidence levels being able to be controlled by the player rather than having them rise and fall according to how Allan was hitting the ball or scoring. He then compared the state of confidence against his state of not being confident. The notable differences, which he could control, were his level of peripheral vision, his level of self-talk and his general level of energisation.

Technique correction was to be achieved through a video analysis comparison of Allan's current swing, his swing when he was playing well, and swings of Tour players whose swings and body shapes were similar to Allan's. This was achieved using the Swinger video analysis program. This particular program allows the use of split screen and overlapping images to create extremely effective analysis. A weekly practice plan was set which included a balance of shots played with different clubs as well as specific technique and competitive drills, the results of which were to be recorded in a practice diary. Overall progress could be easily measured through statistical round analysis. The practice plan and drills were monitored every 2 weeks and adjusted accordingly. One of the drills had Allan hitting 5, 6 and 7-iron shots to a target 10 metres wide. For the shot to score, it had to land either in line with, or in-between, the two target boundaries.

Results
After undergoing the fitness regime, Allan commented on being able to concentrate for longer periods of time during practice, felt fresher after completing a round or multiround event, and had a greater general sense of well-being. His performance on the shuttle run after 6 weeks improved to Level 9 Stage 1. His sit-and-reach test measure improved to 1 cm. The improvements combined with his general sense of well-being have meant that new goals have already been established for further improvement.

Allan already had quite a good understanding of his swing technique, having used the Swinger system previously. However, each time he saw the current state of his swing, he was able to marry the swing feels he had with what it actually looked like. Combining technique drills with the use of video analysis allowed Allan to make the improvements almost immediately.

When exploring the confidence state, Allan hit a number of shots focusing on each of the elements which for him made up his state of being confident. The reason for this was to experiment with different levels of self-talk, peripheral vision and energisation. Once optimal levels were determined, then the three elements were combined. Interestingly, there was an improvement in technique as this state was being developed.

In an ensuing major multiround event, Allan performed his best for the year. Was this a result of improved fitness levels, technique or mental skills? Who can say for sure? Most likely it was a combination of all three, especially as each had an effect on the other. In fact this serves to highlight the importance of addressing all areas of development, rather than just one that may appear (at times misleadingly) to be the obvious one.

Conclusion
While there may be a science to developing each of the areas of preparation, linking them is the art. There are some rules to developing a plan such as reducing volume and increasing intensity as the competition period nears, but there is plenty of flexibility in the plan. As with any plan, use it as a base model, constantly monitor the progress of the plan against the established objectives with the player and make adjustments where appropriate. Planning is an educated guess, you just become better educated with practice.

Acknowledgments

Some parts of this chapter were originally presented at the PGA of Australia's 1998 and 2000 National Coaching Summits and are reproduced with permission.

References

Bacon, T. (1989). The planning and integration of mental training programs. *Sports, 10*(1), 1–8.
Bompa, T.O. (1983). *Theory and methodology of training.* Iowa: Kendall & Hunt.
Chim, J., & McMaster, R. (1994). *Get fit for golf: Part 1.* Melbourne: Graphics Unlimited.
Crampton, J. (1986). *Practice drills for golf.* Unpublished manuscript. Performance Enhancement Associates.

CHAPTER 9

A Performance History of International Golfers in the US Masters

Raymond J. Leigh

The US Masters can be considered to be unique because it differs from the other major championships in a number of respects (Lumb, Hobbs, & Pinner, 1988). Firstly, as indicated by its original name, The Augusta National Invitation Tournament, it is not a championship as such but an invitational event for which qualification is different. Secondly, the number of competitors is limited to a figure considerably lower than that of the other three majors (the mean was 84 for 1966–1999). Thirdly and most obviously, it is the only one of the four majors that is played on the same golf course each year.

The invitational nature of the tournament may take its lead from the original competition, held in 1934, where Bobby Jones was requested to invite the participants and also compete. Its current and more famous name did not come about until 1938. Since then, however, certain rules of qualification have developed and golfers must fall into one or more of the categories in Table 1 in order to be invited.

This policy, with its focus predominantly on the US, has frequently, particularly amongst Europeans, laid the tournament open to the charge of not being representative of the world's current best players. The criticism is clearly justifiable if we look at the qualification referring to past winners.

Many former champions take part who are no longer considered to be prominent and the more that do reduces the chances of invitations to international golfers under the final category of qualification. The purpose of this chapter is to analyse the performance of competitors over the history of the US Masters in order to establish whether there may be any justification for this criticism.

International players from 29 different countries have participated during the 64 years of competition to date, and although there was only one foreign player in 1946, there has never been a competition without any at all. Even during the early years of the Second World War while the tournament was still running (1939–1942), invited players from England and Australia felt able to take up their invitations. From its inauguration in 1934 up to 1957 (the year of the introduction of the 'cut' which reduced the number of players competing over the final two days) that percentage was always in single figures, averaging 5.5%. From that date the figure has risen considerably and overall, international players have averaged around 22% of the

Table 1

Categories of Qualification for Invitation to the US Masters

QUALIFICATIONS FOR INVITATION

1.	Masters Tournament Champions (Lifetime).
2.	US Open Champions (Honorary, non-competing after five years).
3.	British Open Champions (Honorary, non-competing after five years).
4.	PGA Champions (Honorary, non-competing after five years).
5.	Winners of The Players Championship (three years).
6.	Current US Amateur Champion (6-A) (Honorary, non-competing after one year); Runner-up (6-B) to the current US Amateur Champion.
7.	Current British Amateur Champion (Honorary, non-competing after one year).
8.	Current US Amateur Public Links Champion.
9.	Current US Mid-Amateur Champion.
10.	The first 16 players, including ties, in the previous year's Masters Tournament.
11.	The first 8 players, including ties, in the previous year's US Open.
12.	The first 4 players, including ties, in the previous year's US PGA Championship.
13.	The first 4 players, including ties in the previous year's British Open.
14.	The 40 leaders from the Final Official PGA TOUR Money List for the previous calendar year.
15.	The 3 leaders on the current year Official PGA TOUR Money List published during the fourth week prior to the current Masters.
16.	The 50 leaders on the Final Official World Golf Ranking for the previous calendar year.
17.	The 50 leaders on the Official World Golf Ranking published during the fourth week prior to the current Masters.

The Masters Committee, at its discretion, also invites international players not otherwise qualified. (Greenspan, 2000)

field. That figure has risen to over 23% since 1985, the year of the perceived emergence of European golf due to its supremacy in the Ryder Cup. In the past 3 years the proportion of non-US players has risen to above 30%.

Regardless of the measure of qualification, an invitation to the competition is no guarantee of success. It was not until 1961 that the US Masters had its first overseas winner (Gary Player) and it took another 13 years for that same player to be the next international golfer to win. It was not until 1980 that a different foreign player succeeded (Seve Ballesteros). There have been regular international successes since 1985, with 10 winners in those 16 years (see Table 2). Overall, international golfers have provided 23.4% of winners which closely corresponds to their level of participation. The Masters Committee had to wait quite a while, though, for justification via success of its international invitation policy.

Obviously not every golfer can win, but in every tournament there are certain objectives each will strive to achieve. The first of these must be to complete all 4 days of competition. Another is to do well enough to finish in the top 16 places (top 24 until 1999), which guarantees both automatic qualification for the following year and future financial reward as every invitee, regardless of his performance, receives a fee for appearing.

There is a fairly close relationship between the percentage of overseas players competing and the percentage making the cut. In 24 of the 44 competitions since 1957 the percentage of overseas players making the cut was greater than the percentage initially competing. On two occasions the figures have been identical, and relatively fewer made the cut than started in the remaining 18 competitions. Completion rates have been lower than starting percentages on only four occasions since 1985 (1989, 1991, 1995, 1998).

A similar pattern is evident in top-24 finishes. In 23 of the 44 years the field has been cut, the percentage of overseas players finishing among the top 24, including ties, has been higher than that completing the event. This relationship has been sustained in 10 of the 16 years since 1985.

These figures tend to show that by their own standards the international golfers invited to compete are certainly holding their own, particularly most recently. But comparisons do tend to be made between the performances of these golfers and the US golfers taking part, not only informally but also at the formal level (Greenspan, 1996). On the one hand may be the perception that the invited foreigners represent the best that the rest of the world has to offer, measured against a view that in order to be globally representative some of the international players may not be of the same standard as others.

However, the real indicator of players' performance in medal competition is to be found in their scores (Hale & Hale, 1990; Leigh, 1996). If we therefore analyse the 4-day scores for all golfers in all tournaments between 1934

Table 2
List of US Masters Champions (US unless indicated)

Year	Champion	Year	Champion
1934	Horton Smith	1969	George Archer
1935	Gene Sarazan	1970	Billy Casper Jr.
1936	Horton Smith	1971	Charles Coody
1937	Byron Nelson	1972	Jack Nicklaus
1938	Henry Picard	1973	Tommy Aaron
1939	Ralph Guldahl	1974	Gary Player (South Africa)
1940	Jimmy Demaret	1975	Jack Nicklaus
1941	Craig Wood	1976	Raymond Floyd
1942	Byron Nelson	1977	Tom Watson
1943–1945	No competition	1978	Gary Player (South Africa)
1946	Herman Keiser	1979	Fuzzy Zoeller
1947	Jimmy Demaret	1980	Severiano Ballesteros (Spain)
1948	Claude Harmon	1981	Tom Watson
1949	Sam Snead	1982	Craig Stadler
1950	Jimmy Demaret	1983	Severiano Ballesteros (Spain)
1951	Ben Hogan	1984	Ben Crenshaw
1952	Sam Snead	1985	Bernhard Langer (Germany)
1953	Ben Hogan	1986	Jack Nicklaus
1954	Sam Snead	1987	Larry Mize
1955	Cary Middlecoff	1988	Sandy Lyle (Scotland)
1956	Jack Burke Jr.	1989	Nick Faldo (England)
1957	Doug Ford	1990	Nick Faldo (England)
1958	Arnold Palmer	1991	Ian Woosnam (Wales)
1959	Art Wall Jr.	1992	Fred Couples
1960	Arnold Palmer	1993	Bernhard Langer (Germany)
1961	Gary Player (South Africa)	1994	Jose Maria Olazabal (Spain)
1962	Arnold Palmer	1995	Ben Crenshaw
1963	Jack Nicklaus	1996	Nick Faldo (England)
1964	Arnold Palmer	1997	Tiger Woods
1965	Jack Nicklaus	1998	Mark O'Meara
1966	Jack Nicklaus	1999	Jose Maria Olazabal (Spain)
1967	Gay Brewer	2000	Vijay Singh (Fiji)
1968	Bob Goalby		

and 1999 and compare them by nation, we find that the mean for US golfers is 295.01 ± 8.87 strokes and that for international golfers is 292.41 ± 7.48 strokes. Given the small single-figure percentage representation up to 1957, scores were analysed for the period 1957–1999. These show means of 291.54 ± 6.38 strokes for US golfers and 291.34 ± 6.56 strokes for overseas players. In each case there exists a small difference in favour of the overseas golfers but this is not statistically significant. It may be explained, certainly in the early days of the competition, by the very low numbers of international players taking part.

There is no evidence that the better international scores have come about more recently because of a decline in US performance over the period (cf.

Hale, Harper, & Herb, 1994). Nor is it correct simply to consider improvement in the standard of European golf over a similar period (Hale et al., 1994) for, although the number of European players participating in the Masters in recent years may have increased, thus reflecting a recognition of that improvement, the general increase also includes players from other continents, particularly Asia, Australasia and South America.

What is clear from Figure 1 is that there is a general improvement in both sets of mean scores throughout the whole period (1934–2000). The pattern of scoring is almost identical for both US and international players and the yearly fluctuations could quite reasonably be explained by the vagaries of the weather conditions encountered, although a comparison with local weather records might lend greater credibility to this explanation. There may be a number of interrelated reasons why mean scores have fallen overall. It would be easy to say that the course itself has become easier for today's golfer. The necessity of having to accommodate both the average golfer and the world's best professionals would make it difficult to provide a stern test for both types of golfer simultaneously (Jones, 1959; Lumb et al., 1988). When a true test of golf for the modern professional is discussed, however, the recurring theme is the severity of the greens and any explanations referring to increases in golf technology bringing the course to its knees may have difficulty reconciling themselves to this factor.

Technology has enhanced performance and improvements in both club and particularly, ball design and consistency, have had a part to play in

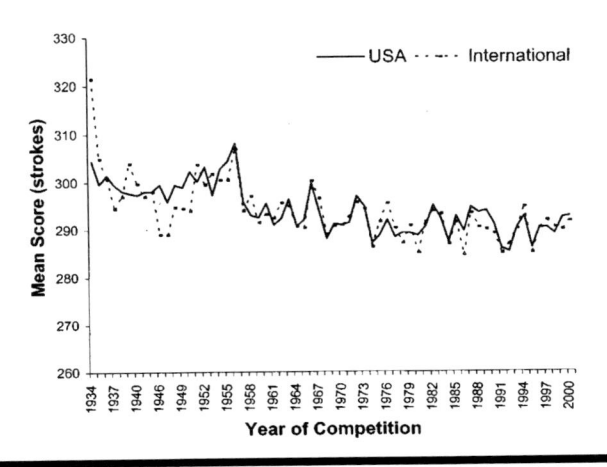

Figure 1
Mean scores for US and international golfers in the US Masters.

improvements in scoring (Cochran, 1990; Thomas, 1994). But, as Thomas says, "science is entering golf" and golfers themselves may well be using a far more scientific and systematic approach to their game in terms of technical, physical and psychological preparation which is having a marked effect on the performance of all golfers, regardless of their nationality.

In conclusion, this chapter has shown that international golfers have performed as well as US golfers in the Masters competition thus, perhaps, belying the criticisms that have been levelled somewhat unfairly at the tournament organisers.

References

Cochran, A.J. (1990). Science, equipment, development and standards. In A.J. Cochran (Ed.), *Science and golf: Proceedings of the First World Scientific Congress of Golf* (pp. 177–186). London: E & FN Spon.

Greenspan, G. (1996). *Masters media guide*. Augusta National Inc.

Greenspan, G. (2000). *New qualifications for invitation to Masters Tournament*. www.masters.org

Hale, T., & Hale, G.T. (1990). Lies, damned lies and statistics in golf. In A.J. Cochran (Ed.), *Science and golf: Proceedings of the First World Scientific Congress of Golf* (pp. 159–164). London: E & FN Spon.

Hale, T., Harper, V., & Herb, J. (1994). The Ryder Cup: An analysis of relative performance 1980–1993. In A.J. Cochran & M.R. Farrally (Eds.), *Science and golf II: Proceedings of the 1994 World Scientific Congress of Golf* (pp. 205–209). London: E & FN Spon.

Jones, R.T. (1959). *Golf is my game*. New York: Doubleday.

Leigh, R.J. (1996). An investigation into the success of US golfers in the Open Golf Championship at St. Andrews. In E. Wallace, B. Deddis, & J. Hanna (Eds.), *Proceedings of the First International Golf — Theory in Practice Conference* (p. 35). University of Ulster, Northern Ireland.

Lumb, N., Hobbs, M., & Pinner, J. (1988). *The complete book of golf*. London: New Burlington.

Thomas, F.W. (1994). The state of the game, equipment and science. In A.J. Cochran & M.R. Farrally (Eds.), *Science and golf II: Proceedings of the 1994 World Scientific Congress of Golf* (pp. 237–246). London: E & FN Spon.

The Physiology of Optimising Golf Performance in Hot Environments

Tom M. McLellan

Humans are homeothermic creatures, and regulate their body temperature within a narrow range over the entire course of their lives (Bligh, 1985). When heat is generated by increased metabolic activity, humans are generally successful in maintaining a thermal steady state by activating heat-loss mechanisms to dissipate the excess heat. A hot and/or humid environment, however, imposes a major stress on the human body's ability to maintain physiological stability during exercise, due to a decrease in the thermal and water vapour pressure gradients between the body and the environment, thus impairing heat exchange (Gonzalez, 1988). Hyperthermia, and its attendant clinical symptoms of heat exhaustion and heat stroke, has become well recognised as a major risk encountered when exercising in hot environments (Gardner et al., 1996).

Golf is a recreational pastime and sport enjoyed by millions of people worldwide. Participation is not restricted by age, gender or race but rather accessibility and cost are probably the most deterring factors. If a round is scheduled on a particular day, participants are not likely to cancel due to inclement weather unless such a policy is endorsed by the course. Some courses even require prepayment, thus cancellation prior to teeing-off may not be an option. With the exception of thunderstorms, today's golfer probably is willing to endure most climatic conditions including rain, wind and temperature extremes. Certainly the professional player has no option during a tournament except to continue playing. Clothing can be worn to reduce the impact of rain and cold temperatures and there are even microclimate heating units available that could be used by golfers in cold weather to maintain warmth in the hands (Brajkovic et al., 1998).

However, how prepared are golfers to meet the challenge of playing during the high temperatures of the summer? It would not be uncommon to reach environmental temperatures in excess of 35°C during the summer months in the popular golfing areas of the world such as Florida, Georgia, the Carolinas, Texas and Arizona in the southern USA, or the Gold Coast in Queensland Australia. Vacationers travelling to these warmer climates during their winter for a 1–2 week holiday are suddenly exposed to warmer environmental temperatures. Does this place them at greater risk to exertional heat injury? What factors are in the control of the player to help reduce the risk of heat injury? What is the impact of elevations in body temperature on golf performance? As a physiologist, this last question is the most difficult for me to address and I refer the reader to other experts in this area (Hancock, 1982, 1986; Ramsey, 1995). Their consensus is that performance of complex motor or mental tasks would be reduced at wet bulb globe temperatures (WBGT which incorporates the influence of both temperature and relative humidity) above 30°C. A WBGT of 30°C represents, for example, an environmental dry bulb temperature of 35°C with a relative humidity close to 60% which are environmental conditions also associated with signs of increased physiological strain, as indicated by an increase in body core temperature (Ramsey, 1995). Thus, factors that reduce the physiological strain of heat exposure either prior to or during the round of golf should optimise one's performance.

The following chapter is divided into three sections. First, an overview of the physical factors governing heat exchange between the body and the environment is presented. As shown in Figure 1, these factors include the environmental temperature, water vapour pressure, solar radiation and clothing. In the second section, details concerning the importance of physiological factors such as hydration, aerobic fitness and heat acclimatisation together with individual characteristics such as body composition, age, gender, menstrual cycle and circadian rhythm are discussed as they pertain to the physiological strain of heat exposure. The final section integrates this previous discussion and presents recommendations for golfers to help optimise their performance in hot environments.

Environmental Factors

Temperature
Relative Humidity
Wind
Solar Radiation

Physiological Factors

Aerobic Fitness
Heat Acclimatisation
Hydration

Individual Characteristics

Gender
Body Composition
Menstrual Cycle
Hormone Replacement Therapy
Oral Contraceptives
Circadian Rhythm
Age

External Factors

Clothing
Sunscreen Protection
Metabolic Rate

Figure 1
Environmental, physiological, individual and external factors that influence heat storage while playing a round of golf.

Heat Exchange

Mechanisms of heat transfer are grouped into two general categories consisting of dry (radiative, conductive, and convective) and wet (evaporative) pathways. Dry heat exchange is dependent on the temperature gradients within the body (e.g., core to periphery) and also between the skin surface and the environment. In addition, the rate of cutaneous blood flow to transport heat from the core to the periphery influences the degree of convective heat exchange. Wet heat loss arises from the evaporation of water, typically secreted by the sweat glands within the skin. The potential for evaporative heat loss is determined primarily by the water vapour pressure gradient between the body surface and the environment, which in turn may be modified both by the environment and clothing (Craig & Moffitt, 1974; Kakitsuba et al., 1988; Kenney et al., 1987; McLellan et al., 1996; Sawka & Wenger, 1988) as well as physiologically due to alterations in sweat gland activity and output (Candas et al., 1979; Taylor, 1986).

The rate of evaporative cooling required to balance the summation of all other sources of heat gains and losses by the body is shown in the following equation:

$$\dot{E}_{req} = \dot{M} - \dot{W} \pm (\dot{C} + \dot{R} + \dot{K}) \pm (\dot{C}_{resp} - \dot{E}_{resp}) \tag{1}$$

where $\dot{M}$ is the metabolic rate, $\dot{W}$ represents the rate of heat loss from the generation of external power, $\dot{R}$, $\dot{C}$ and $\dot{K}$ are the rates of radiative, convective and conductive heat transfer, respectively, $\dot{C}_{resp}$ defines convective heat transfer through respiration, and $\dot{E}_{resp}$ represents evaporative heat loss with respiration. For equations that can be used to derive each of these terms, the reader is referred to other publications (Aoyagi et al., 1997; Fanger, 1970; McLellan et al., 1996; Nishi, 1981).

The maximum cooling power of sweat evaporation at the skin surface is defined by the following equation when clothing is worn (Gonzalez et al., 1997):

$$\dot{E}_{max} = LR \cdot i_m \cdot I_T^{-1} \cdot (P_{sk} - P_a) \tag{2}$$

where LR is the Lewis relation (16.5 °C·kPa^{-1}), i_m is the water vapour permeability coefficient (dimensionless), P_{sk} represents the saturated skin vapour pressure at $\overline{T}_{sk}$, and P_a defines the ambient water vapour pressure.

The heat stress index (HSI) is defined as the ratio of $\dot{E}_{req}$ to $\dot{E}_{max}$. When HSI ≤ 1.0, $\dot{E}_{max}$ equals or exceeds $\dot{E}_{req}$, resulting in a compensable heat stress environment where a new thermal steady-state is achieved for any given rate of heat production. Conversely an uncompensable heat stress is defined when HSI exceeds 1.0 resulting in continued heat storage and rise in body core temperature.

When unclothed, the regulation of thermal energy exchanges between humans and the ambient environment can occur directly across the skin. When the temperature of the ambient environment is similar to that found at the skin, as is the case during exercise in the heat at approximately 35°C, the primary pathway for heat dissipation is from the evaporation of secreted sweat (Wenger, 1972). Maximal evaporative heat dissipation from the body occurs when secreted sweat is vapourised at the skin (Nadel, 1979). When clothing is worn, however, an air layer is formed directly above the skin surface, and this microenvironment forms the initial environmental layer between the body and the environment. In addition, the site of phase change may be raised above the skin due to the clothing microenvironment. In this scenario, a portion of the heat energy of vapourisation may come from the environment rather than the body, thus further decreasing the efficiency of evaporative heat loss (McLellan et al., 1996; Nunneley, 1989). Therefore, the thermal properties of clothing, such as its insulation, ventilation, and permeability to water vapour, have a significant influence on the rate of heat transfer between the skin and the ambient environment (Gonzalez, 1988; Holmer, 1995).

Table 1 presents estimates of the terms in Equations 1 and 2 during a round of golf at 25°C and 35°C with relative humidity of 50%. Obviously, these values will vary depending on how long the round takes to play, whether you walk and carry your clubs or ride in a power cart, and whether the day is sunny or overcast. Estimates for the average metabolic rate of walking 18 holes and pulling or carrying your clubs approximate 150–175 $W \cdot m^{-2}$ (Getchell, 1968; Lampley et al., 1977; Murase et al., 1989) or about 3 times higher than the value for riding (or resting) in a power cart. The external work of walking would be small but would include the work done to overcome the resistance of air and the friction of the foot contacting the ground. The impact of the amount (e.g., shorts versus trousers, short-sleeved versus long-sleeved shirt and a hat) and colour (e.g., light versus dark) of clothing (Blum, 1945; Nielsen, 1990) on heat transfer is also estimated in this table. With the increased awareness of the associated risk of skin melanoma through acute and chronic exposure to ultraviolet radiation, the use of sunscreens and/or protective clothing has become more common (Cummings et al., 1997; Davis et al., 1997). Some trade-off may be necessary, however, since heat transfer away from the body will be reduced if more clothing is worn. There is also some evidence to suggest that the use of effective sunscreens will reduce evaporative heat loss and have a negative impact on temperature regulation during exposure to hot environments (Spaul et al., 1985). The values in Table 1 do show that the heat stress index is less when one uses a power cart due to the lower rate of heat production. However, under most situations while walking the heat stress is still compensable. In the late morning or early afternoon of a bright sunny day at 35°C, wearing more protective clothing (of darker colour) may create a situation that is very close to being defined as uncompensable.

Physiological Factors

Previous exposure to a hot environment is arguably the most specific and direct method of adaptation to exercise in the heat (Wenger, 1988). A high level of aerobic fitness has also been associated with an improved exercise-heat tolerance, and physical training is another treatment that has been used in an attempt to adapt individuals to work in a hot environment (Armstrong & Pandolf, 1988). Primary amongst the adaptations to heat stress appear to be alterations in the body's fluid compartments and overall fluid balance, with an increase in plasma volume a consistent response to both physical training and heat acclimation protocols (Armstrong & Pandolf, 1988). In turn, improvements in body fluid balance with manipulation of hydration status may result in the classic description of an individual who is adapted to hot environments, including the maintenance of a heightened sweating

Table 1

Estimates of Sources of Heat Gain (positive values) and Avenues of Heat Loss (negative values) During a Round of Golf (while either walking or riding in a power cart and wearing different clothing configurations at either 25°C and 50% relative humidity or 35°C and 50% relative humidity). Values are estimated in W·m^{-2}. For convective heat transfer mean skin temperature was assumed to be 34°C and 36°C while walking at the ambient temperatures of 25°C and 35°C, respectively, and 32°C and 35°C while riding, respectively. Total thermal resistance and water vapour permeability were assumed to be increased and decreased 20%, respectively, by wearing long pants and a long-sleeved shirt compared with the wearing of shorts and a short-sleeved shirt because of the surface areas involved (Hardy & Dubois, 1938). It was estimated that golfers were walking for 40% of the time and standing during the remainder of their round (Getchell, 1968). With the power cart, it was assumed that the cart was in motion for 20% of the total time with the remainder being spent seated at rest or standing. Radiant heat load was calculated for a bright sunny day during the late morning or early afternoon assuming a projected surface area of 25% (Blum, 1945; Nielsen, 1990).

	ENVIRONMENTAL CONDITIONS			
	25°C, 50% RH		35°C, 50% RH	
	WALKING	RIDING	WALKING	RIDING
Metabolic Rate	175	60	175	60
External Power	-5	0	-5	0
Convective Heat Transfer				
shorts, short-sleeved shirt and hat	-50	-30	-5	0
trousers, long-sleeved shirt and hat	-40	-25	-4	0
Radiant Heat Transfer				
light coloured clothing	55	30	55	30
dark coloured clothing	100	60	100	60
Conductive Heat Transfer	0	-5	0	3
Respiratory Heat Transfer	-12	-4	-8	-3
Required Evaporative Cooling (E_{req})				
shorts, short-sleeved shirt and hat	163 (light colour) 208 (dark colour)	51 (light) 81 (dark)	212 (light) 257 (dark)	90 (light) 120 (dark)
trousers, long-sleeved shirt and hat	173 (light colour) 218 (dark colour)	56 (light) 86 (dark)	213 (light) 258 (dark)	90 (light) 120 (dark)
Maximum Evaporative Potential (E_{max})				
shorts, short-sleeved shirt and hat	335	230	280	205
trousers, long-sleeved shirt and hat	265	185	220	165
Heat Stress Index ($E_{req} \cdot E_{max}^{-1}$)				
shorts, short-sleeved shirt and hat	0.49 (light colour) 0.62 (dark colour)	0.22 (light) 0.35 (dark)	0.76 (light) 0.92 (dark)	0.44 (light) 0.59 (dark)
trousers, long-sleeved shirt and hat	0.65 (light colour) 0.82 (dark colour)	0.30 (light) 0.46 (dark)	0.97 (light) 1.17 (dark)	0.55 (light) 0.73 (dark)

response, a lowered heart rate, and a lowered internal body temperature (Nadel et al., 1974; Rowell, 1974; Taylor, 1986; Wyndham, 1973).

Hydration Status

Water balance during exercise is determined by a multitude of factors, including the environmental conditions, the nature and intensity of exercise, and the characteristics of the fluid replacement (Sawka, 1988). Two terms related to hydration status that are often mistakenly used interchangeably are dehydration and hypohydration. The former term refers to the dynamic loss of body water due to sweating over the course of exercise without fluid replacement, or where fluid replacement does not match the rate of fluid loss. The latter term refers to the state or level of hydration after the loss of a certain amount of body water from the body. Diuretics such as alcohol or caffeine lead to a progressive state of dehydration. If fluid loss is not replaced, an individual may be hypohydrated the following day prior to beginning their round of golf.

Table 2 presents the calculated sweat rates necessary to match the required evaporative cooling rates shown in Table 1. For example, the required evaporative cooling while walking during a round of golf at 35°C approximated 225 $W \cdot m^{-2}$ (see Table 1). This value is equivalent to an evaporative heat loss of 600 $g \cdot h^{-1}$. Estimated sweat rates required to maintain a thermal steady-state, therefore, would approximate 0.6 $L \cdot h^{-1}$ under these conditions. These rates would represent a total fluid loss of almost 2.5 Litres or 3% of body mass for an 80 kg male during a 4-hour round. Sweat rates would actually exceed these values because the efficiency of evaporative heat loss would not be 100%. Thus, although the required sweat rates shown in Table 2 are similar for when shorts or trousers are worn, the sweat rate would be higher in the latter clothing configuration because of the reduced efficiency of sweat evaporation. It should be evident that without proper fluid replacement golfers could become quite dehydrated by the end of the round. Together with improper rehydration strategies, this situation could lead to an individual being hypohydrated by more than 3% of body mass on a subsequent day that involves exposure to a hot environment.

To a certain extent, mild dehydration during exercise is psychologically tolerated by an individual (Armstrong et al., 1985; Decastro, 1992; Greenleaf, 1992; Hubbard et al., 1984). Even with an adequate fluid supply, the rate of ad libitum fluid intake rarely matches the rate at which fluid is lost, and an individual will gradually dehydrate (Armstrong et al., 1985; Greenleaf, 1992). An involuntary dehydration of 2% or more of body weight may occur before a strong drinking response is observed (Armstrong et al., 1985).

Table 2

Estimated Sweat Rates (L·h^{-1}) (for an 80 kg male with a surface area of 1.8m^2) Necessary to Match the Required Evaporative Cooling Rates (E_{req}) (for the different environmental conditions, metabolic rates and clothing configurations calculated in Table 1).

	ENVIRONMENTAL CONDITIONS			
	25°C, 50% RH		35°C, 50% RH	
	WALKING	RIDING	WALKING	RIDING
shorts, short-sleeved shirt and hat	0.43 (light colour) 0.55 (dark colour)	0.14 (light) 0.22 (dark)	0.57 (light) 0.69 (dark)	0.24 (light) 0.32 (dark)
trousers, long-sleeved shirt and hat	0.45 (light colour) 0.58 (dark colour)	0.15 (light) 0.23 (dark)	0.57 (light) 0.69 (dark)	0.24 (light) 0.32 (dark)

Hypohydration

It is well documented that fluid replacement and hydration status are important determinants of heat tolerance when evaporative heat loss is not restricted by clothing (Candas et al., 1986, 1988; Noakes, 1993; Sawka, 1988). The additional physiological stresses imposed by hypohydration appear to potentiate the effects of heat stress and severely impair the ability of individuals to tolerate exercise. The magnitude of cardiovascular and thermoregulatory impairment due to hypohydration during exercise in the heat appears to be graded in proportion to the severity of hypohydration. Sawka et al. (1985) systematically compared the effects of hypohydration levels of 0, 3, 5, and 7% body weight during exercise in the heat. Comparing the four hydration levels, core temperature linearly increased by approximately 0.15°C and heart rate increased 4 beats·min^{-1} with each percentage decrease in body mass. The increased core temperature and heat storage appear to be largely mediated by an impaired heat loss capacity, as the sweating rate at a given core temperature also decreased for each increasing level of hypohydration.

During uncompensable heat stress, impairments in physiological responses and heat tolerance while hypohydrated are consistently observed regardless of aerobic fitness, exercise intensity or any physiological manipulations such as aerobic training and heat acclimation (Cheung & McLellan, 1998a, 1998b, 1998c).

Fluid Replacement

Fluid replacement during exercise contributes to the maintenance of plasma volume during exercise, aiding thermal and cardiovascular homeostasis (Candas et al., 1986, 1988). In a warm (32°C) environment, Montain and Coyle (1992) elicited graded levels of dehydration during 2 h of moderate cycling exercise by varying the amount of fluid replacement from 0 to 100%

of sweating rate. Graded dehydration resulted in graded physiological responses, including increases in heart rate, decreases in stroke volume, increases in T_{es}, decreases in skin blood flow, and increases in RPE (Montain & Coyle, 1992). The importance of fluid replacement was also illustrated by Candas et al. (1988). During prolonged exercise in the heat, heart rate and T_{re} were significantly higher beyond 2 h in participants who were initially euhydrated but given no fluid replacement compared with when they were 2% hypohydrated prior to the exercise but given fluid replacement throughout.

However, ingested fluid must first be emptied from the stomach and absorbed in the intestine before it can enter the body and affect exercise response. Gastric emptying is dependent on many factors including volume ingested, exercise intensity, and fluid composition and temperature (Murray, 1987). Balanced against ingesting large volumes of fluid to prevent dehydration is the danger of large gastric volumes causing discomfort and impaired performance (Mitchell & Voss, 1991). This is especially dangerous if either heat exposure or exercise impairs gastric emptying. Neufer et al. (1989a) observed an increase in gastric emptying when walking or running at < 70% $\dot{V}O_{2max}$ compared with resting values, possibly due to an increase in stomach motility from the walking motion. Only at exercise intensities > 70% $\dot{V}O_{2max}$ was the rate of gastric emptying decreased. Fordtran and Saltin (1967) found no impairment in gastric emptying of a glucose solution while exercising at 71% $\dot{V}O_{2max}$ on the treadmill. Thermal strain decreased gastric emptying rate, with a lower rate being observed when exercising at 49°C compared with 18°C (Neufer et al., 1989b). While a period of heat acclimation had no effect on the rate of emptying from the stomach, hypohydration of 5% body mass decreased the rate of gastric emptying (Neufer et al., 1989b).

Because the metabolic rate of playing golf is low when expressed as a %$\dot{V}O_{2max}$ (Murase et al., 1989), it is unlikely that carbohydrate supplementation is essential for optimising performance. However, sport drinks that are comprised of up to 8% carbohydrate not only provide caloric content but also contain sodium and other electrolytes which are essential for maintaining fluid balance (Maughan & Leiper, 1995). Following exercise in the heat, the inclusion of sodium in the rehydration beverage has been shown to be the most critical factor in the return to the euhydrated state (Maughan & Leiper, 1995).

Heat Acclimatisation

Classic adaptations following heat acclimatisation include an increase in sweating response and a decrease in heart rate, core and skin temperature, and perceived exertion during exercise in the heat (Nadel et al., 1974; Rowell, 1974; Wyndham, 1973). Sato et al. (1990) have shown both morphological and functional changes of the sweat gland following heat acclimation. The nature of the secreted sweat may also change with heat acclimation (Dill et al., 1938). A strong inverse correlation was observed by Nose et al. (1988) between the loss of free water and the [Na^+] in sweat. Therefore, one adaptation resulting from heat acclimation is the production of a more dilute sweat (Allan & Wilson, 1971; Dill et al., 1938). In situations of compensable heat stress, even short acclimation periods of 4 days appear to be sufficient for significant reductions in physiological strain (Pandolf et al., 1977). Major cardiovascular and thermoregulatory adaptations occur during the first few days of repeated heat exposures, with almost complete adaptation being achieved within 14 days (Armstrong & Maresh, 1991; Pandolf et al., 1977; Senay et al., 1976). Once heat acclimation is achieved, the rate of decay of the adaptations is slow, occurring over several weeks, and the reinduction of heat acclimation can be achieved rapidly (Pandolf et al., 1977).

The benefits that follow a period of heat acclimatisation will be less evident if the environmental conditions and/or clothing that is worn reduce the potential for evaporative heat loss (Cheung & McLellan, 1998b; McLellan et al., 1996). In addition, one should not expect that the magnitude of the reduction in physiological strain that follows heat acclimatisation to a hot and dry environment will be as evident during exposure to a hot and humid environment (McLellan & Aoyagi, 1996).

Aerobic Fitness

A high level of cardiorespiratory fitness has been associated with an improved exercise-heat tolerance since the initial theoretical connection was made by Robinson et al. (1943) and Bean and Eichna (1943). These suggestions were based largely on anecdotal evidence, but have been largely supported by subsequent studies (Armstrong & Pandolf, 1988). Havenith and van Middendorp (1990) reported that inter-individual variations in aerobic fitness and anthropometric measures could account for a significant portion of the variance in heat storage not explained by differences in metabolic rate and environmental conditions. In either temperate, hot-dry (Cadarette et al., 1984; Shvartz et al., 1977), or hot-wet environments (Havenith et al., 1995), maximal aerobic power ($\dot{V}O_{2max}$) was significantly and inversely correlated with core temperature and heart rate. Henane et al. (1977) reported that trained and fit ($\dot{V}O_{2max} - 65$ $mL \cdot kg^{-1} \cdot min^{-1}$) athletes had an improved sweating response and exercise-heat tolerance compared to sedentary and unfit ($\dot{V}O_{2max} - 40$ $mL \cdot kg^{-1} \cdot min^{-1}$) individuals. $\dot{V}O_{2max}$ by itself may not be a reliable indicator of exercise-heat tolerance (Armstrong & Pandolf, 1988; Pandolf et al., 1988). The amount of regular physical activity may be a better indicator of the presence of training-induced adaptations to heat exposure. Cheung and McLellan (1998b) observed distinct differences between high and low fitness groups in the reasons for ending their exposure to uncompensable heat stress and also in both the initial T_{re} and the final T_{re} at which participants terminated the experiment. The highly fit participants had a lower T_{re} at the beginning and were able to tolerate greater increases in T_{re}. Overall, their observations during uncompensable heat stress support the general consensus observed during compensable heat stress that an association exists between the level of cardiorespiratory fitness and improvements in physiological responses to exercise in a hot environment (Armstrong & Pandolf, 1988).

Physical Training

As higher levels of aerobic fitness appear to benefit tolerance to the heat and replicate many of the physiological adaptations reported with heat acclimation, physical training may be an effective complement or replacement for heat acclimation (Armstrong & Pandolf, 1988; Pandolf, 1979). If true, this would be of great interest in many occupational settings, where a temperate ambient environment or lack of facilities may preclude proper heat acclimation. However, aerobic training may differ from heat acclimation both in the nature and also in the magnitude of the adaptive responses, and the compatibility of these physiological treatments remains an active field of research.

Gisolfi and Robinson (1969) were among the first to report a reduction in physiological strain and an improvement in exercise tolerance during compensable heat stress following a relatively long-term (6 weeks) interval training program. Four weeks of interval training also produced significant improvements in exercise-heat tolerance, with the improvement reaching a plateau after 8 or more weeks of training of approximately 50% of the adaptive responses brought about by heat acclimation (Gisolfi, 1973).

The effectiveness of a training program in improving exercise-heat tolerance is dependent on many variables, including the intensity, duration, and frequency of the training. Henane et al. (1977) suggested that a 15-20% increase in $\dot{V}O_{2max}$ is required in order to improve exercise-heat tolerance. Metabolic hyperthermia is the major stimulus for thermoregulatory adaptations (Fox et al., 1963), and the degree and duration of core temperature rise induced by the training may be a determinant of the degree of heat adaptation. It should also be noted that benefits that arise from an improved aerobic fitness during exposure to a hot and dry environment may be less evident in more humid environments (Aoyagi et al., 1994; Cheung & McLelllan, 1998c).

Other factors, besides elevations in sweat rates that accompany improvements in aerobic fitness, must be involved in explaining the differences in heat tolerance between aerobically fit and unfit individuals. Certainly, the lower resting core temperature (Cheung & McLellan, 1998b; Henane et al., 1977) and the higher core temperature tolerated at exhaustion for persons with higher aerobic fitness levels (Cheung & McLellan, 1998b) are factors that will increase performance in the heat. Tolerance for less fit individuals may be related more to the strain on the cardiovascular system in its attempt to dissipate body heat and maintain arterial blood pressure, whereas the increase in body heat content may be the greater limiting factor for more fit individuals. In addition, differences in body fatness between fitness groups (Cheung & McLellan, 1998b) could account for some of the differences in response during the heat-stress exposure.

Individual Characteristics

Individual characteristics can have a significant influence on the response to exercise-heat stress. Gardner et al. (1996) reported that the Marine Corps recruits most at risk for developing exertional heat illness during basic training had a body mass index (BMI = mass·height^{-2}) of over 22 kg·m^{-2} and a time for a 1.5 mile run in excess of 12 min at the start of basic training, suggesting an influence of both anthropometric measures and aerobic fitness. Inter-individual variations in fitness, anthropometric measures, and hydration and acclimation status can significantly influence the response to exercise-heat stress (Havenith & van Middendorp, 1990; Havenith et al., 1995; Kenney, 1985).

Gender

On average, women typically have a lower aerobic fitness and an increased body fatness compared with males (Dill et al., 1977; Shapiro et al., 1980). Also, the advantage of a larger surface area to mass ratio for radiative and convective heat exchange, as is typically documented for females (Nunneley, 1978), disappears in hot climates if the ambient temperature exceeds skin temperature (Shvartz et al., 1973). Thus, in hot-dry environments, a lower rate of heat storage for males is attributed to an earlier onset of sweating (Bittel & Henane, 1975) and an increased rate of sweating and evaporative heat loss to the dry environmental conditions (Fox et al., 1969; Morimoto et al., 1967; Wyndham et al., 1965). However, during exposure to hot and humid conditions, Shapiro et al. (1980) reported that women of lower aerobic fitness and higher body fatness were at a thermoregulatory advantage compared with males during treadmill walking at 4.8 km·h^{-1}. This advantage was attributed to the larger surface area to mass ratio for the women, which allowed a more effective evaporative heat loss to the humid environment. However, our recent findings during uncompensable heat stress conditions would challenge this conclusion as we found that tolerance times were reduced by 25% or 30 min for women during light exercise at 40°C (McLellan, 1998).

Menstrual Cycle

It has been well established that, under conditions of compensable heat stress, the menstrual cycle affects temperature regulation. Basal body temperature exhibits a biphasic rhythm in which core temperature is approximately 0.4°C higher in the luteal phase compared with the follicular phase (Frascarolo et al., 1990; Horvath & Drinkwater, 1982). Likewise, the core temperature thresholds for the onset of thermoregulatory sweating, cutaneous vasodilation and skin blood flow are also higher in the luteal phase compared with the follicular phase (Hessemer & Bruck, 1985; Horvath & Drinkwater, 1982; Kolka & Stephenson, 1989). Tenaglia et al. (1999) reported that tolerance to uncompensable heat stress is reduced during the luteal phase. In very hot environments, therefore, these findings indicate that golf performance may be impaired during the post-ovulatory phase of the menstrual cycle.

Heat tolerance during pregnancy will be reduced because of the continued thermogenic effect of elevated progesterone levels and the progressive decrease in aerobic fitness that occurs (see Gorski, 1985; Wolfe et al., 1989 for review). In addition, large increases in core temperature may place the developing fetus at risk (Gorski, 1985) and thus expectant mothers should take extra care to optimise hydration during their round of golf and limit exposure to very hot conditions.

Oral Contraceptive Use

Recent investigations have shown that, similar to non-users, resting core temperature is higher during the later stages of the quasi-luteal phase (when exogenous estrogen and progesterone are ingested) compared with the quasi-follicular phase (when the pill contains no exogenous steroid) (Charkoudian & Johnson, 1997; Grucza et al., 1993, 1997; Rogers & Baker, 1997) for women using oral contraceptives. The phase-related elevation in core temperature is maintained during exercise in comfortable (Grucza et al., 1993; Rogers & Baker, 1997) and warm (Martin & Buono, 1997) environments, and during passive heat (Charkoudian & Johnson, 1997) exposure. Oral contraceptive use also has little impact on the cardiovascular and thermoregulatory responses to uncompensable heat stress (Tenaglia et al., 1999) and should not impact on golf performance.

Hormone Replacement Therapy

A recent study by Brooks et al. (1997) has shown that postmenopausal women receiving chronic estrogen replacement therapy were at a thermoregulatory adavantage compared with either women receiving no treatment or a group receiving a combined estrogen and progesterone therapy. Core temperatures were approximately 0.5°C lower at rest and during exercise and heat-stress for those receiving the estrogen therapy due to an increased vascular conductance. Postmenopausal women receiving estrogen replacement therapy alone, therefore, should expect to experience less heat strain while playing golf in hot environments.

Body Composition

McLellan (1998) reported that the partitional calorimetric estimate of the rate of heat storage was similar for males and females despite differences in their T_{re} response during a given heat-stress test. These findings imply a different heat capacity of the whole body for males and females. This is not too surprising given the lower heat capacity of fat versus non-fat tissue (Buskirk et al., 1969) and the higher body fatness, in general, of females compared with males. Thus for a given amount of heat production women cannot store as much body heat as men. McLellan (1998) noted that when individuals were matched for body fatness alone or in combination with $\dot{V}O_{2max}$, heat storage per unit of total mass and tolerance times were similar between men and women. McLellan (1998) also reported that when participants, regardless of gender, were grouped according to their final T_{re}, the group with the lower T_{re} and shorter tolerance times had the lower $\dot{V}O_{2max}$ and higher body fatness. These findings supported the data described for the comparisons between the sexes and led to the general conclusion that body composition and aerobic fitness had a significant influence on heat tolerance. Thus, golfers who are otherwise inactive and overweight will be more at risk to exertional heat injury during rounds played in hot environments.

Circadian Rhythm

The normal circadian rhythm leads to oscillations in resting core temperature that can vary by 0.5°C from early morning to mid-afternoon (Kräuchi & Wirz-Justice, 1994) and these differences in core temperature remain during compensable heat stress (Reilly & Garrett, 1998). In a recent study, McLellan et al. (1999) observed that uncompensable heat-stress trials conducted in the early afternoon were associated with an increased rectal temperature tolerated at exhaustion that offset the circadian influence on resting rectal temperature, and thus, maintained tolerance times similar to trials conducted in the morning. Thus, under identical environmental conditions, playing golf in the afternoon should not place an individual at greater risk to heat injury. However, environmental temperatures climb during the day to usually peak in the early afternoon hours such that the environmental heat stress is typically much greater in the afternoon.

Age

Pandolf (1995) and Kenney (1997) have recently summarised the effects of the aging process on temperature regulation. Their overwhelming consensus was that declines in aerobic fitness, rather than the aging process per se, were responsible for differences in the thermoregulatory responses of older individuals compared with their younger counterpart. Certainly if older and younger individuals were matched for aerobic fitness and body fatness (as discussed above for the comparisons between men and women), there would be no reason to expect a difference in work performance in the heat. The chronic use of diuretics for control of hypertension may place older individuals at greater risk to heat injury because of changes to their hydration status. Thus optimal fluid replacement strategies are critical for the older golfer using any medication that affects their normal fluid balance.

Summary and Recommendations

This chapter has provided an overview of the potential problems facing the golfer during exposure to hot and possibly humid environmental conditions. The following summary and recommendations will hopefully help to optimise your golf performance when you play in hot and/or humid environments.

Point 1. Table 1 summarised the sources of heat gain and avenues for heat loss at two different environmental temperatures (25°C and 35°C), rates of heat production (walking versus riding) and clothing configurations. Playing the round of golf during the cooler morning hours would obviously reduce the heat strain but for the tournament player their tee-off times are prescheduled for the first 2 days and dictated by their previous days' play during the final rounds. Playing during the early morning on the weekend for a touring professional is not desirable since it usually means that their performance has left them well back of the leaders during the weekend. I would be the last one to advocate the use of power carts on a regular basis but certainly during exposure to very hot conditions this would be a recommended option. If this is not possible, as is the case during tournament play, then certainly minimising the restriction of evaporative heat loss by wearing shorts and a short-sleeved shirt with appropriate sunscreen protection would be desirable. Again for the touring professional even this is not an option.

Thus the only factor that they can manipulate is the amount of radiative heat absorbed due to their choice of clothing colour.

Point 2. For the vacationer travelling from a cool to a hot climate for a week's golfing holiday, extra caution should be taken during the first few days of the trip. Unfortunately, lifestyle behaviour may place the golfer at greater risk to exertional heat injury because of poor aerobic fitness, improper hydration practices with alcohol consumption and lack of heat acclimatisation during the early days of the holiday. For touring pros who live in cooler climates, attention should be paid to the expected climate of the area that will be hosting the tournament. Arriving the day before the start of the tournament may have a negative impact on the professional's performance during the early rounds and influence whether they make the cut for the final rounds on the weekend. High ambient humidity at coastal or island resorts may reduce the benefits of heat acclimatisation acquired from living in or prior travelling to a hot and dry climatic region.

Point 3. Hydration status is the most important, and most easily manipulated, physiological variable that determines thermoregulatory and cardiovascular responses during heat stress. Individuals should always be well hydrated before beginning their round of golf in a hot environment. Whenever possible, adequate recovery time and fluid must be provided to allow participants to regain normal body weight and fluid balance before initiating a second round of golf. Sodium should be included as part of the rehydration beverage since the consumption of water alone will not restore optimal fluid balance. Being in a hypohydrated state prior to beginning the round will significantly impair thermoregulatory responses regardless of any other countermeasure employed. Even highly fit and heat-acclimatised individuals provided with fluid during exercise will have greatly reduced heat tolerance if they are hypohydrated prior to beginning the round of play.

Point 4. Fluid replacement during the round of golf is another critical factor in optimising performance. Estimated sweat rates required to maintain a thermal steady-state at 35°C approximated 0.6 $L \cdot h^{-1}$ or a total fluid loss of almost 2.5 Litres or 3% of body mass for an 80 kg male during a 4-hour round. These sweat rates will vary depending on the player's level of aerobic fitness and state of heat acclimatisation. Players should not rely on their own sense of thirst for determining the amount of fluid replacement. A strategy for fluid replacement including amounts and type of ingested fluid should be in place at the beginning of the round. Fluid replacement should begin early in the round since the benefits of the ingested fluid are not instantaneous but require time to be absorbed from the intestine.

Point 5. In general, women are at a thermoregulatory disadvantage compared with men because of their lower aerobic fitness and higher body fatness. This disadvantage would be equally demonstrable in men who have an inactive lifestyle or in the elderly population. Improvements in aerobic fitness will confer an advantage during exercise in the heat but these improvements may require a long-term commitment to a change in lifestyle behaviour.

Point 6. Because of concerns of increased risk of skin melanoma, the elderly may be more apt to wear protective clothing including trousers, long-sleeved shirts and hats. This clothing will reduce heat transfer away from the body and increase the heat strain experienced during a round of golf. Following proper hydration strategies becomes more imperative under these conditions.

References

Allan, J.R., & Wilson, C.G. (1971). Influence of acclimatization on sweat sodium concentration. *Journal of Applied Physiology, 30,* 708–712.

Armstrong, L.E., Hubbard, R.W., Szlyk, P.C., et al. (1985). Voluntary dehydration and electrolyte losses during prolonged exercise in the heat. *Aviation Space and Environmental Medicine, 56,* 765–770.

Armstrong, L.E., & Maresh, C.M. (1991). The induction and decay of heat acclimatisation in trained athletes. *Sports Medicine, 12,* 302–312.

Armstrong, L.E, & Pandolf, K.B. (1988). Physical training, cardiorespiratory physical fitness and exercise-heat tolerance. In K.B. Pandolf, M.N. Sawka, & R.R. Gonzalez (Eds.), *Human performance physiology and environmental medicine in terrestrial extremes* (pp. 199–226). Indianapolis: Benchmark Press.

Aoyagi, Y., McLellan, T.M., & Shephard, R.J. (1994). Effects of training and acclimation on heat tolerance in exercising men wearing protective clothing. *European Journal of Applied Physiology, 68,* 234–245.

Aoyagi, Y., McLellan, T.M., & Shephard, R.J. (1997). Interactions of physical training and heat acclimation: The thermophysiology of exercising in a hot climate. *Sports Medicine, 23,* 173–210.

Bean, W.B., & Eichna, L.W. (1943). Performance in relation to environmental temperature: Reactions of normal young men to simulated desert environment. *Federation Proceedings, 2,* 144–158.

Bittel, J., & Henane, R. (1975). Comparison of thermal exchanges in men and women under neutral and hot conditions. *Journal of Physiology (London), 250,* 475–489.

Bligh, J. (1985). Regulation of body temperature in man and other mammals. In A. Shitzer & R.C. Eberhart (Eds.), *Heat transfer in medicine and biology* (pp. 15–51). New York: Plenum Publishing.

Blum, H.F. (1945). The solar heat load: Its relationship to the total heat load and its relative importance in the design of clothing. *Journal of Clinical Investigation, 24,* 712–721.

Brajkovic, D., Ducharme, M.B., & Frim, J. (1998). Influence of localized auxiliary heating on hand comfort during cold exposure. *Journal of Applied Physiology, 85,* 2054–2065.

Brooks, E.M., Morgan, A.L., Pierzga, J.M., et al. (1997). Chronic hormone replacement therapy alters thermoregulatory and vasomotor function in postmenopausal women. *Journal of Applied Physiology, 83,* 477–484.

Buskirk, E.R., Bar-Or, O., & Kollias, J. (1969). Physiological effects of heat and cold. In N.L. Wilson (Ed.), *Obesity* (pp. 119–139). Philadelphia: Davis.

Cadarette, B.S., Sawka, M.N., Toner, M.M., et al. (1984). Aerobic fitness and the hypohydration response to exercise-heat stress. *Aviation Space and Environmental Medicine, 55,* 507–512.

Candas, V., Libert, J.P., Brandenberger, G., et al. (1986). Hydration during exercise: Effects on thermal and cardiovascular adjustments. *European Journal of Applied Physiology, 55,* 113–122.

Candas, V., Libert, J.P., Brandenberger, G., et al. (1988). Thermal and circulatory responses during prolonged exercise at different levels of hydration. *Journal of Physiology (Paris), 83,* 11–18.

Candas, V., Libert, J.P., & Vogt, J.J. (1979). Human skin wettedness and evaporative efficiency of sweating. *Journal of Applied Physiology, 46,* 522–528.

Charkoudian, N., & Johnson, J.M. (1997). Modification of active cutaneous vasodilation by oral contraceptive hormones. *Journal of Applied Physiology, 83,* 2012–2018.

Cheung, S.S., & McLellan, T.M. (1998a). Influence of hydration status and fluid replacement on tolerance during uncompensable heat stress. *European Journal of Applied Physiology, 77,* 139–148.

Cheung, S.S., & McLellan. T.M. (1998b). Influence of heat acclimation, aerobic fitness, and hydration effects on tolerance during uncompensable heat stress. *Journal of Applied Physiology, 84,* 1731–1739.

Cheung, S.S., & McLellan, T.M. (1998c). Influence of hydration status and short-term aerobic training on tolerance during uncompensable heat stress. *European Journal of Applied Physiology, 78,* 50–58.

Craig, F.N., & Moffitt, J.T. (1974). Efficiency of evaporative cooling from wet clothing. *Journal of Applied Physiology, 36,* 313–316.

Cummings, S.R., Tripp, M.K., & Herrmann, N.B. (1997). Approaches to the prevention and control of skin cancer. *Cancer and Metastasis Reviews, 16,* 309–327.

Davis, S., Capjack, L., Kerr, N., et al. (1997). Clothing as protection from ultraviolet radiation: Which fabric is most effective? *International Journal of Dermatology, 36,* 374–379.

Decastro, J.M. (1992). Age-related changes in natural spontaneous fluid ingestion and thirst in humans. *Journal of Gerontology, 47,* P321–P330.

Dill, D.B., Hall, F.G., & Edwards, H.T. (1938). Changes in composition of sweat during acclimatization to heat. *American Journal of Physiology, 123,* 412–419.

Dill, D.B., Soholt, L.F., McLean, D.C., et al. (1977). Capacity of young males and females for running in desert heat. *Medicine and Science in Sports, 9,* 137–142.

Fanger, P.O. (1970). *Thermal comfort: Analysis and applications in environmental engineering.* Copenhagen: Danish Technical Press.

Fordtran, J.S., & Saltin, B. (1967). Gastric emptying and intestinal absorption during prolonged severe exercise. *Journal of Applied Physiology, 23,* 331–335.

Fox, R.H., Goldsmith, R., Kidd, D.J., et al. (1963). Blood flow and other thermoregulatory adaptations with acclimation to heat. *Journal of Physiology (London), 166,* 548–562.

Fox, R.H., Lofstedt, B.E., Woodward, P.M., et al. (1969). Comparison of thermoregulatory functions in men and women. *Journal of Applied Physiology, 26,* 444–453.

Frascarolo, P., Schutz, Y., & Jequier, E. (1990). Decreased thermal conductance during the luteal phase of the menstrual cycle in women. *Journal of Applied Physiology, 69,* 2029–2033.

Gardner, J.W., Kark, J.A., Karnei, K., et al. (1996). Risk factors predicting exertional heat illness in male Marine Corps recruits. *Medicine and Science in Sports and Exercise, 28,* 939–944.

Getchell, L.H. (1968). Energy cost of playing golf. *Archives of Physical Medicine and Rehabilitation, 49,* 31–35.

Gisolfi, C.V. (1973). Work-heat tolerance derived from interval training. *Journal of Applied Physiology, 35,* 349-354.

Gisolfi, C.V., & Robinson, S. (1969). Relations between physical training, acclimatization, and heat tolerance. *Journal of Applied Physiology, 26,* 530–534.

Gonzalez, R.R. (1988). Biophysics of heat transfer and clothing considerations. In K.B. Pandolf, M.N. Sawka, & R.R. Gonzalez (Eds.), *Human performance physiology and environmental medicine in terrestrial extremes* (pp. 45–95). Indianapolis: Benchmark Press.

Gonzalez, R.R., McLellan, T.M., Withey, W.R., et al. (1997). Heat strain models applicable for protective clothing systems: Comparison of core temperature response. *Journal of Applied Physiology, 83,* 1017–1032.

Gorski, J. (1985). Exercise during pregnancy: Maternal and fetal responses. A brief review. *Medicine and Science in Sports and Exercise, 17,* 407–416.

Greenleaf, J.E. (1992). Problem — thirst, drinking behavior, and involuntary dehydration. *Medicine and Science in Sports and Exercise, 24,* 645–656.

Grucza, R., Pekkarinen, H., Timonen, K., et al. (1997). Physiological responses to cold in relation to the phase of the menstrual cycle and oral contraceptives. *Annals of the New York Academy of Science, 813,* 697–701.

Grucza, R., Pekkarinen, H., Titov, E., et al. (1993). Influence of the menstrual cycle and oral contraceptives on thermoregulatory responses to exercise in young women. *European Journal of Applied Physiology, 67,* 279–285.

Hancock, P.A. (1982). Task categorization and the limits of human performance in extreme heat. *Aviation Space and Environmental Medicine, 53,* 778–784.

Hancock, P.A. (1986). Sustained attention under thermal stress. *Psychological Bulletin, 99,* 263–281.

Hardy, J.D., & DuBois, E.F. (1938). The technic of measuring radiation and convection. *Journal of Nutrition, 15,* 461–475.

Havenith, G., Luttikholt, V.G.M., & Vrijkotte, T.G.M. (1995). The relative influence of body characteristics on humid heat stress response. *European Journal of Applied Physiology, 70,* 270–279.

Havenith, G., & van Middendorp, H. (1990). The relative influence of physical fitness, acclimation state, anthropometric measures and gender on individual reactions to heat stress. *European Journal of Applied Physiology, 61,* 419–427.

Henane, R., Flandrois, R., & Charbonnier, J.P. (1977). Increase in sweating sensitivity by endurance conditioning in man. *Journal of Applied Physiology, 43,* 822–828.

Hessemer, V., & Bruck, K. (1985). Influence of menstrual cycle on thermoregulatory, metabolic, and heart rate responses to exercise at night. *Journal of Applied Physiology, 59,* 1911–1917.

Holmer, I. (1995). Protective clothing and heat stress. *Ergonomics, 38,* 166–182.

Horvath, S.M., & Drinkwater, B.L. (1982). Thermoregulation and the menstrual cycle. *Aviation Space and Environmental Medicine, 53,* 790–794.

Hubbard, R.W., Sandick, B.L., Matthew, W.T., et al. (1984). Voluntary dehydration and alliesthesia for water. *Journal of Applied Physiology, 57,* 858–875.

Kakitsuba, N., Gaul, K., Michna, H., et al. (1988). Dynamic moisture permeation through clothing. *Aviation Space and Environmental Medicine, 59,* 49–53.

Kenney, W.L. (1985). A review of comparative responses of men and women to heat stress. *Environmental Research, 37,* 1–11.

Kenney, W.L. (1997). Thermoregulation at rest and during exercise in healthy older adults. *Exercise and Sport Science Reviews, 25,* 41–76.

Kenney, W.L., Lewis, D.A., Hyde, D.E., et al. (1987). Physiologically derived critical evaporative coefficients for protective clothing ensembles. *Journal of Applied Physiology, 63,* 1095–1099.

Kolka, M.A., & Stephenson, L.A. (1989). Control of sweating during the human menstrual cycle. *European Journal of Applied Physiology, 58,* 890–895.

Kräuchi, K., & Wirz-Justice, A. (1994). Circadian rhythm of heat production, heart rate, and skin and core temperature under unmasking conditions in men. *American Journal of Physiology, 267*, R819–R829.

Lampley, J.H., Lampley, P.M., & Howley, E.T. (1977). Caloric cost of playing golf. *Research Quarterly, 48*, 637–639.

Martin, J.G., & Buono, M.J. (1997). Oral contraceptives elevate core temperature and heart rate during exercise in the heat. *Clinical Physiology, 17*, 401–408.

Maughan, R.J., & Leiper, J.B. (1995). Effects of sodium content of ingested fluids on post-exercise rehydration in man. *European Journal of Applied Physiology, 71*, 311–319.

McLellan, T.M. (1998). Sex-related differences in thermoregulatory responses while wearing protective clothing. *European Journal of Applied Physiology, 78*, 28–37.

McLellan, T.M., & Aoyagi, Y. (1996). Heat stain in protective clothing following hot-wet or hot-dry heat acclimation. *Canadian Journal of Applied Physiology, 21*, 90–108.

McLellan, T.M., Gannon, G.A., Zamecnik, J., et al. (1999). Low doses of melatonin and diurnal effects on thermoregulation and heat tolerance to uncompensable heat stress. *Journal of Applied Physiology, 87*, 308–316.

McLellan, T.M., Pope, J.I., Cain, J.B., et al. (1996). Effects of metabolic rate and ambient vapour pressure on heat strain in protective clothing. *European Journal of Applied Physiology, 74*, 518–527.

Mitchell, J.B., & Voss, K. (1991). The influence of volume on gastric emptying and fluid balance during prolonged exercise. *Medicine and Science in Sports and Exercise, 23*, 314–319.

Montain, S.J., & Coyle, E.F. (1992). Influence of graded dehydration on hyperthermia and cardiovascular drift during exercise. *Journal of Applied Physiology, 73*, 1340–1350.

Morimoto, T., Slabochova, Z., Naman, R.K., et al. (1967). Sex differences in physiological reactions to thermal stress. *Journal of Applied Physiology, 22*, 526–532.

Murase, Y., Kamei, S., & Hoshikawa, T. (1989). Heart rate and metabolic responses to participation in golf. *Journal of Sports Medicine, 29*, 269–272.

Murray, R. (1987). The effects of consuming carbohydrate-electrolyte beverages on gastric emptying and fluid absorption during and following exercise. *Sports Medicine, 4*, 322–351.

Nadel, E.R. (1979). Control of sweating rate while exercising in the heat. *Medicine and Science in Sports and Exercise, 11*, 31–35.

Nadel, E.R., Pandolf, K.B., Roberts, M.F., et al. (1974). Mechanisms of thermal acclimation to exercise and heat. *Journal of Applied Physiology, 37*, 515–520.

Nielsen, B. (1990). Solar heat load: Heat balance during exercise in clothed subjects. *European Journal of Applied Physiology, 60*, 452–456.

Neufer, P.D., Young, A.J., & Sawka, M.N. (1989a). Gastric emptying during walking and running: Effects of varied exercise intensity. *European Journal of Applied Physiology, 58*, 440–445.

Neufer, P.D., Young, A.J., & Sawka, M.N. (1989b). Gastric emptying during exercise: Effects of heat stress and hypohydration. *European Journal of Applied Physiology, 58*, 433–439.

Nishi, Y. (1981). Measurement of thermal balance of man. In K. Cena & J.A. Clark (Eds.), *Bioengineering, thermal physiology and comfort* (pp. 29–39). New York: Elsevier.

Noakes, T.D. (1993). Fluid replacement during exercise. *Exercise and Sport Science Reviews, 21*, 297–330.

Nose, H., Mack, G.W., Shi, X., et al. (1988). Shift in body fluid compartments after dehydration in humans. *Journal of Applied Physiology, 65*, 318–324.

Nunneley, S.A. (1978). Physiological responses of women to thermal stress: A review. *Medicine and Science in Sports, 10*, 250–255.

Nunneley, S.A. (1989). Heat stress in protective clothing: Interactions among physical and physiological factors. *Scandinavian Journal of Work, Environment and Health, 15 (Suppl. 1),* 52–57.

Pandolf, K.B. (1979). Effects of physical training and cardiorespiratory physical fitness on exercise-heat tolerance: Recent observations. *Medicine and Science in Sports and Exercise, 11,* 60–65.

Pandolf, K.B. (1995). Aging and human heat tolerance. *Experimental Aging Research, 23,* 69–105.

Pandolf, K.B., Burse, R.L., & Goldman, R.F. (1977). Role of physical fitness in heat acclimatization, decay and reinduction. *Ergonomics, 20,* 399–408.

Pandolf, K.B., Cadarette, B.S., Sawka, M.N., et al. (1988). Thermoregulatory responses of middle-aged men and young men during dry-heat acclimation. *Journal of Applied Physiology, 65,* 65–71.

Ramsey, J.D. (1995). Task performance in heat: A review. *Ergonomics, 38,* 154–165.

Reilly, T., & Garrett, R. (1998). Investigation of diurnal variation in sustained exercise performance. *Ergonomics, 41,* 1085–1094.

Robinson, S., Turrell, E.S., Belding, H.S., et al. (1943). Rapid acclimatization to work in hot climates. *American Journal of Physiology, 140,* 168–176.

Rogers, S.M., & Baker, M.A. (1997). Thermoregulation during exercise in women who are taking oral contraceptives. *European Journal of Applied Physiology, 75,* 34–38.

Rowell, L.B. (1974). Human cardiovascular adjustments to exercise and thermal stress. *Physiological Reviews, 54,* 75–159.

Sato, F., Owen, M., Matthes, R., et al. (1990). Functional and morphological changes in the eccrine sweat gland with heat acclimation. *Journal of Applied Physiology, 69,* 232–236.

Sawka, M.N. (1988). Body fluid responses and hypohydration during exercise-heat stress. In K.B. Pandolf, M.N. Sawka, & R.R. Gonzalez (Eds.), *Human performance physiology and environmental medicine in terrestrial extremes* (pp. 227–266). Indianapolis: Benchmark Press.

Sawka, M.N., & Wenger, C.B. (1988). Physiological responses to acute exercise-heat stress. In K.B. Pandolf, M.N. Sawka, & R.R. Gonzalez (Eds.), *Human performance physiology and environmental medicine in terrestrial extremes* (pp. 97–151). Indianapolis: Benchmark Press.

Sawka, M.N., Young, A.J., Francesconi, R.P., et al. (1985). Thermoregulatory and blood responses during exercise at graded hypohydration levels. *Journal of Applied Physiology, 59,* 1394–1401.

Senay, L.C., Mitchell, D., & Wyndham, C.H. (1976). Acclimatization in a hot, humid environment: Body fluid adjustments. *Journal of Applied Physiology, 40,* 786–796.

Shapiro, Y., Pandolf, K.B., Avellini, B.A., et al. (1980). Physiological responses of men and women to humid and dry heat. *Journal of Applied Physiology, 49,* 1–8.

Shvartz, E., Saar, E., & Benor, D. (1973). Physique and heat tolerance in hot-dry and hot-humid environments. *Journal of Applied Physiology, 34,* 799–803.

Shvartz, E., Shapiro, Y., Magazanik, A., et al. (1977). Heat acclimation, physical fitness, and responses to exercise in temperature and hot environment. *Journal of Applied Physiology, 43,* 678–683.

Spaul, W.A., Boatman, J.A., Emling, S.W., et al. (1985). Reduced tolerance for heat stress environments caused by protective lotions. *American Industrial Hygiene Association, 46,* 460–462.

Taylor, N.A.S. (1986). Eccrine sweat glands: Adaptations to physical training and heat acclimation. *Sports Medicine, 3,* 387–397.

Tenaglia, S.A., McLellan, T.M., & Klentrou, P.P. (1999). Influence of menstrual cycle and oral contraceptive use during compensable and uncompensable heat stress. *European Journal of Applied Physiology, 80,* 76–83.

Wenger, C.B. (1972). Heat evaporation of sweat: Thermodynamic considerations. *Journal of Applied Physiology, 32,* 456–459.

Wenger, C.B. (1988). Human heat acclimatization. In K.B. Pandolf, M.N. Sawka, & R.R. Gonzalez (Eds.), *Human performance physiology and environmental medicine in terrestrial extremes* (pp. 153–197). Indianapolis: Benchmark Press.

Wolfe, L.A., Ohtake, P.J., Mottola, M.F., et al. (1989). Physiological interactions between pregnancy and aerobic exercise. *Exercise and Sport Science Reviews, 17,* 295–352.

Wyndham, C.H. (1973). The physiology of exercise under heat stress. *Annual Reviews of Physiology, 35,* 193–220.

Wyndham, C.H., Morrison, J.F., & Williams, C.G. (1965). Heat reactions of male and female caucasians. *Journal of Applied Physiology, 20,* 357–364.

CHAPTER 11

Golf: Exercise for Health and Longevity

Gi Broman

Most people become less physically active at an older age, ignoring the scientific evidence that physical activity renders physical and mental benefits which contribute to preventing disease and promoting health (Blair, Kohl, Gordon, & Paffenbarger, 1992; Saltin, 1992). However, knowledge itself is probably not sufficient to motivate middle-aged and older people to become more physically active. Golf is one of the few sports where the majority of participants are adults and older persons. This may be partly a result of the combination of low-intensity activity and the extreme interval character of the game of golf. In fact, the exercise intensity while walking the golf course varies from 35% to 70% of maximal aerobic capacity for middle-aged men and women, potentially leading to an improved aerobic fitness (Magnusson, 1999). In middle-aged male golfers the blood lipid profile has been shown to be somewhat improved in combination with a modest weight reduction after one season of regular golf play (Palank & Hargreaves, 1990; Parkkari et al., 2000). These are a few of the factors which indicate that walking the golf course may result in health-related training effects similar to those found after continuous walking programs. Such factors also include a rise in maximal oxygen uptake, reduced body weight, and an improved blood lipid profile (Davison & Grant, 1993; Pollock et al., 1971; Santiago et al., 1987).

The physiological effects from golf, however, may be compromised compared to those from continuous walking programs because of the short walking intervals in golf, each ranging approximately from 50 m to 150 m for an average middle-aged player.

Therefore, the physiological adaptations after a walking program consisting of numerous very short intervals, by means of playing golf, remain to be quantified in middle-aged and older golfers.

Methods
Participants
Fifty-six healthy golfers (30 male and 26 female) aged between 40 and 70 years participated in the study (see Table 1). They had been active golfers during at least the last 5 years. No participant had symptoms of cardiovascular disease nor was any on pharmacological treatment. The participants were divided into three age groups: 40–49, 50–59, and 60–70 years.

Procedures and Measurements
The participants were tested before and after 14 weeks of walking the golf course when playing golf. After arriving at the laboratory in the morning in a fasting state, their resting blood pressure was measured in a sitting position with the arm at heart level using the manual cuff method. Venous blood samples were taken for analysis of blood lipids. The participants were weighed on a calibrated balance scale (Lindells, Jönköping, Sweden). Thereafter they performed a warm-up consisting of 8-minute ergometer cycling with low resistance.

Maximal isometric knee extensor strength was measured, at 90° knee angle, with an isokinetic dynamometer (Cybex II, Lumex Inc, USA). The

Table 1

Mean (SD) Age, Weight and Height Values for the Male and Female Golfers in each Age Group

GROUP	N	AGE (YEARS)		WEIGHT (KG)		HEIGHT (CM)	
Men							
40–49	9	45.2	(2.7)	77.8	(8.1)	180.0	(4.3)
50–59	11	52.5	(2.1)	85.2	(13.3)	181.0	(6.7)
60–69	10	65.7	(3.6)	79.0	(11.3)	178.5	(5.5)
Women							
40–49	9	46.0	(2.5)	67.2	(7.0)	168.6	(4.6)
50–59	11	52.3	(2.1)	60.2	(4.8)	166.0	(3.5)
60–70	6	65.5	(2.9)	64.3	(5.7)	165.5	(3.9)

contraction was maintained for 3 seconds. A total of three trials were performed and 45 seconds of rest was allowed between trials. Right and left handgrip strength was determined with a handgrip dynamometer (Cardionics Inc, Stockholm, Sweden), using an equivalent number of trials and resting periods as for the knee extensor muscle.

Muscular endurance of the knee extensor was also measured in a subgroup of the golfers (17 men and 9 women) using the isokinetic dynamometer. Fifty consecutive maximal concentric contractions were performed at an angular velocity of $180°·s^{-1}$. The remaining capacity to develop force after 50 contractions, expressed as a percentage of the initial force, was defined as a fatigue index (for calculation see Magnusson, Isberg, Karlberg, & Sylvén, 1994).

Maximal pulmonary oxygen uptake was determined using an on-line system (CPX System, Medical Graphic Corporation St. Louis, USA). A modified Åstrand ramp protocol was used for the treadmill.

Body composition was assessed preseason in a subgroup of 19 participants aged 50–70 years, and postseason in 11 participants. (Eight of the golfers were uncomfortable with this test method and did not want to perform it the second time.) Body composition was estimated by underwater weighing, using a water tank with a chair inside connected to a pendulum balance. The underwater weighing procedures were performed according to Pollock et al. (1984). The residual lung volume was assessed with a modified closed circuit oxygen dilution method (Wilmore, Vodak, Parr, Girandola, & Billing, 1980).

Blood lipids (total cholesterol, high- and low-density lipoproteins) were assessed by a bichromatic analysis according to Allain, Poon, Chan, Richmond, and Fu (1974). A Monarch centrifugal analysator (Instrumentation Laboratory Instruments Lexington, USA) was used to measure the blood lipids in 34 individuals.

Training

The participants were instructed to walk and play three 18-hole rounds of golf per week during the 14 weeks. The prescribed minimum amount of activity was 6 hours per week, which corresponds to walking and playing nine holes of golf three times. They were given a protocol, and had to keep an exact record (day by day) of the number of golf rounds they played. They had to walk the golf course and were not allowed to use any type of vehicle. Participants who played less than the minimum time required were excluded from the study. The golfers were instructed to keep their normal dietary habits, and to avoid participation in any form of high-intensity aerobic exercise throughout the intervention period.

Statistics

Values in the text represent means and standard deviations *(SD)*. Analysis of variance was used to test intra- and intergroup differences. Paired *t* tests were applied to analyse intragroup differences and regression analyses were also performed. The level of significance was set at $p < .05$.

Results

Exercise Performed

The participants walked and played an average of 51.3 (17.1) 18-hole rounds of golf during the 14 weeks. The women and men played an equal number of rounds, 49.2 (17.9) and 53.1 (16.4) respectively. The participants walked an approximate distance of 25 km on the golf course in playing an average of 3.6 times per week.

Maximal Aerobic Capacity

The mean maximal aerobic capacity of the golfers was above average when compared to age-matched population data (Shvartz & Reibold, 1990). Thirty-nine of the 56 golfers had a higher than average aerobic capacity in relation to their ages (Figures 1a, 1b). Thirteen golfers had an aerobic capacity 5–7% lower, and two were more than 7% lower than the population mean. Using Shvartz and Reibold's (1990) 7-point fitness scale (where 1 = *excellent*, 2 = *very good*, 3 = *good*, 4 = *average*, 5 = *fair*, 6 = *poor*, and 7 = *very poor*), the golfers aged between 40 and 59 years had good to very good fitness, and those between 60 and 70 years had excellent fitness.

The absolute maximal oxygen uptake was raised after the season in 23 of the golfers (11 above 60 years). Women aged 60–70 years increased their maximal oxygen uptake from 1.71 (0.38) to 1.82 (0.40) l·min^{-1} ($p < .05$).

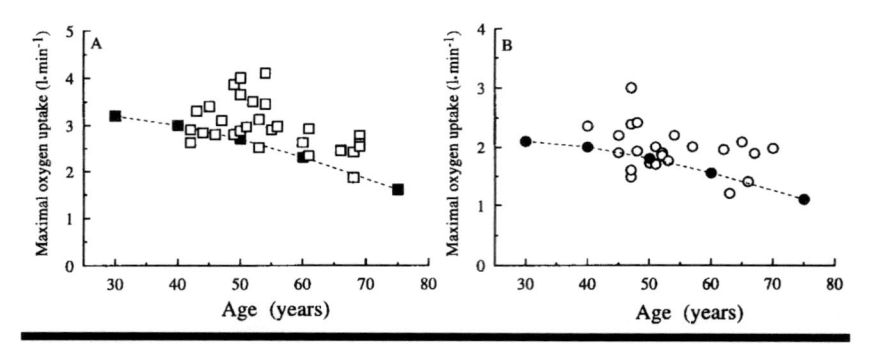

Figure 1a, 1b

Golfers' preseason maximal oxygen uptake relative to population norms (Shvartz & Reibold, 1990). Unfilled symbols represent individual values; filled symbols are population means; men are squares ▫ (Figure 1a); and women are circles ○ (Figure 1b).

However, for the group as a whole, the increase from 2.51 (0.66) preseason to 2.54 (0.66) l·min^{-1} postseason was not significant.

The mean relative oxygen uptake for all golfers was raised from 34.2 (6.2) to 35.1 (6.3) ml·kg^{-1}·min^{-1} ($p < .01$) as shown in Figure 2. Men aged 60–69 years raised their oxygen uptake by 6% from 32.4 (4.3) to 34.3 (5.1) ml·kg^{-1}·min^{-1} ($p < .05$), and women 60–70 years raised theirs by 9% from 26.9 (5.1) to 29.4 (5.4) ml·kg^{-1}·min^{-1} ($p < .05$). One 47-year-old man increased his maximal oxygen uptake by 13% and his relative maximal oxygen uptake by 17%. He played a total of 63.5 rounds and reduced his weight by 2.8 kg. The 57-year-old woman who played the most golf (99 rounds) raised her maximal oxygen uptake by 10% (the relative by 12%), and reduced her weight by 2.0 kg. For the whole group of golfers, however, there was no significant relationship between the rounds of golf played and rise in maximal oxygen uptake.

Weight and Body Fat Percentage

The average weight for the whole group was reduced from 72.8 (12.8) kg to 71.7 (12.6) kg ($p < .01$). The men weighed 80.9 (11.4) kg before and 79.6 (11.3) kg after the season ($p < .01$), and the women 63.6 (6.4) kg and 62.6 (6.3) kg ($p < .01$). Thirty-one of the golfers reduced their weight by 0.5–6 kg; 18 did not alter their weight; and 7 showed a tendency to increase weight, 3 increasing by 1–2 kg. As shown in Figure 3, the number of 18-hole rounds of golf played was significantly correlated with change in body weight ($r = -.29$, $p < .05$).

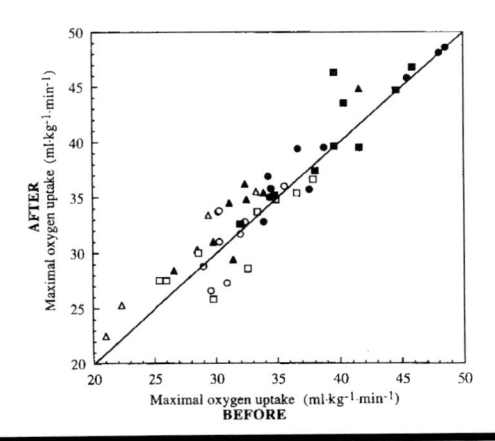

Figure 2

Maximal relative oxygen uptake before and after 14 weeks of active golf play. Unfilled symbols represent women; filled symbols are men; 40–49 years are squares ◻ ■; 50–59 years are circles ○ ●; and 60–70 years are triangles △ ▲.

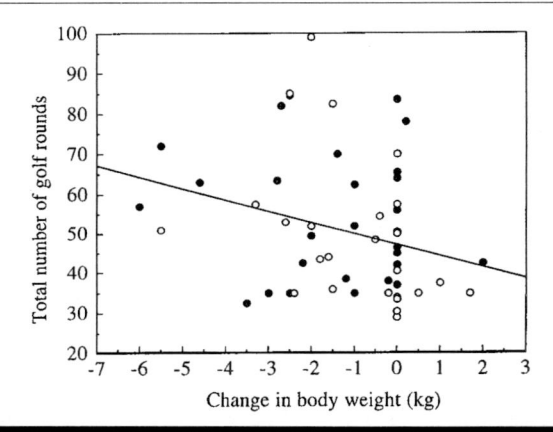

Figure 3

Changes in body weight in relation to the number of 18-hole golf rounds played in 14 weeks. Unfilled circles represent women ○; and filled circles are men ●.

The data from 10 male and 9 female golfers aged 50–70 years indicated initial body fat percentages of 20.8 (5.3) and 25.7 (4.7), respectively. Seven of the men and four of the women tested after the intervention period showed a total reduction of 10.6% in percentage of body fat, from 23.5 (6.4) preseason to 21.0 (4.7) postseason ($p < .01$). The mean body weight reduction for these 11 golfers was 0.7 kg, from 72.6 (10.9) kg preseason to 71.9 (10.5) kg postseason. Three of the participants had reduced percentage body fat without a concomitant reduction in body weight.

Blood Lipids

The total serum cholesterol for 34 of the golfers aged 40–69 years was 6.1 (0.8) mmol·l^{-1}, which is less than the 6.5 mmol·l^{-1} limit for hypercholesterolemia, but similar to age and sex-matched individuals from the Swedish population (Jungner, Walldius, Holme, Kolar, & Steiner, 1992). The women tended to have somewhat lower total cholesterol values than the men (Table 2). Both the high-density lipoprotein (HDL) and low-density lipoprotein (LDL) values for the golfers were within normal values. After the intervention period the total cholesterol was lowered by 3% to 5.9 (0.7) mmol·l^{-1} ($p < .05$). HDL increased by 5% ($p < .05$) and LDL decreased by 8% ($p < .05$) leading to a reduction of the LDL/HDL ratio by 12.5% ($p < .05$).

Blood Pressure

The mean resting blood pressures for the golfers were lower than the respective age and sex norms for the Swedish population (Landahl, Bengtsson,

Table 2
Mean *(SD)* Resting Values for Total Serum Cholesterol (mmol·l⁻¹), High-Density Lipoprotein (HDL, mmol·l⁻¹), Low-Density Lipoprotein (LDL, mmol·l⁻¹), and the LDL/HDL Ratio for each Age Group

GROUP	N	CHOLESTEROL TOT		HDL		LDL		LDL/HDL	
		Pre	Post	Pre	Post	Pre	Post	Pre	Post
Men									
40–49	9	6.1	6.0	1.20	1.30*	4.55	4.21	3.9	3.3*
		(.9)	(.7)	(.26)	(.26)	(.78)	(.59)	(.70)	(.69)
50–59	10	6.3	6.1	1.46	1.52	4.37	3.92*	3.1	2.8*
		(.8)	(.8)	(.29)	(.34)	(.84)	(.86)	(.7)	(.9)
Women									
40–49	9	6.0	5.7	1.42	1.45	4.22	3.81*	3.1	2.7*
		(.5)	(.7)	(.26)	(.28)	(.51)	(.71)	(.8)	(.8)
50–59	6	5.9	5.9	1.56	1.68	4.04	3.84	2.6	2.4*
		(1.2)	(.9)	(.26)	(.32)	(1.0)	(.8)	(.7)	(.6)
Total	34	6.1	5.9*	1.40	1.47*	4.32	3.95*	3.22	2.84*
		(.8)	(.7)	(.29)	(.32)	(.78)	(.73)	(.8)	(.8)

*$p < .05$ for preseason-postseason difference.

Sigurdsson, & Svanborg, 1986). At the start of the season 49 of the golfers had lower than average systolic blood pressure (Figure 4a), and 50 golfers had lower than average diastolic blood pressure (Figure 4b). The mean systolic blood pressure was 118 (15) mm Hg preseason and 119 (15) mm Hg postseason for the whole group. Mean systolic blood pressures were 124 (16) preseason and 126 (13) mm Hg postseason for the men, and 111 (12) preseason and 112 (13) mm Hg postseason for the women. The diastolic blood pressure at rest was 73 (8) mm Hg preseason and 76 (8) mm Hg

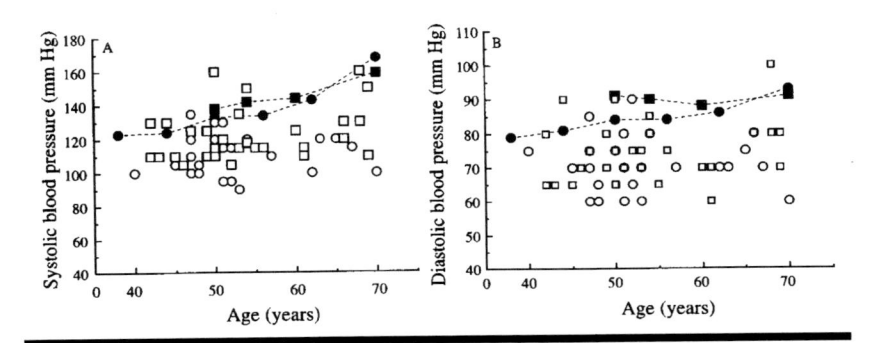

Figure 4a, 4b
Golfers' preseason systolic (Figure 4a) and diastolic blood pressures (Figure 4b) relative to population norms (Landahl et al., 1986). Unfilled symbols represent individual values; filled symbols are population means; men are squares ❑; and women are circles O.

postseason for the whole group. Diastolic pressures were 75 (9) preseason and 79 (7) mm Hg postseason for the men, and 71 (8) preseason and 74 (9) mm Hg postseason for the women. The blood pressures were not altered significantly in any of the male or female age groups after the season.

Strength

The golfers' mean maximal isometric knee extensor strength was approximately 15% lower than the age norms for Swedish men and women (Borges, 1989), as shown in Figure 5a. Maximal isometric knee extensor strength was 148 (51) Nm preseason and 149 (45) Nm postseason for the whole group. This measure of strength remained unchanged for male, 184 (39) preseason and 180 (33) Nm postseason, and female participants, 107 (26) preseason and 111 (23) Nm postseason. Maximal knee extensor strength was approximately 10% lower with each successive age group, except for women aged 60–70 years who had similar strength to women 50–59 years. The women's maximal knee extensor strength was about 40% lower than that for the men of comparable ages.

The golfers' handgrip strength was similar to the Swedish population norms (Engstrom, Ekblom, Forsberg, Koch, & Seger, 1993), as shown in Figure 5b. Female golfers were an average of 9% stronger and male golfers aged 60–69 years were 5% stronger than the norms for their respective age groups.

The mean maximal handgrip strength for the whole group was unaltered for both the right hand, 41.4 (10.8) preseason and 41.7 (11.8) kp postseason; and left hand, 39.6 (10.6) preseason and 40.2 (11.4) kp postseason. The male golfers tended to increase the strength of both the right hand, 49.9

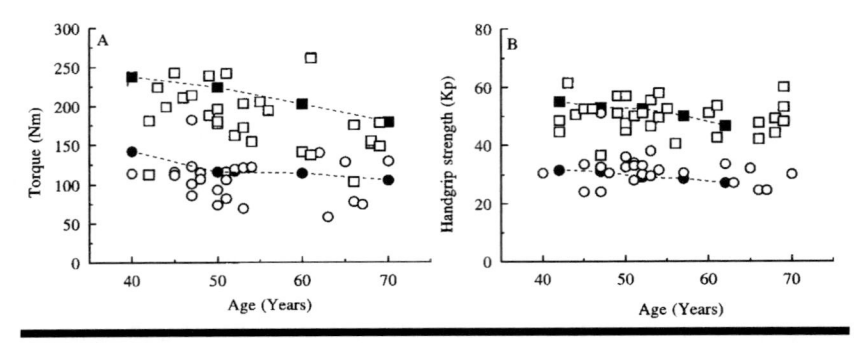

Figure 5a, 5b

Golfers' preseason maximal isometric knee extensor strength (Figure 5a) and maximal handgrip strength (Figure 5b) relative to population norms (Borges, 1989; Engstrom et al., 1993). Unfilled symbols represent individual values; filled symbols are population means; men are squares ▫; and women are circles ○.

(5.8) preseason and 51.3 (6.4) kp postseason; and left hand, 47.8 (6.3) preseason and 49.1 (7.0) kp postseason. The handgrip strength of the female golfers was unaltered in either the right hand, 31.6 (5.4) preseason and 31.0 (5.8) kp postseason; or left hand, 30.1 (5.2) preseason and 30.2 (5.6) kp postseason. The mean handgrip strength was maintained by male golfers from 40 to 69 years, whereas it was 12% lower for female golfers aged 60–70 years compared to those 40–49 years (Figure 5b). Maximal handgrip strength was 4% higher for the right hand than the left hand for the whole group ($p < .05$). This difference was unchanged throughout the season.

Muscular Endurance, Fatigue Index

For 26 of the golfers (17 men, 9 women), the remaining capacity to develop force after 50 maximal knee extensor contractions was 47 (11) preseason and 50 (12) % postseason ($p < .08$). The fatigue index was not significantly different between men and women. Men aged 50–59 years raised their local muscular endurance by 20% from 42 (13) preseason to 51 (16) % postseason ($p < .05$).

Discussion

The present golfers were physically very active in terms of duration. After 14 weeks of very active play they lowered their total body weight and reduced their body fat, and the blood lipid profile was improved. Close to 50% of the golfers improved their already high aerobic capacity. Muscle strength was maintained, and the local muscle endurance of the knee extensors tended to be raised. The low resting blood pressures found in the present golfers further emphasise the important health benefits they seem to gain by walking while playing golf.

Physical inactivity is a major risk factor for developing cardiovascular disease and overall mortality (Blair et al., 1989; Paffenbarger, Hyde, Wing, & Hsieh, 1986; Paffenbarger et al., 1993). Participation in any kind of leisure time physical activity would contribute to preventing disease. The exercise intensity is not critical for protection. Rather the regularity of exercise seems to be a key factor, since several of the physiological health-related effects are gained acutely. Thus, the important issue is how to motivate individuals to keep up with their regular exercise on a lifelong basis. Their sport seems to be an excellent way to motivate golfers, independent of age, to walk the golf course (long distances) on a regular basis. In fact, walking a distance of around 15 km each week has been shown to improve longevity relative to those who walk less (Hakim et al., 1998; Paffenbarger & Lee, 1996). The present golfers walked approximately 25 km each week, which corresponded to about 12.6 hours of active play. This amount of walking while golfing each week may have the potential to add a couple of years to life (Magnusson, 1999).

A high maximal exercise capacity is another factor shown to decrease the risk of dying from all causes, particularly cardiovascular disease (Blair et al., 1989; Blair et al., 1995). Even a change from a sedentary to a more physically active lifestyle will lower the risk (Blair et al., 1995; Paffenbarger et al., 1993). High exercise intensity (70–90% of maximal oxygen uptake) is known to improve aerobic power, but at which exercise intensity is it realistic to expect that the majority of the population, particularly older persons, may become involved? The amount and intensity of exercise decrease with age, and after 50 years the majority of the Swedish population choose low-intensity activities (Engstrom et al., 1993). Consequently, golf may be one option, and interestingly this study found male and female golfers to have a higher than average exercise capacity, according to fitness norms developed by Shvartz and Reibold (1990). The golfers aged between 40 and 59 years were classified as having good to very good fitness, and those 60 to 70 years were rated as having excellent fitness. This high level of fitness, however, may be explained by heredity and a generally active lifestyle in which golf is one of several activities (Wilmore & Costill, 1994).

As a group, only the older golfers succeeded in improving their already high aerobic capacity after the season. It is likely that the relative workload walking the golf course was highest for the oldest golfers, thereby causing a stronger aerobic training stimulus. An alternative explanation could be their participation in other aerobic activities during the experimental period. However, as the golfers were informed to avoid such activities and no one upon request reported having performed high intensity aerobic exercise, this reason is less likely. Therefore, the 6–9% rise in aerobic capacity for the older golfers can be seen as an indication that walking the golf course has the potential to improve maximal aerobic capacity, despite the interval character of the game. Since the present golfers already had a high fitness level before the season, it was not expected that the additional walking on the golf course would result in any dramatic fitness changes. It may, however, be speculated that sedentary individuals who take up golf can improve their aerobic capacity by 10–25%, similar to improvements shown in unfit individuals after walking exercise programs (Pollock et al., 1971; Santiago et al., 1987).

Obesity and overweight are associated with heart disease, hypertension, diabetes and certain types of cancer (Björntorp & Brodoff, 1992). The risk of becoming overweight increases with age. The present golfers, however, remained within the normal weight category, except for the men aged 50–59 years who were slightly overweight. Both for preventive and rehabilitative purposes, body weight may be controlled through diet and regular exercise.

The golfers were instructed to maintain their normal dietary habits throughout the experimental period, but it cannot be proven that the weight changes in the present golfers were due exclusively to increased energy expenditure. The average weight loss in the present golfers was 1 kg which is in line with the mean body weight reduction of 1 kg found in male golfers after 4 months of play (Palank & Hargreaves, 1990), and the Parkkari et al. (2000) finding that male golfers reduced their body weight by 1.4 kg more than non-golfing control participants after one golf season. This amount of weight loss went hand-in-hand with the 11% reduction of body fat percentage in the subgroup of golfers, and it is therefore conceivable that the body fat stores were decreased. Two fairly heavy male golfers reduced their body weight by as much as 6 kg each, further emphasising the impact which low-intensity exercise of long duration may have on body weight. Even if the mean weight loss of 1 kg appears to be marginal, it should be kept in mind that the majority of the present golfers were of normal weight prior to the study. On a long-term basis that 1 kg, if it represents a reduction of fat stores, may be of significant importance for weight control. Equally important is the fact that if overweight persons keep physically active on a regular basis, they will reduce the risk for coronary heart disease associated with overweight, even if they do not reduce their weight (Paffenbarger, Hyde, Wing, & Steinmetz, 1984).

Total plasma cholesterol is an independent risk factor for coronary artery disease (Kannel, Castelli, Gordon, & McNamara, 1971). The number of individuals with high plasma cholesterol (> 6 mmol·l^{-1}) increases with age (Engstrom et al., 1993; Jungner et al., 1992). It is possible, however, to influence the progression of disease even by non-pharmacological treatment (dietary management, physical exercise, stress management, stopping smoking). In fact, Ornish et al. (1990) showed regression of severe coronary atherosclerosis following 1 year of lifestyle changes. Physical activity lowers total cholesterol and low-density lipoprotein cholesterol (LDL), and raises high-density cholesterol (HDL) irrespective of the exercise intensity (Kiens et al., 1980; Puggard, Pedersen, Sandager, & Klitgaard, 1994). The present golfers lowered their serum cholesterol, decreased their LDL and increased their HDL, which led to a lowered LDL/HDL ratio. Other researchers have also reported similar improvements in blood lipid profiles of male golfers after a period of regular golf play (Palank & Hargreaves, 1990; Parkkari et al., 2000). Even though the improvements are small in absolute values, evidence shows that a reduction of total serum cholesterol by 0.6 mmol·l^{-1} in men is coupled with a markedly reduced risk for ischemic heart disease (Law, Wald, & Thompson, 1994). Ten of the present golfers had a serum cholesterol of 6.5 mmol·l^{-1} or higher. All of them improved at least one blood lipid value, and seven lowered their serum cholesterol and LDL, and increased the HDL in combination. Still, seven of the golfers had a serum cholesterol of 6.5 mmol·l^{-1} or slightly higher, which means that they probably also would have to alter their dietary habits in order to further lower their blood lipid levels. Walking when playing golf improves the blood lipid profile in a similar manner to other aerobic exercise activities.

Hypertension shows an increasing impact on the occurrence of chronic heart disease with advancing age (Kannel & Gordon, 1978). There is evidence that low-intensity exercise has an antihypertensive effect, especially in individuals with mild and moderate hypertension (Tipton, 1991). Physical activity cannot treat hypertension; rather it is used as a non-pharmacological treatment in order to lower systolic and diastolic pressures by approximately 10–15%. The present golfers aged between 40 and 70 years had lower systolic and diastolic resting blood pressures relative to age norms for the Swedish population (Landahl et al., 1986). The mean blood pressure values in the golfers are equal to mean values for 20-year-old normotensive males and females. A further lowering of the resting blood pressure in the golfers would not necessarily be beneficial for their health, since a diagnosed low blood pressure will result in some physiological drawbacks. Consequently, both the systolic and the diastolic resting blood pressure values remained at the low preseason level, even after the intervention period. It is possible, however, that the long duration of low-intensity activity pursued over at least 5 years is important for blood pressure regulation, partly contributing to the low resting blood pressures found in the present golfers. Therefore, in addition to a general physically active lifestyle, walking on the golf course may be beneficial for maintenance of a normal to low blood pressure.

Skeletal muscle strength is maintained up to about 50 to 60 years of age, and gradually reduced thereafter (Larsson, Grimby, & Karlsson, 1979; Porter, Vandervoort, & Lexell, 1995). Endurance training seems not to be sufficient to increase leg muscle strength above that of healthy non-active older individuals (Harridge, Magnusson, & Saltin, 1997). In contrast, strength training has been shown to improve muscle strength even at high age (Fiatarone et al., 1990). The handgrip strength of the present golfers was comparable to that of other individuals of the same age (Engstrom et al., 1993). The knee extensor strength was somewhat lower (10–15%) for both males and females compared to values reported for age-matched individuals (Borges, 1989). Neither handgrip nor knee extensor strength was altered after the golf season. Therefore, walking and playing golf will maintain muscle strength at a normal level, but will not result in any major improvements in muscular strength.

Muscular endurance tended to improve for a subgroup of the golfers. This may be partly a result of an improved oxidative capacity and an increased capillary density in the knee extensor muscle (Magnusson et al., 1996). These factors are important for substrate utilisation as well as for the submaximal endurance capacity. Thus, it can be speculated that these and other physiological adaptations located in skeletal muscle are of high importance for the health benefits that will be gained indirectly due to the long duration of golf play.

Further Research

The present data suggest that further investigation of the physiological adaptations of regular golf play would be worthwhile to establish direct cause and effect relationships. The health-related adaptations shown in the present study are similar to those found recently by Parkkari et al. (2000) in 55 male golfers (age 55 ± 4 years) after 20 weeks of regular golf play. However, they also included 55 sedentary non-golfers (age 55 ± 4 years) in order to control for seasonal variations in activity level and dietary habits. Their study design allowed Parkkari et al. to reach stronger conclusions about golfing and its physiological health benefits than the present one-group pretest-posttest design. It is of importance that their findings further support the results from the present study, which in addition shows health-related benefits in female golfers.

Conclusion

The present adult and older golfers who played three or more golf rounds per week maintained or improved their aerobic fitness, blood lipid profile, and blood pressure; reduced their body weight and body fat percentage; and retained their leg and handgrip strength. This indicates that walking while playing the golf course on a regular basis is associated with health-related benefits similar to those found after continuous walking programs.

Acknowledgments

I wish to thank Anne-Britt Olrog and Else Magnusson for excellent help performing the experiments, Eddy Carlsson for technical assistance, and Ewa Sejby for analysing blood lipids.

References

Allain, C.C., Poon, L.S., Chan, C.S.G., Richmond, W., & Fu, P.C. (1974). Enzymatic determination of total serum cholesterol. *Clinical Chemistry, 20,* 470–475.

Björntorp, P., & Brodoff, B.N. (1992). *Obesity.* Philadelphia: Lippincott.

Blair, S.N., Kohl, H.W., Barlow, C.E., Paffenbarger, R.S., Gibbons, L.W., & Macera, C.A. (1995). Changes in physical fitness and all-cause mortality. A prospective study of healthy and unhealthy men. *The Journal of the American Medical Association, 273,* 1093–1098.

Blair, S.N., Kohl, H.W., Gordon, N.F., & Paffenbarger, R.S. (1992). How much physical activity is good for health? *Annual Review of Public Health, 13*, 99–126.

Blair, S.N., Kohl, H.W., Paffenbarger, R.S., Clark, D.G., Cooper, K.H., & Gibbons, L.W. (1989). Physical fitness and all-cause mortality. A prospective study of healthy men and women. *The Journal of the American Medical Association, 262*, 2395–2401.

Borges, O. (1989). Isometric and isokinetic knee extension and flexion torque in men and women aged 20 – 70. *Scandinavian Journal of Rehabilitation Medicine, 21*, 45–53.

Davison, R.C.R., & Grant, S. (1993). Is walking sufficient exercise for health? *Sports Medicine, 16*, 369–373.

Engström, L-M., Ekblom, B., Forsberg, A., Koch, M., & Seger, J. (1993). *Livsstil, prestation, hälsa. Liv 90*. Ödeshög: AB Danagård Grafiska.

Fiatarone, M.A., Marks, E.C., Ryan, N.D., Meredith, C.N., Lipsitz, L.A., & Evans, W.J. (1990). High-intensity strength training in nonagenarians. *The Journal of the American Medical Association, 263*, 3029–3034.

Hakim, A.A., Petrovitch, H., Burchfiel, C.M., Ross, G.W., Rodriguez, B.L., White, L.R., Yano, K., Curb, J.D., & Abbott, R.D. (1998). Effects of walking on mortality among nonsmoking retired men. *The New England Journal of Medicine, 338*, 94–99.

Harridge, S., Magnusson, G., & Saltin, B. (1997). Life-long endurance-trained elderly men have high aerobic power, but similar muscle strength to non-active elderly men. *Aging Clinical Experimental Research, 9*, 80–87.

Jungner, I., Walldius, G., Holme, I., Kolar, W., & Steiner, E. (1992). Apolipoprotein B and A-I in relation to serum cholesterol and triglycerides in 43 000 Swedish males and females. *International Journal of Clinical & Laboratory Research, 21*, 247–255.

Kannel, W.B., Castelli, W.P., Gordon, T., & McNamara, P.M. (1971). Serum cholesterol, lipoproteins, and the risk of coronary heart disease. *Annals of International Medicine, 74*, 1–12.

Kannel, W.B., & Gordon, T. (1978). Evaluation of cardiovascular risk in the elderly: The Framingham study. *Bulletin New York Academy of Medicine, 54*, 573–591.

Kiens, B., Jorgensen, I., Lewis, S., Jensen, G., Lithell, H., Vessby, B., Hoe, S., & Schnohr, P. (1980). Increased plasma HDL-cholesterol and apo A-1 in sedentary middle-aged men after physical conditioning. *European Journal of Clinical Investigation, 10*, 203–209.

Landahl, S., Bengtsson, C., Sigurdsson, J.A., & Svanborg, A. (1986). Age-related changes in blood pressure. *Hypertension, 8*, 1044–1049.

Larsson, L., Grimby, G., & Karlsson, J. (1979). Muscle strength and speed of movement in relation to age and muscle morphology. *Journal of Applied Physiology, 46*, 451–456.

Law, M.R., Wald, N.J., & Thompson, S.G. (1994). By how much and how quickly does reduction in serum cholesterol concentration lower risk of ischaemic heart disease? *The British Medical Journal, 308*, 367–372.

Magnusson, G. (1999). Golf: Exercise for fitness and health. In M.R. Farrally & A.J. Cochran (Eds.), *Science and golf III: Proceedings of the 1998 World Scientific Congress of Golf* (pp. 51–57). Champaign, IL: Human Kinetics.

Magnusson, G., Isberg, B., Karlberg, K.-E., & Sylvén, C. (1994). Skeletal muscle strength and endurance in chronic congestive heart failure secondary to idiopathic dilated cardiomyopathy. *American Journal of Cardiology, 73*, 307–309.

Magnusson, G., Karpakka, J., Rong, H.C., Kaijser, L., Sylvén, C., & Saltin, B. (1996). Exercise capacity in heart failure patients: Relative importance of heart and skeletal muscle. *Clinical Physiology, 16*, 183–195.

Ornish, D., Brown, S.E., Scherwitz, L.W., Billings, J.H., Armstrong, W.T., Ports, T.A., McLanahan, S.M., Kirkeeide, R.L., Brand, R.J., & Gould, K.L. (1990). Can lifestyle changes reverse coronary heart disease? The life style heart trial. *Lancet, 336*, 129–133.

Paffenbarger, R.S., Hyde, R.T., Wing, A.L., & Hsieh, C.C. (1986). Physical activity, all-cause mortality, and longevity of college alumni. *The New England Journal of Medicine, 314,* 605–613.

Paffenbarger, R.S., Hyde, R.T., Wing, A.L., Lee, I.M., Jung, D.L., & Kampert, J. B. (1993). The association of changes in physical-activity level and other lifestyle characteristics with mortality among men. *The New England Journal of Medicine, 328,* 538–545.

Paffenbarger, R.S., Hyde, R.T., Wing, A.L., & Steinmetz, C.H. (1984). A natural history of athleticism and cardiovascular health. *The Journal of the American Medical Association, 252,* 491–495.

Paffenbarger, R.S., & Lee, I.M. (1996). Physical activity and fitness for health and longevity. *Research Quarterly for Exercise and Sports, 67* (3 Suppl.), 11–28.

Palank, E.A., & Hargreaves, E.H. (1990). The benefits of walking the golf course. *The Physician and Sportsmedicine, 18,* 77–80.

Parkkari, J., Natri, A., Kannus, P., Manttari, A., Laukkanen, R., Haapasalo, H., Nenonen, A., Pasanen, M., Oja, P., & Vuori, I. (2000). A controlled trial of the health benefits of regular walking on a golf course. *The American Journal of Medicine, 109,* 102–108.

Pollock, M.J., Miller, H.S., Janeway, R., Linnerud, A.C., Robertson, B., & Valentino, R. (1971). Effects of walking on body composition and cardiovascular function of middle-aged men. *Journal of Applied Physiology, 30,* 126–130.

Pollock, M.L, Wilmore, J.H, & Fox, S.M. (1984). *Exercise in health and disease.* Philadelphia: Saunders.

Porter, M.M., Vandervoort, A.A., & Lexell, J. (1995). Aging of human muscle, structure, function, and adaptability. *Scandinavian Journal of Medicine Science and Sports, 5,* 129–142.

Puggaard, L., Pedersen, H.P., Sandager, E., & Klitgaard, H. (1994). Physical conditioning in elderly people. *Scandinavian Journal of Medicine Science and Sports, 4,* 47–56.

Saltin, B. (1992). Sedentary lifestyle: An underestimated health risk. *Journal of International Medicine, 232,* 467–469.

Santiago, M.C., Alexander, J.F., Stull, A.G., Serfass, R.C., Hayday, M.A., & Leon, A.S. (1987). Physiological responses of sedentary women to a 20-week conditioning program of walking or jogging. *Scandinavian Journal of Sports Science, 9,* 33–39.

Shvartz, E., & Reibold, R.C. (1990). Aerobic fitness norms for males and females aged 6 to 75 years: A review. *Aviation Space Environmental Medicine, 61,* 3–11.

Tipton, C.M. (1991). Exercise, training and hypertension: An update. *Exercise and Sport Science Reviews, 19,* 447–505.

Wilmore, J.H., & Costill, D.L. (1994). *Physiology of sport and exercise.* Champaign, IL: Human Kinetics.

Wilmore, J.H., Vodak, P.A., Parr, R.B., Girandola, R.N., & Billing, J.E. (1980). Further simplification of a method for determination of residual lung volume. *Medicine Science and Sports Exercise, 12,* 216–218.

Aerobic Fitness and Psychophysiological Stress Responses to Competition Golf

John S. Carlson, Jennifer M. McKay, Steve E. Selig, and Tony Morris

Stress is a broad concept, whereby physical and emotional influences (such as those inherent in competition) produce psychological and physiological changes, which disrupt the internal environment of the person (Pfister & Muir, 1992). Sport research has focused on several aspects of the treatment and prevention of stress in athletic competition. In an attempt to enhance performance, imagery, relaxation and psych-up strategies have been used to influence athletes' psychophysiological state (Oxendine, 1970; Prapavessis et al., 1992; Ziegler et al., 1982). Whilst physical (aerobic) fitness is beneficial for general health and well-being (Petruzzello et al., 1991; Roth & Holmes, 1985), subsequent evidence suggests a more direct relationship between aerobic fitness-mediated adaptations in physiological systems and reduced psychophysiological responses to psychological stress (Crews & Landers, 1987). Modulations in stress reactivity including cardiovascular and neuromuscular responses are associated with an increased ability to cope with stress (Rostad & Long, 1996). Therefore, aerobic fitness may be advantageous for reducing psychophysiological stress in golfers during competition; a stressful social paradigm (Herbert, 1987). Reduced psychophysiological responses to stress in golfers may directly influence performance. For example, those individuals unable to cope with competition pressure and high levels of state anxiety may experience a detriment in fine motor skill such as those required in golf performance (Spielberger, 1989; Weinberg & Genuchi, 1980). Physical demands, for example heart rates greater than those required to meet the demands of the physical workload, together with elevated catabolic effects of elevated cortisol, could perceivably lead to early fatigue through increased metabolic load. Crews (1994) suggested low-fit golfers may be distracted during putting by heavy respirations and elevated heart rates, suggesting aerobic fitness may play a role in task-orientated attention.

The stress-reducing benefit of aerobic exercise in sporting contexts is somewhat of an anomaly, because the majority of sports require a degree of aerobic fitness training to compete effectively. However, it may have an important practical application in reducing stress responses during competition in low aerobically demanding sports such as golf. A potential benefit to the competition golfer would be to experience a reduction in psychophysiological stress during play and/or a reduction in fatigue especially over several days of a tournament.

The purpose of this study was to examine the effect of enhanced aerobic fitness in elite male amateur golfers on their psychophysiological stress prior to, during, and at the completion of competition golf play.

Methods

Eight healthy male elite golfers (age 22.1, ± 2.2; height 180.3, ± 1.5; weight 76.2 ± 3.2; handicap 1.9, ± 0.4) participated in the study. All participants were completing a 1-year Australian Institute of Sport (AIS) scholarship. AIS scholarships are awarded to the top-ranking amateur male and female players in Australia to prepare them for professional golf. At the time of study, the golfers were participating in a weight development program but were not receiving aerobic training in addition to playing three to four golf rounds per week. The AIS squad was selected for this study because they represent an elite group of golfers, with the time available to incorporate an 8-week, fully supervised intensive fitness program into their schedule. There was no initial assessment to determine whether these golfers were predisposed to stress.

To determine initial levels of physical fitness, each golfer's maximal aerobic power (VO_2max), heart rate and heart rhythm was measured using a graded walking treadmill (Bruce) protocol. The exercise test is a multistaged treadmill protocol to volitional exhaustion, and was selected because walking exercise is specific to golf. The criterion for termination was volitional fatigue, manifested by one or more of the following: attainment of heart rate to 95% of predicted maximal heart rate, respiratory exchange ratio (RER) greater than 1.1, a plateau in oxygen consumption or an unwillingness to continue. The metabolic data (VO_2max) were measured by open circuit analysis of expired air.

The following week, golfers competed in an organised AIS competition comprising 18 holes of stroke play, where saliva cortisol concentration, heart rates and sport-specific anxiety (CSAI-2) were measured at pre (PRE), hole 6 (H6), hole 12 (H12) and at the completion of the round (H18). Each golfer then completed three aerobic training sessions per week for 8 weeks. Training programs were designed to progressively increase the training heart rates during exercise, as well as the duration and frequency of training over the 8-week period. The exercise training comprised aerobic exercise, including cycle ergometer and treadmill walking/running during a compulsory gymnasium session three times per week. All golfers were presented with their target steady-state heart rate at the start of each training session, and monitored their heart rate by either palpation methods or by heart rate feedback from a Polar Sport Tester heart rate monitor. A qualified physical trainer supervised each training session and recorded exercise details and attendance. At the completion of the 8 weeks, the golfers underwent a second VO_2max test to determine the efficacy of the training program. Each individual's aerobic capacity was assessed by criterion relating to enhanced aerobic capacity. A second competition golf round was played using the same golf format, on the same golf course and tee off time as the initial 18-hole round.

Golf Testing Procedures

On the designated golf testing day at the golf course, a heart rate monitor was fitted and recording commenced. Players followed their normal pregame warm-up routine. Ten minutes prior to their allocated tee time, each golfer collected a saliva sample, then completed the first psychometric measure of competitive A-state (CSAI-2). Saliva was collected prior to the CSAI-2 completion on each occasion, in case anxiety cognitions from the questionnaire confounded the cortisol data. Each golfer was a member of a group of three players. An observer followed the group at a discrete distance behind play, and collected data on sampling times and golf play. After hole 6, the player completed the second saliva collection and CSAI-2 questionnaire. The same procedure was repeated at the completion of holes 12 and 18. Within 1 week of completing the golf round, each golfer completed a basal testing day (Basal 1). Golfers were restricted to mild activity (no golf) and collected six saliva samples at hourly intervals, spanning the hours of the preceding golf round. Individual basal (resting) cortisol curves were established, and subsequently used to control for diurnal changes in cortisol concentration.

Psychophysiological Data Collection and Treatment
Saliva Cortisol

Stress-related HPA activity stimulates the adrenal cortex to release the hormone cortisol into the blood serum (Ur, 1991). The plasma concentration of free (unbound) hormone can be determined from saliva (Walker et al., 1978) and because this was the least intrusive, this was designated the best manner to assess this measure of stress. Saliva was collected by asking participants to accumulate saliva in the mouth for 60 seconds before expelling the sample (usually 1.5 to 2 ml) into a 5-ml screw-top plastic vial. Cortisol in saliva has been reported to be stable for several days at room temperature (Kirschbaum & Hellhammer, 1989). The saliva samples were frozen overnight, then transferred the following day to freezer storage (–80°C) until analysis. As cortisol concentration varies with time of day according to a well defined circadian rhythm (Bailey & Heitkemper, 1991; Krieger et al., 1971), it was necessary to establish basal response curves in each golfer. Golfers selected a suitable day within 1 week of the golf testing round to complete basal data collection. From these collections individual basal curves were generated.

The basal cortisol concentrations and the corresponding golf round cortisol concentrations were used to determine cortisol responses at PRE, H6, H12 and H18 for each golfer. The interpolated baseline value was subtracted from the corresponding golf round cortisol concentration to determine cortisol responses ($nmol.l^{-1}$) at PRE, H6, H12, H18. This study reports cortisol responses ($nmol.l^{-1}$) representing a positive deviation from baseline. The rationale for this is to correct for diurnal changes expected in baseline cortisol over the 5-hour cortisol data collection period (Kirshbaum & Hellhammer, 1989), and to control for golfers commencing their golf rounds at slightly different times of day. Cortisol concentration was determined from duplicate 200-ul non-extracted saliva samples using Radio Immuno Asssay (RIA) techniques (Clinical Assays; Gamma Coat [125-I] Cortisol Radioimmunoassay Kit, CA-1549).

Competitive State Anxiety

Competitive state anxiety was assessed with the Competitive State Anxiety Inventory-2 (CSAI-2; Martens et al., 1990) which is a self-report psychometric inventory of A-state consisting of 27 items. The CSAI-2 assesses two components of state anxiety (A-state), cognitive worry and somatic anxiety, and a related construct, self-confidence, with 9 items representing each subscale. The CSAI-2 has high reliability and validity (Martens et al., 1990) and has been widely used in research on anxiety in sport (Vealey, 1990). Each participant completed four CSAI-2 questionnaires (PRE, H6, H12,

H18) for each golf round, immediately following saliva collection. Each CSAI-2 subscale is rated on a scale from 1 = *not at all* to 4 = *very much so*, relating to extremes of intensity. Each subscale, therefore, has a range from 9 to 36. Higher scores on cognitive and somatic anxiety indicate higher levels of anxiety, whereas higher scores on the self-confidence subscale correspond to higher levels of state self-confidence.

Competition

Competition rounds comprised two 18-hole stroke play events, conducted on a Melbourne metropolitan golf course (The Commonwealth Golf Club). The competition round was organised by the AIS coach, and comprised a format commonly used for tournament preparation. The 18-hole stroke competition comprised the eight male players. The winner was the person with the lowest score at the end of the round. A financial inducement was applied whereby the players must pay the winner for each shot over their handicap at the finish of the event. This format was used to create and maintain the pressure on the players, not only to win but also to score low and reduce the amount of money they forfeit.

Statistical treatment of the data included the following sets of analyses. To examine the effect of the 8-week training program on golfers' aerobic capacity, t tests were used to analyse the metabolic data. Salivary cortisol responses were analysed by a Game x Hole (2 x 4) two-way repeated measures ANOVA. Tukey's post hoc analysis was used whenever statistical significance was determined. To examine the effect of aerobic training and time on golfers' heart rates, a Game x Hole (2 x 4) two-way repeated measures ANOVA was conducted on heart rates for each hole.

Finally, to examine the relationship between aerobic training condition and time on state anxiety and self-confidence, a Game x Hole (2 x 4) repeated measures MANOVA was used on the three CSAI-2 subscale scores. Individual repeated measures ANOVAs were used to analyse the separate CSAI-2 subscales to determine the effects from aerobic training.

Results

The group showed a 9.6 ($\pm$ 2.6) % increase in VO_2max, which was a significant difference between the pretraining and posttraining VO_2max values (54.9 $\pm$ 2.7 and 59.7 $\pm$ 2.9 ml.kg^{-1}.min^{-1} respectively; $p < .008$). There was also a significant change in the pre- and posttraining determinations of anaerobic threshold (43.3 $\pm$ 2.2 and 50.3 $\pm$ 3.2 ml.kg^{-1}.min^{-1} respectively; $p < .006$). Body weight was unchanged between pretest (76.2 kg $\pm$ 3.18) and posttests (76.4 kg $\pm$ 2.8; $p = .89$).

To examine the effects of aerobic training condition and time on the physiological parameters, intraindividual cortisol responses and heart rates were analysed before, during and after the golf games. The mean cortisol responses for $n = 8$ male golfers are illustrated in Figure 1. Salivary cortisol responses analysed by a Game x Hole (2 x 4) two-way repeated measures ANOVA revealed there was no significant difference between the pretrained and posttrained condition for the two competition games ($2.5 \pm .22$ nmol.l^{-1} and $2.1 \pm .78$ nmol.l^{-1} respectively; $p = .50$). There was no time effect for cortisol ($p < .15$).

The heart rate responses are illustrated in Figure 2. The ANOVA revealed that the mean heart rates in the pretraining competition game (105 ± 2.7 b.min-1) were not significantly different from the posttraining competition (108 ± 2.7, $p = .18$).

The CSAI-2 scores during the pre- and posttraining golf games are shown in Figure 3. Individual repeated measures ANOVAs used to analyse the separate CSAI-2 subscales revealed there was no significant effect on cognitive anxiety as a result of the aerobic training condition ($p = .09$). For somatic anxiety and self-confidence, there were no significant differences observed during competition following the aerobic conditioning program ($p = .15$ and $p = .37$, respectively).

Intraindividual comparison using a two-way ANOVA with repeated measures (training condition x hole) for six-hole average performance scores revealed that performance in the pretraining game was not significantly different to the posttraining game (79.3 ± 0.8 and 77.0 ± 0.9 strokes pre- and posttraining respectively; $p = .23$). The golfers took longer to complete

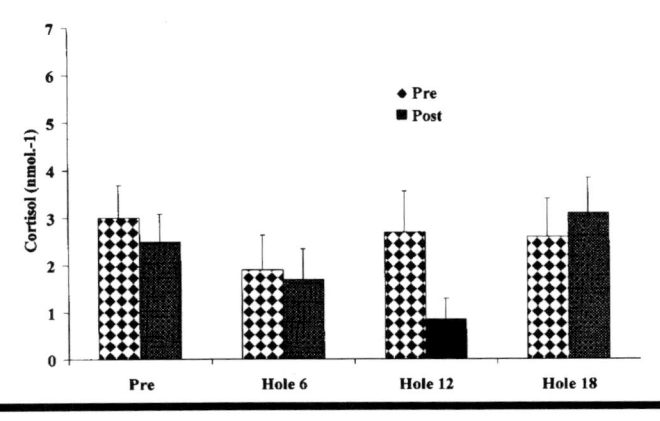

Figure 1

Cortisol responses of elite golfers to competition golf pre- and posttraining.

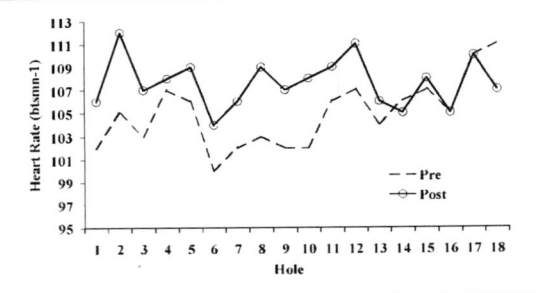

Figure 2
Heart rate responses during competitive golf following an aerobic training program.

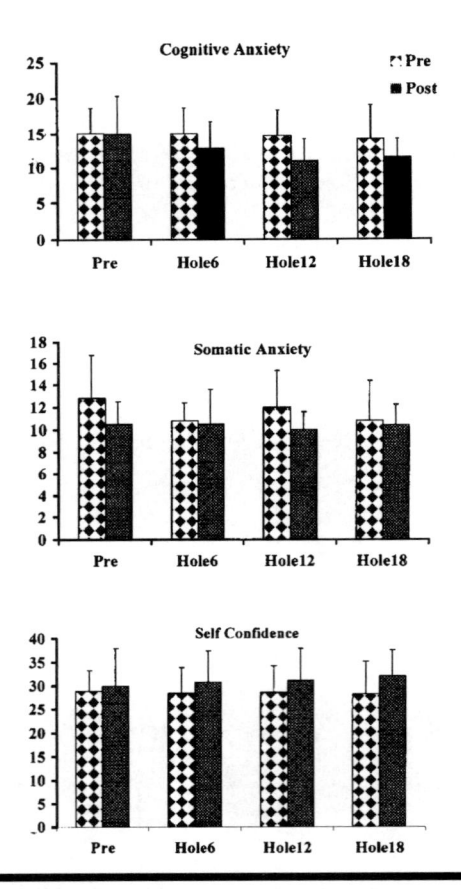

Figure 3
CSAI-2 cognitive, somatic anxiety and self-confidence during competitive golf.

the pretraining round compared to the posttraining round with times of 248.5 min ± 2.65 and 222.8 min ± 8.71 respectively ($p = .014$).

Discussion

The eight male elite golfers in this study showed significant improvements in aerobic capacity after an 8-week training program. However, intraindividual comparisons of psychophysiological stress responses revealed increased aerobic fitness had no influence on salivary cortisol responses, or self-reported state anxiety during competition.

Golfers' salivary cortisol responses in both game conditions were low and remained unchanged in competition before and after aerobic training. Intraindividual analysis confirmed that despite a mean increase in aerobic power of just less than 10%, the adrenocortical response to golf competition was not affected. Previous training studies in controlled laboratory settings by White et al. (1976) and Buono et al. (1987) have found evidence to support the modulation of this physiological system with training. These authors found increased VO_2max resulted in attenuated adrenocorticotropin (ACTH) and cortisol release during exercise at submaximal workloads. The current field study does not provide support for these contentions.

The discrepancies in the results of the present study may be accounted for by the differences in the intensity and nature of the exercise. Golf is played at a start and stop walking pace, averaging around 30–40% VO_2max (Murase et al., 1989). White and colleagues' (1976) study measured attenuated responses whilst athletes exercised at steady-state and a higher (50% VO_2max) exercise intensity. Elements attributed to the less strictly controlled field environment, combined with golf activity being low intensity and intermittent in nature, may have masked the subtle changes in cortisol being observed. A field study by Brooke and Long (1987) found that groups of high and low-fit novice rapellers showed similar plasma cortisol increases, before and after a rapelling manoeuvre. Their study supports the result of the present study that fitness does not appear to modify HPA reactivity to the stressful task. However, unlike the golf competition, rapelling evoked a definite cortisol response which may be due to both the novelty and threatening aspects of the task (Brooke & Long, 1987). In another cross-sectional study design, Sinyor et al. (1983) found that fit and low-fit groups did not show elevated cortisol in response to a psychologically stressful series of laboratory tasks, but heart rate and subjective anxiety were elevated during the stressful period. It would appear that in the present study the competition paradigm was not particularly stress evoking for these golfers.

Physical training and its influence on cardiovascular stress responses have been more thoroughly researched compared to the HPA system. The bradycardia typically associated with trained athletes has been measured in stress studies and typically mainfests as a lower overall heart rate across all testing periods (Brooke & Long, 1987; Holmes & Roth, 1985). However, this effect may be negated when correcting for baseline heart rates within high and low-fit groups (Van Doornen & de Geus, 1989). The current study used intraindividual comparisons and training interventions which control for baseline differences amongst golfers for heart rates. Blumenthal et al. (1990) found support that training reduced heart rate responses during and after 15-minute arithmetic challenge, concluding that aerobic fitness was causal. In the current study, the incremental treadmill tests in the laboratory (VO_2max) showed the golfers' posttraining heart rates were consistently lower than during pretraining, but this was not reflected in the on-course heart rates, which were similar for the two training states.

The elevated heart rates in the posttraining game compared to pretraining may have been due to the fact that the postraining round was completed in a much shorter time (26 minutes), indicating a higher average level of physiological exercise intensity. In the pretrained state, heart rates trended upwards toward the end of the round, possibly indicating a component of fatigue, which was not evident in the posttraining round where heart rates remained relatively flat. The initial fitness levels in this group of golfers may have also influenced the heart rates. Even before training, these golfers may have shown an efficient (trained) cardiac response to golf activity and further increments in fitness may only provide small and nonsignificant changes to golfing performance heart rates.

Whilst aerobic fitness has been implicated in reducing psychological stress, this study provided little evidence for a causal relationship between increased fitness and reduced competitive state anxiety (CSAI-2) during competition. Holmes and Roth (1985) had previously found that during a psychological stressor, cognitive and somatic anxiety was lower in fit individuals. They also observed that despite a significant increase in aerobic fitness, there was no change in cognitive and somatic anxiety and self-confidence with training status. In the present study cognitive and somatic anxiety responses were generally low and self-confidence high, indicating that the golfers were not particularly anxious or nervous about their ability to perform despite the chance of winning or losing money.

In summary, the absence of psychological threat or challenge for golfers in this study is emphasised by low cortisol and heart rate responses together with low levels of reported state anxiety, especially in the pretraining game. Golf competition has previously been found to be a potent stressor in elite golfers (McKay et al., 1997). The competition format used in the current study may partly explain the low psychophysiological responses. Although the golfers were playing against their peers and being assessed by their coach, other factors that are stress evoking such as spectators were absent (Ziegler et al., 1982). Situational factors, together with the initially high level of fitness in these high-ability players, may explain why heart rate, cortisol and state anxiety were not lower in competition play following the aerobic conditioning program. Future studies should continue to examine elite golfers with a view to quantifying the role of aerobic fitness and measuring psychophysiological responses during a series of actual tournament performances, such as consecutive days of tournament play or tournaments played every week for several weeks.

References

Bailey, S.L., & Heitkemper, M.M. (1991). Morningness-eveningness and early-morning salivary cortisol levels. *Biological Psychology, 32*, 181–192.

Blumenthal, J.A., Fredrickson, M., Kuhn, C.M., Ulmer, R.L., Walsh-Riddle, M., & Appelbaum, M. (1990). Aerobic exercise reduces levels of cardiovascular and sympathoadrenal responses to mental stress in subjects without prior evidence of myocardical ischemia. *The American Journal of Cardiology, 65*, 93–98.

Brooke, S.T., & Long, B.C. (1987). Efficiency of coping with a real-life stressor: A multimodal comparison of aerobic fitness. *Psychophysiology, 24(2)*, 173–180.

Buono, M.J., Yeager, J.E., & Sucec, A.A. (1987). Effect of aerobic training on the plasma ACTH response to exercise. *Journal of Applied Physiology, 63(6)*, 2499–2501.

Crews D.J. (1994). Research based golf: From the laboratory to the course. In A.J. Cochran & M.R. Farrally (Eds.), *Science and golf II: Proceedings of the 1994 World Scientific Congress of Golf* (pp. 127–137). London: E & FN Spon.

Crews, D.J., & Landers, D.M. (1987). A meta-analytic review of aerobic fitness and reactivity to psychosocial stressors. *Medicine and Science in Sports and Exercise, 19*(5), s114–s120.

Herbert, J. (1987). Neuroendocrine responses to social stress. Neuroendocrinology of stress. *Bailliere's clinical endocrinology and metabolism — International practice and research*, 1(2) (pp. 468–490). London: Bailliere Tindall.

Holmes, D.S., & Roth, D.L. (1985). Association of aerobic fitness with pulse rate and subjective responses to psychological stress. *Psychophysiology, 22(5)*, 525–529.

Kirschbaum, C., & Hellhammer, D.H. (1989). Salivary cortisol in psychobiological research: An overview. *Neuropsychobiology, 22*, 150–169.

Krieger, D.T., Allen, W., Rizzo, R., & Krieger, H.P. (1971). Characterization of the normal temporal pattern of plasma corticosteroid levels. *Journal of Clinical Endocrinology, 32*, 266–284.

Martens, R., Burton, D., Vealey, R.S., Bump, L.A., & Smith, D.F. (1990). The competitive state-anxiety inventory-2 (CSAI-2). In R. Martens, R.S. Vealey, & D. Burton (Eds.), *Competitive anxiety in sport* (pp. 117–190). Champaign, IL: Human Kinetics.

McKay, J.M., Selig, S.E., Carlson, J.S., & Morris, T. (1997). Psychophysiological stress in elite golfers during practice and competition. *The Australian Journal of Science and Medicine in Sport, 29(2)*, 55–61.

Murase, Y., Kamei, S., & Hoshikawa, T. (1989). Heart rate and metabolic responses to participation in golf. *Journal of Sports Medicine, 29*, 269–272.

Oxendine, J.B. (1970). Emotional arousal and motor performance. *Quest, 13*, 23–32.

Petruzello, S.J., Landers, D.M., Hatfield, B.D., Kubitz, K.A., & Salazar, W. (1991). A meta-analysis on the anxiety-reducing effects of acute and chronic exercise: Outcomes and mechanisms. *Sports Medicine, 11(3),* 143-182.

Pfister, H.P., & Muir, J.L. (1992). Arousal and stress: A consideration of theoretical approaches. In H.P. Pfister (Ed.), *Stress effects on central and peripheral systems* (pp. 1-15). Australia: Australian Academic Press.

Prapavessis, H., Grove, J.R., McNair, P.J., & Cable, N.T. (1992). Self-regulation training, state anxiety, and sport performance: A psychophysiological case study. *The Sport Psychologist, 6,* 213-229.

Rostad, F. G., & Long, B.C. (1996). Exercise as a coping strategy for stress: A review. *International Journal of Sport Psychology, 27,* 197-222.

Roth, D.L., & Holmes, D.S. (1985). Influence of physical fitness in determining the impact of stressful life events on physical and psychological health. *Psychosomatic Medicine, 47(2),* 164-172.

Sinyor, D., Schwartz, S.G., Peronnet, G., Brisson, G., & Seraganian, P. (1983). Aerobic fitness level and reactivity to psychosocial stress: Physiological, biochemical and subjective measures. *Psychosomatic Medicine, 45(3),* 205-217.

Spielberger, C.D. (1989). Stress and anxiety in sports. In D. Hackfort & C.D. Spielberger (Eds.), *Anxiety in sports: An international perspective* (pp. 3-7). New York: Hemisphere.

Ur, E. (1991). Psychological aspects of hypothalamo-pituitary-adrenal activity. In A. Grossman (Ed.), *Bailliere's clinical endocrinology and metabolism — Psychoendocrinology* Vol.5(l) (pp. 79-96). London: Bailliere Tindall.

Van Doornen, L.J.P., & de Geus, E.J.C. (1989). Aerobic fitness and the cardiovascular response to stress. *Psychophysiology, 26(1),* 17-28.

Vealey, R. S. (1990). Advancements in competitive anxiety research: Use of the Sport Competition Anxiety Test and the Competitive State Anxiety Inventory-2. *Anxiety Research, 2,* 243-261.

Walker, R.F., Riad-Fahmy D., & Read, G.F. (1978). Adrenal status assessed by direct radioimmunoassay of cortisol in whole saliva or parotid saliva. *Clinical Chemistry, 24(9),* 1460-1463.

Weinberg, R.S., & Genuchi, M. (1980). Relationship between competitive trait anxiety, state anxiety, and golf performance: A field study. *Journal of Sport Psychology, 2,* 148-154.

White, J.A., Ismail, A.H., & Bottoms, G.D. (1976). Effect of physical fitness on the adrenocortical response to exercise stress. *Medicine and Science in Sports, 8(2),* 113-118.

Ziegler, S.G., Klinzing, J., & Williamson, K. (1982). The effects of two stress management training programs on cardiorespiratory efficiency. *Journal of Sport Psychology, 4,* 280-289.

CHAPTER 13

How Has Research Influenced Golf Teaching and Equipment?

Robert J. Neal, Eric J. Sprigings, and Michael J. Dalgleish

Golfers are continually on a quest to improve their games. This notion was summarised in the foreword to Ben Hogan's (1957) publication which stated that:

> No man who golfs is so stubborn, so conceited, so arrogant or so accomplished that he is not constantly striving to improve his score. He may not admit this to others. He may pretend that mediocrity is enough for him. ... This man is telling a white lie and he knows it. (p. 5)

One would like to believe that such motivation would be the precursor to improved scores, enhanced techniques and optimal movement patterns achieved through dedicated and systematic practice, under the watchful eye of a coach. Unfortunately, this description is not indicative of current-day practice at most golf courses. Golf coaches too often offer band-aid solutions to swing faults without teaching swings to the clients that will ensure long-term success and injury-free golf. We are not implying that golf coaches are entirely to blame. Players frequently do not want to invest the time and effort to improve their technique and seek a quick fix before their Saturday afternoon game.

Manufacturers of equipment have taken advantage of golfers' desires to improve without having to spend time practising the fundamentals of the swing. They advertise and sell to the golfer notions that specific equipment will allow them to "hit the ball straighter and further" than they can with their current models, allowing them to improve their games. They exploit the golfer's wishful thinking and naivety in mechanics by using marketing ploys that appeal to specific sectors of the market. The consumer is usually not in a position to determine whether claims made by manufacturers are true or merely speculation designed to capture the market.

One aim of independent research is to check the efficacy of such claims. By developing models of equipment and selecting realistic conditions (e.g., clubhead speeds obtainable by golfers, mass and mass distribution of clubs, grooves that conform to the current rules, etc.), research can be conducted that allows one to determine if particular club designs are of any likely benefit to golfers.

Another approach is one that attempts to provide insight into golfers' performances by collecting empirical data and then making sense of them. Dave Pelz has adopted this approach over the last 25 years, developing a huge database on performance characteristics of players whose abilities range from poor to the best of the world's touring professionals. This research, while often lacking in theoretical construct, has provided the golfer with information that shows where improvements in skill are most likely to translate into an improvement in score. Furthermore, he has developed a line of teaching that attempts to encourage techniques that optimise these skills and provide a reliable method of consistently performing them (Pelz, 1999).

A third approach, often adopted in biomechanics, is one that relies on selected empirical data coupled with a model of the human golfer and his or her equipment. This method focuses on the biomechanical inputs to the system (golfer plus equipment), and the interaction between the mechanical system (equipment) and the biological system (the human golfer). It offers insight into how technique can be modulated by the equipment, but also provides a conduit allowing one to determine if a particular swing style provides advantages over another one. The advantages in this case could be based on any number of criteria including likelihood to develop injury, greatest clubhead speed, or minimal kinematic variation from swing to swing.

This approach also allows one to examine sequencing in the golf swing and why proximal to distal patterns of segment involvement emerge as the predominant pattern used by golfers of all skill levels. By understanding the complex behaviour of human muscles and how they operate during the golf swing one can begin to understand why certain techniques afford advantages over others, and the potential limitations of various movement patterns.

This chapter will attempt to show how these three approaches have led to changes in coaching principles and philosophies, equipment design and modification, and approaches to training.

Modelling
Improvements in Equipment

Manufacturers of equipment are continually looking for ideas that can improve their product and give them a market edge over their competitors. Until recent times, driving clubs in golf were made from wood (either persimmon or laminates). In the 1980s, metal woods emerged with the promise, from the manufacturers, of increased distance and accuracy. The figures bandied around by the sales and marketing people were that you could expect to increase your driving distance by approximately 20 metres.

The next equipment revolution was the introduction of space-age materials in the construction of the shaft of the club. Graphite and carbon-fibre-based materials offered new potentials for club manufacturers. The mass of these new shafts was considerably smaller than their steel counterparts yet shaft stiffness was not compromised. Furthermore, various positions of the kick-points of the shaft could be produced simply by changing the way in which the materials were assembled in the manufacturing process. With these new shafts (and appropriately weighted clubheads), the marketing people claimed that a 20-metre driving distance increase was possible.

Oversized and titanium clubheads were the next change that promised to bring increased driving distance. The strength and high stiffness of titanium allowed manufacturers to produce clubs that had longer shafts, lighter heads but equivalent swing weights than their predecessors. It was therefore proposed that this combination would increase the distance that one could drive the ball. With the increased shaft length but little or no increase in moment of inertia, the logical deduction was that with the same torques applied, increased angular velocity and hence clubhead speeds were possible. Since clubhead speed is the most important factor relating to driving distance, there was an expectation that increased driving distance was possible.

The most recent development is the so-called trampoline or spring effect. The claim here is that with the very thin-walled, high-strength materials that are available these days, one is able to produce a clubface that stores strain energy during the compression phase of ball contact and then springs back delivering increased energy to the ball. Independent tests conducted by the USGA Research & Test Center show that there is the potential for this phenomenon to occur. In fact, in a driver with an appropriately selected wall thickness, it may be possible to increase the departure velocity of the golf ball by 8–14% (Johnson & Hubbell, 1999). Since departure velocity is directly related to driving distance, one might expect a similar (though not equal) percentage increase in driving distance. The theoretical results obtained by Johnson and Hubbell (1999), assuming an approach velocity between the club and the ball of 49 m/s, are shown in Table 1.

If all the claims of the club manufacturers were true, then we would expect that within the last 20 years there should have been an approximate 60 to 80-metre increase in average driving distance. Perusal of the statistics kept by the Professional Golfers' Association (PGA) Tour in the United States does not show this magnitude of increase at all. In fact the most recent information provided to the golfing community in the form of a press release by the USGA indicates that driving distances on the PGA tour have, between 1968 and 1994, increased at a rate of approximately 30 cm per year. Thus, the total increase in this period would be less than 10 m. While the rate increased to 1.8 m/yr during the next 5 years, and is possibly associated with the move to thin-walled, titanium drivers, the increase has not been as large as marketing groups would have the public believe. While comparable statistics on amateur golfers are not available, it seems highly unlikely that they would be different from the world's best golfers. In summary, while there has been an increase in driving distance over the last 20 years, it is impossible to tease out contributions to this increase that are due to changes in equipment, course presentation, swing technique or any of a number of other confounding variables. In fact, our view is that the increased athleticism of modern-day professional golfers (i.e., increased strength, flexibility, muscular control and improved swing mechanics) is likely to be the variable that accounts for the largest percentage of this improvement. There is certainly no concrete evidence to support the widely held views in the market that golf equipment can have a profound influence on the length and accuracy of tee shots.

Another interesting development in shaft technology was to reshape the shaft using an extrusion process that shifted a portion of the mass of the club

Table 1

Rebound Velocity for Different Titanium Membrane Thicknesses used to Model Modern Driving Clubs

WALL THICKNESS/ BALL TYPE COMBINATION	REBOUND VELOCITY (M/S)	% INCREASE
2.54 mm, 2 piece ball construction	26.36	13.5
3.18 mm, 2 piece ball construction	25.38	9.3
6.35 mm, 2 piece ball construction	23.23	—
3.18 mm, wound ball construction	24.60	7.8
6.35 mm, wound ball construction	22.83	—

distally (toward the head). The manufacturers claimed this would reduce the club's moment of inertia, which would allow the club to be swung faster, thus producing greater clubhead speed than if the mass was uniformly distributed along the length of the shaft. Their claim of enhanced swing speed was supported by a video clip that clearly showed a club fitted with this new shaft oscillated as a pendulum, more quickly than an identical club fitted with a normal shaft.

We (Sprigings & Neal, in press) examined the manufacturer's hypothesis by developing a computer model of a golf club in which we could move a small portion of the mass of the shaft to any position along the length of the shaft. The computer simulation trials, in which the modelled club was allowed to oscillate in simple harmonic (pendula) motion, revealed that there was a point at which a portion of the mass could be located distally down the shaft that would increase the angular velocity of the club (and hence increase clubhead speed).

However, the assumption used in these first simulations (and in the pendulum swing demonstrations provided by the manufacturers) was that there was no external torque applied to the handle of the club; only gravitational torque was used to accelerate the club. In reality this assumption is not true. In golf, the hands produce a substantial torque during the swing, and this moment of force assists in rotating the club. As soon as we included even a small torque (10 Nm) at the grip end of the club, the results changed as we had anticipated. With an external torque applied to the club, the best position to locate this moveable mass was as close as possible to the point on the handle where the torque was being applied. By locating it here, the moment of inertia of the club about the axis of rotation was minimised. With the moment of inertia minimised, the effect of the torque was maximised, and the clubhead speed was maximised too. In conclusion, we believe that testing the merits of a club's shaft by using a pendulum swing is flawed, and that the conclusions of enhanced swing speed, reached by the manufacturer, were unsupported.

Simulation Studies Relating to Swing Mechanics

One of the questions that has perplexed golfers and their coaches over the last few decades relates to the contribution that wrist torque has to clubhead speed at impact. Jorgensen (1999), using a computer simulation approach, decided that an active wrist torque by the muscles crossing the wrist joint was not necessary during the golf swing to accelerate it toward impact. In fact, he maintained that the best notion for a golfer is to have a frictionless wrist joint that allows the club to swing freely.

The modelling approach adopted by Jorgensen was based on a double pendulum (arms and club), swinging on a plane inclined to the horizontal. A torque actuator was placed at the proximal end (shoulder) with the maximum possible torque set to 100 Nm. It is not clear from his description of the model what type of mathematical function was used to simulate the onset and development of torque. It seemed that the torque was speed independent, which is not representative of the way in which mammalian muscles work. In mammalian and therefore human muscle, it takes time for maximum force to build up (i.e., it does not go from 0 to maximum instantly), and the force it can produce is dependent on the speed of shortening. The faster a muscle shortens, the less force it can produce.

To examine the conclusions on wrist torque involvement reached by Jorgensen (1999), we (Neal & Sprigings, 1999; Sprigings & Neal, 2000) developed our own computer model of the swing. The golf swing was modelled as a three-segment, two-dimensional (2-D), linked system with the golf club, arm, and torso segments moving in a plane tilted 60° to the ground (Figure 1). For the purposes of the 2-D representation, the torso was collapsed along its longitudinal axis so that it lay in the movement plane as a rigid rod with a length equal to the distance from the sternal notch of the sternum to the glenoid fossa of the shoulder.

Torque generators were inserted at the proximal end of each segment, and provided the model with the capability of adding energy to the system. The torque generators used in the simulation were programmed such that they were constrained by the activation rate and force-velocity properties of human muscle. These constraints made the torque patterns that were possible at the joint much more realistic of human torques and a far better representation of the system that we were modelling than the model of Jorgensen

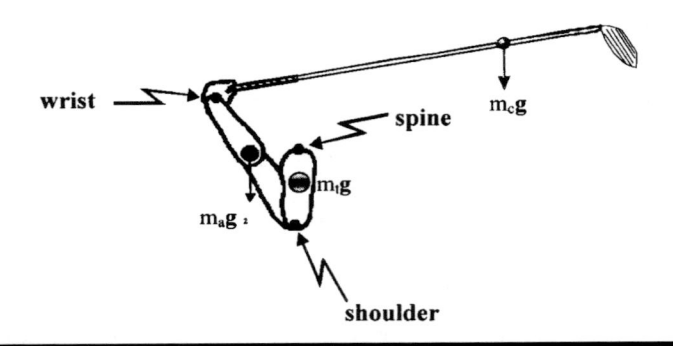

Figure 1
Three-segment model of the golfer.

(1999). The force-length property of muscle was expected to play a second-order role in the outcome of the performance and, as such, was not included in the simulation model. The activation rate and force-velocity properties associated with human muscle were implemented using the calculated instantaneous isometric torque predicted from a linearised Hill model structure (Niku & Henderson, 1985; Sprigings, 1986), as input to the force-velocity approach described by Alexander (1990).

$$\tau = \tau_{max}\left(1 - e^{\frac{-t}{\delta}}\right)\left(\frac{\omega_{max} - \omega}{\omega_{max} + \zeta\omega}\right) \qquad \text{Equation 1}$$

In Equation 1, τ is the instantaneous value produced by a torque generator; τ_{max} is the maximum isometric torque of the torque generator; ω_{max} is the maximum angular velocity of the associated joint; ω is the instantaneous joint angular velocity; ζ is a shape factor controlling the curvature of the torque/velocity relationship; t is the elapsed time from initial torque activation; and δ is the activation time constant (Pandy, Zajac, Sim, & Levine, 1990; Sprigings, 1986). This equation has a hyperbolic shape typical of a Hill-type muscle.

For the present study, τ_{max} was set at 180, 120, 60 Nm for the spine, shoulder, and wrist respectively; ω_{max} was set at 20, 30, 60 rad s^{-1} for the spine, shoulder, and wrist joints respectively; δ was set at 40 ms (Sprigings, 1986); and ζ was assigned a value of 3.0 (Alexander, 1990). The variable chosen for maximisation was clubhead speed and the optimisation routine searched for the onset and offset times of the torque actuators.

The following simulations were run:

1. Enable wrist torque and seek optimal solution
2. Disable the wrist torque and find new optimal solution
3. Activate the wrist torque 50 ms early
4. Activate the shoulder torque 50 ms early

Figure 2 illustrates the timing and magnitudes of torque activation for Simulation 1 which included an optimally timed wrist torque. You see evidence of a proximal to distal pattern of activations that produced a clubhead speed for this simulation of 160 km/hr. Figure 3 shows the results for Simulation 2 in which no wrist torque was applied. Clubhead speed for this situation was 144 km/hr, a 10% reduction. Thus, these data clearly illustrate that, in theory, an optimally timed wrist torque can increase clubhead speed significantly. It also highlights that while the wrist joint can increase the kinetic energy of the clubhead, its effect is relatively small compared to the proximal links in the kinetic chain.

Figures 4 and 5 illustrate the patterns of torque activation when the shoulder torque (Figure 4) and wrist torque (Figure 5) were activated 50 ms earlier than the optimal solution (Simulation 1). The reduction in clubhead speed is approximately 5% from 160 km/hr down to 152 km/hr. Thus, small timing errors in the simulation can have a substantial effect on clubhead speed. In reality, the effects are likely to be much larger than the 5% shown here, because it would be most unlikely that the body would be able to re-organise the timing of the other applied torques on the fly and produce a new optimal swing (which is what the simulation was allowed to do).

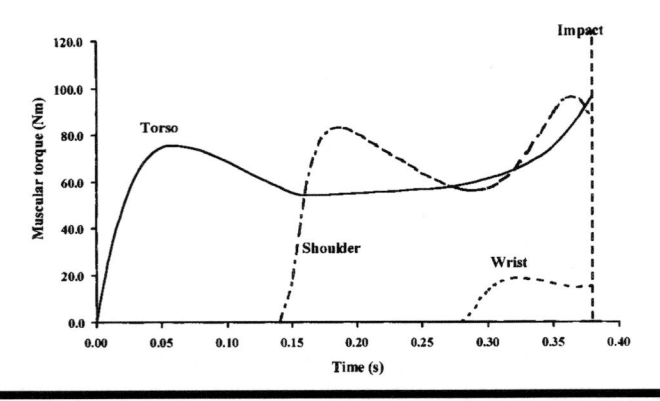

Figure 2
Optimal torque application pattern with three segments and three actuators.

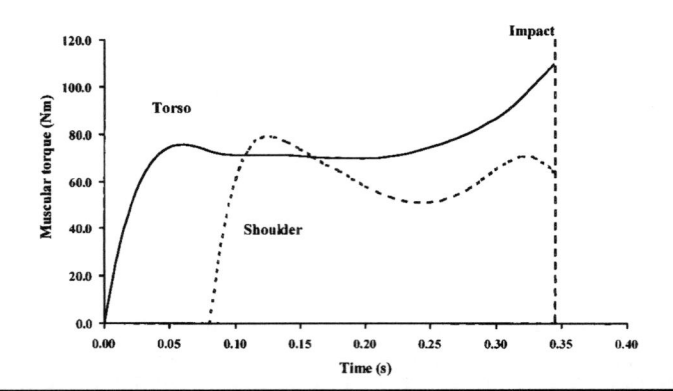

Figure 3
Optimal pattern of torque application when no wrist torque was available.

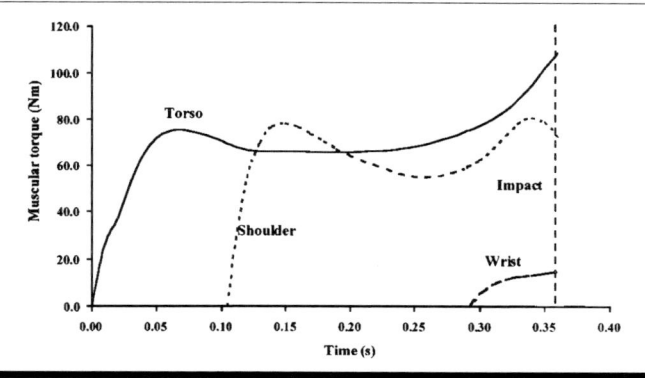

Figure 4
Torque activation patterns when the shoulder torque was applied 50 ms *early* in the downswing.

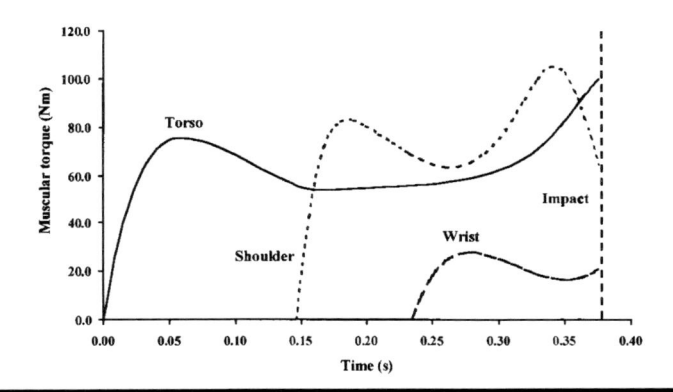

Figure 5
Torque activation patterns when the wrist torque was applied 50 ms *early* in the downswing.

One of the most interesting insights that this simulation study provided related to proximal to distal sequencing of body segment involvement in the swing. In our initial model, we did not include a force-velocity constraint on the torque actuators and we found that the distal torques were turned on very early in the swing. This timing made sense because if the torque is velocity independent then one should apply the torque as soon as possible so that the maximum amount of work can be done. This pattern was not consistent with empirical data collected in our lab (Neal & Wilson, 1985) and thus the inclusion of the velocity constraint was an important modification to our model. It also seems that this characteristic of human muscle (after Hill, 1938) may be the reason that proximal to distal patterns of movement are the ones that have emerged as effective in producing maximum speed at the distal end of a kinematic chain. Specifically for golf, the force-velocity relationship of human muscle dictates that the rotations should proceed distally, commencing with the hips and finishing with the wrists.

While it might well be argued that golf coaches already teach that type of sequencing and that theory has not preceded practice, it is important to realise that understanding why a particular movement pattern is effective is crucial in teaching. Armed with this knowledge, golf coaches can ground their teaching in appropriate theory and explain to their students why particular patterns of movement are better than others.

Empirical and Stochastic Modelling Approaches

As noted earlier in this chapter, there have been a number of authors who have studied the performances of both amateur and professional golfers in an attempt to identify the differences between these groups that allow the professional golfer to perform at such high levels. This approach is very practical and organises performance statistics in a way that logical arguments about differences between players or groups of players can be ascertained. Of course, the shortfall of this approach is that it does not provide alternative approaches for up-and-coming players that may be even better than the approaches used by current-day champions.

Initially a number of scientists used statistical analyses of various performance data made available by the professional golfers' associations around the world to try to discriminate those touring professionals who were the leading money winners from those who lost their touring cards. Interestingly, there were no startling differences between these groups on most of the performance parameters. It seemed that the best players were just slightly better at one part of the game, particularly if they were weak in other aspects. For example, the very accurate drivers of the golf ball hit a lot of greens in regulation, but their putting statistics tended to be worse than their colleagues who were less accurate with their driver and irons. Thus, there appeared no ready formula for success!

Dave Pelz (1999) collected and examined these types of data and was not able to see a pattern emerging that allowed him to conclude that if you had high scores on particular parameters (e.g., greens in regulation) then you could be classed as a very successful touring player. He decided that re-examination of the data and close observation of players needed to be done. Over a number of years, Pelz kept track of the way a number of the touring professionals on the United States PGA Tour performed. He measured (or estimated) a number of variables including driving distance and accuracy, iron play accuracy and consistency, scatter (where balls finished in relation to the intended target), and so forth. After pouring over these data, he came to a number of conclusions about the way in which to measure performance.

His first important notion related to what he termed the Percent Error Index (PEI), which is the ratio of the distance that the ball finishes from the target divided by the distance of the shot, times 100%. That is,

$$\text{PEI} = \frac{\text{Distance away from target}}{\text{Shot distance}} \times 100\% \qquad \text{Equation 2}$$

The PEI allowed him to classify players on their ball-striking ability. The very best players in the world had a PEI of approximately 5%. That is, if they had a 200-m shot, there was a strong probability that the shot would finish, on average, 10 m from the hole. Alternatively, if they only had a 150-m shot, the ball's resting position would be approximately 7.5 m from the target. Although there were small differences between their long, middle and short irons (less than 2%), their relative accuracy did not change much from their driver down through to their 9 iron. There was a startling difference between the PEIs of the full shots and the distance wedges (those shots requiring a less than full swing). For these clubs, the PEIs of the best touring professionals ranged from 13% to 26%. An example of Pelz's data on some touring players is shown in Figure 6.

The data clearly indicated that the shots requiring less than full swings were not hit as accurately (relative to the shot distance) as full shots, but,

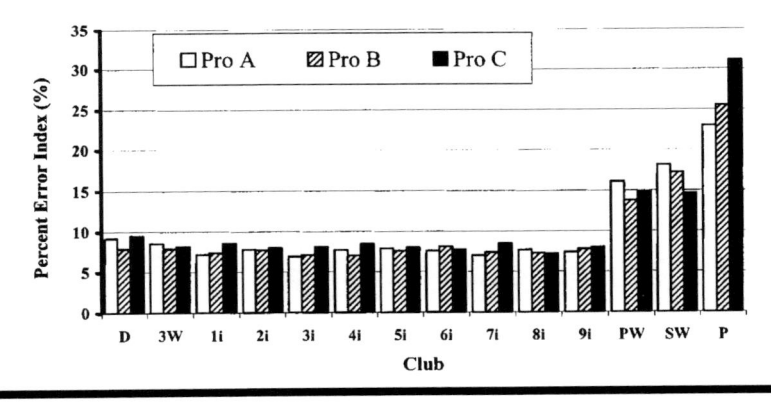

Figure 6
PEIs for three touring professionals (redrawn using data from Pelz, 1999).

more important than this finding was the significant negative correlation between the short-game PEIs and money earned. That is, if your PEI was low for these clubs (but average for the full shots), you could expect to be winning lots of money (and therefore shooting low scores).

The interpretation and thoughtfulness of Pelz must be commended but it is the next phase of the process for which he is due high praise. Pelz has used this research to structure the teaching process that he employs in his clinics and short-game schools. Recently, many teaching professionals, too, have espoused these ideas and developed training regimes based on Pelz's ideas. In a nutshell, he has developed techniques that he believes will help players reduce their PEIs for the short shots in golf, and thereby improve their ability to post low scores (the ultimate performance measure!). He clearly diagnosed that the difficulty with the touch shots was distance control (i.e., the ability to hit the ball a precise distance), and developed training and swing techniques to ameliorate this problem.

The final example that we will use to demonstrate the way in which empirical research has reformed golf practice relates to putting conversion rates. Pelz (1999) collected data on golfers of varying skill levels and developed the putting conversion rate (i.e., the number of putts holed expressed as a percentage of ones attempted) as a function of distance from the hole. These data are illustrated in graphical form in Figure 7.

The message evident from this figure is that unless you consistently hit shots to inside 8 feet (2.4 m), you are more than likely going to miss greater

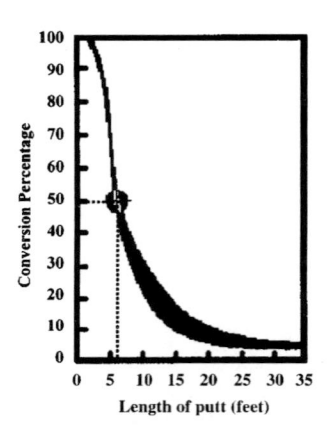

Figure 7

Putting conversion percentage as a function of putt length. From *Dave Pelz's Short Game Bible* (p. 29), by D. Pelz, 1999, New York: Broadway Books. Copyright 1999 by David T. Pelz. Reprinted with permission.

than 50% of your putts. Thus, these data emphasise to the golfer where practice should be directed. Even if you become the very best ball striker in the world, you are unlikely to hit your long, middle and short irons consistently inside 2.4 m. Thus, golf practice needs to be focused on improving the touch shots (pitches and chips) so that you use fewer putting shots. Pelz advocates a particular putting style, and has also developed teaching practices and routines in order to improve players' putting abilities.

Biomechanical Approaches

Biomechanical research has focused on a number of issues relating to the golf swing. We have decided, in this chapter to highlight two issues: the way in which the golf swing is modulated by equipment, and a new notion developed recently in the United States, called the X-Factor Stretch.

While it is evident that club design may not necessarily provide large advantages for the player, appropriate club fitting can have substantial effects on performance. If clubs are not weighted correctly and consistently, are not set at appropriate lie angles, or have inappropriate shafts of incorrect length fitted, performance will be compromised. Some of these effects may be noticeable immediately while others may present themselves later. For example, if incorrectly fitted equipment was used over a long period, swing mechanics may have changed so that ball striking was as effective as if the golfer was using correctly adjusted equipment. However, the altered technique could lead to long-term injury concerns at sites such as the shoulder, wrist and low back.

A recent case study completed by us (Neal & Dalgleish, 2000), showed that a club with a shaft that was 2 inches (5 cm) shorter than optimal length for this golfer, caused the following kinematic swing changes:

With the poorly fitted club, at the top of the backswing, this golfer's hips were 4° and his shoulders were 3° less rotated (i.e., less turn) than with the well-fitted club. Thus, he was unable to turn the hips and shoulders as well when using the short club.[1]

At impact, the hips were 4° and shoulders 3° less open with the badly fitted club compared to the properly fitted club. Because the hips and spine experience more forward flexion with the short club than when using the correct one, the hips and shoulders do not clear the hitting region as well. The reduced range of motion limits the golfer's ability to produce high trunk rotation speeds (and therefore hand and clubhead speeds).

With the poorly fitted club, the hips were 4° more flexed than with the properly fitted club. Furthermore, at impact, with the well-fitted club, the player's spine (the angle between the hips and shoulders) was 8° less flexed than with the badly fitted club.

Thus, even with this simple case analysis, one can see the very important link between technique and equipment. Inappropriately fitted clubs may cause players to adopt techniques that are suboptimal, and ones that may even compromise the integrity of the body. That is, the swing that is used with poorly fitted equipment may lead to soft tissue injury.

The second example of biomechanical research relates to hip and shoulder axial rotations. The term X-Factor was introduced by McLean (1992) to describe the relative rotation of the shoulders with respect to hips during the golf swing, specifically at the top of the backswing. McTeigue, Lamb, Mottram, and Pirozzolo (1994) confirmed McLean's view that a large X-Factor was positively correlated to driving distance when they studied 51 PGA tour professionals and 46 senior PGA tour professionals. They concluded that the long hitters "generated more of the turn" from the X-Factor than the rest of the group and that a large X-Factor at the top of the backswing was the key to generating a large clubhead velocity at impact. Recently, McLean (1996) stated that the separation between the shoulders and the hips during the early downswing was critical in generating clubhead speed. Although this argument seemed logical, it was not until Cheetham, Martin, Mottram, and St. Laurent (2000) completed their biomechanical research, that this idea could be confirmed.

Cheetham et al. (2000) studied the swings of 10 highly skilled golfers (professional or low-handicap amateurs) and 9 less skilled golfers (handicap 15 or higher). Three-dimensional motion of the shoulders and hips was determined using an electromagnetic tracking system and the X-Factor (difference between hip and shoulder rotation) was determined throughout the swing. Discrete values were extracted at the top of the backswing, as well as the maximum value during the downswing.

Statistical analysis indicated that the X-Factor Stretch was significantly greater for the highly skilled golfers than the less skilled golfers. Mean values highlighted that the highly skilled golfers had a 19% increase in the X-Factor due to the stretch at the beginning of the downswing and the less skilled players increased their X-Factor by only 13%.

Biomechanical research has shown that active stretching of muscle (i.e., eccentric muscle contraction) can increase the force of contraction during the concentric phase (Gowitzke & Milner, 1988; Nordin & Frankel, 1989). Although the underlying mechanism responsible for this observation is still not known, various factors mitigate its effect. The speed of the eccentric contraction, the length of the stretch, and the delay (if any) between the eccentric and concentric phases have all been shown to modulate the effect. From the golfer's perspective, it is not particularly important to know what causes the phenomenon but it is important to know how to take advantage of it.

The term *X-Factor Stretch* was coined to describe how much the X-Factor increases during the initial part of the downswing. It is suspected that a large X-Factor Stretch will be highly (positively) correlated to clubhead speed. Since the motion of the hips and shoulders in opposite directions causes the muscles of the torso that rotate these body parts to be highly stretched, they must contract eccentrically at the start of the downswing. The increased level of force in these muscles at this time should allow them to increase the amount of work that they do during their concentric phases (cf. van Ingen Schenau, Bobbert, & de Haan, 1997).

From a coaching perspective, these research findings are very important. If players, by increasing their X-Factor Stretch, are able to increase the forces in the muscles of the trunk, then they should, assuming all other aspects remain the same, be able to increase the clubhead speed. Alternatively, by using these proximal muscles to their maximum, the contribution of the hands can be reduced, thereby providing a mechanism to increase the consistency of ball striking. While these ideas are logical and consistent, further research is required to evaluate their efficacy.

Conclusions

This chapter illustrates the way in which research and development has influenced golf performance, the understanding of the mechanics of the golf swing, and how these two issues, in turn, have impacted on teaching golf. Research can be of many and varied forms. We have highlighted, through computer modelling, how independent research can assess the efficacy of marketing claims of manufacturers. Evaluating the available hard data, we found little evidence to support the notion that very expensive, high-tech golf clubs have made a large impact on driving distance and accuracy. On the other hand, systematic tracking of performances (Pelz, 1999) has led to improved understanding of shot quality and performance for all the clubs from driver to putter. This work has led to an altered philosophy and way of teaching the short (less than full-swing) shots. Finally, biomechanical research has demonstrated that equipment can influence swing mechanics and has helped us to understand why particular movement patterns are advantageous. For example, we recognise the importance of having a large differential between the shoulder and hip rotations during the backswing. Stretching these muscles while they actively contract (eccentric contractions) allows them to develop high levels of force when they shorten. These increased forces applied over a large distance increase the work output of the muscles, and therefore the energy that can be transferred to the club.

As scientists, we would like to believe that systematic analysis of golfers and their swings has led to changes in practice and performance over the last

25 years. In truth, golf-interested scientists have served in an advisory capacity of providing explanations as to why a particular change actually worked, or whether a product is likely to provide the promised benefits. However, after examining the scientific literature, it appears as though golfers and their coaches, as well as equipment manufacturers appear to be the people who have led the revolution of change in golf. This is not a criticism but simply a statement of what has transpired to date.

Footnotes

1   The more that the hips and spine are in forward flexion, the less one is able to rotate about the long axis of the spine. Thus, with the short club, the hips are flexed and so too is the spine, to a greater extent than with the long club. Thus, axial rotation is reduced with the short club.

References

Alexander, R. McN. (1990). Optimum take-off techniques for high and long jumps. *Philosophical Transactions of the Royal Society of London, 329*, 3–10.

Cheetham, P.J., Martin, P.E., Mottram, R.E., & St. Laurent, B.F. (2000). The importance of stretching the "X-Factor" in the downswing of golf: The "X-Factor Stretch." *Proceedings of the 2000 Pre-Olympic Congress.* Brisbane, Australia: International Congress on Sport Science, Sports Medicine and Physical Education.

Gowitzke, B.A., & Milner, M. (1988). *Scientific bases of human movement* (3rd ed.). Baltimore, MD: Williams and Wilkins.

Hill, A.V. (1938). The heat of shortening and the dynamic constants of muscle. *Proceedings of the Royal Society of London, B76*, 136–195.

Hogan, B. (1957). *Modern fundamentals of golf.* London: Nicholas Kaye.

Johnson, S.H., & Hubbell, J.E. (1999). Golf ball rebound enhancement. In M.R. Farrally & A.J. Cochran (Eds.), *Science and golf III: Proceedings of the 1998 World Scientific Congress of Golf* (pp. 493–499). Champaign, IL: Human Kinetics.

Jorgensen, T. P. (1999). *The physics of golf* (2nd ed.). New York: Springer-Verlag.

McLean, J. (1992, December). Widen the gap. *Golf Magazine*, 49–53.

McLean, J. (1996). *The X-Factor swing.* New York: Harper Collins.

McTeigue, M., Lamb, S. R., Mottram, R., & Pirozzolo, F. (1994). Spine and hip motion analysis during the golf swing. In A.J. Cochran & M.R. Farrally (Eds.), *Science and golf II: Proceedings of the 1994 World Scientific Congress of Golf* (pp. 50–58). London: E & FN Spon.

Neal, R.J., & Dalgleish, M.J. (2000, August). *Does club fitting change swing mechanics? A case study.* Technical report to Henry Griffitts Australia.

Neal, R.J., & Sprigings, E.J. (1999). Optimal golf swing kinetics and kinematics. In C. Dillman, B. Elliott, & T. Ackland (Eds.), *Proceedings of the 5th IOC World Congress on Sport Science* (p. 32). Sydney: Sports Medicine Australia.

Neal, R.J., & Wilson, B.D. (1985). 3D kinematics and kinetics of the golf swing. *International Journal of Sport Biomechanics, 1*, 221–232.

Niku, S., & Henderson, J. (1985). Determination of the parameters for an athetotic arm model. *Journal of Biomechanics, 18*, 209–215.

Nordin, M., & Frankel, V.H. (1989). *Basic biomechanics of the musculoskeletal system* (2nd ed.). Philadelphia: Lea and Febiger.

Pandy, M., Zajac, F., Sim, E., & Levine, W. (1990). An optimal control model for maximum-height human jumping. *Journal of Biomechanics, 23*, 1185–1198.

Pelz, D. (1999). *Dave Pelz's short game bible: Master the finesse swing and lower your score.* New York: Broadway Books.

Sprigings, E. (1986). Simulation of the force enhancement phenomenon in muscle. *Computers in Biology and Medicine, 16,* 423–430.

Sprigings, E.J., & Neal, R.J. (2000). An insight into the importance of wrist torque in driving the golf ball: A simulation study. *Journal of Applied Biomechanics,* 16, 356–366.

Sprigings, E.J., & Neal, R.J. (in press). Shifting a portion of the club shaft's mass distally: Does it improve performance? *Sports Engineering.*

van Ingen Schenau, G.J., Bobbert, M.F., & de Haan, A. (1997). Does elastic energy enhance work and efficiency in the stretch-shorten cycle? *Journal of Applied Biomechanics, 13,* 389–415.

CHAPTER 14

The Importance of Stretching the "X-Factor" in the Downswing of Golf: The "X-Factor Stretch"

Phillip J. Cheetham, Philip E. Martin, Robert E. Mottram, and Bryan F. St. Laurent

---

The term X-Factor was coined by John Andrisani of Golf Magazine and was introduced by Jim McLean in a Golf Magazine article titled *Widen the Gap* (McLean, 1992). It was used to describe the relative rotation of shoulders with respect to hips during the golf swing, specifically at the top of the backswing. His article was based on the research done by Mike McTeigue of Sport Sense Inc. (Mountain View, CA) using a measurement device called the Swing Motion Trainer. After analysing tour professionals they found the bigger the rotational difference between the hips and the shoulders, the longer the drives. In his article titled *X-Factor 2: Closing the Gap* McLean (1993) concluded that it was not only important to have a large X-Factor at the top of the backswing but also important to close it very rapidly during the downswing.

McTeigue et al. (1994) studied 51 PGA tour professionals and 46 senior PGA tour professionals and concluded that the long hitters "generated more of the turn" from the X-Factor than the rest of the group. So it was concluded that a large X-Factor at the top of the backswing was key in generating a large clubhead velocity at impact, provided of course that the rest of the swing mechanics are intact. McTeigue et al. also concluded that the majority of tour players begin the downswing with the hips leading the shoulders. They concluded, "Approximately 70 percent of Tour players rotate their hips first in the downswing." They did not, however, go on to quantify how much the hips lead the shoulders at the beginning of the downswing, and how the X-Factor changes early in the downswing.

The initiation of an athletic motion by the rotation of the body's larger proximal segments (hips and shoulders) followed progressively by the more distal segments (arms) has been reported in several sports. It has been recognised in baseball (Hay, 1993), tennis (Marshall & Elliott, 2000) and soccer (Putnam, 1993; Robertson & Mosher, 1985). This has been termed proximal-to-distal sequencing (Bunn, 1972; Kreighbaum & Barthels, 1985; Marshall & Elliott, 2000; Putnam, 1993; Robertson & Mosher, 1985) and the "kinetic link principle" (Kreighbaum & Barthels, 1985). In the golf swing, the hips leading the downswing is just the beginning phase of this sequence.

Parks and Price (1999), from research conducted by GolfTEC Inc. (Denver, CO) on both PGA and Nike tour professionals using the SkillTec 3D-Golf™ system, recommended that, "In order to develop the most efficient X-Factor, you need to limit the rotation of your hips and maximise the rotation of your shoulders." They were referring to the X-Factor at the top of the backswing but did not progress to discuss what happens to the X-Factor early in the downswing. Recently, however, several golf instructors have recommended that the rotational separation between hips and shoulders should increase on the downswing (Hogan, 2000; Leadbetter, 2000; McLean, 1996), but this increase has not been quantified.

The purpose of this study was to quantify the X-Factor's increase on the downswing. Specifically we tested the hypotheses that highly skilled golfers have a higher X-Factor at the top of the backswing (as found by McTeigue et al., 1994), and also have a greater increase in X-Factor early in the downswing than less skilled golfers. We term this increase the "X-Factor Stretch" and consider it to be at least as important as the X-Factor itself.

Methods

Multiple swings of 10 highly skilled golfers and 9 less skilled golfers were captured using the SkillTec 3D-Golf™ system (see Figure 1). The less skilled players all had a handicap of 15 or higher. The highly skilled players included eight playing professionals with handicaps of 0 or better, one long-drive champion, and one highly ranked collegiate player.

The SkillTec 3D-Golf™ system is comprised of the Fastrak (Polhemus Inc., Colchester, VT) electromagnetic tracking system, and the Skill Technologies' motion capture and analysis software. Electromagnetic tracking systems have been found to be accurate for quantification of human

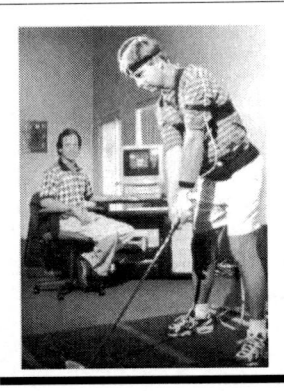

Figure 1
PGA professional golfer Brandel Chamblee being analysed by the SkillTec 3D-Golf™ system.

motion in many different applications (An et al., 1988; Bull et al., 1998; Johnson & Anderson, 1990; Mannon et al., 1997). The tracking system works on an electromagnetic sensing principle (Raab et al., 1979). There is a 2-inch cubic transmitter that has three perpendicular coils. Each coil transmits an electromagnetic signal. This transmitter is used as the global reference frame. Each half-inch cubic sensor also has three coils, and each coil receives the corresponding signal from the transmitter and computes position (x, y, z) and orientation (bend, tilt, twist) of each sensor in realtime. Each sensor is used as a local reference frame for the segment to which it is attached. The golfer's body is transparent to the electromagnetic field and so there are never any missing data samples. From these sensor measurements a virtual-reality, three-dimensional model of the golfer is displayed and the dynamics of the golf swing are calculated, including segment and joint positions, angles, speeds and accelerations.

For this study a sensor harness was used to place sensors on the posterior aspect of the golfer's pelvis, back at T3, forehead, and back of left hand (see Figure 1). All the golfers were right handed and all swings were with a 5 iron. An initial neutral standing position of the golfer was taken before any swings were captured. The golf swing was sampled at a rate of 30 Hz. This sample rate is adequate since only the sensors on the pelvis and back, in the vicinity of the top of the backswing, were used in the calculations. A fourth-order Butterworth digital filter with a cut-off frequency of 12 Hz was used to smooth the position and orientation data. X-Factor was computed as the difference between the rotational position of the pelvis and T3 sensors at all points during the swing.

X-Factor values at the top of the backswing and the X-Factor maximum in the downswing were extracted and averaged over each golfer's swings. To test the hypothesis that highly skilled golfers have a higher X-Factor at the top of the backswing than less skilled golfers, we performed a contrast of the means of each group at this position. To examine the X-Factor trends more broadly and to test the hypothesis that the highly skilled golfers have a greater increase in X-Factor early in the downswing than less skilled golfers, we conducted a two-factor ANOVA. This allowed us to compare the effects of skill level (highly skilled and less skilled) and swing position (top and max) on the X-Factor.

Results

X-Factor trends are shown in Figure 2. On average the highly skilled golfers showed a 19% increase in the X-Factor due to the stretch at the beginning of the downswing and the less skilled only a 13% increase. This difference between groups is supported by a significant interaction of skill level and swing position found using a two-factor ANOVA. This showed that the X-Factor Stretch was significantly greater for the highly skilled golfers than the less skilled golfers, $F(1, 17) = 6.90$, $p = .02$. This supported our hypothesis that highly skilled golfers have a greater increase in the X-Factor early in the downswing (X-Factor Stretch) than less skilled golfers. Further, the results of a direct contrast of the X-Factor means at the top of the backswing showed them not to be significantly different between groups, $t = 1.02$, $p = .33$. This disagrees with our hypothesis that highly skilled golfers have a higher X-Factor at the top of the backswing. These two results suggest that the X-Factor Stretch is more important to an effective swing than simply the X-Factor at the top of the backswing.

The two-factor ANOVA also revealed other relationships. When the X-Factor means were collapsed across swing position (averaged for both top and max for all highly skilled and then again for all less skilled), the resulting mean in the highly skilled golfers was 11% higher than the mean of less skilled golfers but this difference was not statistically significant, $F(1, 17) = 1.93$, $p = .18$. Finally, when the X-Factor means were collapsed across skill level (averaged for both highly skilled and less skilled for the top of the backswing and then again for maximum), the resulting mean at the maximum was 16% higher than the mean at the top of the backswing. This difference was statistically significant, $F(1, 17) = 131.57$, $p < .001$. This shows that both highly skilled and less skilled golfers exhibited an X-Factor Stretch. So even the less skilled golfers did in fact increase their X-Factor somewhat at the beginning of the downswing.

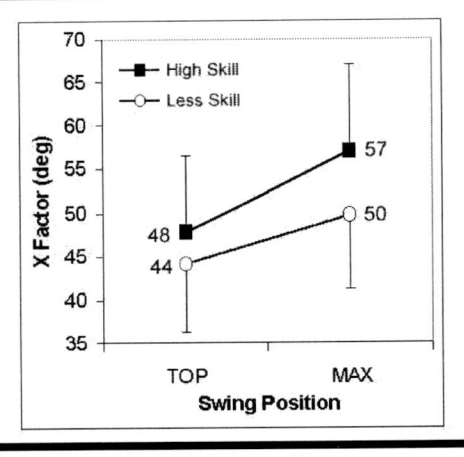

[Figure 2: Graph showing X-Factor (deg) on y-axis (range 35-70) versus Swing Position on x-axis (TOP, MAX). High Skill line rises from 48 at TOP to 57 at MAX. Less Skill line rises from 44 at TOP to 50 at MAX. Error bars shown at each point.]

Figure 2
X-Factor means as a function of swing position for highly skilled and less skilled golfers. The means can be seen to be larger for the highly skilled golfers in both positions, but more so at max.

Discussion

In order to illuminate the differences in the X-Factor Stretch, we will extract two extreme example swings, one from each skill level, and discuss them. Figures 3 and 4 show graphs of the X-Factor throughout the swing for the less skilled golfer and the highly skilled golfer and the models at two points, top of the backswing and maximum X-Factor. The vertical lines mark address (A), top of the backswing (T), impact (I) and finish (F). The X-axis is time and the Y-axis is X-Factor in degrees. The negative direction represents a closed X-Factor, that is, the shoulders are rotated more away from the target than the hips. Two models are shown in each figure, at the positions of top of the backswing and maximum X-Factor. The corresponding X-Factor values are labeled in the graphs.

Figure 3 shows the two positions of a less skilled player. At the top he has an X-Factor of 38.0 degrees. On his downswing he only stretches this to a max of 38.5 degrees, giving an X-Factor Stretch of only 0.5 degrees. In other words his hips and shoulders rotated down virtually together early in the downswing. This is shown by the flat spot on the curve between the top and max.

Figure 4 shows the two positions of a highly skilled player. At the top he has an X-Factor of 60.1 degrees. On the downswing he stretches his X-Factor to 73.5 degrees, an X-Factor Stretch of 13.4 degrees. In the early stage of his downswing his hips have rotated significantly faster than his shoulders

THE "X-FACTOR STRETCH"

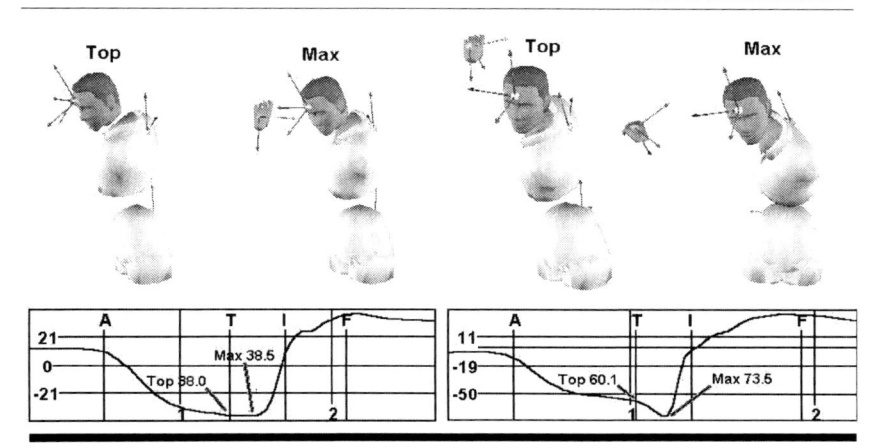

Figures 3 & 4
The less skilled golfer and the highly skilled golfer.

causing a stretch in the torso of 13.4 degrees. This is shown by the rapid change in the graph between the top and max.

For most highly skilled golfers just prior to the transition from the backswing to the downswing, the pelvis slows down and changes direction to rotate forward while the upper body continues to rotate backwards (See Figure 5). This head start of the pelvis moving towards the ball causes an increase in the stretch of the large and powerful rotating muscles of the trunk. Early on in the downswing, the pelvis has a higher rotational velocity than the upper body and so will "outrun" the upper body toward the ball. Because of this initially higher velocity of the pelvis, the X-Factor increases, and in some highly skilled golfers it grew by as much as 15 degrees.

Research has shown that extra stretch on muscle, and active resistance to this stretch, can increase the force of contraction of muscle (Gowitzke & Milner, 1988; Nordin & Frankel, 1989). Several mechanisms are responsible for this. A rapid rotation of the pelvis early in the downswing may trigger sensitive stretch receptors (called muscle spindles) in the muscles to quickly shorten the muscle. Therefore, as the hips initially rotate forward toward the ball, the maximally stretched rotational muscles of the trunk respond by a faster and more forceful contraction. A second mechanism relates to stored elastic energy in the muscles. The opposing directions of the shoulders and hips at the top of the backswing will stretch the torso muscle facilitating storage and finally release of elastic energy. The end result is that the X-Factor Stretch increases the force production on the downswing, facilitating greater clubhead speed at impact.

Figure 5
For an instant at the beginning of the downswing the pelvis rotates forwards into the downswing while the upper body continues to rotate backwards.

Conclusion

After contrasting the X-Factor at the top of the backswing and at its maximum early in the downswing for highly skilled and less skilled golfers, we found that the X-Factor at the top of the backswing was not significantly larger for the highly skilled players than less skilled players. We also found that both highly skilled and less skilled golfers did significantly increase their X-Factor early in the downswing. They did not immediately begin to rapidly close the X-Factor. Finally, we found that this stretch of the X-Factor early in the downswing was significantly greater for the highly skilled golfers than less skilled golfers. This suggests that the X-Factor Stretch is more important to an effective swing than simply the X-Factor at the top of the backswing, and that the X-Factor should actually increase early in the downswing before it rapidly decreases to impact. This research also indicates that the aim of the backswing is not just to put the golfer in the correct position for the downswing, but also to dynamically tension the torso muscles correctly to allow them to contract maximally during the downswing, hence generating optimum power.

Acknowledgments

The authors would like to thank Brandel Chamblee for his cooperation and participation in this study and Jason Bodine for taking the photographs. This chapter was awarded a place in GOLF Magazine's inaugural Science in Golf Prize, conducted in conjunction with the World Scientific Congress of Golf Trust, and is reproduced with permission.

References

An, K.N., Jacobsen, M.C., Berglund, L.J., & Chao, E.Y.S. (1988). Application of a magnetic tracking device to kinesiologic studies. *Journal of Biomechanics, 21,* 613–20.

Bull, A.M.J., Berkshire, F.H., & Amis, A.A. (1998). Accuracy of an electromagnetic device and application to the measurement and description of knee joint motion. *Proceedings of Institute of Mechanical Engineers, 212,* 347–355.

Bunn, J. (1972). *Scientific principles of coaching.* Englewood Cliffs, NJ: Prentice Hall.

Gowitzke, B.A., & Milner, M. (1988). *Scientific bases of human movement* (3rd ed.). Baltimore: Williams and Wilkins.

Hay, J.G. (1993). *The biomechanics of sports techniques* (4th ed.). Englewood Cliffs, NJ: Prentice Hall.

Hogan, B. (2000, July). Golf Digest 50 greatest golfers of all time and what they taught us. In G. Yocum (Ed.), *Golf Digest,* 93.

Johnson, G.R., & Anderson, J.M. (1990). Measurement of three-dimensional shoulder movement by an electromagnetic sensor. *Clinical Biomechanics, 5,* 131–136.

Kreighbaum, E., & Barthels, K.M. (1985). *Biomechanics — A qualitative approach for studying human movement.* Minneapolis, MI: Burgess.

Leadbetter, D. (2000, August). Let me help you hit it farther, straighter, closer. *Golf Digest,* 73–79.

Mannon, K., Anderson, T., Cheetham, P., Cornwall, M.W., & McPoil, T.G. (1997). A comparison of two motion analysis systems for the measurement of two-dimensional rearfoot motion during walking. *Foot and Ankle, 18,* 63–75.

Marshall, R.N., & Elliott, B.C. (2000). Long-axis rotation: The missing link in proximal-to-distal segment sequencing. *Journal of Sports Sciences, 18,* 247–254.

McLean, J. (1992, December). Widen the gap. *Golf Magazine,* 49–53.

McLean, J. (1993, August). X Factor 2: closing the gap. *Golf Magazine,* 28–32.

McLean, J. (1996). *The X-Factor Swing.* New York: Harper Collins.

McTeigue, M., Lamb, S. R., Mottram, R., & Pirozzolo, F. (1994). Spine and hip motion analysis during the golf swing. In A.J. Cochran & M.R. Farrally (Eds.), *Science and golf II: Proceedings of the 1994 World Scientific Congress of Golf* (pp. 50–58). London: E & FN Spon.

Nordin, M., & Frankel, V.H. (1989). *Basic biomechanics of the musculoskeletal system* (2nd ed.). Philadelphia: Lea and Febiger.

Parks, J., & Price, J. (1999, December). X-Factor: An efficient X-Factor for more power and accuracy. *Golf Tips Magazine,* 36–41.

Putnam, C.A. (1993). Sequential motions of body segments in striking and throwing skills: Descriptions and explanations. *Journal of Biomechanics, 26,* 125–135.

Raab, F.H., Blood, E.B., Steiner, T.O., & Jones, H.R. (1979). Magnetic position and orientation tracking system. *IEEE Transactions on Aerospace Electronic Systems, AES-15*(5), 709–718.

Robertson, D.G.E., & Mosher, R.E. (1985). Work and power of the leg muscles in soccer kicking. In D.A. Winter, R.W. Norman, R.P. Wells, K.C. Hayes, & A.E. Patla (Eds.), *International Series on Biomechanics, Biomechanics IX-B* (pp. 533–538). Champaign, IL: Human Kinetics.

CHAPTER 15

Swing Technique Change and Adjunctive Exercises in the Treatment of Wrist Pain in a Golfer: A Case Report

Michael J. Dalgleish, Bill Vicenzino, and Robert J. Neal

Over recent years, biomechanical analysis of the golf swing has led sports medicine and sports science professionals to proffer an ideal technique. The focus has been on understanding those anatomical alignments that create reduced physical stress in load-bearing structures, while still providing the potential for optimal performance. This is borne out of the premise that all athletes have a desire to perform near their maximum while not compromising their longevity.

This chapter outlines the treatment of an elite golfer who had left-wrist pain that caused him to withdraw from the Professional Golfers' Association of Australia (PGA) Tour for 14 months. Clinical examination of the wrist injury and elucidation of the mechanism of injury proved enlightening. Importantly it was the establishment of the link between presumably long-term technique flaws and predisposition to the wrist injury that ultimately led to effective intervention. As a basis for explaining the treatment approach taken with this golf player, this chapter describes the salient features of the clinical interview, the physical examination, and the analysis of the data derived from the examination which is interpreted in light of current knowledge of the golf swing and wrist injuries.

Clinical Interview

The male golfer presented to our clinic in July 1999 and described his major concern as wrist pain that was worse over the ulnar aspect. On occasions he also experienced pain over the dorsal/ventral, radial aspect of the wrist. The pain was provoked when pushing up from a sitting or lying position on the ground. The pain was not present at rest but could be intermittently provoked by squeezing the carpal bones with his other hand, hitting golf balls, pushing up from a chair, and by placing the hands on the hips with the fingers spread. At worst he rated his pain as 6 on a 10-point visual analogue scale for pain where a score of 10 is the most severe pain imaginable.

There was no elbow, forearm or shoulder pain, nor paraesthesia or numbness in the upper limbs. There was some mild left-side cervical and thoracic soreness over the previous 18 months but this did not appear to be related to the original injury or the wrist pain — rather it appeared to be related to a change in mattress.

The player's history highlighted a single episode of left-wrist pain at 16 years of age when he sprained the wrist following a fall onto an outstretched arm. He was able to play a junior tournament, in pain, but with the wrist strapped. The pain subsided over 3 weeks. He was left with no residual symptoms following that injury.

The recent injury, for which treatment was being sought, occurred during a routine swing with the driver in May 1997 while playing a PGA Tour event. The shot did not involve the taking of a divot or even contact with the ground. Pain was felt on the dorsal/ventral radial side of the wrist 1 centimetre distal to the radial styloid. The pain was reported as sharp and deep as it was not palpable. The pain did not recur during that round. At that stage slight pain could be reproduced with circumferential pressure to the carpal bones.

The symptoms became increasingly pronounced over the next 10 weeks at which time a chiropractor diagnosed tendonitis. Rest was recommended but not heeded. On returning home, pain was experienced two to three times per round. The golfer was playing at least 4 days per week. A sports general practitioner was consulted and a plain film was taken and showed no abnormality. Physiotherapy treatment was commenced and included carpal mobilisation and wrist strengthening. Strengthening exercises were completed over 4 weeks up to the Tour Qualifying School. The symptoms appeared to be resolving until they were exacerbated by practice on a hard surface prior to Tour School. The player then attempted to play in the Tour School qualifying rounds but was forced to withdraw during the second round. Pain was being experienced with every shot. A single dose of oral corticosteroid medication the previous night had decreased the pain prior to playing the second round. At this time the pain had progressed to involve the proximal ulnar side of the wrist and caused the dorsum of the hand to ache down to the level of the metacarpophalangeal joints.

Subsequently, the golfer rested for 4 months. He attempted to play on 15 occasions during 1998. The symptoms were decreased but still evident particularly with the driver. He recommenced practising in April 1999, but pain was experienced with every shot by June 1999 when he attempted a return to competition. He consulted a sports physician who requested further x-rays and an ultrasound that showed no abnormality. He was referred to a golf specialist physiotherapist (MD) for assessment and treatment.

Physical Examination

Observation revealed a fit, 28-year-old male in excellent health. There was no obvious swelling over the wrist or hand. Active movement was pain-free except at the end of ulnar deviation. There was a slight loss of range into extension and ulnar deviation. Grip strength testing on a dynamometer demonstrated symmetry between left and right sides to within 10%. Manual muscle testing revealed a relative weakness of radial deviation on the left side compared to the right.

Examination with specific stress tests for the wrist region revealed signs consistent with a general synovitis of the region (LaStayo & Howell, 1995; Skirven, 1996). The original radial-side pain was reproduced with passive gliding of the scapho-trapezium joint. There was some sensitivity to palpation of the peri-scaphoid structures, however the scaphoid shift test was negative. The ulnar-side pain was evoked with testing of the triangular fibrocartilage complex and the distal radio-ulnar joint. The distal radio-ulnar joint exhibited some laxity and joint crepitus. No evidence of ganglion could be found on the clinical examination.

In addition to the conventional clinical evaluation, the golfer's current swing technique was evaluated from video footage. Particular note was taken of the position at address, swing path and the impact position. At address, the golfer stood with his hands elevated and forward, placing the left wrist in flexion and ulnar deviation. This posture places the major extension-producing muscles of the wrist, especially extensor carpi radialis brevis, in a weak position (Lieber & Friden, 1998; McCarthy, 1999). During takeaway, the golfer took the club away vertically and finished across the line at the end of the backswing. The natural motion of the torso from this position is to come over the top with the right shoulder and arm, resulting in a sharply descending blow (characterised by deep divots). In an effort to prevent this outside-to-in swing path, the player's wrists were dropped inside the target line (at the start of the downswing) and the left wrist was bowed. At impact, the amount of compensatory left-wrist extension was large. A sweeping action, where the ball was picked off the turf, was evident as the player attempted to minimise the stress on the wrist at contact. Upon further questioning, the golfer clarified that his impact position had been altered in an attempt to limit the original (radial) wrist pain. This movement involved rapid extension of the left wrist and supination of the forearm immediately following impact. A crossover of the forearms early in follow-through characterised this motion.

Analysis: Wrist Pain in Golfers and Swing Technique

The risk of wrist injury in golf, especially the left hand, is reasonably high as it occurs in 26.7% and 20.1% of professional and amateur male golfers, respectively (Barton, 1997; Cahalan, Cooney, Tamai, & Chao, 1991; McCarroll, 1986; McCarroll & Gioe, 1982; Murray & Cooney, 1996; Sherman & Finch, 1997). A number of risk factors have been identified. For example, the high frequency of practice has been linked with the occurrence of overuse injuries. Hitting objects other than the ball such as the ground, inadequate warm-up procedures, and poor swing mechanics have also been implicated (Cahalan et al., 1991; McCarroll, 1986). With regards to swing technique, it is generally agreed that optimal technique meets the goals of maximum performance and minimal injury risk. Optimal swing technique implies minimal variation from the ideal pattern of movement. It is generally regarded that any significant variation from this optimal swing results in a higher risk of injury (James, 1995; Kohn, 1996; McCarroll, 1986; Stover & Mallon, 1992), although this has yet to be proven (Mallon & Hawkins, 1994; Stover & Mallon, 1992). Correction of swing mechanics, which includes addressing all body segments from the foot up, has been advocated as a means by which to ameliorate acute and chronic golfing injuries (McCarroll, 1986; Pietrocarlo, 1996).

Treatment Program

Following examination and the analysis of the findings in light of current knowledge of swing technique and injuries in golf, it was decided that the golfer should return to his coach with the recommendation that his impact position and swing path be reviewed. Crucially, this request would only be fulfilled if it proved consistent with the desired technical direction of the coach and golfer, which in this case it was. In addition to the technical advice, the golfer was instructed in the use of supportive taping and a resting splint (Prosser, 1995). The golfer was advised to employ these devices when he returned to practice on a daily basis. The role of strengthening for wrist and forearm muscles was discussed with the golfer.

Initial intervention by the coach was to alter the address position. This change was followed by a flatter takeaway and wider angle of attack to the ball. The change in swing technique involved an increase in trunk rotation. This was supplemented with swing-technique-specific stretching exercises devised by the therapist and coach. Within 1 week of daily practice, hitting approximately 100 balls per day, the pain was not being experienced during most practice drills and only occurred on two occasions when using a driver. Practice was increased slowly and supplemented with golf-specific posture exercises devised by the therapist as well as specific technique drills by the coach.

A review 6 weeks after presentation revealed a marked reduction in pain on all tests. Pain was reported as less than 1 on the 10-point visual analogue scale for self-reported pain intensity. Only scapho-trapezial gliding and triangular fibro-cartilage complex load tests were reported as mildly symptom provocative as opposed to strongly provocative at the initial examination. On a daily basis, the golfer reported an awareness of his wrist but was able to practise unimpeded. He hoped to regain his playing card at the Tour School in October.

Discussion

Three distinct features appear to characterise this injured golfer's presentation. Firstly, the initial trauma to the left wrist during adolescence may have left him with some residual painless joint problem. Secondly, the technique analysis highlighted a steep vertical takeaway, an inside-to-out swing path to impact and a bowed left wrist at impact. Repetition of this movement could result in irritation and eventual synovitis of the peri-scaphoid and distal radio-ulnar joint tissues. Thirdly, it is postulated that in an attempt to limit the pain, the golfer may have altered his impact and follow-through position such that the wrist underwent rapid left-wrist extension, ulnar deviation and forearm supination. This action created the crossover position previously described. The resultant repeated compression and shear within the distal radio-ulnar joint and triangular fibro-cartilage complex could have produced the more recent ulnar-side symptoms.

The intervention, a change in swing technique and adjunct exercises, was associated with a resolution of a chronic problem, probably as a result of altered stresses at the wrist joint and soft tissues. The alteration in stresses allowed the resumption of pain-free playing. With subthreshold stress on the irritable structures, the golfer was able to gradually return to golf.

Conclusion

The purpose of this case study was to highlight an unusual therapeutic intervention strategy in the treatment of a golfer with wrist pain. The case reported here involved a touring professional who was unable to compete for 14 months. For the clinician, a knowledge of optimal swing mechanics, the anatomical structures involved, and the likely progression of the pathology were important factors in the treatment of this player. A change to the swing technique, promotion of a rotational action of his trunk, hip and shoulder, an approach to the ball in line with the target, a neutral wrist position, and reduced supination of the left wrist led to excellent ball striking without pain. The player's coach assumed a critical role in the re-education of this player's swing technique and hence in the treatment program.

This type of presentation is not uncommon at any sports-specific clinic. Physiotherapy treatment would commonly involve a poly-modality approach including, for example, manual therapy, taping, splinting and therapeutic exercise. However, understanding the key aspects of the swing technique that would limit stress to the left wrist was paramount to effective therapeutic intervention for this golfer. This case highlights the need to know the sport from all perspectives including technically, physiologically and anatomically so that due consideration is given to sport-specific technique. With this knowledge, the consulting sports health care professional will prove to be valuable to both the coach and the athlete.

References

Barton, N. (1997). Sports injuries of the hand. *British Journal of Sports Medicine, 31,* 191–196.

Cahalan, T.D., Cooney, W.P., Tamai, K., & Chao, E.Y.S. (1991). Biomechanics of the golf swing in players with pathologic conditions of the forearm, wrist and hand. *American Journal of Sports Medicine, 19*(3), 288–293.

James, T. (1995, December). Weakness in the shoulder. *Australian Doctor,* 50.

Kohn, H.S. (1996). Prevention of and treatment of elbow injuries in golf. *Clinics of Sports Medicine, 15,* 65–81.

LaStayo, P., & Howell, J. (1995, January–March). Clinical provocative tests used in evaluating wrist pain: A descriptive study. *Journal of Hand Therapy,* 10–17.

Lieber, R.L., & Friden, J. (1998). Musculoskeletal balance of the human wrist elucidated using intraoperative laser diffraction. *Journal of Electromyography and Kinesiology, 8,* 93–100.

McCarroll, J.R. (1986). Golf: Common injuries from a supposedly benign activity. *Journal of Musculoskeletal Medicine, 6,* 9–16.

McCarroll, J.R. (1994). Golf. In F.H. & D.A. Stone (Eds.), *Sports injuries: Mechanisms, prevention, treatment.* Baltimore, MD: Williams and Wilkins.

McCarroll, J.R., & Gioe, T.J. (1982). Professional golfers and the price they pay. *Physician and Sports Medicine, 10,* 64–70.

McCarthy, A. (1999). *The relationship between extensor carpi radialis brevis and tennis elbow.* Assignment for HM863 — Masters in Physiotherapy Studies (Sports). Brisbane, Australia: University of Queensland.

Mallon, W.J., & Hawkins, R.J. (1994). Injuries in golf. In P.A.F.H. Renstrom (Ed.), *Clinical practice of sports injury prevention and care. Vol 5 Encyclopedia of sports medicine.* Oxford: Blackwell Scientific Publications.

Murray, P.M., & Cooney, W.P. (1996). Golf induced injuries of the wrist. *Clinics in Sports Medicine, 15,* 85–109.

Pietrocarlo, T.A. (1996). Foot and ankle considerations in golf. *Clinics in Sports Medicine, 15,* 129–146.

Prosser, R. (1995). Conservative management of ulnar carpal instability — case presentation. *Australian Journal of Physiotherapy, 41*(1), 41–46.

Sherman, C., & Finch, C. (1997). *On par for preventing golf injuries — A review of the literature.* Melbourne, Australia: Deakin University School of Human Movement Studies.

Skirven, T. (1996, April–June). Clinical examination of the wrist. *Journal of Hand Therapy,* 96–107.

Stover, C., & Mallon, W.J. (1992, October). Golf injuries: Treating the play to treat the player. *Journal of Musculoskeletal Medicine,* 55–72.

CHAPTER 16

Strength and Conditioning for Golf

David K. Chettle and Robert J. Neal

Strength and conditioning has been a major growth area in golf over the past 5 years. Golf has always been thought of as a skill-based sport, with minimal amounts of strength and fitness required. The reality is the golf swing is a highly physical action that requires a great deal of intermuscular coordination utilising flexibility, stability, strength and power to achieve the desired result — a technically and biomechanically sound, reproducible stroke. Today, the players who look and train like athletes are dominating professional golf.

Many of today's touring professionals follow a total golf program comprising technical development, mental skills training, and physical conditioning. The result of this "golfer evolution" is a lean, athletic golfer who appears stronger, more powerful, more flexible and fitter than golfers of previous generations.

The purpose of this chapter is to outline the components of a golf-specific strength and conditioning program and the rationale for their inclusion. Following the review is a case study that illustrates an individualised strength and conditioning program developed for an elite male golfer, and reports on its effects over a 2-year period.

Components of a Strength and Conditioning Program

There are three elements that should be considered when constructing a golf-specific strength and conditioning program: flexibility, strength — including static and dynamic postural control, and cardiovascular fitness. The time spent on each element and the intensity of the activity will be determined by the golfer's relative physical and physiological needs, the person's training history, and access to facilities.

Flexibility

> Increased Flexibility = Decreased Resistance to Goal Swing Path

Stretching is one aspect of the total strength and conditioning program that has been performed by golfers for many years. Information on how to stretch is plentiful, and many golfers take it upon themselves to complete a total body stretching routine at least three times per week. Further, the major tours around the world now have fitness vans that travel from event to event and are therefore available for use by players. These vans are regularly frequented by the treating physical therapists who advise the players on stretching technique.

In practice, each golfer should have an individualised flexibility-training program designed to meet their specific requirements based on physical assessment results. The screening process allows the physical therapist to identify the short and tight muscles. Correct stretches should be undertaken and these should be progressed to advanced stretches as the golfer's abilities increase. Like most elements of physical conditioning, maintenance of attained levels of physical ability is easier than initially reaching them.

Flexibility alone does not guarantee improvements in swing mechanics. Once flexibility has been improved, golfers must learn to coordinate their body segments through their newly found range of motion (ROM). In the vernacular of the physical therapist and strength and conditioning fraternity, the golfer must learn new segmental control. Without this control of the timing of segment involvement (sometimes referred to as segment interactions or sequencing), swing mechanics may become compromised.

Flexibility imbalances must be addressed as they may result in altered joint mechanics (Jobe & Pink, 1996). In the swing, these altered joint mechanics may result in compensatory changes that over time may lead to injury of the joint itself or surrounding soft tissues. Although further golf-specific research is needed to substantiate these relationships, examples of technical problems that may well be related to decreased flexibility are shown in Table 1. It is evident that many physical conditions may contribute to the technical fault, hence individual assessment is essential.

Table 1

Examples of Specific Joint/muscle Inflexibility Proposed as Correlates of Swing Technique Problems

TECHNICAL FAULT	PHYSICAL CORRELATE
Poor position at address	Tight hamstrings
	Tight gluteals
	Tight hip flexors
	Tight levator scapulae
	Tight neck extensors
	Tight pectorals
	Tight latissimus dorsi
	Decreased thoracic extension
Poor body turn	Tight latissimus dorsi
	Tight rectus abdominus
	Tight obliques
	Tight hip flexors
	Tight lateral trunk
	Tight quadratus lumborum
	Decreased trunk rotation
Laid off backswing	Tight latissimus dorsi
	Tight rectus abdominus
Early release	Tight thigh adductors
	Tight quadriceps
	Decreased internal hip rotation
	Decreased external hip rotation

Various authors have concluded that golf performance measures such as clubhead speed and shot reproduction benefit from increased flexibility (Chek, 1999; Draovitch & Wescott, 1999; Duda, 1989; Hetu, Christie, & Faigenbaum, 1998; Jones, 1999; Keir, 1996; Lennon, 1999; Walsh, 1989). The potential benefits of increasing flexibility include:

- Increasing swing length (i.e., muscles and joints can move unrestricted through the dynamic ROM required to execute the desired golf swing, resulting in an increased shoulder turn, and an increased differential between hip and shoulder turn)
- Greater ability to "swing within yourself," therefore not having to utilise 100% of resources on every shot
- Decreased stretch reflex
- Greater ability to withstand tensile forces at the end ROM
- Increased power through conditioning soft tissue to become more elastic
- Assistance in injury prevention
- For the senior golfer, assistance in slowing down the natural decline of muscle and joint function that occurs with age.

Golfers often stretch in random order rather than the sequence that ensures best results. They should start with muscle stretches before moving to joint stretches and finishing with any neural stretches that are required. If the muscles are not stretched first, joint stretches may be less effective due to muscle tension being too great to allow for joint ROM to be challenged. Generally, stretches are held for 20–30 seconds, however, individual variation may result in stretches of longer duration being more effective for some persons. Neural stretches should be "pulsed" in and out of the stretched position for short 1-second holds and repeated 15–20 times rather than held (Laughlin, 1999).

Strength

Increased Strength = Increased Striking Force to the Ball

Strength training was once considered taboo for the golfer. Golfing myth held that lifting weights resulted in an overly muscular physique with poor flexibility. Thus, golfers were taught to believe that weight training was contraindicated and they rarely ventured into the weight room. Fortunately, as years have passed and sports science knowledge has improved, myths such as these have been debunked. A strength-training program designed to meet the individual requirements of the golfer can result in physical adaptations that enhance the technical adaptations the golfer is striving to achieve (Chek, 1999; Draovitch & Wescott, 1999; Keir, 1996; Lennon, 1999). Unfortunately, information on strength training for golfers is often in the form of generic programs that may not be suitable for each individual.

Strength-training programs should progress concomitantly with the athlete's development. Exercises should start at the appropriate level for the golfer based on the physical assessment results, and over time the neurological demand of the exercises should be increased in accordance with the athlete's improvements. The initial strength-training program should focus upon corrective exercises designed to develop sound movement and muscle recruitment patterns. This stage is far more important than gaining large strength increases. Increased strength with poor exercise execution may result in worsening of physical problems and possible injury rather than improvement.

Once exercise techniques have been taught and correct movement skills established, progression should increase the workload (i.e., increased resistance, repetitions, sets, etc.). Initially, exercises in the frontal and sagittal planes should be performed and mastered. Transverse plane (rotational) strength and control exercise may be introduced and perfected over time after the simple planar movements can be well executed. Obviously rotational strength is very specific to the golfer's needs, and should be a medium- and long-term goal of any golf conditioning program.

Golf requires strength and power of many muscles in the body. The muscles act together to create complex movement patterns rather than contracting in isolation (Jobe & Moynes, 1982; Jobe, Moynes, & Antonelli, 1986; Jobe, Perry, & Pink, 1989; Kao, Pink, Jobe, & Perry, 1995; Lennon, 1999; Maddalozzo, 1987). Exercises should utilise complex movements to develop intermuscular coordination. Thus multijoint exercises such as deadlifts, squats and rowing drills should form the foundations of such a program.

Abdominal strength is of great importance to the golfer. Traditionally, great attention is paid to the superficial muscles of the abdomen — the rectus abdominus and the obliques. These muscle groups do have a role in the swing, especially the obliques, however it is the deep-lying stabilising musculature of the trunk that has a greater role in golf than the superficial muscles. Proper functioning of the transversus abdominus and segmental stabilisers such as the multifidus is crucial for injury prevention (of low back), balance, and posture maintenance. This idea is true for both static and dynamic activities.

Initially, correct activation of these muscles must be mastered. We recommend that this skill be taught by a qualified physiotherapist. Once basic activation has been learned, progression to more demanding exercises should occur to allow for continued adaptation. There have been various accounts of the benefits of increased functional abdominal strength (Chek, 1999; Draovitch & Wescott, 1999; Hetu et al., 1998; Jobe & Schwab, 1991; Keir, 1996; Larkin, Larkin, & Larkin, 1990; Lennon, 1999; Walsh, 1989) that include the following:

- Helps to protect the spine and prevent damage or injury to the spine itself through segmental stabilisation
- Increased stabilisation will prevent unwanted movement during the swing and improve posture at address
- Assists rotational power production in the golf swing
- Aids in preventing excessive tilting of the pelvis throughout the swing.

Static Postural Control

Static posture may be defined as the position of the body at rest — sitting, standing, or lying (Chek, 1999). As the golf swing uses one side of the body in differing function to the other, static postural imbalances are common in many golfers. These imbalances may be in the frontal, sagittal or transverse planes. The goal of the strength-training program should be to return the body to "normal" resting posture as postural deviations may be contributing to technical problems, and possibly injury.

Posture is a habit, and increasing strength will not necessarily improve posture. Although strengthening the body's postural muscles is an important step to improving static posture, it is the day-to-day actions which individuals perform that will ultimately determine their success in improving their posture. For example, if the golfer sat or stood in a slumped posture for hours each day, the result will be a continual reinforcement of poor posture. On the other hand, if golfers started to monitor the occasions they returned to poor postural habits, and made immediate corrections, their posture will improve over time. This change occurs because a new postural habit was learned and developed.

The initial phase of any strengthening program should focus on corrective exercises. Thus, one goal of a conditioning program would be to return the body to, and maintain, optimal posture. Ideally all movements should begin from a position of optimal posture, especially strength-training exercises that use an external load. Therefore, this initial phase of the conditioning program must be completed prior to the addition of heavy resistance training exercises.

A simple posture check may be performed using a mirror, or the help of a friend. The following list is not comprehensive but it does provide some key postural alignments — all of which are important for a safe golf swing:

- Head in the middle of the shoulders (sagittal and frontal planes)
- Ears aligned above the shoulders (sagittal plane)
- Shoulders level
- No excessive curvature of upper or lower spine
- Hips level and not excessively rotated up or down
- Kneecaps pointing forward (not in or out)
- Knees not hyperextended
- Feet pointing forwards (not in or out)
- Head not pushing forward
- Shoulders back with scapula sitting flat on rib cage — shoulders not rounded.

Dynamic Postural Control

Once sound static posture has been developed and reinforced, dynamic postural stability should be developed. Chek (1999) defines dynamic postural control as "the ability to keep each and all working joints in optimal alignment during any given movement, such that the efficiency of the movement is facilitated and injury is prevented" (p. 86). Basically, by increasing dynamic postural control/stability, the golfer should improve swing consistency in a manner that best maintains joint and soft tissue health.

Many teaching professionals feel that increasing balance and coordination will improve consistency. There are many drills that may be incorporated to enhance dynamic postural control and balance utilising equipment such as Swiss balls, Dura-discs, wobble boards and free weights. Exercises using these devices should be incorporated as a part of the athletes' strength and conditioning programs as their golf skills develop. The exercises will often be quite different to the "standard" strength-training exercises that are found in books or magazines, and will frequently depend on the athlete's overall strength, balance, and level of postural control.

Cardiovascular (CV) Fitness

A minimum level of cardiovascular fitness is required to complete 18 holes of golf over the 4 days of a tournament. Optimum fitness would have the golfer feeling minimal fatigue (physical or mental) at the conclusion of the event. It is accepted that physical fatigue increases levels of mental fatigue (Wilmore & Costill, 1994). Therefore, inadequate fitness may result in decreased mental abilities including poor concentration and decision making. Lack of adequate aerobic fitness often becomes evident over a 4-day tournament, where cumulative fatigue occurs. Sound levels of CV fitness will not only reduce the effects of fatigue (e.g., skill deterioration, course management, etc.) but also assist one to cope with the effects of extended practice sessions and travel.

Research on aerobic conditioning (Chek, 1999; Draovitch & Wescott, 1999; Jobe & Schwab, 1991; Keir, 1996; Lennon, 1999; Walsh, 1989) identifies the key benefits for the golfer:

- Improved mental concentration
- Prevention of fatigue
- Prevention of skill deterioration (as a result of the above)
- Recovery from training/practice
- Weight loss/weight control
- Protection against many disease states associated with poor cardiovascular function.

Merely playing golf will not substantially increase CV fitness for many individuals. Alternative moderate intensity exercise should be performed 3–4 times per week in addition to time spent on the golf course. Cross-training activities such as walking/jogging, swimming, cycling, indoor steppers, and other sports are all sound choices. Care must be taken that the exercise used is not detrimental to the golfer's physical attributes (e.g., for a golfer exhibiting tight pectorals, abducted and elevated scapula, and tight upper trapezius, swimming freestyle would not be a suitable option due to the nature of the stroke). Choice and variety of exercise will assist in golf athletes adhering to a comprehensive fitness program.

Individualisation

Books on strength and conditioning or fitness for golf have become widely available from a large number of different "experts." These books often provide a recipe for the golfer to follow, implying that everyone has the same physical and physiological needs. The problem with this approach is that golfers are unique in their swing model, physical attributes (including joint and muscle flexibility, strength, postural balance, and cardiovascular fitness), and time/equipment available to address these areas. There is no "cure-all" program that can satisfy all golfers — especially those of varying abilities (e.g., professional vs social golfer).

Most books recommend that strength training be performed using a multitude of machines which isolate individual muscles that have been shown by researchers to be active in the golf swing (Jobe & Moynes, 1982; Jobe et al., 1986; Jobe et al., 1989; Kao et al., 1995; Lennon, 1999). The problem with this approach relates to the way in which the research is interpreted. For example, just because a particular muscle is active within the swing does not mean that we can conclude that merely exercising this muscle will result in performance enhancement. It is surprising that some authors have reached this conclusion given that the research shows that these muscles never act in isolation — rather in conjunction with each other.

The golf swing is an action that recruits groups of muscles in pretrained sequences. The exercises chosen to make up the golfer's conditioning program must integrate the whole body rather than isolate each muscle. We believe that free-weight training has more benefits to the golfer than machine-weight training as free weights allow for variable planes of movement and require the use of the small stabilising muscles to maintain desired postures. The result of using free weights for golf conditioning is a strengthening and recruiting of muscles in real-life, unstable situations — this is not the case when using machines. Free weights provide far more variety and exercise choice for the strength and conditioning specialist to design an individualised program.

The benefit of following an individualised strength and conditioning program for golf is the correction of physical insufficiencies that are specific to a particular golfer. Technical improvements to the swing may be achieved faster than with a standardised program. Rather than following a generic strength and conditioning program that contains stretches and exercises that may be either detrimental or contraindicated for the individual, the athlete's time and efforts would be better spent focusing on individual areas of concern. The likely result would be better adherence to the program and more rapid improvements over time compared to the generic program.

In summary, the research reviewed above indicates that a strength and conditioning program based on the golfer's physical and physiological needs will result in:

- An ability to hit the ball further with more control
- Reduced risk of golf-related injuries
- Increased longevity (longer practice and playing periods without injury; and preservation of ability over time, or minimisation of natural decline in performance due to the effects of aging)
- An increase in concentration levels
- A decrease in effects of fatigue on performance (both muscle endurance and cardiovascular fatigue).

Conclusion

Strength and conditioning should not be seen as the panacea for every golf problem. The primary aim of strength and conditioning programs for golfers is to decrease any or all physical issues that may limit technical improvements or swing consistency. Technical problems highlighted by the teaching professional may be occurring because of an undiagnosed physical issue (e.g., limited range of motion, strength, or control of a body segment or joint). The goal of any strength and conditioning program should be to correct ROM limitations, postural imbalances, stability and basic control issues before trying to improve performance. As golf organisations become increasingly aware of the role of sports medicine and sports science, these initiatives will continue to filter through to our junior ranks.

It is imperative prior to undergoing any strength and conditioning program that the golfer be fully screened/assessed by a qualified sports physiotherapist with experience in identifying specific physical limitations in golfers. The results of this assessment should be coupled with a coach's report of the technical areas of concern. Without these two assessments and open communication between all professionals/clinicians concerned, the program may never be truly individualised. Once the background information is collated, the strength and conditioning program may be designed and implemented. Over time the strength and conditioning specialist should review the program to ensure that correct technique is being adhered to, and progressively increase the workload but maintain appropriate levels of safety. As physical improvements continue, exercises will need to be changed so that more advanced and neurologically demanding exercises promote continued development.

There is a distinct need for further research into the area of strength and conditioning for golf performance. Research to date indicates that strength, cardiovascular and flexibility training enhances measures including clubhead speed, consistency of swing, and decreased fatigue (Jones, 1999; Larkin et al., 1990; Lennon, 1999). There is a need for research that correlates an individual player's weaknesses with the physical changes that accompany a well-designed program. Recently developed three-dimensional biomechanics analysis equipment (e.g., the SkillTec 3-D Golf System) permits accurate measures of technical changes. Such equipment will enable researchers to relate specific kinematic alterations to physical training interventions.

When amateur and social golfers are used as research participants, the data cannot and should not be extrapolated to the elite or professional golfer. Care needs to be taken when designing programs for these athletes as any poor prescription choices may actually be detrimental to their performance. Measures over time of injury states, with and without conditioning, would also be valuable.

The role of strength and conditioning in golf will continue to grow in the years to come. Open communication between professionals working in this field will enhance the quality of programs that are prescribed. It is imperative that strength and conditioning consultants work with the golfer's coaching, physiotherapy and medical team to ensure that common goals are being worked towards in a manner that will result in the golfer making steady and sound improvements over time. Just as the technical components of swing mechanics/models take years to develop, physical conditioning goals should be planned over similar timeframes to ensure the progression from corrective exercises through to performance enhancement is safe and controlled.

Case Study

Following is a case study of an elite male golfer (age = 21 years, handicap = 1.3) over a 24-month period. The golfer had prior weight-training experience (minimal) and ran 5 km twice per week. The athlete had undergone a golf-specific physical screening assessment by a sports physiotherapist specialising in golf performance and injury prevention. The results of the assessment indicated the following areas needed addressing:

- Tight hamstrings, gluteals, pectorals, latissimus dorsi, upper trapezius

- Decreased trunk rotation
- Decreased thoracic extension
- Poor single-leg control (esp. LHS)
- Poor abdominal control
- Poor scapula control.

The athlete's coach had made the following technical notations with the thought of there being a physical underpinning to the technical issues:

- Poor address posture — rounded shoulders and "tucked" bottom
- Occasionally has difficulty in accepting weight onto the left leg on follow-through, thus decreasing distance and at times accuracy
- Arms occasionally become overactive in the swing due to not having consistent trunk turn
- Seems to have difficulty in maintaining spine angle when fatigued.

The athlete followed a flexibility-training program specifically designed to address these issues (see Figures 1–3), coupled with basic abdominal and scapula control exercises over a period of 12 weeks. This program was generated and administrated by the physiotherapist and the strength and conditioning specialist. Daily stretches and control exercises were performed lasting 40 minutes in total.

After the initial 12-week period, the sports physiotherapist re-assessed the golfer to ascertain his improvements. He had now attained the desired ROM in all areas of concern with the exception of thoracic extension which still had a small percentage of improvement expected to come over the following months. Activation and control of abdominal musculature and scapula control musculature (serratus anterior, subscapularis, and lower trapezius) had improved dramatically, resulting in improved posture — both standing and in positions of address. The coach's report noted improvements but felt that the golfer was still having difficulty maintaining posture and getting consistent weight transfer under difficult conditions and fatigue. There was further mention of issues relating to consistency of spine angle, and consistency of weight transfer.

At this point, a specific strength and conditioning program was designed to meet the athlete's needs incorporating weight training and Swiss ball exercises. These were accompanied with a maintenance flexibility program and a general cardiovascular conditioning program. In total, the golfer completed a daily 15–20 minute stretching routine, a twice-weekly 45-minute strength-training program, and three 30-minute cardiovascular fitness sessions per week. As the golfer's playing commitments were now increasing, the timing of these sessions became more important to allow for

Figure 1
Lying hamstring stretch.

Figure 2
Lateral trunk stretch.

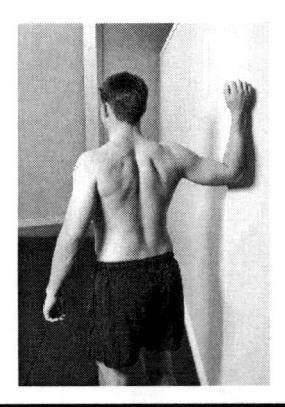

Figure 3
Pectoral stretch position.

sufficient recovery. The two strength-training sessions were performed on Mondays and Thursdays — allowing for ample recovery for weekend competitions.

Table 2 outlines the initial exercise prescription for this particular athlete with a brief rationale for the choice of exercise. Figures 4–14 illustrate these exercises. Goals of this initial strength-training program were to:

- Gain an understanding of the role of strength training in golf
- Generate sound muscle recruitment patterns in set movement skills
- Improve single leg control
- Improve scapula control against external loads
- Advance trunk stability exercises using a Swiss ball to introduce an unstable environment
- Integrate trunk stability exercises in conjunction with other muscle actions.

The athlete was further assessed by the same physiotherapist at 6-month intervals over the 2 years to ensure that desired joint and muscle ROM was maintained, and to ensure that base activation and control of intrinsic stabilising muscles was maintained. The golfer was reviewed regularly by the strength and conditioning specialist, and had his program modified every 8 weeks to cater for adaptations made. Progressions included more advanced single-leg, trunk-stability, and back-strengthening exercises.

Once strength and control in the frontal and sagittal planes had been developed, the athlete was introduced to various rotation strength and rotation control exercises using weights and Swiss balls. Again, these were progressed in accordance with the athlete's neurological and strength developments. Unfortunately, it is beyond the scope of this chapter to detail every exercise modification and program change over the 2-year period.

This particular golfer did not experience any injuries over the 2-year period — however it would be foolish to conclude that this was purely due to the physical training although it is felt that the training certainly contributed.

Videotape evidence demonstrates the technical improvements made over the course of the 2 years. The golfer's handicap was reduced to scratch, and on-course performances became far more consistent. The improvements were a result of adherence to the strength and conditioning program, along with quality technical information with regard to swing technique and course management skills, and quality mental skills training. We believe that further research should be conducted in this area using three-dimensional biome-

Table 2
Initial Exercise Prescription for the Case Study Athlete

EXERCISE	SETS * REPS	RATIONALE
Deadlifts (see Figures 4–6)	2 * 10–13	Maintenance of neutral spine and scapula position against load Increase lower body strength Emphasise role of trunk stability against external loads
Single Leg Squats (see Figures 7–8)	2 * 12–15	Improve single leg strength Improve ability to control hip and knee alignment at neutral when under load Develop equal strength in left and right legs Improve balance
Seated Row	2 * 10–13	Develop correct recruitment pattern of all scapula adductors Activate and strengthen lower trapezius while minimising activation of upper trapezius Maintenance of neutral lumbar posture throughout through trunk stabilisation
Prone DB Flyes (see Figures 9–10)	2 * 12–15	Develop correct recruitment pattern of all scapula adductors Activate and strengthen lower trapezius while minimising activation of upper trapezius
Straight Arm Pulldown (see Figures 11–12)	2 * 12–15	Strengthen scapula stabilisers and neutralisers against external load Maintenance of neutral scapula position while arm moves through frontal plane
Abducted DB External Rotation	2 * 15–20	To strengthen muscles of rotator cuff To achieve balance in left and right side strength
Abducted DB Internal Rotation	2 * 15–20	To strengthen muscles of rotator cuff To achieve balance in left and right side strength
DB Wrist Flexion	2 * 15–20	Strengthen all wrist flexors To achieve balance in left and right side strength
DB Wrist Extension	2 * 15–20	Strengthen all wrist extensors To achieve balance in left and right side strength
Swiss Ball Sit & Alternate Leg Lift	2 * 8 per leg	Activation and utilisation of transversus abdominus in an unstable environment Improve balance
Swiss Ball Bridge & Leg Curl (see Figure 13)	2 * 8 per leg	Integration of trunk stability and gluteal stability in an unstable environment Improve balance
Swiss Ball Oblique Crunch (see Figure 14)	2 * 12–15	Strengthen and balance left and right obliques in an unstable environment Improve balance
Swiss Ball Crunch	2 * 12–15	Strengthen rectus abdominus through complete range of motion in an unstable environment Improve balance

STRENGTH AND CONDITIONING FOR GOLF

Figure 4
Deadlift start.

Figure 5
Deadlift midpoint.

Figure 6
Deadlift finish.

Figure 7
Single leg squat start.

Figure 8
Single leg squat finish.

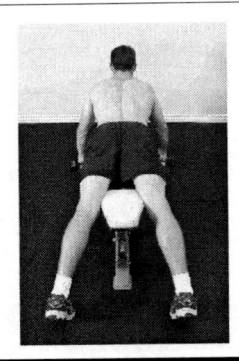

Figure 9
Prone DB Flye start.

Figure 10
Prone DB Flye finish.

Figure 11
Straight arm pulldown start.

Figure 12
Straight arm pulldown finish.

Figure 13
Swiss ball leg curl.

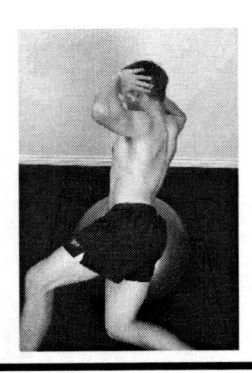

Figure 14
Swiss ball oblique crunch.

chanics analysis equipment to accurately measure technical changes. Only then may kinematic alterations be related to physical training interventions.

References

Chek, P. (1999). *The golf biomechanics manual.* California: C.H.E.K. Institute.

Draovitch, P., & Wescott, W. (1999). *Complete conditioning for golf.* Champaign, IL: Human Kinetics.

Duda, M. (1989). Golfers use exercise to get back into the swing. *The Physician and Sports Medicine, 17*(8), 109–113.

Hetu, F.E., Christie, C.A., & Faigenbaum, A.D. (1998). Effects of conditioning on physical fitness and club head speed in mature golfers. *Perceptual and Motor Skills, 86*(3), 881–815.

Jobe, F.W., & Moynes, D.R. (1982). *30 exercises for better golf.* Inglewood, CA: Champion Press.

Jobe, F.W., Moynes, D.R., & Antonelli, D.J. (1986). Rotator cuff function during a golf swing. *The American Journal of Sports Medicine, 14*(5), 388–392.

Jobe, F.W., Perry, J., & Pink, M. (1989). Electromyographic shoulder activity in men and women professional golfers. *The American Journal of Sports Medicine, 17*(6), 782–787.

Jobe, F.W., & Pink, M. (1996). Shoulder pain in golf. *Clinics in Sports Medicine, 15*(1), 55–63.

Jobe, F.W., & Schwab, D.M. (1991). Golf for the mature athlete. *Clinics in Sports Medicine, 10*(2), 269–282.

Jones, D. (1999). The effects of proprioceptive neuromuscular facilitation flexibility training on the clubhead speed of recreational golfers. In M.R. Farrally & A.J. Cochran (Eds.), *Science and golf III: Proceedings of the 1998 World Scientific Congress of Golf* (pp. 46–57). Champaign, IL: Human Kinetics.

Kao, J.T., Pink, M., Jobe, F.W., & Perry, J. (1995). Electromyographic analysis of the scapular muscles during a golf swing. *The American Journal of Sports Medicine, 23*(1), 19–23.

Keir, D.G. (1996). *The complete guide to physical conditioning for golf.* Sydney: Sports Insight Australia.

Larkin, A.F., Larkin II, W.F., & Larkin, S.L. (1990). Annual torso specific conditioning program for golfers. In A.J. Cochran (Ed.), *Science and golf: Proceedings of the First World Scientific Congress of Golf* (pp. 61–63). London: E & FN Spon.

Laughlin, K. (1999). *Stretching and flexibility.* Sydney, Australia: Simon & Schuster.

Lennon, H.M. (1999). *Physiological profiling and physical conditioning for elite golfers.* In M.R. Farrally & A.J. Cochran (Eds.), *Science and golf III: Proceedings of the 1998 World Scientific Congress of Golf* (pp. 58–64). Champaign, IL: Human Kinetics.

Maddalozzo, G.F.J. (1987). An anatomical and biomechanical analysis of the full golf swing. *NSCA Journal, 9*(4), 6–8, 77–79.

Walsh, B. (1989, July–September). Golf... Let's get physical. *Sports Coach,* 19–24.

Wilmore, J.H., & Costill D.L. (1994). *Physiology of sport and exercise.* Champaign, IL: Human Kinetics.

CHAPTER 17

The Rhetoric and Reality of Warm-up Activity Among Junior Golfers

Raymond J. Leigh

The concept of warm-up prior to exercise is a fascinating one. It is a form of activity undertaken by almost all elite athletes who have learned to recognise its benefits. Children at school in the United Kingdom are also, as a statutory requirement of the National Curriculum, obliged to be taught explicitly "to warm up and prepare appropriately for different activities" (DFEE, 1999) in order that they may eventually undertake such activity on their own when they are taking part in either play or practice related to sport.

While at school, therefore, all pupils should be conducted through some sort of warm-up initially by the teacher and eventually by their peers and themselves for all physical education (PE) lessons. The duration of this type of activity will vary in relation to the lesson time available and almost certainly will not be of the same length or depth as that undertaken by, for example, a track and field athlete before a training session. Its purpose is to educate children as to the benefits, and to provide them with an understanding of its constituent parts in order that it will eventually become an automatic part of their sporting activity.

The benefits of warm-up are largely based around the notions that it prepares the body for exercise both physiologically and psychologically, mobilises joints, and reduces the likelihood of muscle stiffness or soreness and the possibility of injury. The inconclusiveness of the evidence regarding its claims is readily recognised (Bartlett, 1999; Harris & Elbourn, 1992), but a combination of some positive research findings (Alter, 1988; De Vries, 1986), the recommendation of those working in the field of sports injuries (Grisogono, 1984), and a desire to follow the idea of "Pascal's Wager" and err on the side of safety, leads to the inclusion of warm-up activity which generally incorporates "passive stretching, ballistic bouncing, pulse warmers and skill rehearsal" (Grisogono, 1984, p. 5).

If, as Harris and Elbourn (1992) say, "Physical education teachers, exercise leaders and sports coaches all have an important role to play in educating people about exercise" (p. 8), then we should equally find among those involved in the teaching and coaching of golf a similar espousal of positive views towards warm-up activity.

Watching tournament professionals practise before the start of a round, one is immediately struck by the variety of practice methods. But what is noticeable is that the great majority perform some sort of stretching routine prior to hitting balls. Golfers who put their names to teaching texts also recommend similar activity (Lewis, 1995; Trevino, 1971). In a study on back pain among junior golfers, Leigh and Young (1999) recommended some form of prepractice preparation in order to offset the possibility of lower back damage. No less an authority than Harvey Penick (1995) writes, "After you have done your stretching, which you should always take time to do, pull out your wedge and hit five full shots" (p. 36).

It is clear, therefore, that teachers in England and Wales are compelled by law to undertake warm-up activity with their pupils. Those who write about golf support its inclusion, and youngsters should be accepting the notion and bringing it to bear upon their practice. If the rhetoric is correct, then what should be seen are teachers and golf professionals undertaking warm-ups with pupils, and more importantly, youngsters who are doing these things for themselves because they either accept their benefits or because they have become conditioned to do so.

However, the rhetoric and the reality of situations are not always concomitant. Laws (1994) examined the curriculum in terms of layers of practice following work undertaken by Foucault (1982) on the genealogy of knowledge. At the top end is the curriculum that is formally laid down as the ideal, while at the other is that which children actually experience and from which they are expected to have learned. The present study set out to investigate whether this is the case in this instance. It examines whether the perceived layer of the practice of warm-up activity before PE lessons and golf exists, and whether the intended learning outcome of this activity — that children understand its purpose, regardless of whether the claims made on its behalf are valid — is being evidenced by juniors in their undertaking of warm-up activity prior to play and practice.

Method

This study initially investigated whether and what children were being taught about warm-up in school. It then focused on the warm-up activities teaching professionals were doing with junior golfers. Finally, the study examined how this instruction translated into individual play and practice.

The first group of participants consisted of 73 male and 6 female junior golfers aged between 11 and 17 years (Mean age = 12.94 ± 1.63 years). The sample consisted of the 36% of children who responded to the lengthy questionnaire requesting information about the warm-up activity prior to PE lessons in school, and enquiring about the nature and duration of their warm-up habits before play and practice.

The second group of participants consisted of 19 teaching professionals from 13 golf clubs in the south-east of England, all of whom were involved in the teaching of junior golfers either in groups or as individuals. Although small, the sample represented a 59% return rate to a questionnaire containing eight items related to the warm-up activity, if any, which they undertook with their pupils, its nature and its duration.

The information was subjected to a variety of forms of statistical enquiry. Descriptive and frequency statistics were used in accordance with the level of measurement, and a Chi-square and goodness of fit analysis was also undertaken.

Results

The children's responses show that 94.9% undertake some sort of warm-up activity before PE lessons. Modal scores indicate that they spend between 5–10 minutes on warm-up and are engaged in pulse raising, joint mobilising and muscle stretching activity, of which they identify muscle stretching as being the most common form.

Responses from the teaching professionals indicate that 84% undertake warm-up activities with junior golfers. Modal scores indicate that the duration of this activity is up to 5 minutes. As shown in Figure 1, the most commonly undertaken practices are club swinging (75%), arm swinging (56%), trunk twisting (38%), and shoulder mobilising (38%). In 13% of cases professionals recognise short swing shots as part of a warm-up routine.

Modal scores from the juniors indicate that they play golf once per week and practise additionally at the same rate. Prior to playing, 86.1% maintain that they undertake some form of warm-up, but prior to practice this figure reduces to 64.6%. The goodness of fit analysis revealed a Contingency

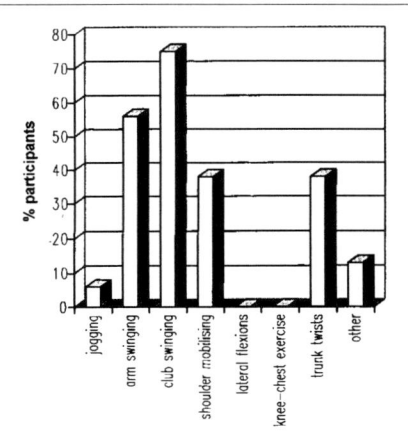

Figure 1
Frequency and nature of warm-up activity supervised by golf teaching professionals.

Coefficient value of 0.363, $p = .001$, showing this to be a significant reduction. A Chi-square analysis showed no significant association between warm-up prior to practice and age, $\chi^2 (6) = 5.497$, $p = .482$. For these juniors, the duration of the warm-up before play and practice is no greater than 5 minutes. The nature of the activities within these warm-up periods can be seen in Figure 2.

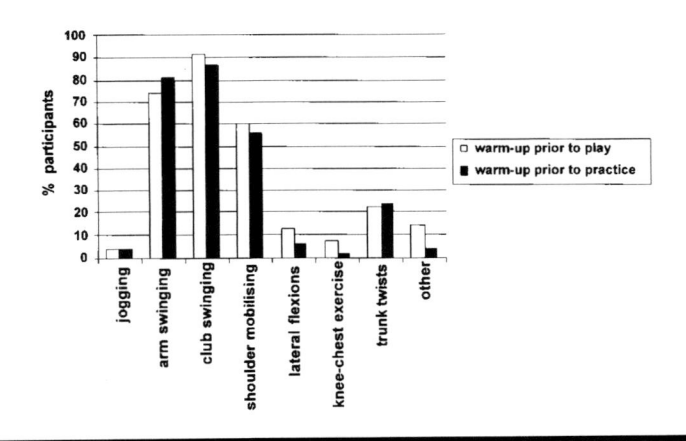

Figure 2
Frequency and nature of warm-up activity prior to play and practice.

Discussion and Conclusions

It is clear that warm-up activity is taking place among juniors. However, its degree seems to be somewhat dependent upon who is overseeing it. As would be expected because of the constraints of the curriculum placed upon them (DFEE, 1992, 1995, 1999), physical education teachers would seem to be the most conscientious in ensuring warm-up is undertaken, its duration is adequate, and its content includes the factors identified by Grisogono (1984). The discrepancy between the actual (94.9%) and the ideal (100%) compliance rate that may be expected from a statutory obligation may be explained by the fact that some private schools are not obliged to subscribe to the government requirements. The type of school attended was not a feature of the analysis undertaken.

Teaching professionals would appear, on the whole, to be following the lead given to them by the accepted authorities in their field, although it may be surprising that this warm-up figure is also not closer to the 100% level. The nature of their warm-up activity contains a variety of practices that cover both mobilising and stretching of the upper and lower back. If the active nature of some of these is accepted, they would also fulfill the pulse-raising requirement to some extent. Some of the activities, however, would appear to run counter to the recommendations of those authorities (Lycholat, 1990) who would decry their rebounding nature, arguing that forced, hurriedly repeated stretching techniques may be more likely to bring about injury to muscle and connective tissue rather than prevent it.

The junior golfer responses revealed a significant reduction in the numbers who warm-up prior to practice compared to those who warm-up prior to play. There may be several reasons for this. The most obvious is that when practising they are likely to be largely unsupervised and therefore there would be no one in authority present to ensure that what takes place under their control is happening outside of it. Youngsters are naturally keen to engage as quickly as possible in what they consider to be the most important aspect of practice, that of hitting golf balls, and anything that may prevent them from quickly doing this may be seen as superfluous. It may also be possible to assume from this disparity in the figures that the lessons of warm-up and its importance, initiated in school and via the golf professional, have not been assimilated by the youngsters. This is not only important for those involved in the teaching of golf, but also for physical education teachers, as it may be giving a signal that what they are hoping to achieve as one of the general requirements of the National Curriculum is not proving to be altogether successful at this moment. Neither is the argument — that continual subjection to warm-up over a long period would result in older pupils being more likely to recognise its value — borne out by the results of the Chi-square analysis.

The content of the warm-ups that are being undertaken by junior golfers is very similar across contexts. This is not surprising. The children will inevitably use those activities with which they are familiar in a golf context and therefore follow the lead given them by adults in this field. What may be surprising though, again, particularly for physical educators, is that juniors are using very little of the material they encounter in their PE lessons in order to either complement the warm-up experience or supplement it. The activities mentioned in the *other* column in Figure 2 consisted largely (80%) of hitting golf balls prior to play, which is consistent with Penick (1995), and a neck rolling exercise. Hitting golf balls was also the only *other* activity identified in the questionnaire directed towards the golf professionals. Understandably, hitting golf balls did not feature as a warm-up activity prior to practice as hitting golf balls is its constituent activity.

The duration of the junior golfers' warm-up period is identical for both play and practice and follows closely the lead given to them by their teaching professionals. The only real issue here is whether it is enough. As a physical educationist, one may believe that the time spent in warm-up prior to a PE lesson may not really be sufficient to prevent injury but is rather part of a process of instilling the notion of good habits. The golf professional may also feel the same way. If this is so, then to some extent there is a degree of success. It would certainly appear that before a round of golf our juniors are preparing in a relatively systematic way and that prior to practice many, but fewer, are preparing similarly.

If the benefits of warm-up activity are accepted, and it should be clearly stated that it was not the function of this paper to examine the validity of that argument but rather to accept warm-up activity as *de jurie*, then the significant discrepancy in warm-up before playing and practice requires addressing. It may be that both physical education teachers and golf professionals need to clearly identify golf as being a physical activity that makes considerable demands upon the body in general and specific parts, such as the lower back, in particular. Because golf is not commonly taught in schools in the UK it may be more appropriate for the professional, in the course of a conducted lesson, to establish a distinct pattern of warm-up activity that pupils are to undertake prior to hitting balls. The importance of the warm-up then needs to be continually reinforced in the hope that, even if pupils do not fully understand the significance of what they are doing, they will still be conditioned to do it. It then remains to the physical educationist to ensure that the underpinning knowledge regarding its purpose is supplied.

References

Alter, M.J. (1988). *Science of stretching* (pp. 66–69, 101–148). Leeds: Human Kinetics.
Bartlett, R. (1999). *Sports biomechanics* (pp. 28–51). London: E & FN Spon.
D.E.S. (1992). *Physical education in the National Curriculum* (p. 3). London: HMSO.
D.F.E. (1995). *Physical education in the National Curriculum* (p. 2). London: HMSO.
D.F.E.E. (1999). *Physical education* (p. 18). London: HMSO.
De Vries, H.A. (1986). *Physiology of exercise* (p. 264). USA: Wm. C. Brown.
Foucault, M. (1982). The subject and power. *Critical Inquiry, 8,* 777–789.
Grisogono, V. (1984). *Sports injuries.* London: John Murray.
Harris, J., & Elbourn, J. (1992). *Warming up and cooling down.* Loughborough: Loughborough University.
Laws, C.J. (1994). Rhetorical justification for new approaches to teaching games: Are physical education teachers deluding themselves? In *Proceedings of 10th Commonwealth & International Scientific Congress* (pp. 175–180).
Leigh, R.J., & Young, D.B. (1999). Back pain among junior golfers. In M.R. Farrally & A.J. Cochran (Eds.), *Science and golf III: Proceedings of the 1998 World Scientific Congress of Golf* (pp. 92–96). Champaign, IL: Human Kinetics.
Lewis, B. (1995). *Play better golf.* London: Tiger Books.
Lycholat, T. (1990). *The complete book of stretching.* London: Crowood.
Penick, H. (1995). *Harvey Penick's little blue golf book.* London: Collins.
Trevino, L. (1971). *I can help your game.* London: W.H. Allen.

CHAPTER 18

An Integrated Approach to the Golfer's Physical and Technical Development

Ramsay McMaster, Ross Herbert,[1] Sandy Jamieson, and Patrick R. Thomas

---

Research presented at the World Scientific Congresses of Golf clearly establishes the importance of physical, technical and mental skills for optimal performance in golf (Cochran, 1990; Cochran & Farrally, 1994; Farrally & Cochran, 1999). Although coaches and players often discuss the relative contributions of these three types of skills to golf performance, their interactions are often overlooked. When considering an athlete's skills profile, a coach needs not only to total the scores across these three areas, but also examine how strengths or weaknesses in one area are impacting on another. Golfers undergoing swing changes, for example, will frequently suffer a drop in confidence until the new technique is mastered, becomes automatic, and performance subsequently improves. So too, a golfer with high anxiety on the first tee is likely to experience muscle tension which affects the execution of the swing or putting action and results in poor performance.

In a similar way, swing techniques are affected by golfers' physical skills and physiological characteristics, and this interaction impacts significantly on

---

[1]Ross Herbert gained international recognition for his initiatives as Head Coach, Australian Institute of Sport Golf Program in Melbourne. After a short battle with cancer, Ross died on January 1, 2001, aged 41. The golfing community mourns a highly respected colleague.

their performance. Spine, shoulder and hip rotations during the swing affect clubhead speed and the distance the ball travels, and are significantly different between amateurs and Tour players (Cheetham, Martin, Mottram, & St. Laurent, 2000; McTeigue, Lamb, Mottram, & Pirozzolo, 1994). Jones (1999) found that an 8-week flexibility training program significantly increased recreational golfers' range of motion in the hips, shoulders and trunk, producing a 7% increase in clubhead speed. Lennon (1999) showed that a golf-specific conditioning program significantly improved junior golfers' weight, grip and leg strength, aerobic endurance, and flexibility. As a result, they were better able to fully rotate the club on an inside plane and straight to target, achieving greater distance with a 5-iron while still remaining balanced. In a second study to measure the effects of a physical conditioning program with European Tour players and elite Irish amateurs, Lennon (1999) reported significant improvements in strength, flexibility and balance that resulted in best-ever performances by golfers in both categories.

Just as important, however, is the reverse relationship where poor set-up and swing techniques result in physical injury to the golfer. There have been a number of recent studies identifying the nature and frequency of golf injuries (Batt, 1992, 1993; Finch, Sherman, & James, 1999; Leigh & Young, 1999; McCarroll, 1996; McCarroll, Rettig, & Shelbourne, 1990; McNicholas, Nielsen, & Knill-Jones, 1999; Sugaya, Tsuchiya, Moriya, Morgan, & Banks, 1999; Van Der Steenhoven, Burdof, & Tromp-Klaren, 1994; Wilks & Jones, 1996). After a comprehensive review of research in this area, Theriault and Lachance (1998) concluded that technical deficiencies leading to overuse injuries were one of the main causes of injuries among golfers. The elbow, wrist, shoulder and lower back are primarily affected. Differences in the patterns of injuries sustained by professional and recreational golfers can be explained by their playing habits and the biomechanical characteristics of their golf swing. Importantly, Theriault and Lachance (1998) also concluded that:

> Many of these injuries can be prevented by a preseason, and year-round, sport-specific conditioning program including: (i) muscular strengthening, flexibility and aerobic exercise components; (ii) a short, practical, pregame warm-up routine; and (iii) the adjustment of an individual's golf swing to meet their physical capacities and limitations through properly supervised golf lessons (p. 44).

Numerous factors contribute to optimal performance in golf including strength, flexibility, muscular endurance, cardiovascular fitness, coordination, proprioception (body awareness), and mental toughness. The purpose of this chapter is to describe the proactive strategies used in an integrated approach to the golfer's physical and technical development aimed at improving performance and preventing injury. Case studies are provided to illustrate the approach to assessment and treatment that has been developed and widely utilised in several programs recently introduced in Australia.

Assessment Processes

The Melbourne Golf Injury Clinic was established in 1993, initially to treat individuals who had incurred injuries while playing golf. More than 3,000 club golfers and 70 Tour players have now been assessed and treated at the Clinic, and its role has expanded to the areas of injury prevention, research and education. The Clinic cross-refers to doctors, specialists, dietitians, podiatrists, psychologists, masseurs, and so forth. Arguably the most significant working relationship we have is with some of Australia's internationally recognised coaches. Under their direction we have gained considerable insight into the technical approach to golf, not only for amateurs of all ages and standards but also for professional golfers.

A multidisciplinary team approach is adopted to optimise performance in golf (Figure 1). Golfers are given practical lectures and workshops in applied anatomy, physiology and biomechanics specific to golf. Topics such as foot care, skin care, muscle imbalances, postural and regional areas that are placed under stress in playing golf (e.g., feet, spine, wrists) are presented through interactive workshops. These workshops provide advice and physical management programs that can be implemented not only on a daily basis but also when travelling (e.g., correct sitting positions, jet lag, lifting and handling luggage). A process of empowerment of health management from practitioner to golfer is established.

Self-testing

Within two or three lessons, the professional golf coach usually detects the physical anomalies of their pupil (e.g., tight muscle groups, poor joint flexi-

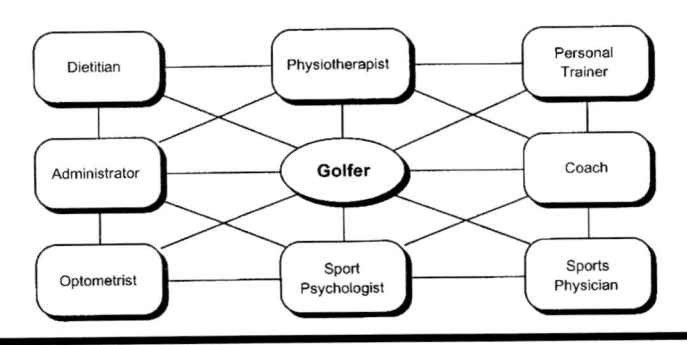

Figure 1
A multidisciplinary team approach to optimising performance and preventing injury.

bility, and poor posture). Initially a subjective form is completed to analyse the lifestyle, practice behaviour and previous injuries sustained by the golfer. Apart from promoting good duty of care, this assessment can indicate potential risk areas and postural weakness as a result of occupation or poor practice regimes. Self-testing drills are given to assist in improving the technical skills of the pupil. For example, they may be recommended to develop awareness of good postural position when addressing the ball; to stretch tight muscles caused by prolonged functional activities prior to arriving at the golf course; to strengthen postural muscles weakened by these activities; or to reduce the risk of spinal injuries and back pain as a result of prolonged bending and twisting in short- and long-game practice.

Figure 2 shows examples of exercises designed to improve shoulder, trunk, hip and heel control in the golf swing (2a, 2b), and to correct muscle imbalance between back and front of the body (2c). These drills can be used as part of a home program to improve posture, flexibility, golf technique and self-regulation. They also optimise performance by providing effective warm-up techniques prior to hitting off on the first tee. Technical benefits from improved postural position at address are evident after 6 weeks of self-testing drills in Figure 3. Pupils who have considerable difficulty performing the self-testing drills are referred by the coach to a golf-specific physiotherapist for a musculoskeletal screening.

Musculoskeletal Screening

This individual assessment outlines the physical anomalies that inhibit improvement in the swing technique. The screening involves all of the main

Figure 2
Self-testing drills (2a, 2b) designed to improve control in the golf swing and correct common anomalies (2c).

INTEGRATED PHYSICAL AND TECHNICAL DEVELOPMENT

Figure 3
Technical benefits from improved postural position are evident after 6 weeks of exercise.

muscle groups and identifies muscle imbalances, postural deviations, proprioceptive deficiencies, and areas of inflexibility within muscle groups and surrounding joints — all of which lead to poor movement patterns.

Following musculoskeletal screening, specific exercise programs including stretches, postural awareness drills, and massage can be prescribed by a physiotherapist to alleviate tightness and postural deviations. Figure 4 shows a golfer with hypermobility detected in the musculoskeletal screening. Her position at the top of the backswing was unstable due to poor core stability in the gluteal and latissimus dorsi muscle groups (4a). Included in her exercise program was knee squat positioning to improve balance and stabilise her pelvis (4b). The result was a noticeable improvement in her address position after 3 months (4c). Note particularly how she has less lower body rotation and more control of her body segments, particularly her arms.

Figure 5 shows a golfer diagnosed with kyphosis, an increase in thoracic curvature producing a rounded upper back (5a). Such postural dysfunction may result from maintaining a forward flexed position for long periods when carrying out putting drills and practice regimes. At address the spine is curved, shoulders slumped forward, and head tucked down (5c). This restricts upper body rotation in the golf swing causing the arms and hands to be overactive, which is often a major factor in swing plane deviations.

Upper and lower back extension on a Swiss ball was recommended together with other exercises to reduce kyphosis (Figure 5b). These exercises were designed to stretch the tight pectoral, sternomastoid and upper trapezius muscle groups, and strengthen the weak deep abdominals, rhomboids

Figure 4
Hypermobility detected in musculoskeletal screening can be treated through appropriate exercise.

and middle trapezius. The result was improved postural functioning after 6 months. At the address position the shoulders are back and the head is no longer tucked down, allowing trunk rotations and making it easier to get the club on plane (5d).

Swiss ball exercise programs can be easily implemented when travelling. A personal trainer with golf-specific credentials can also prescribe a gym-based strength and conditioning program. A full screening report is given to the coach and trainer to be implemented in the pupil's program. Potential injury areas are prioritised with specific advice and exercise regimes given. This makes the athlete more accountable and becomes part of their objectives in golf for specific time periods. Communication lines are built between the coach, physiotherapist and personal trainer to ensure the athlete addresses these physiological requirements. Rescreening is carried out at the end of a given time period, for example 6 months to 1 year depending on the intensity of golf practice and competition, and an update can be made on the athlete's physical progress.

A case study of an elite amateur golfer illustrates the integrated approach used in his physical and technical development. Figure 6 shows that his initial set-up and backswing positioning were poor because the top of his spine was closer to the target than its base (6a, 6e). This creates what is known as a reverse pivot whereby weight is transferred toward the target on the backswing and away from it on the downswing. From a physiological perspective he had a sway-back where the curve in the thoracic and upper lumbar spine is exaggerated, as seen here by the gap between the wall and his back (6c). This was also found to be a major cause of his reverse pivot as the extra curve in his spine pushed his upper body towards the target during its

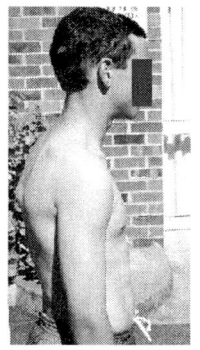

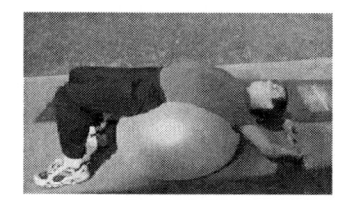

Figure 5
Swiss ball extension and other exercises reduce kyphosis, a rounded upper back, and produce technical improvements in the set-up position.

rotational movement in the backswing. To improve his postural position and reduce the risk of spinal injuries, an exercise program was implemented for a period of 8 weeks. The exercises included the crucifix position, held for 10-30 seconds while keeping the small of his back against the wall, and repeated three times (6c, 6d). The program resulted in improved set-up and pivot motion during the swing (6b, 6f).

Resources
Various resource materials have been published by McMaster and associates to assist coaches and players achieve their fitness objectives and prevent golf injuries. *Get Fit for Golf Part 1* is a pocket manual that explains the benefits of exercising before, during and after golf, and provides insight into basic stretching, golf injuries and their prevention. *Get Fit for Golf Part 2* provides a comprehensive account of the 12 physical requirements for game improve-

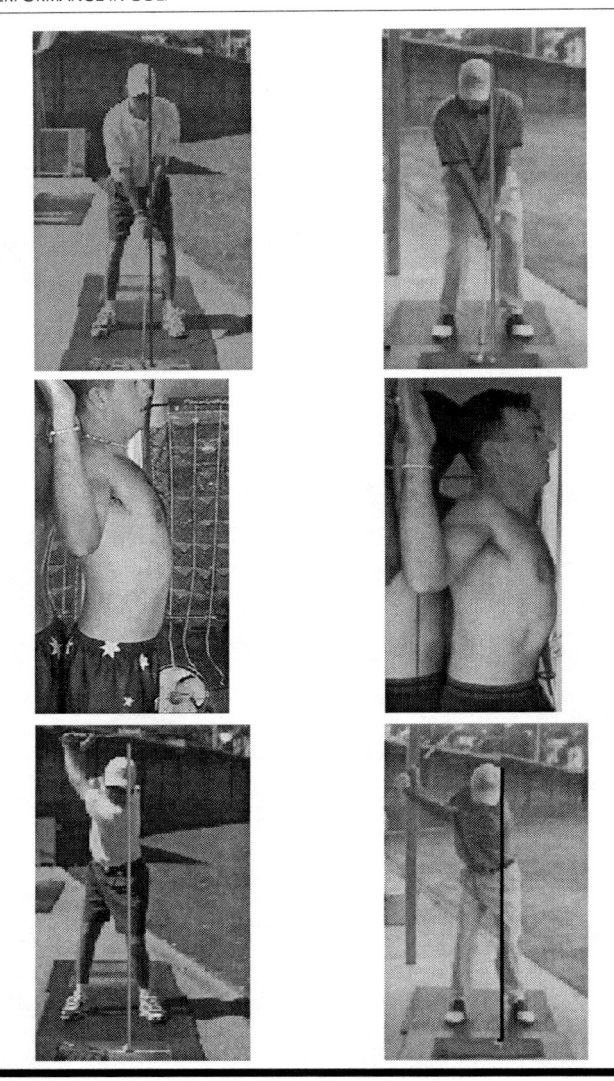

Figure 6
Self-testing drills and other exercises result in technical and physiological improvements in an elite amateur golfer.

ment addressed in the musculoskeletal screening, and recommends appropriate exercises for golfers in each of the areas. This book, together with the self-testing drills, screening forms and many other materials pertinent to golf performance and injury prevention, is also available on *The Golf Fitness*

System CD-ROM (James, Girvan, & McMaster, 2000). Further information is available on the Clinic's web site: www.golfmed.net.

Proactive Programs

Proactive programs have been designed and customised for institutes of sport, golf governing bodies, and clubs in Australia. To ensure they have a positive effect, the programs are all conducted under the title, *Get Fit for Golf.*

Australian Institute of Sport

On commencing an AIS Scholarship Program, an athlete is given a personalised musculoskeletal screening. This screening focuses on the individual's physical requirements and outlines any specific area of their body that could be susceptible to injury. The physiotherapist then compiles a list of priority areas for the athlete to work on, giving them exercises specific to each individual's needs. This makes the athlete aware of their strengths and weaknesses and responsible for their physical well-being. Copies of the musculoskeletal assessment are also given to the coach and the qualified strength and conditioning consultants. These are discussed in a meeting forum to outline any physical weaknesses that the individual athlete may have and to reinforce specific programs when practising or at the gymnasium. Coaches also reinforce the importance of quality practice by implementing warm-up and warm-down exercise regimes, and ensure the athletes receive early intervention if they experience the onset of injury. Postural exercises are also implemented to improve good address positions in the golf swing.

Early screening is essential so that the anomalies associated with intensive golf practice and competition at the highest levels can be addressed throughout the year. Meetings are also held formally and informally with administrators and other medical science professionals. A full syllabus of golf-specific health lectures and workshops is presented throughout the year involving coaches and physiotherapists. The information presented includes applied anatomy, physiology and self-care programs. These have resulted in the athletes having a greater knowledge of the stresses their bodies are placed under, and also gives them an opportunity to be in a 'train-the-trainer' situation, in order that they can give specific exercises and advice to their students in the future. Recent graduates of the AIS Scholarship Program include Tammie Durdin, Matthew Goggin, and James McLean.

Victorian Institute of Sport

This live-at-home program targets an older age group. It includes male and female amateur and professional athletes who are preparing themselves for professional competition, and has been responsible for former athletes such as Robert Allenby, Stuart Appleby, Stephen Allan and Geoff Ogilvy. Musculoskeletal screening and rescreening are compulsory, and as these athletes are preparing themselves towards a professional golf career, proactive programs are geared towards their physical needs on tour or at practice ranges. User-friendly, self-management programs have been designed by coaches, physiotherapists and strength and conditioning consultants. Coaches also integrate quality practice with stretching and postural reeducation programs. Posture ball classes and onsite sport science professionals are available on a weekly basis to prevent potential injuries and ensure the best advice can be given.

New South Wales Institute of Sport
The Victorian and New South Wales Institutes have a similar structure, however the latter has a major logistical problem as a result of athletes having to travel vast distances from home to the Institute. Screening, rescreening and health awareness workshops are therefore presented on a block basis, and the use of web sites and an email system is currently being researched in order that the athletes can have access to injury prevention and health awareness advice.

Women's Golf Victoria
This governing body sponsors the Victorian Institute of Sport program and takes an active role in reinforcing the importance of injury prevention and health awareness in golfers. Those in the Victorian women's amateur team are all screened, rescreened and encouraged to attend the lectures and workshops presented at the Institute. Medical science professionals, administrators, coaches and elite athletes attend the annual junior golf camp. A 12-point screening is given to each junior female golfer and stretching programs are emphasised throughout their stay at camp. Health awareness and injury prevention is also a major focus of Women's Golf Victoria at the Australian Women's Open each year. Information and free advice on injury prevention are given to the golfing public at the Open.

Victorian Golf Association
This governing body also sponsors the Victorian Institute of Sport athletes. They have encouraged compulsory screening, rescreening and injury prevention workshops for those in the Victorian men's amateur team. The State team of junior male golfers have also been screened and implement stretching programs as part of their precompetition routine. The VGA also utilises the Institute's sports medical science team at the Victorian Open to promote the importance of injury prevention and conditioning of golfers.

Professional Golfers' Association of Australia

The PGA sponsors athletes at all of the national institutes, and has incorporated these lectures and workshops into the trainee programs where screening and rescreening are now strongly recommended. In addition, injury prevention and strength and conditioning specific to golf are presented as part of the points system associated with the PGA's Professional Development Program. Professional golf coaches at national and club level also have access to the information at the institutes. National coaching summits include the latest information available on injury prevention and strength and conditioning specific to golf. Many of the PGA's international Tour players access the screening, stretching and postural programs to ensure they maximise their performance and prevent injury while on tour.

Australian Golf Union

The AGU sponsors the Australian Institute of Sport Golf Program. In addition to this they have a State School Camp program. This allows younger golf students to reside in Melbourne and access these programs produced by the AIS. Screening, stretching, and strength and conditioning programs are made available to these students.

Golf Clubs

Many clubs now have yearly seminars which include speakers from the institutes. This allows golfers at grass roots level to access injury prevention programs. Representatives from these golf clubs can also visit the institutes to gain knowledge from their sports medicine database. Public awareness is also achieved through *Get Fit For Golf* articles in journals and segments on television. Injury prevention seminars have also been established by Deakin University in Melbourne and are available to all golfers.

These programs ensure that golfers of all levels have access to injury prevention information and that they understand the importance of personalised physical preparation for golf. Early results have shown a dramatic decrease in chronic golf injuries and a faster return to golf participation as a result of early physiotherapeutic intervention. The detection of potential injury risk factors during musculoskeletal screening assessments of elite male and female golfers at the Australian Institute of Sport and the Victorian Institute of Sport has reduced incidence of injury, reduced injury treatment time, increased practice time, and enabled golfers to increase the potential to be fit specifically for golf and life in general, which should in turn prolong their golf careers.

This success has been achieved with all age and golfing levels largely by an holistic approach with golf administrators, medical science professionals and golf coaches working together to promote early screening of golfers and design specific *Get Fit For Golf* programs. These programs are continually being developed and improved to ensure that all golfers will benefit from being fit for golf.

Conclusion

Australia has enjoyed a most enviable reputation as a producer of some of the world's finest golfers. It is also recognised for its high standard of sports medicine and continues to be a leader in medical science in relation to elite athletes. These factors have now produced programs which not only treat specific golf-related injuries, but also assist in injury prevention at the grass roots through to elite levels. This in turn allows golfers to play more intensively for longer participation periods, enables them to be self-managed, and assists in optimising their performance. This system is now being utilised at all levels of golf, is continually being improved, and is a well-accepted aspect of golf coaching and development in Australia.

Although there is now an integrated approach to the golfer's physical and technical development, further improvements will result from understanding and harnessing the interactions between physical, technical and mental skills. The use of mental rehearsal techniques to visualise swing corrections prior to their physical practice is one such example. Imagery techniques also have much promise in allowing golfers to maintain technical skills during periods of illness and accelerating their rehabilitation process after injury (Green, 1992).

Indeed, it might be argued that an understanding of the interaction between the three skill areas is of fundamental importance for the effectiveness of most, if not all golf science interventions. Lennon (1999) concluded that, "The quality of training in golf has suffered from an overriding concentration by coaches and players on parts of the golf swing without sufficient attention being given to the process of integrating physical development, swing mechanics, and mental skills into one picture" (p. 63). A player preoccupied with a 2° inconsistency in shoulder rotation may experience paralysis by analysis with disastrous consequences for performance. Sports medicine consultants have acknowledged that their work is more effective when they are aware of what the golfer is doing with other members of the team (Thomas, in press). An holistic approach is clearly essential for the effectiveness of golf improvement programs.

Acknowledgments

Some parts of this chapter were originally presented at the PGA of Australia's 1998 and 2000 National Coaching Summits and are reproduced with permission.

References

Batt, M.E. (1992). A survey of golf injuries in amateur golfers. *British Journal of Sports Medicine, 26,* 63–65.

Batt, M.E. (1993). Golfing injuries: An overview. *Sports Medicine, 16,* 64–71.

Cheetham, P.J., Martin, P.E., Mottram, R.E., & St Laurent, B.F. (2000). The importance of stretching the "X-Factor" in the downswing of golf: The "X-Factor Stretch". *Proceedings of the 2000 Pre-Olympic Congress.* Brisbane, Australia: International Congress on Sport Science, Sports Medicine and Physical Education.

Chim, J., & McMaster, R. (1994). *Get fit for golf — Part 1.* Melbourne, Australia: Unlimited Graphics.

Cochran, A.J. (Ed.). (1990). *Science and golf: Proceedings of the First World Scientific Congress of Golf.* London: E & FN Spon.

Cochran, A.J., & Farrally, M.R. (Eds.). (1994). *Science and golf II: Proceedings of the 1994 World Scientific Congress of Golf.* London: E & FN Spon.

Farrally, M.R. & Cochran, A.J. (Eds.). (1999). *Science and golf III: Proceedings of the 1998 World Scientific Congress of Golf.* Champaign, IL: Human Kinetics.

Finch, C., Sherman, C., & James, T. (1999). The epidemiology of golf injuries in Victoria, Australia: Evidence from sports medicine clinics and emergency department presentations. In M.R. Farrally & A.J. Cochran (Eds.), *Science and golf III: Proceedings of the 1998 World Scientific Congress of Golf* (pp. 73–82). Champaign, IL: Human Kinetics.

Green, L.B. (1992). The use of imagery in the rehabilitation of injured athletes. *The Sport Psychologist, 6,* 416–428.

James, T., Girvan, S., & McMaster, R. (2000). *The golf fitness system.* [CD-ROM]. Melbourne, Australia: Melbourne Golf Injury Clinic.

Jones, D. (1999). The effects of proprioceptive neuromuscular facilitation flexibility training on the clubhead speed of recreational golfers. In M.R. Farrally & A.J. Cochran (Eds.), *Science and golf III: Proceedings of the 1998 World Scientific Congress of Golf* (pp. 46–50). Champaign, IL: Human Kinetics.

Leigh, R.J., & Young, D.B. (1999). Back pain among junior golfers. In M.R. Farrally & A.J. Cochran (Eds.), *Science and golf III: Proceedings of the 1998 World Scientific Congress of Golf* (pp. 92–96). Champaign, IL: Human Kinetics.

Lennon, H.M. (1999). Physiological profiling and physical conditioning for elite golfers. In M.R. Farrally & A.J. Cochran (Eds.), *Science and golf III: Proceedings of the 1998 World Scientific Congress of Golf* (pp. 58–64). Champaign, IL: Human Kinetics.

McCarroll, J.R. (1996). The frequency of golf injuries. *Clinics in Sports Medicine, 15,* 1–7.

McCarroll, J.R., Rettig, A.C., & Shelbourne, K.D. (1990). Injuries in the amateur golfer. *Physician and Sports Medicine, 18,* 122–126.

McMaster, R., & Chim, J. (1998). *Get fit for golf — Part 2.* Melbourne, Australia: Flash Print.

McNicholas, M.J., Nielsen, A., & Knill-Jones, R.P. (1999). Golf injuries in Scotland. In M.R. Farrally & A.J. Cochran (Eds.), *Science and golf III: Proceedings of the 1998 World Scientific Congress of Golf* (pp. 65–72). Champaign, IL: Human Kinetics.

McTeigue, M., Lamb, S.R., Mottram, R., & Pirozzolo, F. (1994). Spine and hip motion analysis during the golf swing. In A.J. Cochran & M.R. Farrally (Eds.), *Science and golf II: Proceedings of the 1994 World Scientific Congress of Golf* (pp. 50–58). London: E & FN Spon.

Sugaya, H., Tsuchiya, A., Moriya, H., Morgan, D.A., & Banks, S.A. (1999). Low back injury in elite and professional golfers: An epidemiological and radiographic study. In M.R. Farrally & A.J. Cochran (Eds.), *Science and golf III: Proceedings of the 1998 World Scientific Congress of Golf* (pp. 83–91). Champaign, IL: Human Kinetics.

Theriault, G., & Lachance, P. (1998). Golf injuries: An overview. *Sports Medicine, 1998, 26,* 43–57.

Thomas, P.R. (in press). Professional practice in sport psychology: Developing programs with golfers and orienteers. In G. Tenenbaum (Ed.), *The practice of sport and exercise psychology: International perspectives*. Morgantown, WV: Fitness Information Technology.

Van Der Steenhoven, G.A., Burdorf, A., & Tromp-Klaren, E.G.M. (1994). Back pain in novice golfers, a one-year follow-up. In A.J. Cochran & M.R. Farrally (Eds.), *Science and golf II: Proceedings of the 1994 World Scientific Congress of Golf* (pp.20–25). London: E & FN Spon.

Wilks, J., & Jones, D. (1996). Golf-related injuries seen at hospital emergency departments. *The Australian Journal of Science and Medicine in Sport, 28*, 43–45.

Performance Under Pressure: A Little Knowledge is a Dangerous Thing?

Lew Hardy and Richard Mullen

Few sport contexts present better opportunities than golf to observe the dramatic loss of performance effects that are a characteristic of catastrophe models of anxiety and performance. The catastrophe models were developed by the first of the present authors in conjunction with various other researchers because of dissatisfaction with the then available descriptions of the anxiety-performance relationship based on the inverted-U hypothesis (Broadhurst, 1957; Oxendine, 1970; Yerkes & Dodson, 1908). From that researcher's perspective, it seemed that before one could seriously consider the more interesting question of *how* stress affected performance, one must have at least a reasonably accurate description of *what* these effects were. The first part of the present chapter will focus upon research that has examined the catastrophe models of anxiety and performance. The second part will then focus upon more recent research that has examined possible explanations for catastrophe effects. Most of the data presented will be from golf studies, but occasionally data from other contexts will be presented where it is felt that this may help our understanding. Finally, some "educated guesses" will be presented regarding the control processes that we think may underpin anxiety effects, together with some future directions that researchers might like to pursue and the applied implications for golf.

Catastrophe Models of Anxiety and Performance

The catastrophe models of anxiety and performance (Hardy, 1990, 1996a) make use of a multidimensional conceptualisation of anxiety in which at least two components can be identified. According to this conceptualisation, cognitive anxiety (worry) is operationalised in terms of negative concerns about performing well and the consequences of failing to do so (i.e., fear of failure). Somatic anxiety, on the other hand, is operationalised in terms of performers' perceptions of the physiological symptomatology that is associated with their anxiety state (e.g., racing pulse, butterflies in the stomach, and sweaty hands). A considerable amount of research has supported this two-component conceptualisation (see, e.g., Davidson & Schwartz, 1976; Morris, Davis, & Hutchings, 1981; Martens, Vealey, & Burton, 1990).

The cusp catastrophe model is the simplest of the catastrophe models. According to this model, cognitive anxiety is a splitting factor that determines whether the effects of physiological arousal upon performance will be small and continuous (when cognitive anxiety is low) or large and discontinuous (when cognitive anxiety is high). In catastrophe theory terminology, physiological arousal is called an asymmetry factor and cognitive anxiety is called a splitting factor (see, e.g., Zeeman, 1976). The behaviour surface that is defined by the cusp catastrophe model has two regions of relative stability — an upper performance surface and a lower performance surface. The splitting factor determines the distance between these two regions, whereas the asymmetry factor determines the proximity of a given performance to a point where a critical (discontinuous) change in performance may take place (see Figure 1; Hardy, 1990, 1996a).

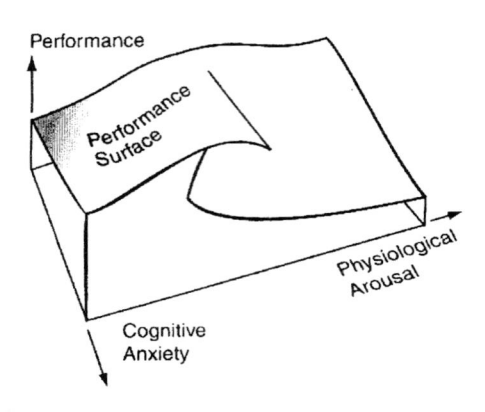

Figure 1

The catastrophe model of anxiety and performance (Hardy, 1990).

An important characteristic of the cusp catastrophe model is that it uses physiological arousal rather than somatic anxiety as the asymmetry factor. Although several studies have shown that physiological arousal, as measured by heart rate, follows a similar time course to somatic anxiety prior to an important event (Parfitt, Jones, & Hardy, 1990), there are important distinctions regarding the means by which physiological arousal and somatic anxiety might exert an influence upon performance (see Hardy, 1996a). A second distinguishing characteristic of the cusp catastrophe model is that it makes predictions about how cognitive anxiety and physiological arousal should interact with each other to influence performance. More specifically, it predicts that increases in cognitive anxiety should lead to enhanced performance when physiological arousal is moderate or low (left hand side of Figure 1), but impaired performance when physiological arousal is high (right hand side of Figure 1). Evidence has been produced that provides both direct (Edwards & Hardy, 1996) and indirect (Deffenbacher, 1977; Woodman, Albinson, & Hardy, 1996) support for an interaction hypothesis. However, it should be noted that although these studies provide clear evidence of *an* interaction, none of them has produced exactly *the* interaction predicted by the cusp catastrophe model.

A third characteristic of the cusp catastrophe model is its prediction that, under conditions of high cognitive anxiety, *hysteresis* should occur; that is to say, the point at which performance suddenly drops from the upper performance surface to the lower performance surface when physiological arousal is increasing, is different from the point at which performance suddenly jumps from the lower performance surface to the upper performance surface when physiological arousal is decreasing (see the front edge of Figure 1, and Hardy, 1990). Under conditions of low cognitive anxiety, hysteresis should not occur; and changes in performance will be smooth and follow the same path, whether physiological arousal is increasing or decreasing (compare the front and back edge of the behaviour surface in Figure 1). To date, the hysteresis hypothesis has been directly tested on two occasions, by Hardy and Parfitt (1991) and by Hardy, Parfitt, and Pates (1994). On both of these occasions, significant three-factor interactions between cognitive anxiety, physiological arousal, and the direction of change of physiological arousal upon performance have confirmed the hypothesis. However, it is also worth observing that both of these studies manipulated physiological arousal via physical exercise, which may or may not be similar to manipulating it via psychological stress.

Hardy (1996b) attempted to clarify the role of self-confidence in the stress performance relationship. He proposed (and tested) a higher order butterfly catastrophe model that included self-confidence as a third control parameter alongside cognitive anxiety and physiological arousal. In this higher order model, self-confidence was hypothesised to act as a *bias* factor, that is, to have the effect of swinging the front face of the catastrophe surface displayed in Figure 1 to the right (high self-confidence) or to the left (low self-confidence). Thus, according to the butterfly catastrophe model, highly confident golfers should be able to tolerate higher levels of physiological arousal when they are cognitively anxious before experiencing a loss in performance. Using putting performance as the criterion variable, Hardy (1996b) found some support for the butterfly catastrophe model. However, he used a fairly complex surface-fitting procedure devised by Guastello (1982, 1987) that has been severely criticised by Alexander, Herbert, DeShon, and Hanges (1992). Consequently, this finding needs to be regarded with some circumspection.

More recently, Hardy, Woodman, and Carrington (in preparation) have produced rather more direct evidence supporting the self-confidence hypothesis using golf driving as the criterion variable. In their study, the median split technique was used to identify four groups of participants who were: high in cognitive anxiety and high in somatic anxiety; high in cognitive anxiety, but low in somatic anxiety; low in cognitive anxiety, but high in somatic anxiety; and low in both cognitive anxiety and somatic anxiety. A two-factor (quadrant) analysis of variance was then performed to examine the interactive effects of cognitive and somatic anxiety upon performance. The effect size for the interaction effect was noted. The data were then redistributed, again using the median to divide participants into high and low groups on cognitive anxiety, but this time using the median plus 0.1 standard deviation to divide the participants into high and low somatic anxiety groups. The two-factor quadrant analysis was again performed, and the effect size of the interaction noted. This procedure was repeated a number of times, increasing the splitting point for somatic anxiety by 0.1 standard deviation at each repetition. The procedure was then repeated a number of times with the splitting point for somatic anxiety starting at the median minus 0.1 standard deviation, and being reduced by 0.1 standard deviations at each repetition. In this way, a point on the somatic anxiety axis was identified that created the maximum effect size for the cognitive anxiety by somatic anxiety interaction. In fact, this "point" was usually a small range of somatic anxiety scores, and this range represents the bifurcation set in which hysteresis occurs (i.e., the range of somatic anxiety scores where performance flips from the upper to the lower performance surface and vice versa). In order to examine the influence of self-confidence on the cognitive anxiety by somatic anxiety interaction, the above procedure was applied separately to two sub-samples that had been obtained by splitting the data into high and low self-confidence groups. The resulting analyses of variance supported the hypothesis that the bifurcation set (and therefore the maximum interaction effect size) would occur at higher levels of somatic anxiety for golfers who were high in self-confidence than for golfers who were low in self-confidence (see Figure 2).

In summary, although it would be extremely premature to make any great claims for the validity of the catastrophe models of anxiety and performance, there is certainly enough supporting evidence to at least consider some potential explanations of them.

Potential Explanations of Catastrophe Effects
Processing Efficiency Theory

Perhaps the most obvious potential explanation of catastrophe effects is provided by Eysenck and Calvo's (1992) processing efficiency theory. This proposes two mechanisms by which cognitive anxiety can exert an influence upon performance. First, cognitively anxious performers have a reduced attentional capacity to focus on the task in hand because they use up part of these resources by worrying. Second, worry signals the importance of the event to the performer, and this signal leads the performer to invest additional effort in the task in order to allay his or her concerns. However, according to earlier versions of the theory (Eysenck, 1982), such increases in effort will occur only when performers perceive themselves to have at least a moderate subjective probability of succeeding; that is, they are moderately confident. If performers do not perceive themselves to have at least a moderate subjective probability of success then they will withdraw all effort from the task because, as Revelle and

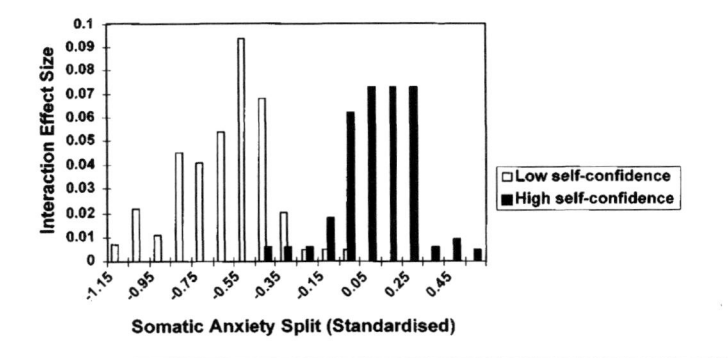

Figure 2
Interaction effect sizes obtained when performance data are partitioned at different points of the somatic anxiety axis (Hardy, Woodman, & Carrington, in preparation).

Michaels (1976) have succinctly put it, "the tough get going when the going gets tough," but "wise men do not beat their heads against brick walls"! Finally, processing efficiency theory does not ascribe any performance effects directly to physiological arousal or somatic anxiety, but proposes that any increases in effort will be reflected by a corresponding increase in physiological arousal or somatic anxiety (Eysenck, 1982). Thus, according to processing efficiency theory, anxiety may enhance performance if the task is not too attentionally demanding, but will impair performance if the task is attentionally demanding. Furthermore, whatever the effects of anxiety upon performance effectiveness, performance efficiency is always diminished because of the increased effort that is used to try and sustain performance.

The strongest evidence in support of the cusp catastrophe model has come from the two studies by Hardy and Parfitt (1991) and Hardy et al. (1994) that examined the hysteresis effect. These studies manipulated physiological arousal by means of physical work. However, it is entirely plausible that, when physiological arousal is manipulated in this way, it reflects the effort required to perform the task, rather than physiological arousal generated by anxiety associated with the environmental conditions. Assuming this to be the case, processing efficiency theory offers a highly plausible explanation for the hysteresis effects observed in these studies. For, as worry and effort required (physiological arousal) increase, one would quite reasonably expect that a point would be reached when performers no longer perceive themselves to have a moderate probability of success, and so withdraw their effort from the task at hand. In essence, they "give up" and performance on the task shows a corresponding catastrophic drop in performance. Of course, once performers have "given up," it is not surprising that a considerable change in their perceptions of the effort required to perform the task would need to occur before they would feel able to re-invest effort in the task. As an aside, it is worth noting that another implication of this line of reasoning is that the asymmetry factor for the cusp catastrophe model may need to be re-labelled effort required rather than physiological arousal (cf. Hardy, 1999).

Eysenck and Calvo (1992) have reviewed an impressive volume of research that is consistent with the predictions of processing efficiency theory. Unfortunately, published tests of these predictions in sports contexts have been extremely rare (Beuter, Duda, & Widule, 1989; Weinberg & Hunt, 1976) and are non-existent in golf settings. However, Mullen and Hardy (2000), and Mullen and Hardy (in preparation) report anxiety-induced increases in effort (both cognitive and physiological) in golfers when putting; and these changes in effort were not accompanied by corresponding improvements in putting performance (see next section), thereby offering some support for that prediction of processing efficiency theory.

The Conscious Processing Hypothesis

The conscious processing hypothesis (Baumeister, 1984; Masters, 1992a) proposes that highly skilled performance often breaks down in competitive situations because anxiety leads performers to focus inwardly upon the process of performing. More precisely, they attempt to use explicit "rules" about the process of performing to consciously control movements that have been overlearned to such an extent that they are normally performed automatically. However, it is well known that conscious control is relatively crude compared to automatic control (Keele, 1973; Kimble & Perlmuter, 1970; Langer & Imber, 1979), and so skilled performance breaks down. The conscious processing hypothesis provides a plausible explanation of the performance decrements associated with catastrophes, but it can only account for hysteresis effects if one makes the additional assumption that human information processing systems have a tendency to continue to operate in whatever way they are already operating; that is to say, if the operating system is using conscious control it has a tendency to continue to do so, and if it is using automatic control then it has a tendency to continue in that mode. If this additional assumption were true, then the reinstatement of automatic control would be difficult once it had been disrupted by conscious control, thereby accounting for the hysteresis effect.

A substantial number of studies have now used golf putting to examine the conscious processing hypothesis. Masters (1992a) conducted a study in which novice golfers learned to putt under different conditions. In one of these conditions, the golfers were given explicit instruction about the rules of golf putting, whereas in another they were stopped from forming such rules by being required to generate random letters throughout their practice sessions. Masters hypothesised that this second group in which participants acquired their skill without any explicit instruction would be less prone to anxiety effects because they had no explicit knowledge that they fall back on to try and consciously control their movements. After 400 practice trials, each participant performed a further 100 trials under a stress condition. In this stress test, the performance of the golfers who had acquired their skill by explicit instruction deteriorated, whereas the performance of the golfers who had acquired their skill by implicit means (i.e., without explicit rules) continued to improve. Masters interpreted these findings as support for the conscious processing hypothesis.

Bright and Freedman (1998) partially replicated Masters' (1992a) study, but failed to find a significant interaction between implicit versus explicit learning and anxiety. However, the participants in Bright and Freedman's study had only 160 practice putts as opposed to 400 in Masters' study, so there is no reason to expect that they would have reached an automatic state of control prior to stress testing. Consequently, there would be no reason to predict that the use of explicit rules would interfere with performance. In light of this argument, it is the present authors' contention that Bright and Freedman's study should be discounted as evidence on the conscious processing hypothesis. However, having said all that, conscious processing is not the only viable interpretation of Masters' data.

Under stress, the implicit learning group in Masters' (1992a) study continued to improve, whereas the explicit learning group did not. However, the implicit learning group was not asked to continue the random letter generation task during their stress test. As a result, their continued improvement could be attributed to a reduction in task difficulty. Hardy, Mullen, and Jones (1996) controlled for this possible confound by replicating Masters' study with the addition of an extra implicit learning group that continued to perform the random letter generation task in the high-anxiety condition. It was hypothesised that the new implicit learning group would suffer performance impairment under stress. The results failed to support this hypothesis, both implicit learning groups showing virtually identical performance in the stress test, thereby adding support to Masters' conscious processing hypothesis. However, the Hardy et al. study was not without its own limitations. Another possible confound was identified. In performing the random letter generation task over 400 learning trials, participants in both the Masters and Hardy et al. studies may have become desensitised to self-generated verbalisations and this desensitisation could have rendered them at least partially immune to the effects of competitive state anxiety. Indeed, in another study on golf putting by Lewis and Linder (1997), "choking" effects were equally attenuated by desensitising participants to self-awareness or by having them count backwards from 100 during their learning trials.

Although not on golf, a study by Hardy, Mullen, and Martin (under review) was designed to provide a test of the conscious processing hypothesis that was not confounded by such desensitisation effects. A performance, rather than learning, paradigm was adopted. Experienced trampolinists were asked to perform using explicit knowledge under low- and high-anxiety conditions. Explicit knowledge was provided for the performers by means of a shadowing technique, as suggested by Masters (1992b). The performers' coach called out a coaching point for each specific move as performers went through their voluntary competition routines and participants were asked to concentrate on using the explicit cues to guide their performance. The combination of explicit knowledge and high state anxiety resulted in the trampolinists registering a decrement in performance, thereby supporting the predictions of the conscious processing hypothesis (see Figure 3). However, yet again, these performance decrements can be explained by an alternative attentional threshold hypothesis. It is well known that anxiety leads to an attentional deficit in working memory (Eysenck, 1992; Wine, 1971). Performance decrements may therefore have been caused by relevant cues taking up a portion of attentional capacity and anxiety taking up a further portion, thereby depleting attentional capacity beyond the threshold required for high-level performance.

The purpose of Mullen and Hardy's (2000) study was to control for both the desensitisation and attentional threshold hypotheses. Golf putting was again used as the criterion task, and the performance paradigm used by Hardy, Mullen, and Martin (under review) was retained but with an additional condition included in the experimental design. Retaining the performance paradigm avoided the problem of desensitisation associated with the learning paradigm used by Masters (1992a) and Hardy, Mullen, and Jones (1996). The additional condition required the skilled golfers who were participants to putt while simultaneously performing the random letter generation task used by Masters. The addition of the random letter generation task afforded an examination of the attentional threshold explanation identified by Hardy, Mullen, and Martin (under review). From a conscious processing perspective, the random letter generation task should have prevented performers accessing their explicit knowledge base, while the shadowing task should have encouraged lapses into conscious processing. However, according to the attentional threshold hypothesis, both the task-relevant shadowing task and the task-irrelevant random letter generation task should consume attentional resources, thereby impairing performance when

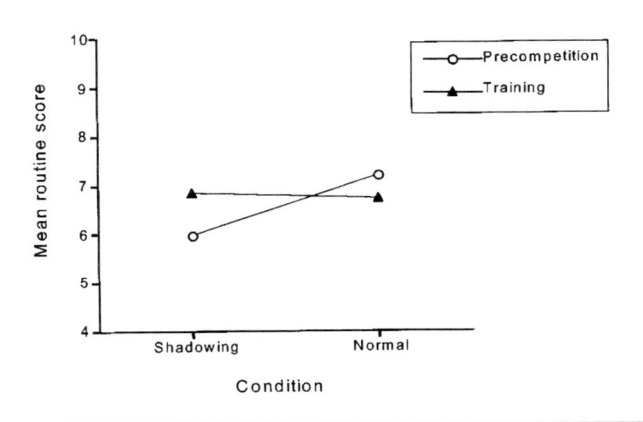

Figure 3
Mean performance scores (Hardy, Mullen, & Martin, under review).

they appeared in conjunction with high levels of cognitive anxiety. Mullen and Hardy (2000) also extended previous research in two additional ways: (a) a self-report scale was included to examine the patterning of effort invested by performers because this had been shown to vary as a function of anxiety (Eysenck, 1992); and (b) an exploratory, in vivo, two-dimensional kinematic analysis of the golf putting stroke was included. Finally, it is worth observing that participants were required to use three swing thoughts (process goals) when they were in the shadowing condition.

Differences were identified in skill levels across the sample, resulting in a median split based on putting ability in the low-anxiety control condition. For better putters, the results partially supported the conscious processing hypothesis, as performance deteriorated when the better golfers putted using explicit knowledge in the high-anxiety condition (see Figure 4). However, there were no significant differences in the performance of the poorer putters in any of the experimental conditions. The patterning of self-reported effort supported the processing efficiency theory prediction that anxious performers would increase the amount of effort they invested in the task. The kinematic analysis revealed little in the way of effects that could be interpreted as offering firm support for conscious processing.

Jackson and Willson (1999) used a slightly different paradigm to examine the effect of swing thoughts (process goals) upon choking under pressure. They had experienced golfers putt using a variety of different attentional strategies, including swing thoughts, process goals during the set-up phase, and focusing on a spot on the ball. They found that a *single* swing

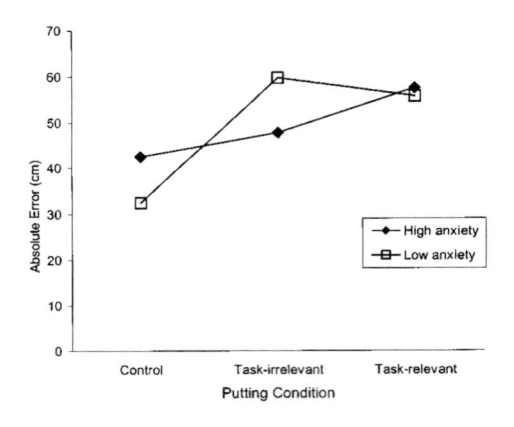

Figure 4
Absolute error scores (cm) for better putters (Mullen & Hardy, 2000).

thought could be used to significantly reduce the negative impact of competitive stress upon putting performance.

Mullen, Hardy and Tattersall (in preparation) performed yet another golf-putting study using a refinement of the design used by Mullen and Hardy (2000). Additionally, the interdisciplinary focus was extended to include a three-dimensional, in vivo kinematic analysis using a more complex model of joint dynamics, and spectral analysis of heart rate variability as a cardiovascular index of effort (Jorna, 1992; Mulder, 1985; Mulder & Mulder, 1987). The results lent themselves to an attentional threshold interpretation in that putting performance was impaired in the high-anxiety condition by both the shadowing and task-irrelevant (tone counting) conditions (see Figure 5). However, the performance impairment experienced by the golfers in the high-anxiety, shadowing condition means that conscious processing effects can not be totally discounted. Furthermore, although self-reported effort remained stable as a function of both anxiety and putting conditions, heart rate variability scores partially mirrored those found for performance (see Figure 6). Heart rate variability in the high frequency bandwidth (HRV-HF) is associated with respiratory sinus-arrythmia, with high spectral power associated with increased parasympathetic activity or decreased respiratory frequency (Grossman, 1992). Consequently, the findings could reflect attempts on the part of the golfers to actively cope with the demands of the tone counting and shadowing conditions. More precisely, when challenged by dual task conditions while putting, golfers may respond by employing a breathing-based relaxation strategy, which decreases

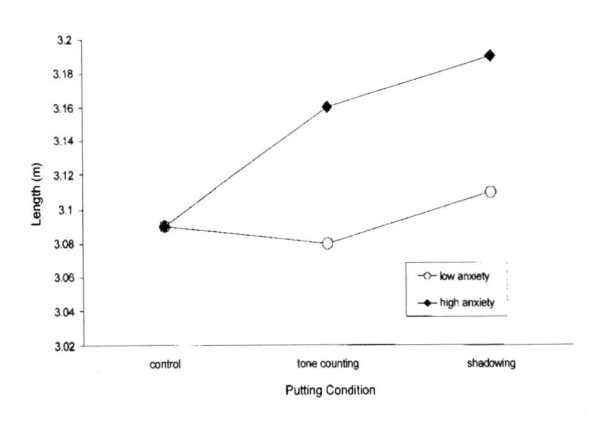

Figure 5
Mean performance scores for length of putt (Mullen, Hardy, & Tattersall, in preparation).

Figure 6
Mean HRVHF difference scores (N.B. Scores are original values prior to logarithmic transformation for ease of interpretation; SMI = squared modulation index; Mullen, Hardy, & Tattersall, in preparation).

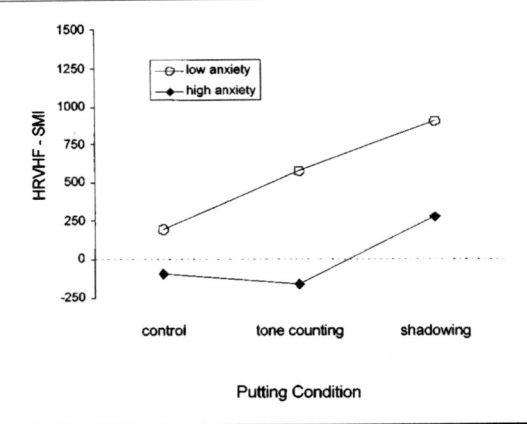

respiratory frequency and increases spectral power in the HRV-HF, provided they are not anxious. However, under stress, this effect is countered by anxiety-induced sympathetic activity. Thus, although in the high-anxiety tone counting and shadowing conditions power in the HRV-HF band returns to levels similar to the control condition, this pattern is now indicative of a suboptimal activation pattern. Of course, this interpretation is somewhat speculative and should therefore be treated with caution.

The kinematic data showed evidence that anxious performers attempted to regain movement control by "re-freezing" degrees of freedom in the distal (wrist) joint (see Figure 7). This finding was also interesting because re-freezing of degrees of freedom is the dynamic systems theory equivalent of the basic tenet of the conscious processing hypothesis — regression to an earlier stage of learning (Handford, Davids, Bennett, & Button, 1997; Vereijken, van Emmerik, Whiting, & Newell, 1992). The finding is also interesting because it is counter-intuitive to the notion of increased wrist break that is usually associated with the "yips."

As Hardy et al. (1996) have indicated, the conscious processing hypothesis does present a problem for advocates of the use of swing thoughts (process goals) by highly skilled golfers. For, if swing thoughts direct attention to the process of performing, they may lead anxious but skilled golfers to reinvest conscious control in their swings and thereby suffer severe loss of performance. However, it should be noted that Jackson and Willson's (1999) golfers did not experience performance loss when they used only a single

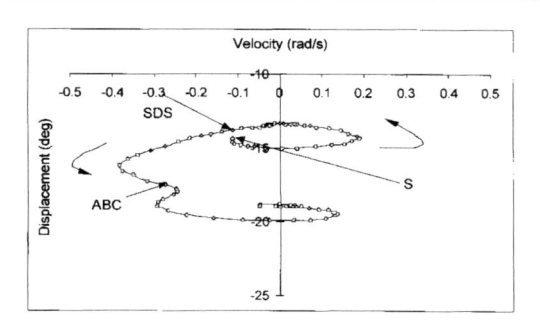

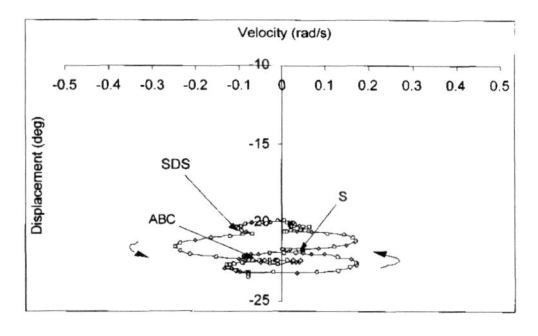

Figure 7
Typical phase plane portraits for the left wrist for the low-anxiety (upper) and high-anxiety (lower) conditions. S = start of putt; SDS = start of downswing; ABC = approximate ball contact (Mullen, Hardy, & Tattersall, in preparation).

swing thought (as opposed to the three that have typically been used elsewhere). Furthermore, it is possible that the nature of the swing thought also has some bearing on its impact upon performance. Hardy et al. (1996) suggest that regression effects may be less likely to happen when expert golfers use holistic swing thoughts that focus upon the whole skill (e.g., tempo) than when they use part swing thoughts that focus upon a part of the skill (e.g., release the clubhead through the ball). Some empirical support for this suggestion has recently been obtained in an as-yet-unpublished study on long jumpers by Hardy and Walker (1999; see Figure 8).

The Role of Self-Confidence

The most obvious variable that has been rather studiously ignored in the previous section is self-confidence. Both Eysenck (1982), and Carver and Scheier (1988, 1998), hypothesise that self-confidence is a key determinant

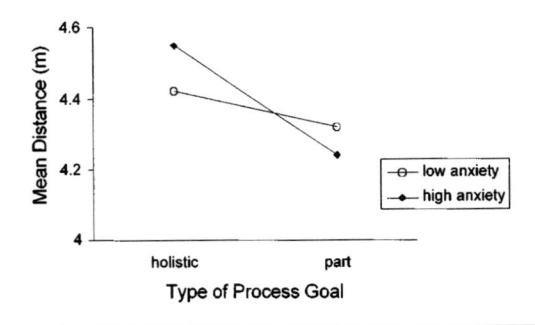

Figure 8
Hardy and Walker's (unpublished) data.

of continued effort in the face of anxiety or adversity. These hypotheses mirror Bandura's (1977, 1997: p. 141) stronger claim that "the stronger the sense of efficacy (situationally specific self-confidence), the bolder people are in taking on the problematic situations that breed stress and the greater their success in shaping things more to their liking." Furthermore, in the context of golf, Hardy (1996b) has presented evidence that self-confidence predicts putting performance over and above any effect that cognitive anxiety and physiological arousal may have. Another finding by Jones, Swain, and Hardy (1993) showed that cognitively anxious, but self-confident, gymnasts had a tendency to interpret their cognitive anxiety symptoms in a positive way. Cumulatively, these findings led Hardy (1996b) to conclude that high levels of self-confidence may protect performers against the debilitating effects of cognitive anxiety. Exactly how self-confidence might protect golfers from such effects is not clear, but it is possible that high self-confidence enables performers to trust their body to perform the actions required by any given situation (cf. Moore & Stevenson, 1994), and therefore allows them to maintain high levels of effort without lapsing into conscious control.

Some Educated Guesses About What is Going on

From the collection of studies that have been discussed above it can be concluded that: 1) attempts to maintain high levels of performance under stress may lead at least moderately self-confident golfers to invest additional effort in their performances when they are under pressure; 2) if they can resist the temptation to try and consciously control their golf/putting swing, this increased effort may lead to enhanced performance; 3) when golfers do regress into conscious control, they are likely to experience a dramatic loss of performance; 4) once high-level performance has been lost it is very difficult to recover it; 5) performance decrements are less likely to occur when golfers use a single swing thought than when they use three swing thoughts; 6) the nature of the swing thought may have some bearing upon whether or not it induces a lapse into conscious control.

It should perhaps be noted at this point that the present chapter has taken a very traditional cognitive approach towards explaining stress effects upon performance. It is entirely plausible that mediating variables other than effort and conscious control also influence such effects. For example, Mullen, Hardy, and Tattersall's (in preparation) kinematic analysis suggested that re-freezing of degrees of freedom might be the cause of lost performance. Other possibilities that may be more or less related to regression include: dechunking (MacMahon & Masters, 1998); attentional narrowing (Easterbrook, 1959); selective attention to threatening stimuli (Eysenck, 1992); and ironic effects — doing the very thing one does not want to do (Wegner, 1994). Indeed, Wegner, Ansfield, & Pilhoff (1998) have reported ironic effects under conditions of counter suggestion in golf putting. More precisely, both experienced and novice golfers putted long when told not to overshoot. Unfortunately, a detailed discussion of these possible effects is beyond the scope of this chapter, but further research is warranted in each of these areas.

Applied Implications

A number of applied implications can be derived from the above evidence and arguments. First, although effort may not appear to play a major role in golf swing production, this view may be a considerable over-simplification. For example, most serious golfers will have experienced occasions when they have been highly stressed and seemed to hit the ball a very long way. This sort of effect would be a classic prediction of processing efficiency theory. It could also be highly disruptive to a golfer's course management to suddenly (and possibly unpredictably) find that he or she was apparently over clubbing every hole. The cure is, of course, obvious once the cause has been identified.

Second, and we apologise for stating the obvious, self-confidence is almost certainly a major factor in high-quality swing production. It is possible that self-confidence is related to an ability to trust one's bodily mechanics to do what they know best how to do and let them "get on with the job" of producing a high-quality swing. However, personal experience suggests that very few club golfers (and possibly even few professional golfers) actually structure their practices to test their self-confidence and trust by putting themselves under a lot of pressure. This is not difficult to do. It simply requires a little bit of imagination and the will to practise the real skill of golf (performing under pressure) as opposed to the apparent skill of golf (having an elegant swing, hitting the ball a long way, or being very accurate with the short game).

One way in which golfers may be able to reduce lapses into conscious processing may be to automatise their preshot routines (Kingston & Hardy, 1994). It is well established that highly skilled golfers have very well established preshot routines that they do not vary for any given club selection/situation (Boutcher & Crews, 1987). By ensuring that preshot routines are automatised, golfers should enter their swing production phase in an automatic state, thereby increasing the likelihood that they will remain in that automatic state throughout swing production. It may also be the case that there is a place for swing thoughts immediately prior to the shot production phase. As Jackson and Willson (1999) suggest, it is possible that such swing thoughts give the mind something constructive to focus on instead of "fiddling" with the control of movement. However, we would recommend that only a single swing thought is ever used and that skilled golfers use holistic swing thoughts rather than part swing thoughts.

Finally, it should be clear that one of the problems that confronts golfers is the need to constantly switch from a conscious analytical state of action during the shot selection phase to an automatic state of action during the swing production phase. It might help to have well-rehearsed triggers to start and end these phases so as to ensure that one is in the most appropriate state. Boutcher and Rotella's (1987) suggestion to briefly employ a relaxation strategy immediately after shot selection may be a very appropriate one in this context.

References

Alexander, R.A., Herbert, G.R., DeShon, R.P., & Hanges, P.J. (1992). An examination of least-squares regression modelling of catastrophe theory. *Psychological Bulletin, 111,* 366–374.

Bandura, A. (1977). Self-efficacy: Toward a unifying theory of behavioural change. *Psychological Review, 84,* 191–215.

Bandura, A. (1997). *Self-efficacy: The exercise of control.* New York: W.H. Freeman.

Baumeister, R.F. (1984). Choking under pressure: Self-consciousness and paradoxical effects of incentives on skilful performance. *Journal of Personality and Social Psychology, 46,* 610–620.

Beuter, A., Duda, J.L., & Widule, C.J. (1989). The effect of arousal on joint kinematics and kinetics in children. *Research Quarterly for Exercise and Sport, 60,* 109–116.

Boutcher, S.H., & Crews, D.J. (1987). The effect of a pre-shot routine on a well-learned skill. *International Journal of Sport Psychology, 18,* 30–39.

Boutcher, S.H., & Rotella, R.J. (1987). A psychological skills educational program for closed-skill performance enhancement. *The Sport Psychologist, 1,* 200–207.

Bright, J.E.H., & Freedman, O. (1998). Differences between implicit and explicit acquisition of a complex skill under pressure. *British Journal of Psychology, 89,* 249–263.

Broadhurst, P.L. (1957). Emotionality and the Yerkes-Dodson law. *Journal of Experimental Psychology, 54,* 345–352.

Carver, C.S., & Scheier, M.F. (1988). A control perspective on anxiety. *Anxiety Research, 1,* 17–22.

Carver, C. S., & Scheier, M.F. (1998). *On the self-regulation of behaviour.* New York: Cambridge University Press.

Davidson, R.J., & Schwartz, G.E. (1976). The psychobiology of relaxation and related states: A multiprocess theory. In D. Mostofsky (Ed.), *Behavioral control and modification of physiological activity* (pp. 399–442). Englewood Cliffs, NJ: Prentice-Hall.

Deffenbacher, J.L. (1977). Relationship of worry and emotionality to performance on the Miller analogies test. *Journal of Educational Psychology, 69,* 191–195.

Easterbrook, J.A. (1959). The effect of emotion on the utilisation and the organisation of behaviour. *Psychological Review, 66,* 183–210.

Edwards, T., & Hardy, L. (1996). The interactive effects of intensity and direction of cognitive and somatic anxiety and self-confidence upon performance. *Journal of Sport & Exercise Psychology, 18,* 296–312.

Eysenck, M.W. (1982). *Attention and arousal.* New York: Springer-Verlag.

Eysenck, M.W. (1992). *Anxiety: The cognitive perspective.* Hove: Erlbaum.

Eysenck, M.W., & Calvo, M.G. (1992). Anxiety and performance: The processing efficiency theory. *Cognition and Emotion, 6,* 409–434.

Grossman, P. (1992). Respiratory and cardiac rhythms as windows to central and autonomic biobehavioural regulation: Selection of window frames, keeping the panes clean and viewing the neural topography. *Biological Psychology, 34,* 131–161.

Guastello, S.J. (1982). Moderator regression analysis and the cusp catastrophe: Application of a two-stage personnel selection, therapy and policy evaluation. *Behavioral Science, 27,* 259–272.

Guastello, S.J. (1987). A butterfly catastrophe model of motivation in organisations: Academic performance. *Journal of Applied Psychology, 72,* 161–182.

Handford, C., Davids, K., Bennett, S., & Button, C. (1997). Skill acquisition in sport: Some applications of an evolving practice ecology. *Journal of Sports Sciences, 15,* 621–640.

Hardy, L. (1990). A catastrophe model of anxiety and performance. In J.G. Jones & L. Hardy (Eds.), *Stress and performance in sport* (pp. 81–106). Chichester, UK: Wiley.

Hardy, L. (1996a). Testing the predictions of the cusp catastrophe model of anxiety and performance. *The Sport Psychologist, 10,* 140–156.

Hardy, L. (1996b). A test of catastrophe models of anxiety and sports performance against multidimensional models using the test of dynamic differences. *Anxiety, Stress and Coping: An International Journal, 9,* 69–86.

Hardy, L. (1999). Stress, anxiety and performance. *Journal of Science and Medicine in Sport, 2,* 227–233.

Hardy, L., Mullen, R., & Jones, G. (1996). Knowledge and conscious control of motor actions under stress. *British Journal of Psychology, 87,* 621–636.

Hardy, L., Mullen, R., & Martin, N. (under review). Effect of task-relevant cues and state anxiety on motor performance. *Perceptual and Motor Skills.*

Hardy, L., & Parfitt, G. (1991). A catastrophe model of anxiety and performance. *British Journal of Psychology, 82,* 163–178.

Hardy, L., Parfitt, G., & Pates, J. (1994). Performance catastrophes in sport: A test of the hysteresis hypothesis. *Journal of Sports Sciences, 12,* 327–334.

Hardy, L., & Walker, A. (1999). unpublished data.

Hardy, L., Woodman, T., & Carrington, S. (in preparation). *Is self-confidence a bias factor in higher order catastrophe models? An exploratory analysis.*

Jackson, R.C., & Willson, R. (1999). Using 'swing thoughts' to prevent paradoxical performance effects in golf putting. In M.R. Farrally & A.J. Cochran (Eds.), *Science and golf III: Proceedings of the 1998 World Scientific Congress of Golf* (pp. 166–173). Champaign, IL: Human Kinetics.

Jones, J.G., Swain, A.B.J., & Hardy, L. (1993). Intensity and direction dimensions of competitive state anxiety and relationships with performance. *Journal of Sports Sciences, 11,* 525–532.

Jorna, P.G.A.M. (1992). Spectral analysis of heart rate and psychological state: A review of its validity as a workload index. *Biological Psychology, 34,* 237–257.

Keele, S.W. (1973). *Attention and human performance.* Pacific Palisades, CA: Goodyear.

Kimble, G.A., & Perlmuter, L.C. (1970). The problem of volition. *Psychological Review, 77,* 361–384.

Kingston, K.M., & Hardy, L. (1994). Factors affecting the salience of outcome, performance and process goals in golf. In A.J. Cochran & M.R. Farrally (Eds.), *Science and golf II: Proceedings of the 1994 World Scientific Congress of Golf* (pp. 144–149). London: E. & F.N. Spon.

Langer, E.J., & Imber, L.G. (1979). When practice makes perfect: Debilitating effects of overlearning. *Journal of Personality and Social Psychology, 37,* 2014–2024.

Lewis, B.P., & Linder, D.E. (1997). Thinking about choking? Attentional processes and paradoxical performance. *Personality and Social Psychology Bulletin, 23,* 937–944.

MacMahon, K., & Masters, R. (1998). *From novice to expert and back again: Chunking and dechunking in motor skills.* Paper presented at the Third Annual Congress of the European Congress of Sport Science, Manchester, UK.

Martens, R., Vealey, R.S., & Burton, D. (1990). *Competitive anxiety in sport.* Champaign, IL: Human Kinetics.

Masters, R.S.W. (1992a). Knowledge, knerves and know-how: The role of explicit versus implicit knowledge in the breakdown of a complex motor skill under pressure. *British Journal of Psychology, 83,* 343–358.

Masters, R.S.W. (1992b). *Implicit knowledge, stress and skill failure.* Unpublished Doctoral Dissertation, University of York, York, UK.

Moore, W.E., & Stevenson, J.R. (1994). Training for trust in sports skills. *The Sport Psychologist, 8,* 1–12.

Morris, L.W., Davis, M.A., & Hutchings, C.H. (1981). Cognitive and emotional components of anxiety: Literature review and a revised worry-emotionality scale. *Journal of Educational Psychology, 73,* 541–555.

Mulder, G. (1985). Attention, effort and sinus arrythmia: How far are we? In J.F. Orlebeke, G. Mulder, & L.P.J. van Doornen (Eds.), *The psychophysiology of cardiovascular control* (pp. 407–424). New York: Plenum Press.

Mulder, L.J.M., & Mulder, G. (1987). Cardiovascular reactivity and mental workload. In O. Rompelman & R.I. Kitney (Eds.), *The beat-by-beat investigation of cardiovascular function* (pp. 216–253). Oxford: Oxford University Press.

Mullen, R., & Hardy, L. (2000). State anxiety and motor performance: Testing the conscious processing hypothesis. *Journal of Sports Sciences, 18,* 785–799.

Mullen, R., & Hardy, L. (in preparation). *Conscious processing and the part process goal paradox.*

Mullen, R., Hardy, L., & Tattersall, A. (in preparation). *Conscious processing and motor performance: An interdisciplinary investigation.*

Oxendine, J.B. (1970). Emotional arousal and motor performance. *Quest, 13,* 23–32.

Parfitt, C.G., Jones, J.G., & Hardy, L. (1990). Multidimensional anxiety and performance. In J.G. Jones & L. Hardy (Eds.), *Stress and performance in sport* (pp. 43–80). Chichester: Wiley.

Revelle, W., & Michaels, E.J. (1976). The theory of achievement motivation revisited: The implication of inertial tendencies. *Psychological Review, 83,* 394–404.

Vereijken, B., van Emmerik, R.E.A., Whiting, H.T.A., & Newell, K.A. (1992). Free(z)ing degrees of freedom in skill acquisition. *Journal of Motor Behaviour, 24,* 133–142.

Wegner, D.M. (1994). Ironic processes of mental control. *Psychological Bulletin, 101,* 34–52.

Wegner, D.M., Ansfield, M., & Pilloff, D. (1998). The putt and the pendulum: Ironic effects of the mental control of action. *Psychological Science, 9,* 196–199.

Weinberg, R.S., & Hunt, V.V. (1976). The interrelationships between anxiety, motor performance and electromyography. *Journal of Motor Behaviour, 8,* 219–224.

Wine, J.D. (1971). Test anxiety and the direction of attention. *Psychological Bulletin, 76,* 92–104.

Woodman, T., Albinson, J.G., & Hardy, L. (1997). An investigation of the zone of optimal functioning hypothesis within a multidimensional framework. *Journal of Sport & Exercise Psychology, 19,* 131–141.

Yerkes, R.M., & Dodson, J.D. (1908). The relation of strength of stimulus to rapidity of habit formation. *Journal of Comparative Neurology and Psychology, 18,* 459–482.

Zeeman, E.C. (1976). Catastrophe theory. *Scientific American, 234,* 65–82.

CHAPTER 20

Preperformance Routine Training Using Holistic Process Goals

Kieran M. Kingston and Lew Hardy

Implementing cognitive-behavioural strategies to regulate psychological and physiological states is viewed as an important determinant of effective performance (Gould, Weinberg, & Jackson, 1980; Shelton & Mahoney, 1978; cf. Gould, Eklund, & Jackson, 1992). According to Boutcher (1990), this skill is especially important for those involved in self-paced, closed skills. In such cases, there are relatively few perceptual and decision-making demands (Hardy, Jones, & Gould, 1996). The non-reactionary nature of the task provides extensive opportunities for athletes to focus on both internal (thoughts and feelings) and external (environmental) distractions.

Under the general guise of cognitive-behavioural techniques (Mace, 1990), a number of specific strategies have facilitated the execution of motor skills across a variety of sports; for example, those addressing attentional focus, self-talk, relaxation, imagery and preparatory arousal. In supporting the notion that cognitive-behavioural techniques may positively affect cognitions in competition, Murphy and Woolfolk (1987) added that this did not automatically result in improved performance.

Preperformance Routines
One cognitive-behavioural strategy commonly used with sports performers is preperformance routine training. Routines typically comprise of a combina-

tion of cognitive and behavioural strategies the purpose of which is to prepare the athlete optimally for skill execution, normally within self-paced sports. They are in essence a collection of well-learned process goals linked together to form a coherent flowing routine (Hardy, Jones, & Gould, 1996; Kingston & Hardy, 1994, 1997). Process goals specify physical and cognitive processes which the performer seeks to engage during task execution (Kingston & Hardy, 1997). One of the earliest studies in this area defined the routine as "a set pattern of cue thoughts, actions and images consistently carried out before performance of the skill" (Crews & Boutcher, 1986, p. 291). According to Cohn (1990), these routines should be highly individualised, taking into consideration such factors as the nature of the task and the skill level of the participant.

Boutcher and Rotella (1987) proposed a psychological skills enhancement program for closed-skill performance, and cited Crews and Boutcher's (1986) observational analysis of the preshot behaviours of professional golfers. According to these researchers, a typical preperformance routine of professional golfers might comprise the following:

1. Setting (establishing optimal arousal level)
2. Imagery (visualising the flight and/or the outcome of the shot)
3. Kinaesthetic coupling (visualising and feeling the upcoming shot)
4. Set-up (the address position)
5. Waggle (small movements of the club)
6. Swing thought (e.g., think 'tempo' or 'rhythm').

Although this model clearly outlines a number of central components of routines, the challenge for the athlete is to find the most efficient 'cocktail' of strategies which can be integrated into a coherent, repeatable routine prior to each shot (Boutcher, 1990).

A number of theories have been forwarded to explain the positive effects of preperformance routines (see Cohn, 1990, for a review). Whereas the mechanisms that underlie the positive effects are somewhat contentious, all explanations seem to involve directing attention and establishing an appropriate, task-specific activation state. According to Boutcher and Zinsser (1990), achieving this desired state may be enhanced by using routines (cf. Hardy, Jones, & Gould, 1996).

Research into Preperformance (Preshot) Routines

Crews and Boutcher in particular have pioneered research into the application of preperformance routines in golf (Boutcher & Crews, 1987; Crews & Boutcher, 1986, 1987). They confirmed (through observation of LPGA professionals) the existence of well-defined consistent routines for both putts and full-swings (Crews & Boutcher, 1987) and suggested that routines might have positive effects for certain athletes (Boutcher & Crews, 1987; Crews & Boutcher, 1986). More recent studies (Beauchamp, Halliwell, Fournier, & Koestner, 1996; Cohn, Rotella, & Lloyd, 1990) have further supported the use of preperformance routines in golf, although it is interesting to note that neither study reported any immediate improvements in performance.

In spite of the equivocal nature of results, researchers in this area have pointed out a number of positive effects on specific subcomponents of performance that might provide an indirect channel through which positive performance effects could be accrued. These include: adherence to the routine; perception of beneficial effects (Cohn et al., 1990); increased attention to the task (Boutcher & Crews, 1987; Cohn et al., 1990); lower arousal levels (Boutcher & Crews, 1987); increased intrinsic motivation; and less negative introspection (Beauchamp et al., 1996). It is also worth noting that Murphy and Woolfolk's (1987) study, which examined the effect of a cognitive-behavioural intervention (involving imagery and self-talk) on golf-putting performance, also elicited reductions in competitive anxiety, but no improved performance. Interestingly, Beauchamp et al. (1996) suggested that there may be a significant time lag between the adoption of a particular routine and its capacity to effect performance improvements.

Although there is consistent support for routine training reducing the variability of preperformance behaviours (Beauchamp et al., 1996; Boutcher & Crews, 1987; Cohn et al., 1990), these do not always translate to performance improvements. A variety of individual difference factors may contribute, but perhaps the most salient factor that distinguishes between participants in the studies discussed to date is their skill level.

The positive effects of consistent preperformance routines with elite golfers have been well documented (Crews & Boutcher, 1986). Singer (1988) suggested that great golfers must be able to go 'trance-like' to focus attention and execute automatically. The key may be that in order to perform optimally, the athlete needs to achieve a degree of automaticity, where the skill is performed smoothly with little cognitive effort and a high degree of consistency. Preperformance routines may provide a vehicle through which to elicit automatic functioning. The importance of automatic functioning for expert golf performance has been demonstrated elsewhere (see Cohn, 1991). One of its characteristics is a high degree of stability in the timing of the well-learned task. Boutcher and Zinsser (1990) supported the ability-automaticity link in noting that elite golfers possessed significantly less variable preshot routines.

Stability of Routines

A high degree of consistency in the timing of the preperformance routine implies that the performer is carrying out similar cognitive and behavioural strategies (a necessary prerequisite for automatising routines). If we accept that consistent, well-learned routines tailored to the specific demands of the client and their sport have a positive effect upon performance (e.g., Crews & Boutcher, 1987), then it follows that a precursor to these positive effects is the establishment and stabilising of the routine. Indeed, there is some evidence to suggest that one of the initial consequences of preperformance routine training is a reduction in the variability of the time taken to complete the routine (e.g., Beauchamp et al., 1996; Boutcher & Crews, 1987; Cohn et al., 1990). Cohn et al. (1990), however, failed to substantiate these findings, and attributed this lack of increased consistency to the participants being in the early stages of new routine development.

For highly skilled golfers, a lack of stability (time) in a previously established preperformance routine can be logically attributed to two major factors. The first is the tendency of performers to attempt an explicit focus (on task components normally performed automatically). The second is excessive internalising (focusing on thoughts and feelings) caused by worries and concerns regarding effective execution of the skill.

Conscious Processing and Holistic Process Goals

According to the conscious processing hypothesis (Baumeister, 1984; Hardy, Mullen, & Jones, 1996; Masters, 1992) anxiety can cause a relapse towards a focus on explicit rules associated with the task. When basic skills are normally performed automatically the consequence of this explicit focus may be a reduction in automaticity and associated decrements in performance. In golf, for example, this might take the form of trying to steer the ball towards the intended target (i.e., focusing on the direction of the stroke) rather than trusting the swing and focusing on a smooth "tempo." The conscious processing hypothesis provides something of a paradox regarding the use of process-oriented goals (Kingston & Hardy, 1994, 1997). The literature on process goals contends that, for non-elite athletes, single process goals may have an important role in reducing the variability of task performance. However, highly skilled performers refine movement sequences until, at the advanced stage, they are performed with efficient automaticity (Fitts & Posner, 1967; Reber, 1993) with no recourse to conscious control. Hardy, Mullen, and Jones (1996) argue, therefore, that a focus on single discrete process goals might elicit conscious processing and cause decrements in task performance through a disruptive effect on automaticity.

The goal of a preperformance routine training program with a skilled athlete should be to minimise the potential for performers to regress to a more explicit focus when placed under more stressful conditions. Consequently, although the routine may comprise a series of individual process goals, the key is to ensure that these are chunked effectively (and automatised) in order to focus on a more holistic representation of the to-be-performed action. Initiating the action using a cue word (or holistic process goal) which avoids a more explicit focus should reduce the potential for regression to more crude control strategies (Kingston & Hardy, 1994, 1997). Examples of holistic process goals and what they may represent to the performer include: TEM-PO (representing the temporal patterning of the backswing and downswing); SMOOTH (representing the feeling of striking through the ball); and PUSH (representing the feeling of the follow-through). Basically, the holistic process goal can be any word (or thought) that, to the performer, can serve to represent a thought or feeling associated with the desired action. It should be appreciated, however, that the exact nature of the holistic process goals used by performers could, by their nature, be highly idiosyncratic.

Purpose of the Investigation

The primary purpose of this study was to examine the effects of a more formalised preperformance routine training program involving the development and use of preperformance routines that used holistic process goals as cues. It was hypothesised that there would be immediate reductions in the variability (mean absolute error of routine time) of the preshot behaviours, and that this would translate to improvements in performance.

Method

Client

The current investigation involved the provision of psychological support for a 32-year-old professional golfer.

Initial Assessment

A consultancy approach to providing psychological support was adopted (Hardy & Parfitt, 1994). Within this approach, both the client and the consultant are viewed as bringing expert knowledge to the situation. Having clarified the aims and objectives of the consultancy, the early meetings with the client involved observation at practice and in competitions. Additionally, the consultant and client discussed extensively the client's game, his goals and his motivation for those goals.

Upon questioning, the client indicated that he would normally enter a competition feeling confident and he would invariably start reasonably well (in terms of his score). However, in spite of his start he would then have a few bad holes in succession. Following this relapse, his game would recover and he'd finish strongly (although he would be too far adrift to make any impact on the leaders). This was a typical pattern for the major events he entered.

Detailed Observation

It appeared that one of the principal reasons for dropping shots was the failure to recover from situations where recovery was a realistic possibility. For example, typically the client would miss a green with an approach shot, and rather than chipping and putting to make a par, he would confound the problem by hitting a relatively poor chip, and then take two or sometimes three putts. The client attributed the problem to his putting when it appeared that the problem lay elsewhere. It was noted that when the client did hit bad shots, he seemed to become agitated, rushed, or even at times took noticeably longer to play his shots. This was confirmed by unobtrusively timing the preshot intervals for each particular type of shot throughout a number of practice and competition rounds. It was also noted that when he performed well, his routines were highly systematic and fairly consistent.

The Intervention

One method to reduce the variability in the timing of the preparation for strokes is establishing highly consistent preperformance routines, which are cued using holistic process goals. The efficacy of performance routines per se is well documented (see Boutcher, 1990; Boutcher & Crews, 1987; Boutcher & Rotella, 1987; Crews & Boutcher, 1987), a primary purpose being to elicit a state of automatic functioning during shot execution. The development and refinement of these routines may have a 'double-hit' effect by influencing performance through other channels (e.g., setting and achieving goals has implications for gaining the self-confidence to trust the automatic processes). Furthermore, preperformance routines of this nature should reduce the tendency to revert to conscious control, because developing the routine in a holistic manner should prevent the golfer from focusing on specific aspects of the skill, which may prevent smooth coordinated movement (Boutcher & Crews, 1987).

An holistic process goal was incorporated into the routine by identifying a single thought or word that could represent a target behaviour consisting of a number of discrete components. For example, if the performer was imagining the line of the putter going through to the target and wanting to execute a smooth stroke, we tried to establish a word that served to represent both component behaviours. So rather than thinking about the line of the putter *and* the execution of the stroke, the word PUSH represented an holistic desired thought or feel (for the individual) associated with chunking the discrete elements together. The key for the performer was to chunk the key components of each stroke, and integrate them using a cue thought (holistic process goal) that could be practised and repeated consistently. The holistic goals would likely be altered for markedly different shots (e.g., driving & putting).

To recap, the purpose of the intervention was: (a) to develop a more systematic, and consistent preperformance routine prior to putting and chipping; and (b) to move on to developing and refining the routines for approach play and drives.

Summary of Training and Data Collection

Baseline. Collect data on timing of preperformance routines according to protocol advocated by Cohn et al. (1990).

Intervention — Phase 1 (10 weeks). Develop and refine new routines for chip shots and putting.

Data collection — Phase 1. Collect data on timing of preperformance routines and subjective performance assessments for each stroke during two complete rounds of golf.

Intervention — Phase 2 (10 weeks). Develop and refine new routines for approach play and drives. Continue with practice on routines for chip shots and putting.

Data collection — Phase 2. Collect data on timing of preperformance routines and subjective performance assessments for each stroke during two complete rounds of golf.

Results

To analyse the data, four one-way ANOVAs were carried out on each aspect of the game (putting, chipping, approach play and drives). A multiple-baseline approach was used with baseline measures on two occasions for putting and chipping, and on four occasions for approach shots and drives. Conversely, postintervention measures were collected on four occasions for the putting and chipping components of the game, and on two occasions for approach shots and drives. The two dependent variables were stability (absolute deviation from the mean time for each shot type at each session), and performance (a subjective rating of each shot from 0–10). The independent variable was training (six sessions).

Stability (timing error)

Table 1 shows the means and standard deviations (in seconds) of the variations in time taken on the routines for each shot type across the six sessions. The one-way analyses of variance on the absolute values of the difference from the session means revealed a number of significant results. There were significant changes in timing variability for putts, $F(6, 107) = 5.56$, $p < .001$; for chip shots, $F(5, 46) = 3.77$, $p < .01$; and for approach shots, $F(6, 103) = 2.38$, $p < .05$. Tukey's post hoc tests showed lower variability in the time to complete the putting routine at Sessions 4, 5, and 6 than at Session 2; and variability at Session 5 was also significantly lower than at Sessions 1 and 3 (see Figure 1). Post hoc tests also indicated that the variability in timing of chip shots at Session 5 was significantly lower than at Session 1 (see Figure 1). Finally, there was significantly less variability in the timing of approach shots at Sessions 5 and 6 than at Session 1 (see Figure 2).

Performance

Table 2 shows the client's subjective ratings of performance (0–10) for each type of shot across sessions. Analysis revealed a significant change in chip shot performance, $F(5, 46) = 3.62$, $p < .01$. Tukey's post hoc tests indicated an improvement in chip shots from Session 1 to Sessions 4 and 5 (see Table 2 and Figure 3). There were no significant changes in performance for any of the other shot types.

Discussion

In congruence with the primary hypothesis, the results of this study provide evidence that the training intervention had the effect of reducing variability in the timing of preperformance routines. This effect was most notable with regards to putting and chipping, and to a lesser extent with approach shots.

Table 1
Means (and Standard Deviations) for Timing Errors (seconds)

	SESSION					
	1	2	3	4	5	6
Drives	1.55	1.70	1.32	1.54	.93	.64
	(1.33)	(1.11)	(1.81)	(1.30)	(.65)	(.48)
Approaches	2.42	1.93	1.58	1.45	1.12[1]	1.00[1]
	(1.92)	(1.50)	(1.24)	(1.11)	(0.87)	(0.84)
Chips	2.07	1.98	1.75	.88	.26[1]	.50
	(.85)	(1.08)	(1.99)	(.78)	(.25)	(.45)
Putts	1.46	2.06	1.53	.80[2]	.42[1,2,3]	.61[2]
	(1.06)	(1.43)	(1.45)	(.99)	(.33)	(.39)

[1] significantly < Session 1; [2] significantly < Session 2; [3] significantly < Session 3

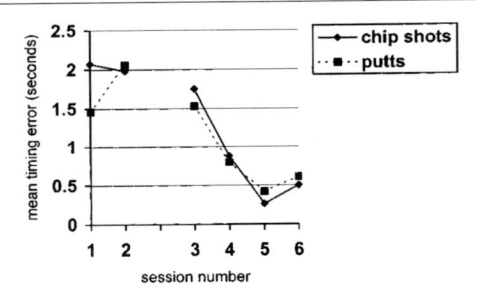

Figure 1
Mean absolute error (seconds) for chips and putts with intervention initiated between Sessions 2 & 3.

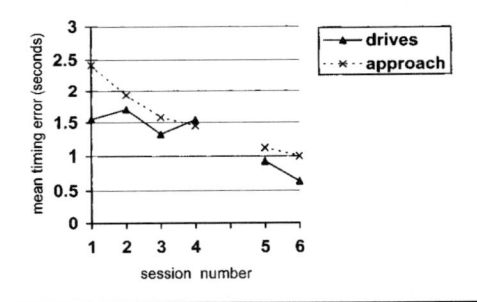

Figure 2
Mean absolute error (seconds) for drives and approach play with intervention initiated between Sessions 4 & 5.

It was somewhat disappointing (if not entirely unsurprising) that these reductions in variability were not accompanied by widespread performance improvements. It is also interesting to note that the most pronounced reductions in the variability of the routines over time were in those areas of the game which had originally been targeted as areas of weakness in the client's game (putting and chip shots). It could be argued, however, that the greater length of time spent applying the refined routines for chipping and putting may have increased the likelihood of observing more pronounced effects.

Research Implications

In addition to the implications that might help to guide best practice, a number of theoretical issues arise from the current study which might help to guide future research in the area of holistic process goals and their use within the framework of preperformance routines. Firstly, however, it is important to

Table 2
Means (and Standard Deviations) for Subjective Ratings of Performance

	SESSION					
	1	2	3	4	5	6
Drives	8.40	6.86	8.14	6.79	7.79	7.36
	(1.59)	(1.88)	(1.56)	(1.58)	(1.76)	(1.74)
Approaches	5.88	6.78	6.25	6.83	6.94	7.11
	(1.89)	(1.99)	(1.84)	(2.04)	(1.92)	(1.74)
Chips	5.14	6.38	6.22	7.78[1]	8.29[1]	6.86
	(2.54)	(1.41)	(1.86)	(.83)	(1.11)	(1.57)
Putts	7.28	7.94	6.78	7.78	6.83	7.67
	(1.49)	(1.26)	(1.90)	(1.99)	(2.07)	(1.65)

[1] significantly > Session 1

make a comment regarding the multiple-baseline design that was used. Although it can be criticised at a number of levels, this type of design provides an opportunity to assess intervention effectiveness across a number of different aspects of the client's game. In the interests of studies with high levels of ecological validity, it is important to acknowledge that researchers may have to apply imaginative (and dare we say it, less psychometrically valid) methodologies to address important applied research questions.

Stability as a precursor to performance effects. According to Crews (1994), consistent behavioural and cognitive patterns facilitate a consistent psychophysiological state which is conducive to best performance. Southard, Miracle, and Landwer (1989) described the objectives of such ritualised behaviours as being consistency of duration, and consequential reductions in the variability of performance. Consequently, it is reasonable to surmise that increased consistency in time to complete the routine may be an initial step towards realising performance benefits. Further longitudinal studies are required to establish conclusively the progression from stabilisation to performance improvements.

Performance assessment. One of the principal shortcomings of the present study was the lack of reliable performance data. Asking the performer to subjectively assess performance on each shot after a completed round (which may have taken upward of 4 hours) is somewhat problematic. Most notably, the golfer's perception of performance on each shot is likely to be influenced by a number of factors independent of that shot (e.g., where the ball came to rest, the final score achieved on the hole, etc.). Furthermore, it is necessary to ensure that each performance measure is assessed using consistent criteria. It is clear that the effective assessment of performance (perhaps including

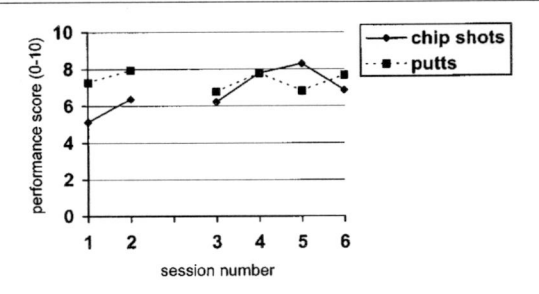

Figure 3
Performance scores for chips and putts with intervention initiated between Sessions 2 & 3.

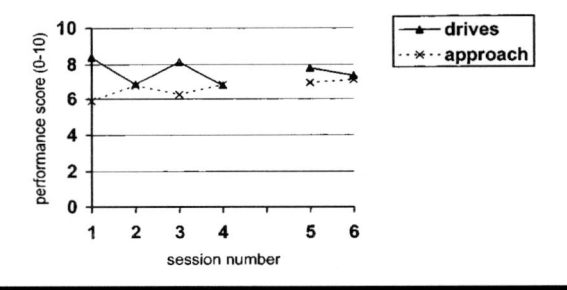

Figure 4
Performance scores for drives and approach play with intervention initiated between Sessions 4 & 5.

more objective methods) has to be balanced with the need to ensure that such measures do not impinge on the task performance. This is undoubtedly a major challenge when assessing the impact of behavioural interventions.

Tailoring training to the skill level of the performer. There appears to be a logical evolution from single process goals to performance routines (Kingston & Hardy, 1994, 1997). It would be reasonable to suggest that the mechanisms thought to underlie the effectiveness of process-oriented goals might also in part contribute to the positive impact of routines, especially if initiated using a cue which has a holistic focus. It may simply be that novices benefit from the increased attentional focus brought about by using single process goals. For more able performers, preperformance routines containing or initiated using holistic process-oriented goals may provide an equally strong process focus, yet prevent the focus on specific aspects of the skill which have been shown to undermine automaticity and hence skilled performance

(Baumeister, 1984; Masters, 1992). This certainly helps to explain the paradox that has been identified between process-oriented goals and conscious processing (see Hardy, Jones, & Gould, 1996; Hardy, Mullen, & Jones, 1996). More detailed (longitudinal) studies into the effects of process goals and preperformance routines on performance, cognitions and affective variables might help to address the issue of the efficacy of preperformance routines as a function of skill level.

Make-up of routines. It is clear that the routines are individualistic in nature, and as Cohn (1990) contended, a number of individual difference factors should be considered. Nevertheless, it also apparent that routines may need to have a number of central components (see Boutcher & Rotella, 1987). A final consideration for future research might be to conduct comparison studies on the efficacy of different types of routines with the purpose of guiding best practice across different ability groups.

Applied Implications

Accelerating automatisation. Although performance effects remained elusive on the whole, it is clear that effects on timing variability were immediate. Since an increase in timing stability is believed to represent consistent cognitive and behavioural processes, one might suggest that incorporating holistic process goals that might reduce the tendency to regress to an explicit focus could further accelerate the automatisation of routines.

Latency of performance effects. One of the more important practical implications of the current research relates to the possible time lag between acquiring and refining preperformance routines, and the subsequent realisation of any discernible improvement in performance. This phenomenon is not unique (see Beauchamp et al., 1996; Cohn et al., 1990). Indeed, it could be argued that, until the routines are well learned, the high level of cognitive resources required precludes performance benefits. Shambrook and Bull (1996) intimated as much when suggesting that drops in the rate of improvement in basketball free-throw shooting may be caused by adjusting to a new preshot routine. The implication for coaches and performers is that routine development and refinement should take place when the frequency of competitions is low and the opportunity to practise is high, for example during the off-season. Equally, it is important that practitioners make explicit the point that performers may experience short-term decrements in performance as their routines are refined or developed. An effective program of realistic goal setting may help to reduce the potential for motivational decrements to occur during the initial stages of routine development.

Effects upon subcomponents of performance. Although the participants in Cohn et al.'s (1990) study did not consistently demonstrate immediate improvements in performance, posttreatment interviews indicated that the golfers perceived the intervention to have had a positive effect upon performance. This highlights an interesting issue. Although immediate improvements in performance may not be realised, it may be more important that the athletes actually perceive that they are making a progression towards enhanced performance. The implications in terms of adherence to mental training programs are obvious. It also implies that we as practitioners should make more explicit the short-term goals of the interventions we suggest as well as the additional benefits of utilising such routines. For example, routine training may help to focus attention, increase adherence to routines, enhance self-confidence, increase intrinsic motivation and reduce controlling tendencies (see Cohn et al., 1990).

Targeting routine training. The results presented here clearly indicate differential effects of routine training across different aspects of the golf game. While this may not be surprising given the design of the study, this model may have important implications in terms of the delivery of a routine training program. Firstly, the approach enabled the client to place an emphasis on those areas of his game that required pressing attention. Secondly, targeting aspects of the game reduces the potential for information overload, as refining routines in all areas simultaneously may appear complicated and daunting for the client. As an adjunct, experiences gained when developing routines in one area might guide routine development in other areas.

Conclusion

This intervention study provides a rationale for the incorporation of holistic process goals into preperformance routine development. The results provide some support for this notion, certainly with respect to reducing the variability of preperformance processes which are argued to precede positive performance effects. Furthermore, the discussion provides some important guides for future research within this area, and from a more applied perspective forwards a number of practical suggestions for engaging athletes.

The efficacy of consistent preperformance routines has received widespread anecdotal and empirical support. It is hoped that adopting an approach that further reduces the potential for recourse to crude methods of conscious control under stressful situations might help to increase the effectiveness of preperformance routine application and training.

References

Baumeister, R.F. (1984). Choking under pressure: Self-consciousness and paradoxical effects of incentives on skilful performance. *Journal of Personality and Social Psychology, 46,* 610–620.

Beauchamp, P.H., Halliwell, W.R., Fournier, J.F., & Koestner, R. (1996). Effects of cognitive-behavioural psychological skills training on the motivation, preparation, and putting performance of novice golfers. *The Sport Psychologist, 10,* 157–170.

Boutcher, S.H. (1990). The role of performance routines in sport. In J.G. Jones & L. Hardy (Eds.), *Stress and performance in sport* (pp. 231–245). Chichester: Wiley.

Boutcher, S.H., & Crews, D.J. (1987). The effect of a preshot routine on a well-learned skill. *International Journal of Sport Psychology, 18,* 30–39.

Boutcher, S.H., & Rotella, R.J. (1987). A psychological skills educational program for closed-skill performance enhancement. *The Sport Psychologist, 1,* 200–207.

Boutcher, S.H., & Zinsser, N.W. (1990). Cardiac deceleration of elite and beginning golfers during putting. *Journal of Sport and Exercise Psychology, 12,* 37–47.

Cohn, P.J. (1990). Preperformance routines in sport: Theoretical support and practical applications. *The Sport Psychologist, 4,* 301–312.

Cohn, P.J. (1991). An exploratory study on peak performance in golf. *The Sport Psychologist, 5,* 1–14.

Cohn, P.J., Rotella, R.J., & Lloyd, J.W. (1990). Effects of a cognitive behavioural intervention on the preshot routine and performance in golf. *The Sport Psychologist, 4,* 33–47.

Crews, D.J. (1994). Research based golf: From the laboratory to the course. In A.J. Cochran & M.R. Farrally (Eds.), *Science and golf II: Proceedings of the 1994 World Scientific Congress of Golf* (pp. 127–137). London: E & FN Spon.

Crews, D.J., & Boutcher, S.H. (1986). The effect of structured preshot behaviours on beginning golf performance. *Perceptual and Motor Skills, 62,* 291–294.

Crews, D.J., & Boutcher, S.H. (1987). An observational analysis of professional female golfers during tournament play. *Journal of Sport Behavior, 9,* 51–58.

Fitts, P.M., & Posner, M.I. (1967). *Human performance.* Belmont, CA: Brooks/Cole.

Gould, D., Eklund, R.C., & Jackson, S.A. (1992). 1988 U.S. Olympic wrestling excellence: I Mental preparation, precompetitive cognition and affect. *The Sport Psychologist, 6,* 358–362.

Gould, D., Weinberg, R., & Jackson, A. (1980). Mental preparation strategies, cognitions, and strength performance. *Journal of Sport Psychology, 2,* 329–339.

Hardy, L., Jones, J.G., & Gould, D. (1996). *Understanding psychological preparation for sport: Theory and practice of elite performers.* Chichester: John Wiley.

Hardy, L., Mullen, R., & Jones, J.G. (1996). Knowledge and conscious control of motor actions under stress. *British Journal of Psychology, 87,* 621–636.

Hardy, L., & Parfitt, G. (1994). The development of a model for the provision of psychological support to a national squad. *The Sport Psychologist, 8,* 126–142.

Kingston, K., & Hardy, L. (1994). Factors affecting the salience of outcome, performance and process goals in golf. In A.J. Cochran & M.R. Farrally (Eds.), *Science and golf II: Proceedings of the 1994 World Scientific Congress of Golf* (pp. 144–149). London: E & FN Spon.

Kingston, K., & Hardy, L. (1997). Effects of different goals on processes that support performance. *The Sport Psychologist, 11,* 277–293.

Mace, R. (1990). Cognitive behavioural interventions in sport. In J.G. Jones & L. Hardy (Eds.), *Stress and performance in sport* (pp. 203–230). Chichester: Wiley.

Masters, R.S.W. (1992). Knowledge, knerves and know-how. *British Journal of Psychology, 83,* 343–358.

Murphy, S.M., & Woolfolk, R.L. (1987). The effects of cognitive interventions on competitive anxiety and performance on a fine motor skill accuracy task. *International Journal of Sport Psychology, 18,* 152–166.

Reber, A.S. (1993). *Implicit learning and tacit knowledge.* Oxford: Oxford University Press.

Shambrook, C.J., & Bull, S.J. (1996). The use of a single-case research design to investigate the efficacy of imagery training. *Journal of Applied Sport Psychology, 8,* 27–43.

Shelton, A.O., & Mahoney, M.J. (1978). The content and effect of "psyching-up" strategies in weightlifters. *Cognitive Therapy and Research, 2,* 275–284.

Singer, R.N. (1988). Strategies and metastrategies in learning and performing self-paced athletic skills. *The Sport Psychologist, 2,* 49–68.

Southard, D., Miracle, A., & Landwer, G. (1989). Ritual and free-throw shooting in basketball. *Journal of Sports Sciences, 7,* 163–173.

CHAPTER 21

The Preshot Routine: A Prerequisite for Successful Performance?

Robin C. Jackson

Self-paced skills, such as golf, place different demands on the performer when compared to externally paced skills. The latter require performers to respond to what might be a rapidly moving stimulus, such as when a tennis player attempts to return the serve of his or her opponent. In self-paced skills on the other hand, the performer decides when to initiate the action, and the perceptual demands in terms of responding to moving stimuli are minimal. For example, the golfer decides when to start her backswing and the rugby ball remains static while the goal-kicker decides when to initiate his run-up. In addition, at the elite level these skills are usually overlearned to the extent that they are performed with very little "cognitive involvement" (Wrisberg, 1993). This has been referred to as the autonomous phase of motor learning, in which skills are performed without conscious attention to the mechanics of the desired movements (Fitts & Posner, 1967).

Paradoxically, it has been argued that because overlearned skills require so little conscious attention, elite performers may be more susceptible to distraction from task-irrelevant stimuli that could disrupt performance (Beauchamp, Halliwell, Fournier, & Koestner, 1996; Boutcher & Rotella, 1987). It has been suggested, therefore, that when performed in the competitive environment, self-paced skills require a considerable degree of attentional control (Boutcher & Crews, 1987; Nideffer, 1993) and that performers may benefit from utilising cognitive-behavioural skills in order to attain an appropriate attentional focus prior to each shot (Beauchamp et al., 1996).

Similarly, Boutcher (1992) suggests that attentional training programs for closed skills should focus on establishing preperformance routines containing behavioural, physiological and cognitive cues. Boutcher goes on to suggest that developing a consistent preperformance routine is central to the development of an effective attention-focusing strategy and that performers might benefit from analysing the temporal and behavioural consistency of their routines (Boutcher, 1990, 1992; Boutcher & Rotella, 1987). Underlying this recommendation is the assumption that increasing routine consistency will result in improved performance and assessing the validity of this assumption is the primary focus of the present chapter. In order to do this, research investigating the link between consistency of preperformance routines and subsequent performance is critically reviewed. This is followed by consideration of research relating to the proposal that preperformance routines have a primarily attentional function.

Routine Consistency and Performance

A preperformance routine is a "sequence of task-relevant thoughts and actions which an athlete engages in systematically prior to his or her performance of a specific sport skill" (Moran, 1996, p. 177). Anecdotally, it is apparent that elite golfers go through a consistent set of preperformance behaviours before initiating their golf swing and observational studies support this view. For example, Crews and Boutcher (1987) observed 12 LPGA tour players over 12 holes of tournament play, recording a number of behavioural measures including their total and partial routine times, the number of practice swings taken and the number of times they glanced towards the hole. They concluded that all of the golfers displayed a remarkable level of consistency with regard to their routine times and behavioural actions prior to each shot. With respect to the latter, the authors describe the most common behavioural sequence before a full shot as follows: (1) stand behind the ball, (2) move beside the ball, (3) set the club behind the ball with one glance at the target, (4) set the feet, (5) a combination of three waggles with two glances towards the target, (6) swing.

Golfers themselves also report using consistent preshot routines and there appears to be a link between the consistency of preperformance routines and level of performance. For example, Boutcher and Zinsser (1990) also looked at the pattern of preperformance behaviours and found that elite golfers used their predominant preputt pattern on 62% of putts whereas beginner golfers used theirs on only 35% of putts. This link is also apparent in the study by Thomas and Over (1994) who designed a questionnaire to assess the psychological and psychomotor skills associated with performance in golf. In a study of 165 club golfers, they found a significant correlation between reported preshot routine consistency and handicap, with better players reporting more consistent routines. The relationship between routine consistency and performance has also been found in other self-paced skills. For example, Wrisberg and Pein (1992) calculated the standard deviation of the preshot interval for the basketball free-throw and found a significant negative correlation between this measure and the success percentage of collegiate players. Once again more successful players were found to have more consistent routine times.

Although the number of studies addressing this issue is limited, the link between routine consistency and performance does appear to be a robust finding. However, the correlational nature of the findings means that a *causal* link has not been established. In other words, while it is apparent that better performers have more consistent routines it is not possible to conclude that their greater routine consistency has *caused* their superior performance. This is clearly important in terms of any recommendation that performers increase the consistency of their routines because the implication is that doing so will *cause* an improvement in performance. However, the correlational nature of the results does not preclude the possibility that increased temporal and behavioural consistency of routines is merely a consequence of performing well. For example, it could be argued that a golfer will be less likely to make changes to his or her preshot routine following a series of good shots but might spend varying amounts of time attempting to ensure that their set-up was correct after several poor shots. This would result in a correlation between routine consistency and performance but with the direction of causality being from performance to consistency. If this is the case then there would be no performance benefit to be gained from interventions that increase the temporal or behavioural consistency of a performer's preshot routine.

From a behavioural perspective, the greater consistency of experienced performers' routines compared to beginners may also be due to well-established principles of operant learning. Thus, behaviours that are reinforced become more likely, whereas those that are not become less likely (Catania, 1992). A direct prediction from this is that the comparatively variable response pattern of the beginner would become progressively more consistent as successful preperformance behaviours are reinforced and unsuccessful ones are extinguished. Because the preperformance routine consists of a chain of responses, successful golf shots could reinforce not only the swing but also the preceding components in the chain (Skinner, 1948), resulting in a consistent routine that is primarily a by-product of experience rather than a cause of superior performance. With these alternative explanations in mind it is informative to consider the outcome of studies that have attempted to introduce preshot routines and/or increase the consistency of performers' routines.

Again, there are very few studies in this area. One of the first was conducted by Crews and Boutcher (1986) who taught a specific preshot routine to male and female beginner golfers after they had completed 8 weeks of their beginners' class. After a further 8 weeks of using the routine only the male golfers showed a significant improvement on an objective measure of performance (accuracy of 7-iron shots). The subjective assessment of an LPGA teacher was that no improvement had occurred for either the male or female experimental groups in terms of ball flight trajectory, distance or direction. Based on these results, Crews and Boutcher (1986) suggested that golfers may need to attain a certain skill level before the preshot routine positively affects performance.

In a subsequent study, Boutcher and Crews (1987) taught male and female collegiate golfers to use a consistent preputt routine, for example establishing a set number of practice swings and glances towards the hole for each player. After the 6-week program the two experimental groups displayed more consistent routine times than the control groups. However, the results of the intervention in terms of performance were decidedly mixed. On the one hand, the female experimental group demonstrated improved performance, as indicated by a 30% increase in the number of putts holed and a 17% decrease in the mean absolute error (distance from the hole) of each putt. On the other hand, the male experimental group holed 38% fewer putts in the posttest with mean absolute error increasing by 91%. Caution should be expressed when attempting to draw any conclusions from this study due to the fact that there were only three participants in each group. In addition, only one assessment of putting performance was conducted for each participant before and after the intervention. At the very least, however, it seems advisable to downplay any apparent benefits of the intervention given its detrimental effect on the male group.

Another study in this area was conducted by Cohn, Rotella, and Lloyd (1990) who used a single-subject design to investigate the effects of a cognitive-behavioural intervention using three collegiate golfers. The intervention primarily focused on improving the behavioural consistency of the participants' preshot routines, but also stressed the importance of "increasing commitment and reducing doubt." As with the previous study the results of the intervention were mixed, with a clear increase in adherence to the preshot routine being apparent in addition to one of the players demonstrating a clear increase in routine time consistency. However, none of the golfers showed any immediate improvement in terms of the number of shots taken on the course and although improvements were apparent 4 months later it is not clear whether this can be attributed to the intervention.

The above studies suggest that there is little, if any, benefit to be gained from striving to increase the consistency of preperformance routines. Furthermore, a recent study by Jackson and Baker (in press) indicates that routine times may vary naturally with the difficulty of the shot. They conducted a case study of Neil Jenkins, a prolific rugby goal-kicker and holder of the world record for the number of points scored in international matches. Rugby goal-kicking has similarities with golf in that it is a self-paced skill, requires a combination of both distance and accuracy, and it involves striking a stationary ball off a tee. In their study, Jackson and Baker assessed the behavioural and temporal consistency of his prekick routine across kicks of varying difficulty. They found that, while certain behavioural aspects of his routine remained consistent across different levels of difficulty, Jenkins' concentration times and physical preparation times were longer on more difficult kicks (see Figure 1).

The extent to which these findings generalise either to other rugby goal-kickers or to other self-paced skills such as golf has yet to be established. It is worth noting, however, that although Crews and Boutcher (1987) reported that the professional golfers in their study "were remarkably consistent with regard to time and behavioural actions" (p. 51), the mean standard devia-

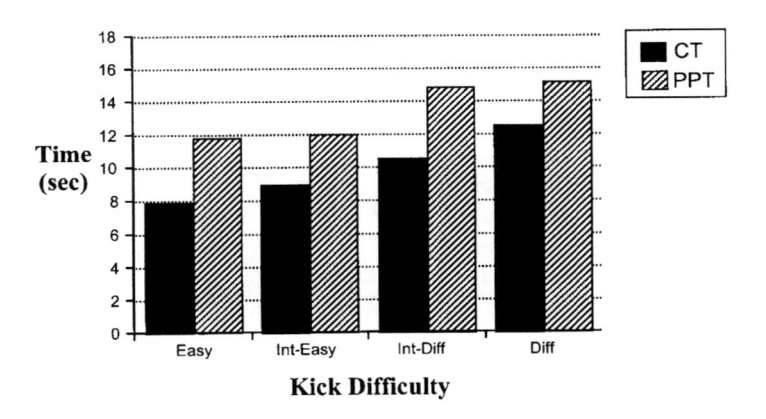

Figure 1
Mean concentration times (CT) and physical preparation times (PPT) for easy, intermediate-easy, intermediate-difficult and difficult rugby goal-kicks taken by Neil Jenkins under experimental conditions.

tions of their total routine time were 3.75 and 5.27 seconds for the full swing and putt respectively. These figures are less impressive when set against mean standard deviations of approximately 0.6 seconds for the preshot interval in the basketball free-throw (Wrisberg & Pein, 1992) and approximately 1.0 seconds for concentration and physical preparation times in rugby goal-kicks performed under competitive conditions (Jackson & Baker, in press). Because Crews and Boutcher (1987) did not attempt to measure the difficulty of each golf shot, it is not possible to determine whether this factor contributed to the higher standard deviations recorded in their study. At least at an intuitive level, however, it seems sensible for performers to spend more time ensuring that they are correctly aligned to the target when there is less margin for error.

Overall then, there appears to be little evidence that having a consistent preperformance routine is a prerequisite for success in golf. This is not to say, however, that the preperformance routine has no functional significance. For example, more positive results have been found with interventions that use preperformance routines as a vehicle for the teaching of psychological skills. The aim of such an approach is to help athletes to develop general mental skills that can then be used in competitive situations. For example, Boutcher and Rotella (1987) outlined a four-phase psychological skills education program for enhancing performance in closed skills. Support for the effectiveness of this program in golf is evident in a study by Beauchamp et al. (1996) who examined the psychological and performance consequences of a 14-week program using novice golfers.

During the program, golfers in the cognitive-behavioural group learned several psychological skills including stress management, mental rehearsal and thought control and then integrated them into a preputt routine. In addition to demonstrating an increase in intrinsic motivation, the cognitive-behavioural group also showed greater performance benefits than either the control group or a group that received technical instruction. Specifically, the cognitive-behavioural group improved steadily over the course of the program whereas the other two groups showed a similar rate of improvement during the first 6 weeks of the study followed by little improvement thereafter. Reviewing the effects of all the different cognitive-behavioural skills is beyond the scope of the current chapter, however, given the perceived importance of attentional control in self-paced skills, evidence that preperformance routines may serve an attentional function is now considered.

The Attentional Function of Preperformance Routines

From an attentional perspective, it has been suggested that preperformance routines can help cue well-learned movements and prevent the performer from focusing attention on the mechanics of movement (Boutcher, 1990; Boutcher & Crews, 1987; Moran, 1996). The theoretical support for these functions comes from the observation that as individuals learning a skill progress from novice to expert, so the amount of conscious attention to the mechanics of performance decreases. Indeed, the amount of conscious control apparent during the early phase of learning a skill led Adams (1971) to refer to it as the "verbal-motor" stage of learning. At the other end of the spectrum, performers describing their peak experiences in sport typically allude to the lack of conscious control associated with their performance (McInman & Grove, 1991).

Experimental evidence to support these functions comes from psychophysiological studies in which cerebral and/or cardiac activity is recorded in the few seconds prior to movement execution. For example, in a study of female European tour golfers Crews, Lutz, Nilsson, and Marriott (1999) found that confident putting performance was related to lower levels of cerebral activity in the final second before initiation of the putting stroke. In another study of golf putting, Boutcher and Zinsser (1990) found that collegiate golfers had lower heart rates than beginner golfers immediately before and after 12-foot putts. Posttask interviews revealed that 86% of the collegiate golfers, but only 20% of the beginner golfers, used a nonanalytical attentional strategy leading Boutcher and Zinsser (1990) to suggest that cardiac deceleration in self-paced skills may be related to having a nonanalytical or kinesthetic attentional focus.

Molander and Bäckman (1993) made a similar suggestion following their analysis of golfers' cardiac activity in the concentration phase prior to putting. They found distinct age-related differences, with younger golfers displaying cardiac deceleration and older golfers displaying cardiac acceleration in the 7 seconds before the putt. Molander and Bäckman (1993) suggest that these results might reflect different attentional strategies, and specifically that "older players may try to retrieve consciously all the steps that are needed to execute a good shot" (p. 244). That such a strategy adversely affects performance is apparent in a study by Bäckman and Molander (1991) in which they asked highly skilled miniature-golf players to attend to a variety of technical aspects of their set-up and putting stroke. The resulting deterioration in putting performance supports the view that "the act of paying attention to such performances... tends to destroy the automaticity of such behaviour" (Kimble & Perlmuter, 1970, p. 375).

The role of preperformance routines in suppressing conscious control may become increasingly important as the pressure associated with performance increases. For example, Baumeister (1984) argues that performers are most likely to try to consciously control their behaviour when under pressure. Using cognitive terms, Masters (1992) made a similar suggestion by proposing that stress might cause performers to "reinvest" explicit knowledge about how to perform their skill. He hypothesised that if this was the case, then preventing them from accumulating explicit knowledge should eliminate poor performance under pressure. Masters tested his hypothesis using a golf putting task and found that a group who learned the skill while performing a secondary random letter generation task continued to improve when placed in a stressful, evaluative situation. In contrast, the groups that accumulated a pool of explicit knowledge performed more poorly when placed under stress.

From a practical point of view, Jackson and Willson (1999) questioned the efficacy of this approach arguing that progressing from novice to skilled performer without building up a pool of explicit knowledge would be extremely difficult. They suggested that a more effective method of preventing reinvestment might be to incorporate verbal or visual cues into the preperformance routine. In a series of studies with recreational golfers, they found qualified support for this proposal. Certain verbal and visual cues did appear to prevent performance decrements under pressure, however, other factors appeared to moderate their effectiveness. For example, a participant-generated verbal cue relating to the putting stroke appeared to be effective whereas one generated by the experimenter did not. However, cues referring to some aspect of the set-up were effective whether they were self-formulated or given by the experimenter.

Previously, Singer, Lidor, and Cauraugh (1993) demonstrated the effectiveness of incorporating cues into a preperformance routine using a *Five-step strategy* consisting of readying (preparing for the act), imaging (visualising the movement), focusing (on a meaningful cue), executing (with a quiet mind) and evaluating (the effectiveness of each of the previous steps). Participants using this strategy on a novel throwing task showed clear benefits compared to a control group but, interestingly, participants using a *nonawareness strategy*, essentially consisting of the *focus* and *execute* steps of the five-step strategy showed almost identical performance benefits. The common function of both strategies is that they discourage performers from attending to the mechanics of their skill thereby enabling them to perform with minimal conscious activity.

In conclusion, there appears to be two answers to the question posed in the title of this chapter. On the one hand, support for the effectiveness of cognitive-behavioural interventions alongside research alluding to the importance of "not thinking" when performing well-learned skills suggests that performers may benefit from incorporating strategies into their preperformance routine that help to prevent conscious control, particularly in pressure situations. On the other hand, there is presently no evidence that increasing the temporal and/or behavioural consistency of a routine will result in improved performance. It would seem that attaining an appropriate attentional focus should be the priority, irrespective of how long it takes.

References

Adams, J.A. (1971). A closed-loop theory of motor learning. *Journal of Motor Behaviour, 3,* 111–150.

Bäckman, L., & Molander, B. (1991). Cognitive processes among skilled miniature golf players: Effects of instructions on motor performance, concentration time, and perceived difficulty. *Scandinavian Journal of Psychology, 32,* 344–351.

Baumeister, R.F. (1984). Choking under pressure: Self-consciousness and paradoxical effects of incentives on skilful performance. *Journal of Personality and Social Psychology, 46,* 610–620.

Beauchamp, P.H., Halliwell, W.R., Fournier, J.F., & Koestner, R. (1996). Effects of cognitive-behavioural psychological skills training on the motivation, preparation, and putting performance of novice golfers. *The Sport Psychologist, 10,* 157–170.

Boutcher, S.H. (1990). The role of performance routines in sport. In J.G. Jones & L. Hardy (Eds.), *Stress and performance in sport* (pp. 231–245). Chichester, UK: John Wiley & Sons.

Boutcher, S.H. (1992). Attention and athletic performance: An integrated approach. In T.S. Horn (Ed.), *Advances in sport psychology* (pp. 251–265). Champaign, IL: Human Kinetics.

Boutcher, S.H., & Crews, D.J. (1987). The effect of a preshot attentional routine on a well-learned skill. *International Journal of Sport Psychology, 18,* 30–39.

Boutcher, S.H., & Rotella, R.J. (1987). A psychological skills educational program for closed-skill performance enhancement. *The Sport Psychologist, 1,* 127–137.

Boutcher, S.H., & Zinsser, N.W. (1990). Cardiac deceleration of elite and beginning golfers during putting. *Journal of Sport & Exercise Psychology, 12,* 37–47.

Catania, A.C. (1992). *Learning.* Englewood Cliffs, NJ: Prentice-Hall.

Cohn, P.J., Rotella, R.J., & Lloyd, J.W. (1990). Effects of a cognitive-behavioural intervention on the preshot routine and performance in golf. *The Sport Psychologist, 4,* 33–47.

Crews, D.J., & Boutcher, S.H. (1986). Effects of structured preshot behaviours on beginning golf performance. *Perceptual and Motor Skills, 62,* 291–294.

Crews, D.J., & Boutcher, S.H. (1987). An exploratory observational behaviour analysis of professional golfers during competition. *Journal of Sport Behavior, 9,* 51–58.

Crews, D., Lutz, R., Nilsson, P., & Marriott, L. (1999). Psychophysiological indicators of confidence and habituation during golf putting. In M.R. Farrally & A.J. Cochran (Eds.), *Science and golf III: Proceedings of the 1998 World Scientific Congress of Golf* (pp. 158–165). Champaign, IL: Human Kinetics.

Fitts, P.M., & Posner, M.I. (1967). The measurement of skills. In D. Legge (Ed.), *Skills* (pp. 67–80). Harmondsworth, UK: Penguin Books.

Jackson, R.C., & Baker, J.S. (in press). Routines, rituals and rugby: Case study of a world class goal-kicker. Paper to appear in *The Sport Psychologist.*

Jackson, R.C., & Willson, R.J. (1999). Using 'swing thoughts' to prevent paradoxical performance effects in golf putting. In M.R. Farrally & A.J. Cochran (Eds.), *Science and golf III: Proceedings of the 1998 World Scientific Congress of Golf* (pp. 166–173). Champaign, IL: Human Kinetics.

Kimble, G.A., & Perlmuter, L.C. (1970). The problem of volition. *Psychological Review, 77,* 361–384.

Masters, R.S.W. (1992). Knowledge, knerves and know-how: The role of explicit versus implicit knowledge in the breakdown of a complex motor skill under pressure. *British Journal of Psychology, 83*, 343–358.

McInman, A.D., & Grove, J.R. (1991). Peak moments in sport: A literature review. *Quest, 43*, 333–351.

Molander, B., & Bäckman, L. (1993). Performance of a complex motor skill across the life-span: General trends and qualifications. In J. Cerella, W. Hoyer, J. Rybash, & M.L. Commons (Eds.), *Adult information processing: Limits on loss* (pp. 231–257). San Diego, CA: Academic Press.

Moran, A.P. (1996). *The psychology of concentration in sport performers: A cognitive analysis.* Hove, UK: Psychology Press.

Nideffer, R.N. (1993). Concentration and attention control training. In J.M. Williams (Ed.), *Applied sport psychology: Personal growth to peak performance* (2nd ed., pp. 243–261). Mountain View, CA: Mayfield.

Singer, R.N., Lidor, R., & Cauraugh, J.H. (1993). To be aware or not aware? What to think about while learning and performing a motor skill. *The Sport Psychologist, 7*, 19–30.

Skinner, B.F. (1948). 'Superstition' in the pigeon. *Journal of Experimental Psychology, 38*, 168–172.

Thomas, P.R., & Over, R. (1994). Psychological and psychomotor skills associated with performance in golf. *The Sport Psychologist, 8*, 73–86.

Wrisberg, C.A. (1993). Levels of performance skill. In R.N. Singer, M. Murphey, & L.K. Tennant (Eds.), *Handbook of research on sport psychology* (pp. 61–72). New York: Macmillan.

Wrisberg, C.A., & Pein, R.L. (1992). The preshot interval and free throw shooting accuracy: An exploratory investigation. *The Sport Psychologist, 6*, 14–23.

CHAPTER 22

How Do We Define Success? Differences in the Goal Orientations of Higher and Lower Ability Golfers

Kieran M. Kingston and Lew Hardy

The cognitive mechanistic approach to goals contends that, for any given situation, "goals are immediate regulators of human action" (Weinberg, 1992, p. 182), and function like a psychological state. Contemporary motivation theorists, however, suggest that goal preferences are like personality characteristics — they imply a dispositional underpinning for individual performance objectives. In this context, goals relate to how the individual construes his or her level of ability, and reflect the personal meaning of achievement to the athlete. Although attempts to converge these contrasting conceptualisations of goals have met with some resistance, it is accepted that there is a meaningful association between dispositional factors, the situation and psychological states (see, Hardy, Jones, & Gould, 1996). Further understanding this relationship will enable sport psychologists and other applied practitioners to more effectively intervene when performers experience motivational problems or exhibit maladaptive (inappropriate) motivational behaviour and cognitions.

Goal Perspectives
One theory, which is increasingly utilised as a basis for examining the relationship between dispositions and situational factors in sport, is goal

perspectives theory (Dweck & Leggett, 1988; Nicholls, 1989, 1992). The theory originated as a social-cognitive approach to understanding motivation in achievement settings. According to the theory, there are two major goal perspectives operating in achievement-related contexts, and it is these that determine the criteria by which individuals conceptualise ability and judge success. An ego-involved perspective exists when individuals construe subjective success by comparing their own ability with that of others. A task-involved perspective is held when subjective success is based upon self-referenced improvements in performance and/or learning or mastering the task. Accordingly, individuals can be classified as being task and/or ego orientated according to their dispositional tendency to employ or favour task- and ego-involved perspectives.

The existence and measurement of these two goal perspectives in sport has been confirmed using a number of assessment tools. One of the more widely used is the Task and Ego Orientation in Sport Questionnaire (TEOSQ; Duda & Nicholls, 1992) which assesses individuals' proneness to be task and ego involved (i.e., their goal orientation). The two-factor structure of the TEOSQ has been found to be stable, with two internally consistent orthogonal (independent) factors. The independence of these factors has been supported in studies of both elite and non-elite sport participants (Duda & White, 1992).

Goal Orientations Research in Sport

Goal orientations represent the tendency for athletes to judge success and failure in terms of normative and/or self-referenced criteria. The research into goal orientations in sport and exercise settings has been reviewed extensively (see, for example Duda, 1992; Duda & Whitehead, 1998; Roberts, 1992). One of the most robust findings within this body of research is that a high level of ego orientation combined with a low perception of ability has negative implications for performance and affect. Similarly, a high as opposed to a low level of task orientation is associated with adaptive beliefs and cognitions (Duda, 1992, 1993; Hardy et al., 1996).

An important consideration when looking at individual goal orientations is their independence. Although Nicholls' (1989, 1992) original conceptualisation of task and ego goal perspectives clearly implies that the two goal orientations are independent, individuals high in task orientation are often compared with individuals high in ego orientation. The independence (orthogonality) of the goal orientations measured by the TEOSQ, however, renders such comparisons meaningless, unless of course it is acknowledged that these are simply dominant perspectives. It is quite possible for an individual to possess simultaneously high or low levels of task and ego orientations. Furthermore, comparing individuals who are ostensibly high in task orientation with those high in ego orientation ignores the potentially important interactive effects between task and ego orientations (Hardy, 1997).

Goal Orientation Profiles

One approach to examining the effects of different levels of goal orientations has utilised the notion of goal orientation profiles. In their simplest forms, these profiles make use of the independent nature of task and ego orientations as measured by the TEOSQ to categorise an individual into one of four goal orientation sub-sets: high task, high ego; high task, low ego; low task, high ego; and low task, low ego. The principal advantage of this approach is that it enables researchers to test hypotheses regarding the interactive effects of task and ego orientations using relatively straightforward research designs. Although there are undoubtedly shortcomings with the use of quadrants to describe goal orientation profiles, this approach has led to an increased appreciation of the need to consider the combined patterning of task and ego orientations (see Hardy, 1997). As Fox, Goudas, Duda, Biddle, and Armstrong (1994) suggest with reference to goal orientations, "...their impact in combination may be somewhat different from their effect examined separately" (p. 255).

Studies that have utilised a profile approach to examining goal perspectives have generally focused on their relationships with aspects of motivation and beliefs about causes of success (Fox et al., 1994; Roberts, Treasure, & Kavussanu, 1996; Walling & Duda, 1995; White, 1998). Although researchers have discussed the possibility that the profiles of highly skilled performers are distinguishable from those of their less able counterparts (e.g., Brunel & Avanzini, 1997; Hardy et al., 1996), there is little direct evidence to support this contention. Fox et al. (1994) did, however, suggest that higher level performers possessed a combination of high ego and high task orientations simultaneously. Furthermore, interviews with elite performers have supported this contention (see Hardy et al., 1996; Jones & Hardy, 1990; Orlick & Partington, 1988). To summarise, it may be possible to discriminate between ability levels on the basis of the patterning of task and ego goal orientations, and while causality cannot be reliably inferred, this association may have implications for the types of goals and strategies that performers use across situations. Furthermore, examination of relative levels of task and ego orientations as a function of ability is of interest because of the emphasis that much of the goal perspectives literature has placed on the downplaying of an ego orientation.

It has become widely accepted that the type of involvement an individual prefers in achievement settings is a product of a disposition by situation interaction (e.g., Duda & White, 1992). According to Dweck and Leggett (1988), situational factors influence individual tendencies to adopt a state of involvement, which is reflective of the dispositional orientation they hold. Furthermore, the literature pertaining to goal-setting practices (e.g., Burton 1992; Kingston & Swain, 1999) makes a number of predictions regarding performance, anxiety, confidence and attributions.

Preliminary research has indicated that in sports settings (or indeed in the context of upcoming sporting scenarios) goal orientations fluctuate in a systematic rather than a random manner according to perceived situational factors. Indeed, Kingston and Swain (1999) have presented empirical data that support the fluctuating nature of athletes' dispositional goal orientations as measured by the TEOSQ. Subsequently, it is important to identify if such patterns of change are a function of the performers' level of ability.

The purpose of the current study was, therefore, to determine the extent to which composite levels of task and ego orientations can be used to differentiate between athlete ability levels, and to establish whether the nature of the discrimination was consistent across a number of situations. Assessing goal orientation profiles across a number of contexts will provide information regarding the situations under which goal orientations can best discriminate ability. It was hypothesised that goal orientation profiles could indeed distinguish between ability levels, and that higher ability performers would possess generally higher levels of task and ego orientation. However, the nature of the relationship between goal orientations and ability might be mediated by prevailing situational factors.

Method
Participants

Seventy-nine male golfers from British golf clubs in Cheshire, Derbyshire and North Wales participated in this study. The sample consisted of two ability groups. The high-ability group ($n = 30$) consisted of club professionals ($n = 13$) and county representative golfers ($n = 17$) with handicaps ranging from +2 to −2 (mean handicap = 0.95, $SD = \pm 0.44$). The low-ability group consisted of club golfers ($n = 49$) with handicaps ranging from 6 to 28 (mean handicap = 17.60, $SD = \pm 8.21$). Participation was voluntary, and participants were required to complete a single 13-item questionnaire on three occasions throughout the year.

Instrumentation

Task and Ego Orientation in Sport Questionnaire (TEOSQ). The TEOSQ (Duda & Nicholls, 1992) was developed to assess individuals' proneness for task and ego involvement in the athletic context. TEOSQ is a modified, sport-specific version of the inventory developed by Nicholls and his colleagues to assess task and ego orientation in the academic context (Nicholls, 1989). All 13 items reflecting task and ego orientations to subjective success contain the stem, "I feel most successful in sport [golf] when...", and participants indicate their degree of agreement by responding on a scale anchored from *strongly disagree* (1) to *strongly agree* (5). Mean scores were calculated on the two subscales of the TEOSQ.

Procedure

Participants were required to respond to the TEOSQ on three separate occasions. The first occasion was in the middle of the closed season for golf (preseason) when participants were neither practising nor competing on a regular basis. In the UK, this period usually coincides with poor weather and course conditions, and occurred in late January. The second occasion was the day prior to beginning practice for a major competition (prepractice). This was typically 5-6 days prior to a relatively high-status competition, depending on the ability of the participants. Finally, participants were asked to complete the questionnaire 1 day prior to a major competition, but not the competition for which they had been preparing at the previous data collection (precompetition). On each occasion, participants completed the questionnaire without any assistance and in the privacy of their own home. This was to control, as far as possible, for the direct effects of the situation on the responses to the questionnaire items.

Results

To assess the ability of goal orientation profiles to distinguish between higher and lower ability golfers, discriminant function analyses were performed. This analysis identifies whether the composite pattern of task and ego goal orientations distinguishes between the higher and lower ability groups. It also indicates the extent to which each goal orientation makes a contribution to the discrimination (i.e., do levels of task or ego orientation, or both, determine high- versus low-ability group membership?). This is ascertained by examining the standardised structure coefficients where a value above 0.3 represents a significant contribution to group separation.

On each of the three occasions that goal orientation levels were assessed, composite levels of task and ego orientations significantly discriminated between the lower and higher ability groups (Wilks' Lambda values between 0.70 and 0.72, $p < .001$). However, the standardised structure coefficients, which assessed the extent to which each of the goal orientations contributed to the classification of group membership, did not show consistent results.

Preseason

The standardised structure coefficients shown in Table 1 indicate that preseason task and ego orientation levels contributed significantly to the classification of group membership ($r = .81$ and $.66$, respectively). Analysis of the group means showed that the high-ability group had significantly ($p < .001$) higher levels of both task and ego orientation than the low-ability group (see Table 2). The high association between the groups and the predictor variables resulted in 81% of the golfers being correctly classified as higher or lower ability on the basis of their goal orientation profiles.

Prepractice

The standardised structure coefficients in Table 1 also indicate that prepractice task and ego orientation levels contributed to the discrimination between groups ($r = .70$ and $.83$, respectively). Similar to the preseason results, the group means indicate that the higher ability group had significantly ($p < .001$) greater levels of task and ego orientation than the lower ability group (see Table 2). Overall, composite scores again correctly classified 81.0% of the golfers (76.7% of the higher ability group, and 83.7% of the lower ability group).

Precompetition

Contrary to the preseason and prepractice results, the standardised structure coefficients in Table 1 indicate that only the precompetition task orientation scores contributed to the ability classification (for task orientation $r = .83$, and for ego orientation $r = .20$). Analysis of the group means indicated that although the higher ability group had significantly ($p < .001$) greater levels of task orientation than the lower ability group, there were no significant differences between the levels of ego orientation (see Table 2). Nevertheless, 81.0% of cases were still correctly classified on the basis of their precompetition task and ego orientation levels (76.7% of the higher ability group, and 83.7% of the lower ability group).

Discussion

The current study sought to establish whether goal orientation profiles measured by the TEOSQ could be used to discriminate between golfers of higher and lower ability as defined by golf handicap. Furthermore, it sought to determine if this classification based on goal orientations was consistent across a variety of situations. The issues addressed in this study are important for two main reasons. Firstly, there have been no studies to date providing empirical data on the association between goal orientation profiles and skill level. Secondly, if one assumes that high-ability golfers have a more adaptive

Table 1

Standardised Structure Coefficients

	PRESEASON	PREPRACTICE	PRECOMPETITION
Task Orientation	0.81	0.70	0.83
Ego Orientation	0.66	0.83	0.20

Note. Values above .30 are regarded as representing significant contributors to the classification of group membership (higher or lower ability golfers).

Table 2

Group Means and Standard Deviations for Preseason, Prepractice and Precompetition Levels of Task and Ego Orientations

	PRESEASON		PREPRACTICE		PRECOMPETITION	
	TASK	EGO	TASK	EGO	TASK	EGO
High Ability	3.95[a]	3.67[a]	3.85[a]	3.58[a]	3.78[a]	3.94
	(.40)	(.85)	(.34)	(.57)	(.43)	(.51)
Low Ability	3.48	3.03	3.45	2.88	3.13	3.81
	(.47)	(.69)	(.47)	(.65)	(.70)	(.55)

[a] Significantly different from Low Ability Group ($p < .001$)

(or perhaps protective?) profile as a function of their higher ability, then a useful objective for less able golfers would be to develop similarly adaptive profiles.

There are three principal findings that have arisen from this study. Firstly, as hypothesised, composite levels of task and ego goal orientations do discriminate between higher and lower ability golfers. Furthermore, the results indicate that the extent to which goal orientation profiles discriminate golfers is not situationally consistent. The second major finding is that higher ability golfers generally have significantly higher levels of task and ego goal orientations than lower ability golfers. The exception to this pattern constitutes the third major finding, that lower ability golfers have comparable levels of ego orientation to higher ability golfers just prior to competition.

The first two results lend further credence to the contention that higher level performers have goal orientation profiles that are markedly different from their less able contemporaries (Brunel & Avanzini, 1997; Hardy et al., 1996). The results also suggest that higher level performers can be generally characterised by relatively high levels of both task and ego goal orientations. Such performers appear to use multiple criteria for success based upon social comparison (e.g., exceeding the performance of others) and self-referenced performance objectives (e.g., learning or mastering the task). Although performance per se was not measured, there is empirical evidence elsewhere (see Kingston & Swain, 1999) which suggests that having multiple criteria for success (i.e., a combination of high levels of task and ego orientation) can have positive effects on the performance of golfers.

The third major finding of this study is that the precompetition levels of ego orientation for the lower ability golfers were similar to those of higher ability. This result suggests that competition may cause lower ability performers to modify their criteria for success towards an increased focus on social comparison. This may not be surprising given sport's pervasive preoccupation with winning. However, reference to the goal perspectives literature might lead one to conclude that such a focus is not entirely appropriate for these performers. For example, Roberts et al. (1996) argued that high levels of task orientation provide a buffering or protective role against the potentially debilitating effects of a high level of ego orientation (see for example, Duda, 1992). It is apparent in this study that the lower ability performers held and maintained a relatively low level of task orientation compared to their more able counterparts. It might also be argued that lower ability players tend to have relatively lower perceptions of their ability in major competitions. When combined with lower perceptions of ability, high levels of ego orientation have consistently been shown to lead to negative motivational consequences (Duda, 1992, 1993; Hardy et al., 1996).

Research Implications

From a methodological perspective, the current study could be criticised for the broadness of the high- and low-ability categories. Within the lower ability group, individuals with handicaps of 6 and 28 are markedly different in skill level. The cut-off for distinguishing between the ability groups could be argued to be somewhat arbitrary. However, it was felt that a 6-handicap characterised a good club player, whereas a 2-handicap identified a golfer of representative standard, and so the 4-stroke difference represented distinct variation in ability level. Future studies should perhaps ensure more distinctive group identities, and balance this with a need to provide meaningful comparison groups (e.g., high, moderate and low ability).

Another potential criticism is the use of the TEOSQ. A number of researchers have questioned the construct validity of the measure (see for example, Hardy, 1997). However, in spite of these concerns, it was felt that its use was warranted because of the absence of a psychometrically valid and reliable alternative at the time of collecting the data. Researchers do, however, need to consider the use of a measure of goal orientations that is based on the definitions or operationalisations of task and ego orientations rather than the behavioural correlates of each, as TEOSQ appears to be.

Practical Implications

It is apparent that simultaneously high levels of task and ego orientations have potential benefits in terms of performance and associated cognitions. However, it is also evident that golfers of different ability levels possess contrasting goal orientation profiles. The implication for applied practitioners (e.g., coaches, sport psychologists) is that high ability golfers should be encouraged to maintain high levels of both task and ego goal orientations. This gives golfers multiple criteria for success so that if they fail to win a competition, having criteria for success based on personal performance allows them a further opportunity to gain motivationally from the experience.

With golfers of lower ability or perceived ability, it is somewhat problematic to advocate a carte-blanche approach to developing task- and ego-based criteria for success. Lower ability golfers should be encouraged to set goals that both enhance their task orientation (e.g., focus on criteria for success based around learning, mastery and enjoyment) and increase their level of perceived competence. The purpose of elevating the task focus is twofold. Firstly, it enables the lower ability golfers to protect themselves against the potentially debilitating effects of a high level of ego orientation in competitive situations. Secondly, maintaining a focus on goals relating to personal performance, rather than the performance of others, allows these golfers to exert higher levels of control over the goals that they set, and hence increase their opportunities to be successful. Therefore, a more specific objective for coaches should be to foster both task- and ego-based criteria for success by attempting to socialise golfers towards utilising multiple criteria for success. The adjunct to this suggestion is that coaches need to consider the ability levels of the golfers and the situation when attempting to encourage a more ego-involved perspective. It is clearly important to balance the emphasis placed on outperforming others with that placed on realising personal performance objectives.

Finally, when skill level increases as a function of extensive practice, athletes are likely to modify or prioritise their criteria for success (i.e., the types of goals that they set) as they become increasingly aware of the consequences of holding such goals (i.e., their criteria become more adaptive). This can help to ensure that practice remains stimulating and golfers maximise their opportunity to achieve success by self-referenced and/or other-referenced criteria in the competition environment.

Conclusion

This study demonstrates that the criteria golfers use to judge success and failure vary as a function of their ability. More specifically, it shows that higher ability golfers use multiple criteria to ascertain success and failure to a greater extent than do lower ability golfers. It is assumed, based on previous research and anecdotal accounts, that higher ability performers hold generally more adaptive goal orientation profiles. On this basis, a number of suggestions have been made to guide both research and applied practice.

Goal orientations are regarded as underlying tendencies towards setting different types of goals. However, situational factors influence these preferences. For applied work to move forward it is important that we understand more about the relationship between these two factors, as well as the motivational consequences. The current study enables applied practitioners to understand the criteria for success that golfers of different ability levels might have in various situations. Perhaps more importantly, it provides useful insights into potentially adaptive ways of defining success that may optimise performance in golf.

References

Brunel, P.C., & Avanzini, G. (1997). Achievement orientation and intrinsic motivation at the Olympic Games. *Journal of Sport and Exercise Psychology, 19*, S36.

Burton, D. (1992). The Jekyll/Hyde nature of goals: Reconceptualizing goal setting in sport. In T. S. Horn (Ed.), *Advances in sport psychology* (pp. 267–297). Champaign, IL: Human Kinetics.

Duda, J.L. (1992). Motivation in sport settings: A goal perspective approach. In G.C. Roberts (Ed.), *Motivation in sport and exercise* (pp. 57–92). Champaign, IL: Human Kinetics.

Duda, J.L. (1993). Goals: A social-cognitive approach to the study of achievement motivation in sport. In R.N. Singer, M. Murphey, & L.K. Tennant (Eds.), *Handbook of research on sport psychology* (pp. 421–436). New York: Macmillan.

Duda, J.L., & Nicholls, J.G. (1992). Dimensions of achievement motivation in schoolwork and sport. *Journal of Educational Psychology, 84*, 290–299.

Duda, J.L., & White, S.A. (1992). Goal orientations and beliefs about the causes of sport success among elite skiers. *The Sport Psychologist, 6*, 334–343.

Duda, J.L. & Whitehead, J. (1998). Measurement of goal perspectives in the physical domain. In J.L. Duda (Ed.), *Advances in sport and exercise psychology measures* (pp. 21–48). Morgantown, WV: Fitness Information Technology.

Dweck, C.S., & Leggett, E.L. (1988). A social-cognitive approach to motivation and personality. *Psychological Review, 95*, 256–273.

Fox, K., Goudas, M., Biddle, S., Duda, J.L., & Armstrong, N. (1994). Children's task and ego goal profiles in sport. *British Journal of Educational Psychology, 64*, 253–261.

Hardy, L. (1997). The Coleman Roberts Griffith Address: Three myths about applied consultancy work. *Journal of Applied Sport Psychology, 9*, 277–294.

Hardy, L., Jones, J.G., & Gould, D. (1996). *Understanding psychological preparation for sport: Theory and practice of elite sports performers.* Chichester: John Wiley.

Jones, J.G., & Hardy, L. (1990). *Stress and performance in sport.* Chichester: John Wiley.

Kingston, K., & Swain, A. (1999). Goal orientations and state goals: Research in golf and implications for performance. In M.R. Farrally & A.J. Cochran (Eds.), *Science and golf III: Proceedings of the 1998 World Scientific Congress of Golf* (pp. 150–157). Champaign, IL: Human Kinetics.

Nicholls, J.G. (1989). *The competitive ethos and democratic education.* Cambridge, MA: Harvard University Press.

Nicholls, J.G. (1992). The general and the specific in the development and expression of achievement motivation. In G.C. Roberts (Ed.), *Motivation in sport and exercise* (pp. 31–56). Champaign, IL: Human Kinetics.

Orlick, T., & Partington, J. (1988). Mental links to excellence. *The Sport Psychologist, 2*, 105–131.

Roberts, G.C. (1992). Motivation in sport and exercise: Conceptual constraints and convergence. In G.C. Roberts (Ed.), *Motivation in sport and exercise* (pp. 3–29). Champaign, IL: Human Kinetics.

Roberts, G.C., Treasure, D.C., & Kavussanu, M. (1996). Orthogonality of achievement goals and its relationship to beliefs about success and satisfaction in sport. *The Sport Psychologist, 10*, 398–408.

Walling, M., & Duda, J.L. (1995). Goals and their associations with beliefs about success in and perceptions of the purposes of physical education. *Journal of Teaching Physical Education, 14*, 140–156.

Weinberg, R.S. (1992). Goal setting and performance in sport and exercise settings: A synthesis and critique. In G.C. Roberts (Ed.), *Motivation in sport and exercise* (pp. 177–197). Champaign, IL: Human Kinetics.

White, S.A. (1998). Adolescent goal profiles, perceptions of the parent-initiated motivational climate, and competitive trait anxiety. *The Sport Psychologist, 12*, 16–28.

CHAPTER 23

Self-Efficacy, Confidence Judgments, and Self-Monitoring in Golfers

Gerard J. Fogarty, Chris Graham, and David Else

"Every golfer scores better when he learns his capabilities" (Tommy Armour, 1965, p. 26).

Some readers may recognise this quote, it is taken from one of the classic books on golf instruction. There are a number of these epigrams scattered through Tommy Armour's book, they are printed in red ink in a publication that is otherwise devoid of eye-catching devices, and they do tend to make a point. It is appropriate that we use Tommy Armour to introduce the theme of this chapter.

The measurement and study of self-confidence is a central concern in sport psychology because of the perceived dramatic effect it has on performance. This impact is both positive, as when the presence of confidence leads to better performance (George, 1994), and negative, as evidenced by the sometimes dramatic effect that a loss of self-confidence has on performance in an experience commonly referred to as 'choking' (Vealey, Hayashi, Garner-Holman, & Giacobbi, 1998). Several major theoretical paradigms have been put forward to explain how confidence relates to external behaviour such as performance, and internal states such as motivation. Bandura's (1977) theory of self-efficacy is perhaps the best known of these. Bandura (1986) defined self-efficacy as "peoples' judgments of their capabilities to organise and execute courses of action required to attain designated types of performances" (p. 391). In Bandura's model, self-efficacy is derived from four major sources of information: performance accomplishments, vicarious experiences, verbal persuasion, and physiological states.

Over the years, a number of researchers have explored the relationship between self-efficacy and performance in sports settings. Although the overall weight of research findings supports the positive link suggested by self-efficacy theory, there are many instances where expected relations did not emerge. In reviewing this evidence, George (1994) concluded "the extent to which self-efficacy predicts performance under variable, dynamic conditions found in many sport settings remains unclear" (p. 382). One of the problems that has hindered research on self-efficacy in sport concerns the generality of the measures used. McAuley and Gill (1983) argued that general measures of self-efficacy would not predict sporting performance whereas task-specific measures would. Wurtele (1986) made the same suggestion, noting that few studies in sport psychology have analysed the degree of congruence between self-efficacy judgments and performance at the level of individual tasks. We address this issue in the present study.

The constructs of self-confidence and self-efficacy are closely related, indeed in many situations it is not possible to separate the two. Vealey (1986), in developing a model of self-confidence that was based on sport, distinguished between trait self-confidence (SC-trait), which is defined as the belief or degree of certainty individuals usually possess about their ability to be successful, and state self-confidence (SC-state), which refers to "right now" feelings of their ability to be successful in a specific situation. SC-state is very similar to task-specific self-efficacy and we will treat the two as synonymous in the present chapter. Vealey's model also included a competitive orientation construct to account for individual differences in perceptions of success. Vealey (1986) developed two separate 13-item inventories to measure trait confidence and state confidence. The former is measured by the Trait Sport Confidence Inventory (TSCI) whereas the latter is measured by the State Sport Confidence Inventory (SSCI). Vealey stated that SC-state is "predicted to be the most important mediator of behaviour as it is based on the mutual influence of situational factors and individual differences" (Vealey, 1986, p. 224). Unfortunately, however, the same uncertain outcomes have plagued research on the relationship between SC-state and performance as was noted earlier for research on self-efficacy and sporting performance.

Apart from the question of generality versus specificity, which Vealey's model does address, there are more fundamental methodological issues that cloud research on the relationship between self-efficacy, self-confidence, and sport. Measures of both constructs are usually based on self-report. For example, when using Vealey's SSCI, athletes are asked to rate their level of confidence compared to the most confident athlete they know. Feltz and Chase (1998) have pointed out that this inadequate frame of reference can produce unsystematic variance depending on whom the participants select as their standard of confidence. Therefore, while Bandura (1978) argued that in situations where individuals have no reason to distort their reports, self-reports can be quite representative of cognitions, we have no guarantee that we are dealing with such situations in the sports domain. How well do these subjective judgments about self-efficacy and self-confidence match actual performance capabilities? That is, are golfers' self-reported beliefs about their competence actually in accordance with what they can do, or do these estimates represent systematic biases in self-judgment that lead to states of under-confidence or over-confidence? If this is so, what are the possible implications in terms of coaching, mental preparation, and performance enhancement? Gaining a greater understanding of the cognitive processes that underlie self-confidence will enable practitioners to better assist in the development of sport programs.

To assist in this aim, we turned to the literature on metacognition. Metacognition refers to "knowing about knowing" and its essence is probably best captured by Lichtenstein and Fischoff's (1977) famous query: "Do those who know more also know more about how much they know?" (p. 159). The measurement operations employed by researchers in metacognition have particular relevance to the aims of the present study. Participants are typically asked a question and then asked to state how confident they are that the answer they gave is correct. This confidence is expressed in terms of a percentage. If this procedure is repeated over a number of trials, three measures can be obtained: the average number of items correct; the average confidence rating for the set of items; and the difference between these two, which is usually called the bias score. The bias score has been found to be highly reliable and can be taken as an estimate of where a respondent is positioned on the underconfidence-overconfidence dimension. A person with a large positive difference when confidence is subtracted from accuracy is underconfident. A person with a large negative difference, on the other hand, is overconfident. A person whose average confidence rating corresponds with the actual percentage correct is said to be well calibrated. The relationship between bias scores and performance is often difficult to obtain because the former is derived partly from the latter and few calibration studies have collected independent measures of performance. What is known is that the confidence ratings obtained in this paradigm (bias = score – confidence) tend to be strongly correlated with performance, with correlations typically around the 0.50 region (Fogarty, Burton, & Baker, 2000;

Lichtenstein & Fischoff, 1980; Stankov & Crawford, 1996). The strength and consistency of this relationship is in contrast with the research reported earlier on the relationship between measures of self-confidence and performance in the sporting domain.

Although metacognitive processes have assumed some prominence in the areas of developmental and cognitive psychology, the study of these processes in relation to sporting performance has been neglected. To our knowledge, there has been no attempt to apply the calibration techniques introduced by Lichtenstein and Fischoff (1977) to see whether there are differences in overconfidence across age, gender, or level of expertise in a sport. Nor have any attempts been made to compare measures of self-confidence obtained from this paradigm with those obtained using standard self-report techniques such as Vealey's (1986) SSCI. The present study was designed to explore the applications of calibration techniques in the sport of golf. It was hypothesised that expert golfers would be better calibrated (show less bias) than non-expert golfers. Because the calibration paradigm necessitates the use of task-specific predictions of performance, it was also hypothesised that these measures would be more closely related to golf expertise than task-specific but non-objective measures of self-confidence.

Method

Participants

A total of 24 male golfers were recruited from golf clubs located in the Queensland city of Toowoomba. Average age was 37 years. The participants were recruited through personal contact and represented a range of handicap levels ($M = 12$; $SD = 7.13$). All participants received tickets in a small lottery ($2,000) for taking part in the study.

Measures

Materials consisted of two short questionnaires assessing self-confidence in putting skill and chipping short distances, a putting task and a chipping task that formed the basis of the calibration measures, a four-item self-confidence measure that was used in conjunction with the calibration paradigm, and golf club handicap. The source of all measures was the present study. Each measure is described below with the Cronbach alpha internal consistency reliability estimates shown in brackets.

Putting Confidence Test *($\alpha = .70$)*. Participants were asked to indicate the extent to which they agreed with a series of 10 statements that employed a 5-point Likert response format wherein 1 indicated strong disagreement with the statement and 5 indicated strong agreement. The items included in the scale were as follows:

- My putting skills are generally very good.
- I am confident about short putts.
- I would have more than 36 putts in an average game of golf (r).
- I am very good at picking the line of the putt.
- I am very good at judging distance when putting.
- With long putts, I am confident that I can get close to the hole.
- Sloping greens do not worry me.
- I rarely leave the ball short of the hole when I putt.
- I tend to get anxious when putting (r).
- In general, I putt better in practice than in competition (r).

Reverse-scored items are indicated with (r). Total score was converted to a percentage to enable easy comparison across measures.

Chipping Confidence Test (α = .84). This test was identical to the Putting Confidence Test except that the questions all referred to chipping skills. The items included in this scale were as follows:

- My chipping skills are generally very good.
- I am confident about landing my chip shots where I want them to land.
- I am good at getting "up and down."
- I feel confident about lobbing over a hazard to the green.
- I am very good at judging distance when chipping.
- I have a delicate touch when chipping.
- I don't feel comfortable chipping off hard lies (r).
- I like to attack chip shots.
- Chipping is the best part of my game.
- I chip better in practice than in competition (r).

Putting Task 1 (α = .66). Participants were required to hit 20 putts on a carpeted floor through an 11.43 cm (4.5 inches) target set 2.5 metres away. They were allowed 10 practice putts and then asked to estimate how many putts out of 20 they could hit through the target. Instructions emphasised that what we were seeking was a realistic estimate of their likely score. This procedure was similar to that employed by Ryckman, Robbins, Thornton, & Cantrell (1982) in their attempt to operationalise self-confidence. Participants then answered four items that assessed their level of confidence that they could achieve this target (α = .91). The purpose of administering these four items was to check that participants were giving realistic estimates.

(Data relating to these items will not be reported here.) Participants then completed the 20 putts. Three scores were obtained from this task: Putting Estimate 1 (converted to a percentage), Putting Score 1 (converted to a percentage), and Putting Bias 1; the Bias score being the difference between obtained and estimated scores, where negative scores suggest overconfidence and positive scores underconfidence.

Chipping Task 1 (α = .80). Participants were required to hit 20 chip shots so that they landed in a circle with a diameter of 3 metres with its centre 17.5 metres from the teeing spot. The same procedure was followed as for Putting Task 1, with three outcome measures: Chipping Estimate 1 (converted to a percentage), Chipping Score 1 (converted to a percentage), and Chipping Bias 1.

Putting Task 2 (α = .57). The putting task was repeated immediately after the completion of Chipping Task 1, giving a further three measures: Putting Estimate 2, Putting Score 2, and Putting Bias 2. Five practice putts were allowed.

Chipping Task 2 (α = .75). The chipping task was also completed a second time, giving Chipping Estimate 2, Chipping Score 2, and Chipping Bias 2. Five practice chips were allowed.

Putting Estimate 3 and Chipping Estimate 3. At the completion of the two "rounds," participants were asked to estimate what they would score on the putting and chipping tasks if they were given the opportunity of one more round. These data will not be reported here.

Golf Knowledge Test. A further set of questions was designed to assess calibration in knowledge of golf rules. These data will not be reported here.

Handicap. Golf club handicaps as measured by the Australian Golf Union were recorded at the commencement of the test sessions.

Procedure

All data were collected at the University's Centre for the Assessment of Human Performance and in its environs, or at the practice facilities of a local golf club. Participants completed the questionnaires and the tasks in the order in which they appear above. Average testing time was 45 minutes.

Results

To gain some impression of overall trends, descriptive statistics were computed for all measures. These data are shown in Table 1.

Table 1
Descriptive Statistics for All Tasks

VARIABLE	MIN	MAX	MEAN	SD
Putting Confidence Test	42.00	82.00	63.08	10.27
Chipping Confidence Test	32.00	78.00	57.75	12.08
Putting Estimate 1	25.00	85.00	62.29	17.38
Putting Task 1	15.00	100.00	59.38	17.96
Putting Bias 1	−30.00	45.00	−2.92	19.94
Chipping Estimate 1	30.00	80.00	47.92	14.66
Chipping Task 1	0.00	90.00	40.63	21.58
Chipping Bias 1	−45.00	20.00	−7.29	17.57
Putting Estimate 2	25.00	95.00	63.13	17.43
Putting Task 2	40.00	100.00	65.83	15.79
Putting Bias 2	−30.00	40.00	2.71	20.38
Chipping Estimate 2	20.00	80.00	49.79	17.60
Chipping Task 2	5.00	85.00	40.21	19.48
Chipping Bias 2	−45.00	10.00	−9.58	16.01

The first point to note about these data is that the participants were generally more confident about their putting skills than their chipping skills, although the difference just failed to reach statistical significance with this small sample ($p = .054$). These differences were mirrored when participants confronted the actual putting and chipping tasks, where their estimates and actual scores were both 10–15% lower for chipping than for putting. The fact that the sample did better at putting than chipping is not of any great interest, the experiment could have been set up differently so that chipping was the easier task. What is more important is that, as a group, when they saw the actual experimental tasks and had the opportunity of practising for 10 shots, the participants seemed to be able to estimate their performance levels with a reasonable degree of accuracy for both tasks. The bias scores reflect this general accuracy. Although participants tended to be overconfident (a negative bias score), it was only on the second chipping task that the difference between estimated and actual scores was significant. We can conclude from these data that, as a group, this sample of golfers was reasonably well calibrated.

Mean scores can be deceptive, however, and when the range of scores and the standard deviations for each of the bias measures is examined, it is clear that there were big individual differences in calibration, with some individuals grossly overestimating their scores on the chipping tasks in particular. To determine whether this tendency was associated with golfing ability, the sample was divided into two groups: a low-handicap group comprising participants with golf club handicaps below 14 ($n = 15$) and a high-handicap group comprising the remainder of the sample ($n = 9$). The mean age for both groups was 35 years. We also decided to look only at the second-round variables, on the grounds that participants were familiar with the tasks by this stage and had feedback on earlier performance. It was felt that if differences emerged between the two groups in the second round, these differences were likely to be reliable. Descriptive statistics for both groups are shown in Table 2.

Some of the differences in Table 2 were very predictable. Low-handicap golfers had significantly better scores on the putting and chipping tasks, as one would expect. Not so predictable, however, was the lack of difference between the low and high handicappers on the Putting Confidence Test and the Chipping Confidence Test where the groups recorded almost identical scores. The items for both of these tasks have been included in the Method section. When the items for both scales were examined individually, the only item on which the groups differed was one which read "I would have more than 36 putts in an average game of golf," a reverse-scored item where the low-handicap group tended to disagree with the statement but the high handicappers tended to agree. The difference between this item and all the others is that it provided a performance standard against which the golfers could assess their competence. The importance of a performance standard is further demonstrated by the significant differences between the low and high handicappers when they were given an opportunity to practise and then to

Table 2
Comparison Between Low-Handicap and High-Handicap Golfers

VARIABLE	GROUP	MEAN	S.E.	$F(6, 17)$	P
Putting	Low-handicap	63.73	2.70		
Confidence Test	High-handicap	62.00	3.49	0.15	0.70
Chipping	Low-handicap	58.67	3.17		
Confidence Test	High-handicap	56.22	4.10	0.22	0.64
Putting	Low-handicap	62.00	4.59		
Estimate 2	High-handicap	65.00	5.92	0.16	0.69
	Low-handicap	71.00	3.76		
Putting Task 2	High-handicap	57.22	4.85	5.04	0.04
	Low-handicap	9.00	4.91		
Putting Bias 2	High-handicap	−7.78	6.34	4.37	0.04
Chipping	Low-handicap	56.00	4.11		
Estimate 2	High-handicap	39.44	5.31	6.08	0.02
	Low-handicap	48.33	4.29		
Chipping Task 2	High-handicap	26.67	5.54	9.55	0.01
	Low-handicap	−7.67	4.17		
Chipping Bias 2	High-handicap	−12.78	5.39	0.56	0.46

estimate their likely performance levels. High-handicap golfers considered themselves to be as good as low-handicap players when the task involved putting short distances on a flat surface. The results (see Table 2) suggested that this might have been an unrealistic expectation with a significant difference between the groups. In the case of the chipping task, however, there was a clear difference in both expectations and actual performance levels between the two groups, with the low handicappers much better at this task.

In terms of calibration, there were interesting differences between the low- and high-handicap golfers. On the putting task, the low-handicap golfers were underconfident whereas the high-handicap group tended to be overconfident. It is tempting to say that the high-ability group was more aware of just how easy it is to miss putts at a distance of 2.5 metres, and accordingly made more modest estimates relative to their ability level, but we have no direct evidence of this. On the chipping task, both groups tended to be overconfident, especially the high-handicap group. On the basis of these data, we tentatively suggest that better golfers are more aware of their own limitations. There are other questions generated by these data that we are not prepared to address until a much larger dataset has been gathered. Some of these questions concern relations among the variables. The late Hans Eysenck once advised the first author of this chapter that one should not have confidence in correlations unless the sample size upon which they were based numbers in the thousands. We are not going to that length but we will defer the interesting analysis of relations until a later date.

Discussion and Conclusions

The present study has demonstrated the danger of assessing golfers' confidence levels at any aspect of the game by simply asking them to fill in self-report measures that use general items, even though those items may be very situation-specific and relate to particular features of the game (e.g., putting across a slope). Golfers at all levels will respond in a similar way to these items. Introduce elements of objectivity (e.g., by mentioning the number of putts taken in an average round) and differences between various ability levels will begin to emerge. However, to get clear separation between ability levels, it may be necessary to introduce actual skills tests or, at the very least, to ascertain performance expectancies (Ryckman et al., 1982). In the present study, all golfers responded in a similar way to general items about chipping skills but when introduced to an actual chipping task, low-handicap and high-handicap golfers gave different estimates of what they could achieve, and at the group level these estimates were reasonably accurate.

Before setting their estimates in Round 1, the golfers in the present study had 10 practice shots, and these practice shots would have influenced the estimates themselves. By Round 2, participants had played 35 putts and chip shots, giving them substantial recent feedback on performance levels. Work is currently underway at this laboratory to determine whether differences in estimates between ability levels will emerge in the absence of practice shots. If differences do emerge in this situation, it would indicate that the mere description of the task itself is sufficient to achieve separation in the estimates of low- and high-ability golfers. Such an outcome would have appeal to researchers and coaches who want to use self-report rather than performance-based measures of confidence.

Our conclusions regarding calibration remain tentative at this stage. There is so much variation among individuals that we will need a much larger dataset before we can make confident statements about general trends. With just 24 participants in our study to this point, it is too early to say whether people who are biased in one task will be biased in another. Early indications suggest that this will be the case. The variability in golf performance is another threat to the reliability of our findings. Every golfer knows that performance varies from week to week, even among the professionals. Our small sample of 24 is far from adequate to settle questions relating to calibration. At this stage, it appears likely that high-handicap golfers overestimate their skills at putting and chipping, even in the midst of a series of putting and chipping tasks. Although not reported in this chapter, they also overestimated their knowledge of golf rules. Low-handicap golfers appear to be less inclined towards overestimation and perhaps inclined towards underestimation on simple golf tasks.

In the meantime, our advice to coaches, researchers, and players is to be mindful of the fact that players need a frame of reference if they are to make meaningful judgments about their own abilities. This can be done by mentioning performance standards when questioning golfers about their own abilities. Coaches also need to be mindful that some players will tend to overestimate their abilities, others will tend to underestimate, and some will be well calibrated. If we take Tommy Armour's advice to heart, it is membership of this group to which all golfers must aspire.

References

Armour, T. (1965). *How to play your best golf all the time* (3rd ed.). London: Hodder and Stoughton.

Bandura, A. (1977). Self-efficacy: Toward a unifying theory of behavioral change. *Psychological Review, 84*(2), 191–215.

Bandura, A. (1978). Reflections on self-efficacy. In S. Rachman (Ed.), *Advances in behaviour research and therapy* (Vol. 1, pp. 237–269). Oxford: Pergamon.

Bandura, A. (1986). *Social foundations of thought and action: A social cognitive theory*. Englewood Cliffs, NJ: Prentice Hall.

Feltz, D.L., & Chase, M. A. (1998). The measurement of self-efficacy and confidence in sport. In J. L. Duda (Ed.), *Advances in sport and exercise psychology measurement* (pp. 65–80). Morgantown, WV: Fitness Information Technology.

Fogarty, G., Burton, L., & Baker, S. (2000, April). *Using calibration techniques to improve correlations between self-report and objective measures of visual imagery.* Paper presented at the 27th Annual Conference of the Australasian Experimental Psychology Society, Queensland.

George, T. R. (1994). Self-confidence and baseball performance: A causal examination of self-efficacy theory. *Journal of Sport and Exercise Psychology, 16,* 381–399.

Lichtenstein, S., & Fischoff, B. (1977). Do those who know also know more about how much they know? *Organisational Behaviour and Human Performance, 20,* 159–183.

Lichtenstein, S., & Fischoff, B. (1980). Training for calibration. *Organisational Behaviour and Human Performance, 26,* 149–171.

McAuley, E., & Gill, D. (1983). Reliability and validity of the Physical Self-Efficacy Scale in a competitive sport setting. *Journal of Sport Psychology, 5,* 410–418.

Ryckman, R. M., Robbins, M. A., Thornton, B., & Cantrell, P. (1982). Development and validation of a Physical Self-Efficacy Scale. *Journal of Personality and Social Psychology, 42,* 891–900.

Stankov, L., & Crawford, J. (1996). Confidence judgements in studies of individual differences. *Personality and Individual Differences, 21,* 971–986.

Vealey, R. S. (1986). Conceptualization of sport-confidence and competitive orientation: Preliminary investigation and instrument development. *Journal of Sport Psychology, 8,* 221–246.

Vealey, R.S., Hayashi, S. W., Garner-Holman, M., & Giacobbi, P. (1998). Sources of sport-confidence: Conceptualization and instrument development. *Journal of Sport & Exercise Psychology, 20,* 54–80.

Wurtele, S.K. (1986). Self-efficacy and athletic performance: A review. *Journal of Social and Clinical Psychology, 4,* 290–301.

CHAPTER 24

The Role of Imagery Ability in the Learning and Performance of Golf Skills

J. Robert Grove, Vicki de Prazer, Robert S. Weinberg, and Russell Pitcher

---

Athletes, coaches, and sport psychologists believe that the use of mental rehearsal can improve sport performance, and imagery techniques are often incorporated into sport-related psychological skills training programs (Hall, Rodgers, & Barr, 1990; Murphy, 1994; Vealey, 1988). Research evidence supports the use of these techniques by confirming that, under certain conditions, systematic application of imagery strategies is associated with improvements in motor performance (Feltz & Landers, 1983; Garza & Feltz, 1998; Hardy & Callow, 1999; Hinshaw, 1991–92; Moran, 1993; Murphy & Jowdy, 1992).

Golfers have long recognised the potential of mental rehearsal for improving performance in their sport and have described a number of ways in which it might be used. Nicklaus (1974, p. 79), for example, provided the following description of how he used imagery to create an association between a desired outcome and a desired swing:

> I never hit a shot, not even in practice, without having a very sharp, in-focus picture of it in my head... First I 'see' the ball where I want it to finish... Then... I 'see' the ball going there: its path, trajectory, and shape... The next scene shows me making the kind of swing that will turn the images into reality.

Other well-known players and coaches have provided insight into how mental rehearsal can be used to improve the quality of practice, learn new swing habits, reduce anxiety during competition, boost self-confidence, and/or modify self-defeating thoughts and behaviours (Cohn, 1994; Cohn & Winters, 1995; Graham, 1990; Owens & Bunker, 1992; Wiren & Coop, 1978).

Despite such endorsements, the academic literature in this area suggests that some people may benefit more than others from the use of mental rehearsal strategies. More specifically, imagery ability needs to be considered, because it has frequently been shown to mediate the effects of imagery interventions (Hall, Schmidt, Durand, & Buckolz, 1994; Isaac, 1992; Martin, Moritz, & Hall, 1999; Moran, 1993; Murphy, 1994; Sheikh, Sheikh, & Moleski, 1994). Although it seems obvious that the impact of imagery manipulations will differ as a function of one's ability to produce or control mental representations of a movement, researchers often fail to consider this factor when attempting to evaluate the impact of imagery interventions (Hall, 1998; Hinshaw, 1991-92). Two studies investigating the relationship between imagery ability and golf performance are reported here.

Study 1
Participants and Assessment of Imagery Ability

Sixty-four female golfers volunteered to participate in this study.[1] On average, the women were 47 years of age (SD = 11), had 10 years of golfing experience (SD = 7.9), currently played twice a week (SD = 0.8), and took 53 strokes to play 9 holes (SD = 9.8).

Imagery ability was assessed using a modified, 12-item version of the Vividness of Movement Imagery Questionnaire (VMIQ; Isaac, Marks, & Russell, 1986). A specific subset of items was selected from the VMIQ that emphasised sport-like actions and included a variety of movement patterns (e.g., throwing, catching, hitting, kicking, running, jumping). Participants were asked to imagine themselves performing each of the 12 movements and then rate the vividness of their images on a 5-point scale ranging from *perfectly clear and as vivid as normal vision* (1) to *no image at all; you only know you are thinking of the skill* (cf. Isaac et al., 1986; Sheehan, 1967). Responses were then summed to obtain a one-number index of imagery ability. The original VMIQ has acceptable psychometric properties for motor skills research (Hall, 1998; Hall & Martin, 1997; Isaac et al., 1986; Moran, 1993), and total scores for the 12 items used in this study correlate extremely well with scores on the original scale (r = .95; Isaac, personal communication, July 29, 1996).

Experimental Task and Imagery Intervention

The experimental task was a pitching-wedge golf shot over a distance of 40 metres (44 yards). Participants hit 12 of these "half-wedge" shots at a flagstick set in the ground before exposure to an imagery intervention and then hit 12 more shots after exposure to the intervention. The outcome measure of interest was shot accuracy which was defined as the final distance of the ball from the hole on each shot (in metres).

The imagery intervention contained an introduction followed by relaxation, modelling, and mental rehearsal components. The introduction consisted of a brief overview of mental imagery and its potential benefits to golfers. The relaxation component made use of abdominal breathing and muscular awareness exercises. During the modelling phase, participants watched a videotape of a professional golfer hitting 60 wedge shots (Golf with Patty Sheehan, 1983). After viewing the model, participants mentally rehearsed 20 wedge shots. They were instructed to rehearse the swings with their eyes closed and to execute them at the same rhythm and tempo as the swings they had seen on the videotape.

Procedure

Participants completed the modified VMIQ in their own time and returned it through the mail. They were subsequently stratified into groups with high or low imagery ability using a median split of VMIQ scores and tested on an individual basis. Upon arrival at the laboratory, they completed an informed consent form and hit their 12 pretreatment shots. After the pretest, they entered a soundproof room, sat comfortably in a padded chair, and viewed a television monitor. The imagery intervention was delivered via videotape for standardisation purposes, but one of the researchers remained in the room to answer questions about the procedure. After exposure to the imagery intervention, participants hit their 12 posttest shots. Procedures for the posttest were identical to those employed during the pretest.

Results

The hypothesis investigated in this study was that the accuracy of half-wedge shots would improve following an imagery intervention, but primarily among golfers with high levels of imagery ability. This hypothesis was tested by using a two-way analysis of covariance to compare the average distance from the hole on the pretest and posttest for players scoring above the median or below the median on the VMIQ. Skill level (defined as each player's average score for 9 holes) was used as a covariate to control for differences due to golfing ability.

Performance scores for the high imagery ability and low imagery ability groups are shown in Figure 1. The ANCOVA on these scores revealed a significant main effect for imagery ability, $F(1, 61) = 5.61$, $p < .025$, but no general difference between the pretest and posttest means, $F(1, 62) = 1.43$, $p < .24$. Inspection of adjusted means for the imagery ability effect revealed that golfers with high imagery ability (average distance from hole = 4.72 m) performed better than those with low imagery ability (average distance from hole = 5.74 m). Contrary to expectations, however, the interaction effect was not significant, $F(1, 62) = 0.04$, $p < .84$. Thus, there was evidence that golfers with relatively high imagery ability executed half-wedge shots more accurately than those with relatively low imagery ability, but there was no evidence that their superior performance was a result of greater sensitivity to the imagery intervention.

Study 2

This study employed a more comprehensive assessment of imagery ability than Study 1 and exposed non-golfers to multiple imagery treatments in an effort to investigate the influence of imagery ability on the initial learning of a golf skill.[2]

Participants and Imagery Assessment

Forty-two first-year university students who had never played a round of golf participated in this study. These individuals were selected from a larger group of 160 first-year university students on the basis of extreme scores on a battery of imagery ability tests. The test battery included the Vividness of

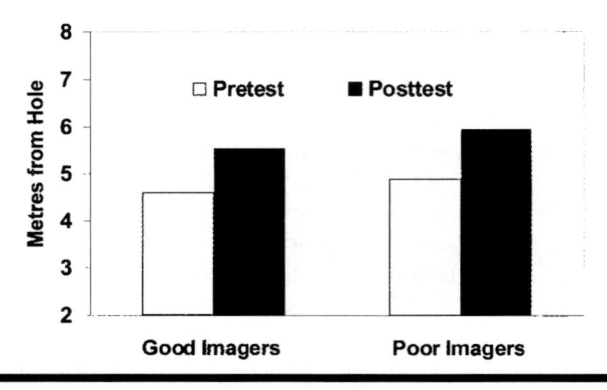

Figure 1
Distance from hole for half-wedge shots hit by players with good or poor imagery ability.

Visual Imagery Questionnaire (VVIQ; Marks, 1973), the Short Form of the Betts Questionnaire upon Mental Imagery (QMI; Sheehan, 1967), and the Gordon Test of Visual Imagery Control (TVIC; Gordon, 1949). These tests have been widely used in imagery research, and they have been shown to be valid measures of both imagery vividness and imagery control (Hall, 1998; Moran, 1993; White, Sheehan, & Ashton, 1977).

Twenty-one participants were classified as high in imagery ability because they scored less than 33 on the VVIQ, less than 30 on the QMI and, at the same time, responded *Yes* 9 or more times out of a possible 12 *Yes* responses on the TVIC.[3] Another 21 participants were classified as low in imagery ability because they scored more than 40 on the VVIQ and the QMI while, at the same time, responding *Yes* fewer than 9 times on the TVIC.

Experimental Task and Imagery Intervention

Participants were advised they would be learning a golf skill under experimental conditions. The skill acquisition task required them to putt a golf ball on a carpeted surface into a plastic putting disk. The putting area consisted of a 24-foot square marked in white masking tape with the putting disk in the centre of this square. Performance was measured using a point system devised by Boutcher and Zinsser (1990). This system allocated 15 points for holing the putt, 10 points for hitting the hole, 5 points for finishing 1–10 inches from the hole, 4 points for finishing 11–20 inches away, 3 points for finishing 21-30 inches away, 2 points for finishing 31–40 inches away, and 0 points for finishing more than 40 inches away. As noted by Boutcher and Zinsser (1990), this system rewards both accurate line (e.g., hitting the hole but not making the putt) and accurate length (e.g., finishing a short distance from the hole).

The imagery intervention had three levels, and each participant was randomly assigned to only one of these levels. In a No Imagery condition, participants read an instructional sheet containing putting tips between each block of trials. In a Full Imagery condition, they received instructions about how to use imagery in putting after every block of trials. In a Partial Imagery condition, they received imagery instructions but only after the second, third, and fourth block of trials.

Procedure

All participants completed 50 putts from a distance of 12 feet. These putts took place in 5 separate 10-putt blocks, with a 2-minute interval between blocks. The intertrial interval allowed one minute for review of the randomly-assigned practice strategy as noted above and another minute for rest. The rest phase was included to minimise any work decrement that could occur with massed practice.

Results

A preliminary analysis was conducted to determine whether there were pre-existing differences in putting skill between the groups at baseline. This analysis consisted of a 2 x 3 ANOVA using point totals from just the first block of trials. Factors in this analysis were imagery ability (high, low) and treatment group (no imagery, partial imagery, full imagery). Results indicated no significant differences in baseline putting scores related to either factor (all $Fs < 1.35$, all $ps > .25$).

A similar 2 x 3 ANOVA was conducted on the point totals from Trial 5 to determine if the groups differed at the conclusion of the study. This analysis revealed a significant interaction between imagery ability and treatment, $F(2, 36) = 6.98$, $p < .003$. This interaction is illustrated in Figure 2 which shows that individuals with good imagery ability performed better in the two imagery conditions than in the non-imagery condition. Conversely, individuals with poor imagery ability performed better on the final block of trials when they were not required to use imagery during the learning process.

Discussion

Taken together, the findings from these studies suggest that imagery abilities play an important role in the learning and performance of golf skills. More specifically, novice golfers were found to learn a putting skill better when the

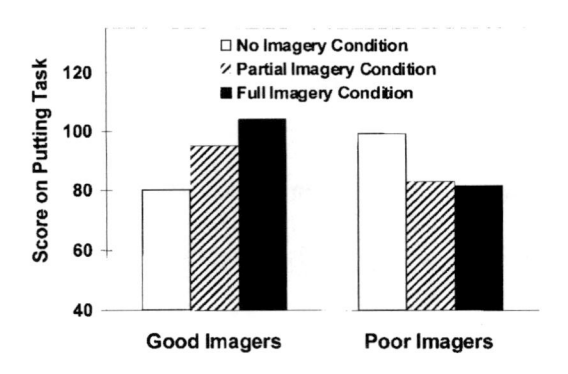

Figure 2
Performance on a golf putting task as a function of imagery ability and practice condition.

practice conditions took their imagery abilities into account. As shown in Figure 2, those with poor imagery ability benefited most from instruction that was primarily verbal in nature rather than imagery-based. On the other hand, those with good imagery ability benefited most from instructional conditions that included an imagery component (cf. O'Halloran & Gauvin, 1994). At the same time, experienced golfers with good imagery abilities performed better on a half-wedge shot than those with poor imagery abilities (Figure 1). Although this latter finding could not be attributed to differential sensitivity to an imagery-based intervention, it is possible that vivid representation of distance to the target and/or swing mechanics helped the good imagers perform better because the half-wedge shot required adjustments to the full swing for accurate performance.

Given that imagery abilities are related to the learning and performance of golf skills, it is pertinent to ask, "Can these abilities be improved?" and, "If so, how might one go about improving them in a task-specific manner?" An examination of the literature indicates that the answer to the first question is "yes." Studies outside of the sport domain as well as sport-specific studies have documented improvements in imagery ability as a function of imagery practice. For example, early research reported by Richardson (1984) showed that imagery training increased ratings of vividness as well as physiological reactivity to imagined stimuli. More recent work has shown similar improvements on image generation and image rotation tasks as a function of training (Seele & Doerr, 1994; Shubbar, 1990; Wallace & Hofelich, 1992). Transfer effects have been also documented for these training protocols, with such effects influenced by task similarity (Wallace & Hofelich, 1992). Moreover, training-induced changes in imagery ability are not restricted to concrete representations of objects or movement. Improvements have also been found in the ability to vividly imagine emotional states that are associated with specific events (Kim, de Jong-Meyer, & Engberding, 1996).

Studies focusing specifically on imagery in sport settings have also found improvements in imagery abilities as a function of training. For example, McKenzie and Howe (1997) used a multiple baseline design to evaluate the effects of a 15-session imagery training program on visual and kinesthetic imagery abilities among competitive dart throwers. All six of the participants reported improvements in either visual or kinesthetic imagery in response to the intervention, and four of them reported improvements in both types of imagery. Similar results were obtained in a group-based study conducted by Rodgers, Hall, and Buckolz (1991). They examined changes in imagery ability and imagery use as a function of participation in an imagery training program or a verbalisation training program over a 16-week period. Findings indicated that imagery training produced significant increases in imagery ability as measured by scores on the Movement Imagery Questionnaire (MIQ; Hall & Pongrac, 1983). Imagery training also led to increased use of mental rehearsal before and after practice as well as improvements in the ability to "feel" (i.e., kinesthetically imagine) themselves skating. Corresponding changes were not observed in the verbalisation training group or an untrained control group. Finally, the specific benefits of imagery training on the imagery abilities of golfers have been documented by Thomas and Fogarty (1997). In that study, a composite measure of imagery ability was examined for changes over time in response to participation in a series of workshops that included training in the use of imagery techniques. Results indicated significant improvement in the composite measure which included an assessment of visual, auditory, and kinesthetic imagery dimensions as well as the controllability and mood-generating impact of the images.

Given that imagery ability can be enhanced via training, how should golfers structure such training to produce the most benefit? We believe there is a two-part answer to this question: (a) Adhere to generally-accepted principles of effective imagery use; and (b) Use imagery frequently and in a variety of task-specific forms.

General Guidelines for Improving Imagery Ability

Imagery is a perceptual experience, and, as such, its nature, informational content and value are subjective. Imagery strategies should therefore be individualised to complement personal abilities, needs, and cognitive styles (Johnston & McCabe, 1993; Rotella & Boutcher, 1990). At the same time, certain general principles should be followed in order to maximise the development of imagery skills.

Regular use of sensory-rich images. As a cognitive skill, imagery is not limited to discrete visual images but is instead a perceptual experience that relies on an array of sensory input. Most importantly, it is a skill that, with practice in appropriate conditions and an understanding of its utility, can enhance skill acquisition and performance. As such, it has been suggested that imagery should be "drilled" regularly in much the same way as physical skills (Munroe, Giacobbi, Hall, & Weinberg, 2000; Rushall, 1991). We agree with this observation and recommend adherence to structured imagery practice as part of the normal weekly training routine.

Imagery is also based on information from all senses (Lee, 1999). Therefore, athletes should use not only visual information, but also tactile, olfactory, auditory, and kinesthetic information to construct their imagined experiences. Utilising images that are rich in sensory information strengthens the neural links between the image and the actual experience, and it also reduces the potential for distraction by other inputs. Research findings by Hardy and Callow (1999) reinforce the value of incorporating kinesthetic components into imagery for closed skills, and it is therefore not surprising that outstanding golfers make regular use of such "feeling images" (Spearman & Allen, 1999).

Multiple purposes/functions. Although rehearsal of specific skills is an important and useful application of imagery in sport, the implementation of this strategy can (and should) go beyond skill rehearsal. Martin et al. (1999) provide a conceptual framework for organising different types of imagery according to their intended outcomes, and this model provides guidance on these other uses. Martin et al. (1999) distinguish between cognitive and motivational uses of imagery and, at the same time, between specific and general uses. Mental rehearsal of a discrete skill such as hitting a long iron or stroking a putt represents the use of imagery for cognitive-specific purposes. On the other hand, mental rehearsal of a preshot routine would represent the use of imagery for cognitive-general purposes. Other potential uses could be to imagine successful performance in a particular event (motivational-specific) or to imagine desired states of arousal, confidence and composure between shots (motivational-general). All of these applications deserve attention within a structured imagery training program.

Incorporate relaxation exercises. Relaxation training is thought to enhance the effectiveness of imagery interventions (Gould & Damarjian, 1996; Sheikh et al., 1994). The ability to create a relaxed mental and physical state as part of imagery practice improves attentional focus, helps the athlete to identify inappropriate muscular tension, and reduces the occurrence of negative images that can undermine motivation and/or performance (Fairweather & Potgieter, 1993; Woolfolk, Murphy, Gottesfeld, & Aitken, 1985). A variety of relaxation techniques can be employed, ranging from the traditional Jacobsonian method, to autogenic training, meditation, and simple breathing exercises (Greenberg, 1990). When used as a precursor to imagery exercises, these relaxation strategies lower heart rate, slow respiration, and create a physical state where vivid and controlled images can be more easily generated.

Rehearse for learning, refinement and transfer. There is evidence that imagery can have beneficial effects on golf performance during initial skill acquisition as well as during the later (skill-refinement) stages of learning. With respect to initial learning, Meacci and Pastore (1995) found that imagery combined with physical practice produced better results for novice golfers than physical practice by itself. Our own research (see Study 2 and Figure 2) reinforces this finding but also suggests that the benefits of imagery during skill acquisition may be dependent upon the extent to which the athlete's imagery capabilities have been developed. At the same time, Thomas and Fogarty (1997) have shown that more experienced golfers can also benefit from imagery-based interventions, both in terms of perceived capabilities and in terms of actual performance. Consequently, we recommend that imagery training be undertaken both for the learning of new golf skills and for the refinement of existing skills.

The benefits of imagery training are most likely to generalise when the training takes place under conditions that simulate the actual performance environment. For that reason, it is important that imagery is incorporated into the practice routine and is utilised in a variety of on-course circumstances (e.g., on the putting green, on the driving range, during practice rounds, etc.). It is also recommended that the mental rehearsal be accurate in terms of both process and outcome. For example, the mental rehearsal of specific shots should occur at a level that is superior to current performance but, at the same time, not so perfect that the result is unrealistic (Kirschenbaum & Bale, 1984). Additionally, it is important to put images into context by imagining specific environmental conditions under which shots will be played. Relevant contextual factors include weather conditions (wet, dry, etc.), strength and direction of wind, consistency and condition of turf, and competitive circumstances (leading, behind, etc.). Incorporation of such details into imagery practice will not only provide a context for the skills being rehearsed, but it will also make the images more vivid (and therefore more powerful).

Specific Applications of Imagery Training in Golf

As with any skill, the more time one spends practising imagery, the more refined, automatic, and useful it becomes. For this reason, serious golfers should take every opportunity to combine mental imagery with physical practice so that, over time, it becomes a natural, unconscious part of their general approach to competition as well as each shot that they hit (Perry & Morris, 1995).

Getting started. Assess your imagery ability by recalling a hole played in a recent round of golf. Attempt to experience this image utilising a range of sensory input. Did you imagine it like you were actually doing it (internal perspective), or was it more like watching a video replay (external perspective)? If both perspectives were used, which one was most comfortable and vivid? Did you rely heavily on a particular type of sensory input, or were your images based on multiple sensory systems? To improve your ability to use information from all your senses, practise writing out a detailed mental rehearsal of several different types of shots. These descriptions should include details related to: smell/taste (e.g., the smell of fresh-cut grass); vision (e.g., how the shot looks from a particular position on the course); kinesthesis (e.g., the position and feel of various body parts at setup and during the swing); touch/feel (e.g., the weight of the club and the sensation of hitting through the ball); and sound (e.g., the sound of solid contact and the content of positive self-talk following the shot). This information can be used to guide your initial mental rehearsal sessions, and the images can be refined over time to include the unique elements that you want to build into different types of shots.

Using audio-visual aids. A number of verbal and visual aids are available to supplement mental rehearsal in golf. These aids can be particularly useful in the early stages of imagery training because they provide concrete templates around which more personalised images can be developed. They can also be used by more experienced golfers to reinforce the mental and behavioural elements of specific shots. For example, Cook, Horvath, and Connelly (1989) found this sort of guided imagery to be effective in enhancing putting proficiency even for experienced players. In that study, 30 low-handicap golfers completed a 9-hole putting course on two occasions, and half of them listened to a taped imagery script between rounds. The group that listened to the audiotape between rounds showed a significant improvement from the first round to the second, but the other group did not.

Video information is also a very powerful visualisation aid and can be used in a variety of ways. Videotapes of high-level players (such as the one we used in Study 1) are an effective modelling tool and may promote what Syer and Connelly (1987) have referred to as "ideal model rehearsal." By watching a well-known player execute specific shots, other golfers acquire a template of fundamental movement patterns and sequences. They can then try to project themselves into the scene and copy these fundamental patterns. A variation on this theme involves making a highlights tape of shots you would like to play and perhaps adding some inspirational music to this video (Templin & Vernacchia, 1995). If the same music is then played at the course while you are practising or preparing to play, it can serve as a "trigger" for reproduction of the positive images as well as the feelings of inspiration and confidence that accompanied them.

Practising with a purpose. Imagery abilities will improve more quickly if mental rehearsal takes place away from the course as well as during formal practice sessions. Away from the course, imagery can be used to reinforce correct technique by focusing on the desired feel and timing of various shots. This kind of mental rehearsal can be accompanied by actual body movements, either with or without the club. Additionally, imagery can be used to re-create feelings such as the satisfaction or pride that accompanies hitting a solid drive or sinking a difficult putt. When used in this way, images of the shot can be linked to affirmations (positive self-statements) that help build trust and confidence in one's abilities. Off-course mental rehearsal can also be used to prepare oneself for competition by visualising the sequence of events that will take place prior to performance. For example, consideration could be given to such things as how you will warm up, what your key thoughts will be for this event, how you intend to play the first few holes, and what you will do to manage unexpected challenges.

On the practice range, it is useful to establish a series of training drills that incorporate imagery into the hitting of actual shots. For example, you might select a particular shot and then create drills that contain both mental rehearsal and physical practice components. The mental rehearsal component might involve seeing the line, rehearsing the feel and tempo of the shot, imagining the swing, and watching the path of the ball in the air. The physical practice component might involve swinging the club with the eyes closed and then, finally, hitting the shot. This kind of systematic practice will be more valuable if you also keep a logbook that contains a description of the drills, a list of imagery goals (e.g., shot acquisition or swing modification), and an evaluation of progress. Owens and Bunker (1992) outline a number of drills that utilise imagery in this way.

Rehearsing preshot routines. Automaticity is an important component of peak performance states (Jackson & Roberts, 1992; McInman & Grove, 1991), and automaticity is promoted by the use of preshot routines that include an imagery component (Cohn, 1990, 1994). Imagery of the line, the swing itself, or the desired outcome might be simply one part of the overall routine. On the other hand, mental rehearsal could also be used as a meta-strategy to help program or automate the routine itself. For example, one could mentally rehearse a preshot routine that involved taking one or two practice swings from behind the ball, visualising the line, selecting the target, addressing the ball, hitting the shot and feeling solid contact, seeing the flight of the ball, watching it come to rest near the target, and feeling a sense of pride and satisfaction with the result. Doing so on a regular basis during practice would make it more likely that such a routine would occur during competition, and there is evidence that the use of routines benefits golf performance (Beauchamp, 1999; Boutcher & Crews, 1987; Fairweather & Potgieter, 1993).

Conclusion

Mental rehearsal has been shown to improve the learning and performance of golf skills, and imagery abilities are an important determinant of how much impact mental rehearsal is likely to have. Imagery abilities can be improved by regular use of task-specific mental rehearsal strategies that follow the general principles outlined above. The effective implementation of these strategies requires some thought and creativity, but, given the potential benefits, it is a challenge that serious golfers should readily accept.

Footnotes

1. A more comprehensive discussion of the procedures and findings in this study is provided by Grove, Weinberg, & Pitcher (2000). The current report focuses on a limited subset of measures from the same data set.
2. This study formed the basis of a dissertation submitted by V. de Prazer as part of a Master of Cognitive Science degree at The University of Western Australia.
3. Low scores indicate better imagery ability on the Betts QMI and the Gordon TVIC.

References

Beauchamp, P.H. (1999). Peak putting performance: Psychological skills and strategies utilized by PGA Tour golfers. In M.R. Farrally & A.J. Cochran (Eds.), *Science and golf III: Proceedings of the 1998 World Scientific Congress of Golf* (pp. 181–190). Champaign, IL: Human Kinetics.

Boutcher, S.H., & Crews, D.J. (1987). The effect of a preshot attentional routine on a well-learned skill. *International Journal of Sport Psychology, 18,* 30–39.

Boutcher, S.H., & Zinsser, N.W. (1990). Cardiac deceleration of elite and beginning golfers during putting. *Journal of Sport & Exercise Psychology, 12,* 37–47.

Cohn, P.J. (1990). Preperformance routines in sport: Theoretical support and practical applications. *The Sport Psychologist, 4,* 301–312.

Cohn, P. (1994). *The mental game of golf: A guide to peak performance.* South Bend, IN: Diamond Communications.

Cohn, P., & Winters, R. (1995). *The mental art of putting: Using your mind to putt your best.* South Bend, IN: Diamond Communications.

Cook, D.L., Horvath, M.J., & Connelly, D. (1989). The effects of an imagery audiotape on putting a golf ball. *Journal of Applied Research in Coaching and Athletics, 4,* 195–205.

Fairweather, K.G., & Potgieter, J.R. (1993). The effect of pre-shot strategies on golf putting. *South African Journal for Research in Sport, Physical Education and Recreation, 16*(1), 35–40.

Feltz, D.L., & Landers, D.M. (1983). The effects of mental practice on motor skill learning and performance: A meta-analysis. *Journal of Sport Psychology, 5,* 25–57.

Garza, D.L., & Feltz, D.L. (1998). Effects of selected mental practice on performance, self-efficacy, and competition confidence of figure skaters. *The Sport Psychologist 12,* 1–15.

Golf with Patty Sheehan. (1983). San Leandro, CA: Sybervision Systems, Inc.

Gordon, R. (1949). An investigation into some of the factors that favour the formation of stereotyped images. *British Journal of Psychology, 39,* 156–167.

Gould, D., & Damarjian, N. (1996). Imagery training for peak performance. In J.L. Van Raalte & B.W. Brewer (Eds.), *Exploring sport and exercise psychology* (pp. 25–50). Washington, DC: American Psychological Association.

Graham, D. (1990). *Mental toughness training for golf.* New York: Viking.

Greenberg, J.S. (1990). *Comprehensive stress management* (3rd ed.). Dubuque, IA: W.C. Brown.

Grove, J.R., Weinberg, R.S., & Pitcher, R. (2000). *Slow-motion imagery and modelling of the golf swing: Effects on movement form and outcome.* Manuscript submitted for publication.

Hall, C.R. (1998). Measuring imagery abilities and imagery use. In J.L. Duda (Ed.), *Advances in sport and exercise psychology measurement* (pp. 165–172). Morgantown, WV: Fitness Information Technology.

Hall, C.R., & Martin, K.A. (1997). Measuring movement imagery abilities: A revision of the Movement Imagery Questionnaire. *Journal of Mental Imagery, 21*, 143–154.

Hall, C.R., & Pongrac, J. (1983). *Movement Imagery Questionnaire.* London, Ontario: University of Western Ontario.

Hall, C.R., Rodgers, W.M., & Barr, K.A. (1990). Imagery use among athletes. *The Sport Psychologist, 4*, 1–10.

Hall, C.R., Schmidt, D., Durand, M-C., & Buckolz, E. (1994). Imagery and motor skills acquisition. In A.A. Sheikh & E.R. Korn (Eds.), *Imagery in sports and physical performance* (pp. 121–134). Amityville, NY: Baywood Publishing.

Hardy, L., & Callow, N. (1999). Efficacy of external and internal visual imagery perspectives for the enhancement of performance on tasks in which form is important. *Journal of Sport & Exercise Psychology, 21*, 95–112.

Hinshaw, K.E. (1991–92). The effects of mental practice on motor skill performance: Critical evaluation and meta-analysis. *Imagination, Cognition and Personality, 11*, 3-35.

Isaac, A. (1992). Mental practice — Does it work in the field? *The Sport Psychologist, 6*, 192–198.

Isaac, A., Marks, D.F., & Russell, D.G. (1986). An instrument for assessing imagery of movement: The Vividness of Movement Imagery Questionnaire (VMIQ). *Journal of Mental Imagery, 10*, 23–30.

Jackson, S.A., & Roberts, G.C. (1992). Positive performance states of athletes: Toward a conceptual understanding of peak performance. *The Sport Psychologist, 6*, 156–171.

Johnston, B., & McCabe, M.P. (1993). Cognitive strategies for coping with stress in a simulated golfing task. *International Journal of Sport Psychology 24*, 30–48.

Kim, T., de Jong-Meyer, R., & Engberding, M. (1996). Examination of a training sequence aimed at improving emotional imaging capability. [German]. *Verhaltenstherapie, 6*, 124–134.

Kirschenbaum, D.S., & Bale, R.M. (1984). Cognitive-behavioral skills in sports: Application to golf and speculations about soccer. In W.F. Straub & J.M. Williams (Eds.), *Cognitive sport psychology* (pp. 275–288). Lansing, NY: Sport Science Associates.

Lee, B. Y. B. (1999). An overview of psychological techniques used for performance enhancement in golf. In M.R. Farrally & A.J. Cochran (Eds.), *Science and golf III: Proceedings of the 1998 World Scientific Congress of Golf* (pp. 138–144). Champaign, IL: Human Kinetics.

Marks, D. F. (1973). Visual imagery differences in the recall of pictures. *British Journal of Psychology, 64*, 17–24.

Martin, K.A., Moritz, S.E., & Hall, C.R. (1999). Imagery use in sport: A literature review and applied model. *The Sport Psychologist, 13*, 245–268.

McInman, A.D., & Grove, J.R. (1991). Peak moments in sport: A literature review. *Quest, 43*, 333–351.

McKenzie, A.D., & Howe, B.L. (1997). The effect of imagery on self-efficacy for a motor skill. *International Journal of Sport Psychology, 28*, 196–210.

Meacci, W.G., & Pastore, D.L. (1995). Effects of occluded vision and imagery on putting golf balls. *Perceptual and Motor Skills, 80,* 179–186.

Moran, A. (1993). Conceptual and methodological issues in the measurement of mental imagery skills in athletes. *Journal of Sport Behavior, 16,* 156–170.

Munroe, K.J., Giacobbi, P.R., Hall, C., & Weinberg, R. (2000). The four Ws of imagery use: Where, when, why, and what. *The Sport Psychologist, 14,* 119–137.

Murphy, S.M. (1994). Imagery interventions in sport. *Medicine and Science in Sports and Exercise, 26,* 486–494.

Murphy, S.M., & Jowdy, D. (1992). Imagery and mental rehearsal. In T.S. Horn (Ed.), *Advances in sport psychology* (pp. 221–250). Champaign, IL: Human Kinetics.

Nicklaus, J. (1974). *Golf my way.* New York: Simon & Schuster.

O'Halloran, A-M., & Gauvin, L. (1994). The role of preferred cognitive style in the effectiveness of imagery training. *International Journal of Sport Psychology, 25,* 19–31.

Owens, D., & Bunker, L.K. (1992). *Advanced golf: Steps to success.* Champaign, IL: Leisure Press.

Perry, C., & Morris, T. (1995). Mental imagery in sport. In T. Morris & J. Summers (Eds.), *Sport psychology: Theory, applications and issues* (pp. 339–385). Brisbane: John Wiley & Sons.

Richardson, A. (1984). *The experiential dimension of psychology.* Brisbane: University of Queensland Press.

Rodgers, W., Hall, C., & Buckolz, E. (1991). The effect of an imagery training program on imagery ability, imagery use, and figure skating performance. *Journal of Applied Sport Psychology, 3,* 109–125.

Rotella, R.J., & Boutcher, S.H. (1990). A closer look at the role of the mind in golf. In A.J. Cochran (Ed.), *Science and golf: Proceedings of the First World Scientific Congress of Golf* (pp. 93–97). London: E. & F.N. Spon.

Rushall, B.S. (1991). *Imagery training in sports: A handbook for athletes, coaches, and sport psychologists.* Spring Valley, CA: Sport Science Associates.

Seel, N.M., & Doerr, G. (1994). The supplantation of mental images through graphics: Instructional effects on spatial visualization skills of adults. In W. Schnotz & R.W. Kulhavy (Eds.), *Comprehension of graphics* (pp. 271–290). Amsterdam: North-Holland/Elsevier Science Publishers.

Sheehan, P.W. (1967). A shortened version of Betts' Questionnaire upon Mental Imagery. *Journal of Clinical Psychology, 23,* 386–389.

Sheikh, A.A., Sheikh, K.S., & Moleski, M. (1994). Improving imagery abilities. In A.A. Sheikh & E.R. Korn (Eds.), *Imagery in sports and physical performance* (pp. 231–248). Amityville, NY: Baywood Publishing.

Shubbar, K. E. (1990). Learning the visualisation of rotations in diagrams of three dimensional structures. *Research in Science & Technological Education, 8,* 145–154.

Spearman, M., & Allen, D. (1999). Picture this: Use these images to fix your faults. *Golf Magazine, 41(8),* 98–103.

Syer, J., & Connolly, C. (1987). *Sporting body, sporting mind: An athlete's guide to mental training* (revised edition). London: Simon & Schuster.

Templin, D.P., & Vernacchia, R.A. (1995). The effect of highlight music videotapes upon the game performance of intercollegiate basketball players. *The Sport Psychologist, 9,* 41–50.

Thomas, P.R., & Fogarty, G.J. (1997). Psychological skills training in golf: The role of individual differences in cognitive preferences. *The Sport Psychologist, 11,* 86–106.

Vealey, R. S. (1988). Future directions in psychological skills training. *The Sport Psychologist, 2,* 318–336.

Wallace, B., & Hofelich, B.G. (1992). Process generalization and the prediction of performance on mental imagery tasks. *Memory & Cognition, 20,* 695–704.

White, K., Sheehan, P.W., & Ashton, R. (1977). Imagery assessment: A survey of self-report measures. *Journal of Mental Imagery, 1*, 145–170.

Wiren, G., & Coop, R. (1978). *The new golf mind.* New York: Simon & Schuster.

Woolfolk, R.L., Murphy, S.M., Gottesfeld, D., & Aitken, D. (1985). Effects of mental rehearsal of task motor activity and mental depiction of task outcome on motor skill performance. *Journal of Sport Psychology, 7*, 191–197.

Preperformance Mood and Elite Golf Performance: What are the Optimal Mood Factors Before Competition?

John F. Mathers and Richard L. Cox

The ability to achieve the optimal emotional state (or mood) before competition is thought to be an important characteristic of successful performance (Ogilvie, 1993; Prapavessis & Grove, 1991; Spielberger, 1989). However, the ability to predict performance on the basis of precompetition mood state has met with limited success (Heyman, 1982; LeUnes, Hayward, & Daiss, 1988; Miller & Edgington, 1984; Renger, 1993; Rowley, Landers, Kyllo, & Etnier, 1995; Stadulis, MacCracken, Levan, & Fender-Scarr, 1993; Terry, 1995). Despite the absence of empirical evidence to suggest an optimal precompetition mood state for golf performance, many authors (e.g., Fahey, 1984; Glad & Beck, 1999; Mackenzie & Denlinger, 1990; Wall, 1993) seem to encourage golfers to create a positive precompetition mood profile for effective performance. This discrepancy between empirical evidence and general guidelines suggests a need to clarify the relationship between precompetition mood state and performance in golf.

Performance in sport is enhanced when the athlete generates the physical and mental state to meet specific situational demands (Cox, 1998; Hahn, 1989: Hanin, 2000; Martens, 1982). Morgan (1979, 1980) suggested that successful elite athletes tend to exhibit a psychological profile of a mentally healthy individual and that mental health has been found to be an effective discriminator of success in elite athletic events. However, most researchers would suggest that prediction of athletic success from Morgan's mental health model has often failed to survive empirical scrutiny (Prapavessis & Grove, 1991). Some of the studies offering support for the predictive capability of the mental health model have utilised a between-subject rather than a within-subject comparison and have been unable to establish precompetition mood state as a reliable indicator of performance. An extensive review of mental health research by Rowley et al. (1995) revealed that, although the successful athlete is likely to enjoy positive mental health, the ability to predict performance from precompetition mood state was not reliable. They suggested that the relationship between precompetition mood and performance provided a "snapshot of mental health and successful performance" (p. 187) and was correlational rather than causal.

The present study aimed to examine the relationship between precompetition mood and performance in elite amateur golf and to identify the precompetitive mood factors most closely associated with positive (and negative) performance.

Method

The present study was carried out with 30 elite amateur golfers from Great Britain and Ireland. The age of the golfers ranged from 18 years to 33 years ($M = 21.38$ years, $SD = 3.07$) and consisted of 24 males and 6 females. All participants volunteered for the study and completed an informed consent form in accordance with ethical guidelines for research. The ability level of the participants was determined by playing handicap which ranged from +1 to 4 strokes ($M = 1.5$ strokes, $SD = 1.4$) and was in accordance with the Confederation of the National Golf Unions (CONGU) handicapping scheme (Confederation of the National Golf Unions, 1997).

Preperformance mood state was assessed using a semantic differential (SD) version of the bipolar form of the Profile of Mood States (POMS-BI) (Lorr & McNair, 1984). This version of the POMS-BI was suggested by Cox, Mathers, and Sinnott (2000) as an alternative method of assessing the mood states of athletes in the minutes immediately prior to competition. This version of the POMS-BI (SD-POMS-BI) requires athletes to select the 12 adjectives (from the list of adjectives used in the POMS-BI) that best describe each end of the mood factors contained within the Profile of Mood States (McNair, Lorr, & Dropleman, 1971) namely: Tension, Anger, Depression, Vigour, Fatigue, and Confusion. These adjectives are then presented in a semantic differential format, the reliability and validity of which were explored and established by Warr and Knapper (1968) in their seminal work on person perception.

The semantic differential version of the POMS-BI was chosen for this investigation for the following reasons. Firstly, the SD-POMS-BI requires no more than six responses, is much quicker to use than all other versions of the POMS and is less intrusive in the minutes prior to competition. Secondly, the SD-POMS-BI has face validity insofar as its content (adjectives) is generated by the athletes themselves and has content validity because the dimensions involved (mood factors) were regarded by the athletes as being comprehensive for their requirements. Finally, since the same six dimensions of mood represented in the POMS-BI are always present in the semantic differential version then, logically at least its construct validity must be equally high.

The adjectives chosen for the SD-POMS-BI were identified by the group of elite golfers, each of whom was required to indicate those adjectives from the original POMS-BI that he or she would have used to describe their feelings, either before or during a round of golf within the last 6 months. The most popular adjective from each group was chosen to represent the bipolar aspect of each mood factor on the SD-POMS-BI, and the result of this exercise can be seen in Figure 1.

The pairs of adjectives that were chosen to represent each mood factor were separated by a 7-point Likert scale that allowed participants to record their overall mood in the minutes before the start of the round of golf.

Mood Factor		-3 Extremely	-2 Very	-1 Quite	0 50/50	1 Quite	2 Very	3 Extremely	
Tension	Composed								Nervous
Depression	Light-hearted								Dejected
Anger	Friendly								Annoyed
Vigour	Tired								Energetic
Fatigue	Confident								Self-doubting
Confusion	Able to Concentrate								Mixed-up

Name: _____ Date: _____
Tournament: _____ Venue: _____
Time of Tee off: _____ Time of SD POMS-BI Completion: _____

Gross Score: _____ Playing Handicap: _____ Net score: _____
C.S.S. Score: _____ Differential: _____ (C.S.S. score - Net score)

Figure 1
The semantic differential version of the POMS-BI created by the participants and used to measure precompetition mood. Participants recorded their precompetition mood and quantitative measure of performance for each competitive round of golf.

Precompetition mood was scored on a scale of −3 to +3 for each mood factor. Participants completed the SD-POMS-BI during the final 30 minutes before their respective tee times, prior to each of 10 consecutive competitive rounds of golf. The level of competition varied from low (i.e., club medal tournament) to high (i.e., County, District or National amateur event) for all participants.

Performance was measured according to the stroke difference between a person's net score (actual score minus handicap) and the course difficulty score (C.S.S.) adjusted on the day of competition (e.g., an actual [gross] score of 75 strokes for a participant with a playing handicap of 2 would yield a net score of 73 strokes). This score would then be compared to the C.S.S. on the day of competition to gain a relative measure of the overall performance. A net score that was lower than the C.S.S. score (a good performance) was given a positive numerical value that quantified the difference between the net score and C.S.S. score (e.g., a net score of 69 strokes against a C.S.S. of 72 yielded a value of +3). A net score that was higher than the C.S.S. score (a poor performance) was given a negative numerical value that quantified the difference between the net score and C.S.S. score (e.g., a net score of 78 strokes against a C.S.S. of 72 yielded a value of −6).

Results and Discussion

The performance variation accounted for by mood was predicted by a multiple regression statistical technique which indicated the extent to which the quantitative measure of performance (dependent variable) was influenced by the six mood factors contained within the Profile of Mood States (McNair et al., 1971) namely: Anger, Confusion, Depression, Fatigue, Tension, and Vigour (independent variables). The regression analysis was carried out for each of the 10 rounds of competitive golf and produced a multiple correlation coefficient (R) between the quantitative measure of performance and precompetition mood states. The raw data were checked for skewness and R^2 values were adjusted according to standard Statistical Package for the Social Sciences (SPSS) protocol (Statistical Package for the Social Sciences, 1988).

The results of the multiple regression analysis shown in Table 1 revealed that the amount of performance variation that could be accounted for by differences in the precompetition mood varied from 0% (Event 7) to 43% (Event 4) across the 10 events. The mean performance variation that could be explained by precompetition mood state was 19%, though it should be noted that the standard deviation was large ($SD = 14$). An indication of the relative importance of each mood factor within the prediction equation was provided by the beta weights. Table 1 shows the beta weights for each of the precompetition mood factors for performance in the 10 rounds of competitive golf.

Table 1

Mood Factor Beta Weights for the Prediction of Golf Performance in 10 Competition Events

EVENT	ANGER	CONFUSION	DEPRESSION	FATIGUE	TENSION	VIGOUR	SD	R^2
1	0.08	−0.37	−0.07	−0.19	0.14	−0.61	1.82	0.02
2	0.06	−0.06	0.53	−0.33	−0.06	0.36	2.13	0.15
3	0.08	0.17	0.28	−0.45	−0.32	0.45	1.98	0.16
4	0.24	−0.76	0.20	0.01	−0.13	0.12	2.55	0.43
5	0.16	−0.82	0.07	0.19	−0.18	0.05	3.46	0.41
6	−0.10	0.64	−0.09	−0.31	0.15	0.71	2.07	0.17
7	−0.03	0.05	0.08	−0.06	−0.40	−0.13	0.64	0.00
8	−0.07	−0.21	−0.18	−0.06	−0.17	0.19	2.70	0.17
9	−0.53	−0.48	0.37	0.58	−0.52	0.19	2.78	0.15
10	−0.13	−0.05	−0.13	−0.40	0.12	0.14	2.05	0.21
Means	−0.02	−0.19	0.11	−0.10	−0.14	0.15	2.22	0.19

The impact on predicted performance made by a change (of 1 *SD*) of each mood factor is shown in Table 2. Results of the change score data revealed the relative importance of each mood factor within precompetition mood state on the predicted performance for each event.

The results revealed that factor C (Confusion) was the most important mood factor within the prediction for 3 of the 10 events (Events 4, 5 and 8). The amount of performance that could be explained by precompetition mood in these three events was 43%, 41% and 17% respectively. In each of these events, a negative score on the Confusion scale was associated with increased performance and provided some additional support for previous research on elite golf performance (Beauchamp, 1999; Duda, 1994).

Table 2

The Impact on Golf Performance of a Change of 1 *SD* in the Precompetition Mood Score

EVENT	ANGER	CONFUSION	DEPRESSION	FATIGUE	TENSION	VIGOUR	R^2
1	0.15	0.67	0.13	0.35	0.25	0.58	0.02
2	0.13	0.13	1.13	0.70	0.13	0.77	0.15
3	0.16	0.34	0.55	0.89	0.63	0.89	0.16
4	0.61	1.93	0.51	0.03	0.33	0.30	0.43
5	0.55	2.84	0.24	0.66	0.62	0.17	0.41
6	0.21	1.32	0.19	0.64	0.31	1.47	0.17
7	0.02	0.03	0.05	0.04	0.03	0.08	0.00
8	0.19	0.57	0.49	0.16	0.46	0.51	0.17
9	1.47	1.33	1.47	1.61	1.45	0.53	0.15
10	0.27	0.10	0.27	0.82	0.24	0.29	0.21
Means	0.38	0.93	0.50	0.59	0.45	0.56	0.19

Although the multiple regression technique allowed the most important factor within precompetition mood to be identified, it was not possible to quantify the significance of each factor within this analysis.

The results also revealed that factor V (Vigour) was the most important factor in precompetition mood on 2 of the 10 events (Events 1 and 6) and jointly (with Fatigue) the most important factor in Event 3. A positive Vigour score was associated with increased predicted performance in two of these events (Events 3 and 6), although a negative score on the Vigour subscale was associated with improved performance in Event 1. The amount of performance that could be explained by precompetition mood in Events 1, 3 and 6 was 2%, 16% and 17% respectively. These results provide very little support for Morgan's (1980) view that increased vigour is a requirement for success in sport.

Factor F (Fatigue) was the most important mood factor in 2 of the 10 events (Events 9 and 10) and jointly the most important factor in Event 3. The amount of performance that could be explained by precompetition mood in Events 9 and 10 was 15% and 21% respectively, and was 16% in Event 3. In two of the events where Fatigue was considered to be the most important precompetition mood factor (Events 3 and 10), a lower score on the Fatigue scale was associated with increased performance. This suggests that players could have benefited by reducing their level of Fatigue prior to performance in these events. In the other event, where Fatigue was the most important factor (Event 9), a higher score on the Fatigue scale was associated with increased performance. This finding was rather surprising given that physiological indices of fatigue have been found to cause a decrement in golf performance (Crews, 1994; Lennon, 1999). It is possible that slight fatigue had a dampening effect on potentially harmful anxiety or overarousal in this event, although more research would be required to provide support for this explanation.

Factor D (Depression) was the most important factor in precompetitive mood in 1 of the 10 events (Event 2) with a low score on Depression being associated with increased predicted performance. The amount of performance that could be explained by precompetition mood in Event 2 was 15%. This suggests that it would be beneficial for golfers to reduce their level of precompetition Depression prior to an event and supports previous findings about the relationship of negative emotions and cognitions with golf performance (Thomas & Over, 1994).

Factor T (Tension) was the most important factor in 1 of the 10 events under investigation (Event 7), but it is clear from Table 2 that a change of 1 *SD* in this precompetition mood had almost no impact on performance in this event. This finding seems to contradict the view of some traditional reference texts (Oxendine, 1984) that suggest that decreased tension is *essential* for success in sports involving fine motor control.

Finally, factor A (Anger) was not found to be the most important factor in the prediction of performance in any of the 10 events, although a change in this factor had a noticeable impact on performance in Event 9. This finding may seem rather surprising given the perceived importance of anger management for optimal golf performance. It should be emphasised, however, that the present study examined the impact of precompetition mood (as opposed to within-competition mood) on golf performance, and did not explore the impact of emotions or mood during the competition round. It is very likely that performance during one part of the golf round will have a bearing on the level of emotions and mood during subsequent parts of the round, which in turn bring about a change in the level of performance.

Conclusion

The results of the study suggested that the extent to which variations in the dependent variable (quantitative performance) can be predicted by changes in the independent variables (precompetition mood factors) is low. The results of the study also failed to uncover any precompetition mood factor that was consistently associated with positive, or indeed negative, performances for this group of elite golfers and casts some doubt on the efficacy of general advice given to groups of golfers prior to performance in competition. However, the extent of common variance between precompetition mood state and performance in a sport with many contributing variables suggests that the relationship between individual precompetition mood profiles and performance is worthy of further investigation. This may be particularly relevant to the elite golfer who seeks to make improvements to performance, however small, over the course of a season. The degree of technical parity of elite golfers would suggest that any improvement may be worth considering in a sport where minimal margins of advantage can be translated into significant outcomes. An improvement in performance that translates to a reduction of even one shot over a championship event (four competitive rounds) would be regarded as very important by an elite player.

Future Directions

Future research should be undertaken to help individual athletes identify the extent to which precompetition mood can account for variations in golf performance on a longitudinal basis. Performers should be encouraged to record their mood state prior to performance on an individual basis using a valid and reliable method of mood assessment that does not compromise the normal preparation of an athlete in the final few minutes before competition. Although the validity of sport-specific semantic differential formats of the POMS-BI appears to be theoretically sound (see Cox et al., 2000, for a more detailed review), efforts should be made to test the reliability of the SD-POMS-BI on an empirical basis. A reliability study within the present investigation would have required the participants to complete the POMS-BI and the SD-POMS-BI in the minutes prior to competition, and would have been too time consuming and intrusive for the athletes in the present study. Given that the most popular methods of mood assessment in sport and exercise settings (i.e. POMS, POMS-BI etc.) propose six independent mood factors, and that the ratio between dependent variables and independent variables should be about 1:20 for quantitative investigations (Tabachnick & Fidell, 1989), the optimal precompetition mood state could take at least 120 events to identify. This may represent a useful time investment for the sport of golf where the longevity of elite competition can spread over some decades. Golfers who identify the precompetition mood state most closely associated with peak performance could then embark on psychological training to learn appropriate mood alteration techniques to create their optimal mood state prior to performance and increase the likelihood of successful performance in competition.

Future research should also aim to investigate the effect of mood state on performance within a performance itself. It is possible, for example, that a poor performance on a particular golf shot or hole may have an impact on mood state that may, in turn, be beneficial or detrimental to subsequent golf shots. Perhaps the impact of mood could be assessed during a competitive event at the naturally occurring breaks in competitive golf such as between holes or when walking on the fairway between golf shots. There is also a need to explore the impact of mood state on other variables believed to influence golf performance such as mental preparation (Thomas & Fogarty, 1997), swing technique, course management skills, speciality shot-making skills, physical conditioning and other psychomotor factors identified in the Golf Performance Survey (Thomas & Over, 1994). Future research should examine the impact of mood on some, or all of these performance criteria rather than a single outcome score (e.g., number of shots taken for 18 holes) often influenced significantly by variables such as *rub of the green* that are more difficult to control.

References

Beauchamp, P. H. (1999). Peak putting performance: Psychological skills and strategies utilised by PGA tour golfers. In A.J. Cochran & M. R. Farrally (Eds.), *Science and golf III: Proceedings of the 1998 World Scientific Congress of Golf* (pp. 181–189). Champaign, IL: Human Kinetics.

Confederation of National Golfing Unions (CONGU). (1997). *The standard scratch score and handicapping scheme 1983.* (Amended Edition, 1997). CONGU.

Crews, D.J. (1994). Research based golf: From the laboratory to the course. In A.J. Cochran & M. R. Farrally (Eds.). *Science and golf II: Proceedings of the 1994 World Scientific Congress of Golf* (pp. 127–137). London: E. & F. N. Spon.

Cox, R.H. (1998). *Sport psychology: Concepts and applications* (4th ed.). Dubuque: McGraw-Hill.

Cox, R.L., Mathers, J.F., & Sinnott, K. (2000). *Assessing mood states: An alternative approach: Part 1 Conceptual considerations.* Manuscript submitted for publication.

Duda, J.L. (1994). Promotion of the flow state in golf: A goal perspective analysis. In A.J. Cochran & M. R. Farrally (Eds.). *Science and golf II: Proceedings of the 1994 World Scientific Congress of Golf* (pp. 156–161). London: E. & F.N. Spon.

Fahey, T.D. (1984). *Basic golf.* Mountain View, CA: Mayfield.

Glad, W., & Beck, C. (1999). *Focused for golf.* Champaign, IL: Human Kinetics.

Hahn, E. (1989). Emotions in sport. In D. Hackfort & C.D. Spielberger (Eds.), *Anxiety in sports: An international perspective* (pp. 153–162). New York: Hemisphere.

Hanin, Y.L. (2000). Successful and poor performance and emotions. In Y.L. Hanin (Ed.), *Emotions in sport* (pp. 157–188). Champaign, IL: Human Kinetics.

Heyman, S. R. (1982). Comparisons of successful and unsuccessful competitors: A reconsideration of methodological questions and data. *Journal of Sport Psychology, 4,* 295–300.

Lennon, H.M. (1999). Physiological profiling and physical conditioning for elite golfers. In A.J. Cochran & M. R. Farrally (Eds.), *Science and golf III. Proceedings of the 1998 World Scientific Congress of Golf* (pp. 58–64). Champaign, IL: Human Kinetics.

LeUnes, A., Hayword, S.A., & Daiss, S. (1988). Annotated bibliography on the Profile of Mood States 1975–1988. *Journal of Sport Behavior, 11,* 213–240.

Lorr, M., & McNair, D.M. (1984*). Profile of Mood States manual: Bipolar form (POMS-BI).* San Diego: Educational and Industrial Testing Service.

McNair, D.M., Lorr, M., & Droppleman, L.F. (1971). *Profile of Mood States manual.* San Diego: Educational and Industrial Testing Service.

Mackenzie, M.M., & Denlinger, K. (1990). *Golf: The mind game.* New York: Dell.

Martens, R. (1982). *Sport Competition Anxiety Test.* Champaign, IL: Human Kinetics.

Miller, B.P., & Edgington, G.P. (1984). Psychological mood state: Distortion in a sporting context. *Journal of Sport Behavior, 7,* 91–94.

Morgan, W.P. (1979). Prediction of performance in athletics. In P. Klavora & J.V. Daniel (Eds.), *Coach, athlete and the sport psychologist* (pp. 173–186). Champaign, IL: Human Kinetics.

Morgan, W.P. (1980, July). Test of champions: The iceberg profile. *Psychology Today,* 92–99.

Ogilvie, B.C. (1993). Applications of psychometrics in performance enhancement. In S. Serpa, J. Alves, V. Ferreira & A. Paula-Brito (Eds.), *Proceedings of the VIII World Congress of Sport Psychology* (pp. 484–489). Lisbon: International Society of Sport Psychology.

Oxendine, J.B. (1984). *Psychology of motor learning.* (2nd ed.). Englewood Cliffs, NJ: Prentice-Hall.

Prapavessis, H., & Grove, J.R. (1991). Precompetitive emotions and shooting performance: The mental health and zone of optimal function models. *The Sport Psychologist, 5,* 223–234.

Renger, R. (1993). A review of the Profile of Mood States (POMS) in the prediction of athletic success. *Journal of Applied Sport Psychology, 5,* 78–84.

Rowley, A.J., Landers, D.M., Kyllo, L.B., & Etnier, J.L. (1995). Does the iceberg profile discriminate between successful and less successful athletes? A meta-analysis. *Journal of Sport and Exercise Psychology, 17,* 185–199.

Spielberger, C.D. (1989). Stress and anxiety in sports. In D.Hackfort & C.D. Spielberger (Eds*.), Anxiety in sports: An international perspective* (pp. 3–17). New York: Hemisphere.

Stadulis, R.E., MacCracken, M.J., Levan, C., & Fender-Scarr, L. (1993). Using both quantitative and qualitative methodology in sport psychology research: A competitive golf example. In S. Serpa, J. Alves, V. Ferreira, & A. Paula-Brito (Eds.), *Proceedings of the VIII World Congress of Sport Psychology* (pp. 493–497). Lisbon: International Society of Sport Psychology.

Statistical Package for the Social Sciences. (1988). *SPSS-X users guide* (3rd ed.). Chicago: Author.

Tabachnick, B.G., & Fidell, L.S. (1989). *Using multivariate statistics*. Cambridge, MA: Harper and Row.

Terry, P.C. (1995). The efficacy of mood state profiling with elite performers: A review and synthesis. *The Sport Psychologist, 9,* 309–324.

Thomas, P.R., & Fogarty, G.J. (1997). Psychological skills training in golf: The role of individual differences in cognitive preferences. *The Sport Psychologist, 11,* 86–106.

Thomas, P.R., & Over, R. (1994). Psychological and psychomotor skills associated with performance in golf. *The Sport Psychologist, 8,* 73–86.

Wall, N. (1993, February). How to obtain that winning look. *Golf Australia,* 50–53.

Warr, P.B., & Knapper, C. (1968). *The perception of people and events.* London: John Wiley and Sons.

CHAPTER 26

Cognitions, Emotions and Golf Performance

Patrick R. Thomas

There is now strong theoretical interest in how emotions influence sport performance (Hanin, 2000; Lazarus, 2000), as well as practical interest in how golfers can improve emotional control. Requests for help in addressing these issues come from State golf associations responsible for the preparation of representative teams prior to national championships, professional golf coaches working with squads or individuals, and parents of young players. There is also strong media interest in this issue, particularly after a dramatic finish to a major tournament. Individual consultations with professionals and elite amateur players often include psychological skills training in emotional control to optimise performance in golf. The purpose of this chapter is to draw on findings from our research with athletes and golfers in particular, outline the theoretical framework on which my professional practice in sport psychology is based, and briefly describe some materials and activities that can be included in psychological skills training programs to enhance golf performance.

Research Findings

Factor analyses of items from the Golf Performance Survey (GPS) provide evidence of a strong link between cognitions and emotions in golf (Thomas

& Over, 1994b). The first factor, labelled Negative Emotions and Cognitions, consists of 10 items that describe emotions (nervous, flat, anxious, angry and frustrated, unsettled) and cognitions (self-talk, thinking of past mistakes) associated with poor performance (choking under pressure, putting yips, playing better at practice than in competition). This subscale has a Cronbach alpha coefficient of .81 indicating that cognitions and emotions combine to form an internally consistent dimension, and a test-retest reliability coefficient of .90 indicating that scores on this dimension are highly consistent over a 3-month period.

Intercorrelations between scores on the GPS subscales indicate that high levels of Negative Emotions and Cognitions are associated with low levels of Concentration ($r = -.49$, $p < .001$), Automaticity ($r = -.35$, $p < .001$), Mental Preparation ($r = -.28$, $p < .01$), and Putting Skill ($r = -.26$, $p < .01$). Thomas and Over (1994b) also found that highly skilled golfers report fewer negative emotions and cognitions than less skilled players, $F(1, 66) = 8.58$, $p < .01$. Hierarchical regression analysis confirms that psychological skills explain a significant portion of the total variance in golf performance after differences in shot-making skills, levels of involvement, and psychomotor skills are taken into account (Thomas & Over, 1994a).

The extent to which golfers experience negative emotions and cognitions decreases significantly as their age increases (Thomas & Over, 1994b). Indeed, negative emotions and cognitions in response to poor performance maximally discriminate groups of younger and older golfers who are equivalent on overall performance (Over & Thomas, 1995). The differences in psychological and psychomotor skills suggest that older golfers employ tactics and strategies that compensate for an age-related reduction in their physical strength.

Further evidence of strong links between emotions and cognitions is available from research on participants in another specific sport and from athletes generally. Negative emotions and cognitions combined to form a single dimension in a study of ten-pin bowling (Thomas, Schlinker, & Over, 1996), the subscale showing high internal consistency ($\alpha = .75$) and reliability over time ($r = .82$). In developing subscales for the Test of Performance Strategies (TOPS), Thomas, Hardy, and Murphy (1999) reported that various factor analyses were unable to separate the items dealing with cognitions and emotions. For example, "When I make a mistake in competition, I have trouble getting my concentration back on track" loaded most highly on the Emotional Control subscale rather than on Attentional Control as intended. Athletes generally, from recreational to international performance standard, clearly associate cognitions and emotions in sport.

Professional Practice Framework

These research findings have implications for professionals working with golfers to improve their performance. When sport psychologists conduct interventions, they often start with tests or interviews to measure their clients' strengths and weaknesses and determine their needs (Morris & Thomas, 1995). These measures might be obtained from sport-specific tests like the GPS, or instruments like the TOPS that are intended for use by athletes across a wide variety of sports.

Performance profiling is an alternative approach recommended by Butler and Hardy (1992). Rather than passively responding to test items or interview questions deemed important by the consultant, the athletes identify the skills most pertinent to their needs at the time, assess their current standing on those selected skills, and set targets that can be achieved with deliberate practice. The performance profiling approach empowers the athlete and is particularly effective with golfers. We often start a squad training program by reflecting on previous performances and analysing the skills needed to cope with the demands of situations such as national or international championships. Players have nominated different types of skills needed for optimal performance in golf as shown in Figure 1.

After considering the skills identified in Figure 1 and their own particular needs, players select specific areas they will address at practice. For each of the areas selected, players use a 10-point scale ranging from *very poor* to

Optimal Performance in Golf

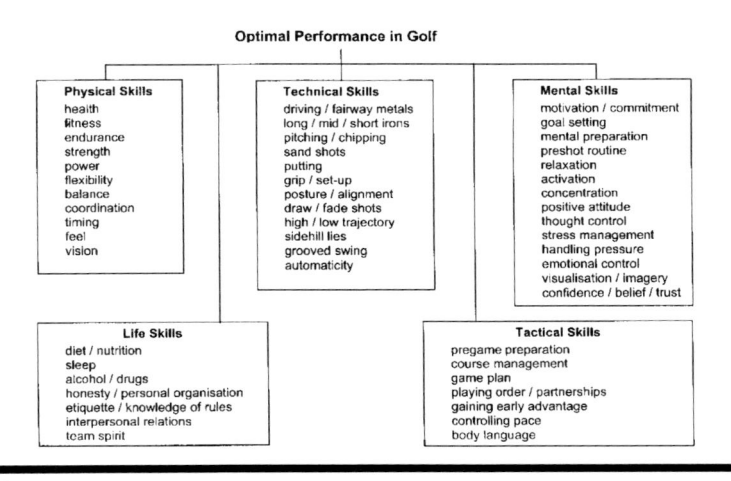

Physical Skills	Technical Skills	Mental Skills
health	driving / fairway metals	motivation / commitment
fitness	long / mid / short irons	goal setting
endurance	pitching / chipping	mental preparation
strength	sand shots	preshot routine
power	putting	relaxation
flexibility	grip / set-up	activation
balance	posture / alignment	concentration
coordination	draw / fade shots	positive attitude
timing	high / low trajectory	thought control
feel	sidehill lies	stress management
vision	grooved swing	handling pressure
	automaticity	emotional control
		visualisation / imagery
		confidence / belief / trust

Life Skills	Tactical Skills
diet / nutrition	pregame preparation
sleep	course management
alcohol / drugs	game plan
honesty / personal organisation	playing order / partnerships
etiquette / knowledge of rules	gaining early advantage
interpersonal relations	controlling pace
team spirit	body language

Figure 1

Skills needed for optimal performance in golf (Thomas, in press). Reproduced by permission of Fitness Information Technology.

excellent to rate their current level of performance and set target ratings to be achieved by specified dates. I have found such target ratings preferable to the ideal ratings suggested by Butler and Hardy (1992) as golfers tend to set 10 as the ideal which can be unrealistic and create unnecessary pressure and frustration. Figure 2 shows the proforma used by players to record ratings. Figure 3 shows the performance profile of a young golfer who was about to commence the training program. The gains achieved by the start of the following season are evident in Figure 4. In the subsequent year, this player was successful in national and international junior golf championships. The profiles display realistic target goals for a wide range of skills and convey a wealth of information in a way that is of benefit to the player, the consultant and the coach. Periodic checks are carried out to determine progress made towards achieving the set goals, and coaches' ratings are obtained to confirm or challenge the players' self-ratings.

Simply knowing their psychological skills profiles, however, is not sufficient for golfers to improve their performance (Thomas, 1993). Psychological skills training is needed for such improvement. There is now considerable evidence of the efficacy of such training (Greenspan & Feltz, 1989; Meyers, Whelan, & Murphy, 1996; Vealey, 1994; Weinberg & Comar, 1994). Our own research shows that golfers can learn how to use imagery and self-talk techniques, with consequent improvement in performance (Thomas & Fogarty, 1997). Golfers who participated in a comprehensive training program conducted by Kirschenbaum, Owens, and O'Connor (1998) also showed significant improvement in self-talk,

Skill / Characteristic / Strategy needed for optimal performance	Current Rating	Target Rating

Figure 2
Players record current and target ratings on selected skills.

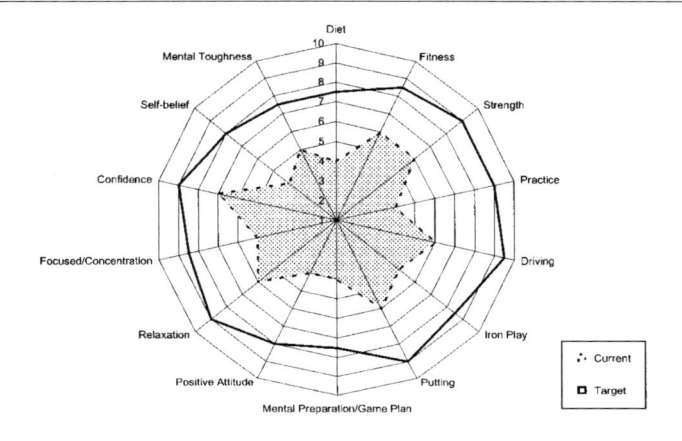

Figure 3
Performance profile of a young player at the commencement of training.

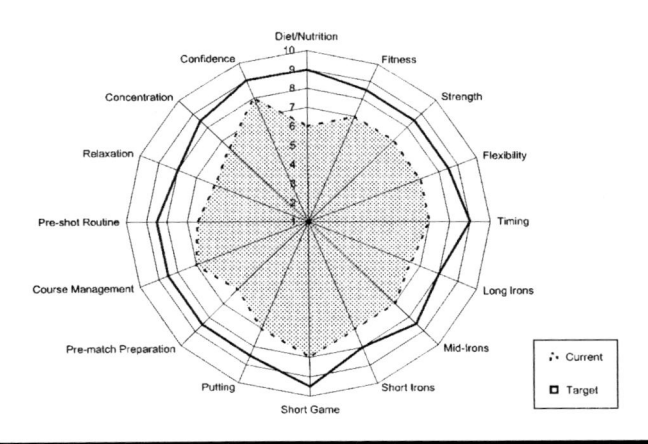

Figure 4
Performance profile of the same player at the start of the following season.

emotional control and relaxation during competition, and in all cases their scoring averages and handicaps improved after the intervention.

As is now the case for many applied sport psychologists, much of my professional work with golfers is based on the principles of cognitive-behaviour theory (Meichenbaum, 1977; Perna, Neyer, Murphy, Ogilvie, & Murphy, 1995). As shown in Figure 5, this theory proposes that our thoughts about a situation determine how we feel and, in turn, how we react or perform in that situation. This framework for professional practice reflects the strong links between cognitions and emotions that have emerged from our research, and emphasises the important role that feelings and emotions have in performance. It also indicates that our emotional states are influenced by how and what we think, say or imagine. Our cognitions can be restructured with training, and many practitioners view this process as the key to improving performance.

Psychological Skills Training

In reflecting on my own professional practice with elite amateur golfers, it is clear that there are significant benefits to be gained from drawing on the players' wealth of experience, encouraging them to take ownership of the program and tailor its contents to their needs (Thomas, in press). My purpose here is to supplement that account by focusing on some of the psychological skills concepts and training materials that have helped elite and recreational golfers gain control of their emotions and cognitions and improve performance. When I began working with State representative teams, I asked the players what areas they wanted the psychology program to address. Topping the list were stress management, self-confidence and emotional control, followed by relaxation techniques, thought control and attentional control. Although each of these topics can be addressed specifically, the framework presented in Figure 5 shows the importance of understanding their strong interrelationships.

Stress Management

To develop effective strategies for managing stress, we begin by considering the sport psychology literature on the relationship between arousal and

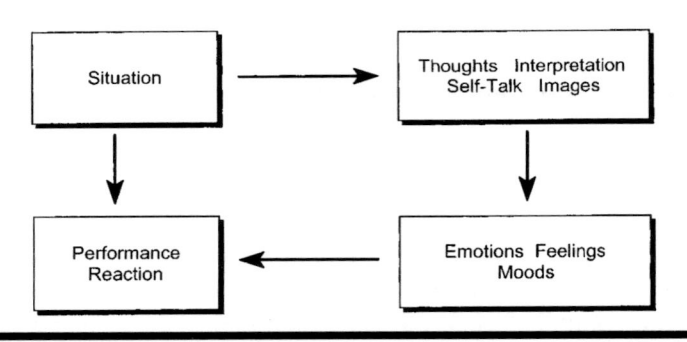

Figure 5

Players' thoughts about a situation determine how they feel and how they react or perform in that situation.

performance. Some players initially believe that the more "pumped up" they are before a round, the better they will perform. However, drive theory's proposition of a linear relationship between arousal and performance was rejected many years ago in favour of the inverted-U hypothesis (Oxendine, 1970; Yerkes & Dodson, 1908). In this curvilinear relationship, performance increases as arousal increases up to a point, after which further increases in arousal are associated with a decline in performance. There are individual differences in optimal levels of arousal for peak performance, just as there are differences between sports.

However, subsequent research indicated that the arousal dimension consists of separate components having opposite effects on performance. King, Stanley, and Burrows (1987) argued that arousal (feelings of physical or mental activation) enhances performance, whereas stress (a state of unacceptable divergence between perceived demands and capabilities to adapt, or doubts about coping) has a simple deleterious effect. Martens (1987) adopted a similar position in suggesting the zone of optimal performance was characterised by high levels of positive energy and low levels of negative energy.

Using questions adapted from Orlick (1986, p. 181), I asked 111 club golfers (60% male, 40% female) to identify their ideal levels of activation and anxiety/worry for peak performance. Their answers indicate that most do not achieve peak performance with maximum levels of activation. Rather, the mean response is 7.5 (SD = 2.09) on a 10-point scale. Similarly, low levels of anxiety rather than no worry or anxiety are seen as ideal for peak performance (M = 2.3, SD = 2.17). The activation responses are typically negatively skewed (–0.82), whereas the distribution of anxiety responses is positively skewed (+0.79). These distributions are consistent with the patterns shown in Figure 6. Interestingly, when golfers are asked to reflect on their best performance, many acknowledge that it was achieved with lower levels of activation (M = 6.36, SD = 1.97) and higher levels of anxiety (M = 2.89, SD = 2.44) than they considered ideal. The important point to be taken from these findings is that, consistent with the notion of eustress, some stress can be beneficial for golf performance. Understanding this relationship helps players manage some of the symptoms of stress commonly experienced before a championship or tournament round.

The idea that cognitive anxiety can be beneficial for performance, providing there is little if any physiological arousal, is one of the interesting predictions of catastrophe theory (Hardy, 1990). The data gathered from club golfers, however, suggest there may well be limits to the benefits gained as only 4 of the 111 golfers believed they performed at their best with anxiety levels higher than 6 (max = 8). Players have also found Csikszentmihalyi's

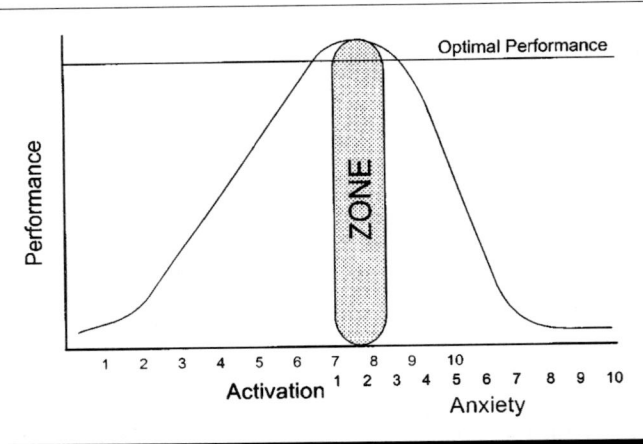

Figure 6
Players' perceptions of ideal levels of activation and anxiety for optimal performance in golf.

(1990) theory of flow helpful in understanding the psychology of optimal performance, particularly the notion that the zone of optimal functioning is not attained when the demands of competition exceed perceived skills or ability (stress from anxiety), or conversely, perceived skills or ability exceed the demands of the situation (stress from boredom).

Relaxation Techniques

Golfers can use a range of relaxation and energising techniques to regulate arousal and achieve optimal performance under pressure (Williams & Harris, 1998). David Feherty (1993) once commented that under conditions of intense competition, top golfers sometimes forget to breathe. Deep, slow complete breathing techniques are therefore used to produce a relaxation response, and they can be coupled with an appropriate attentional focus to implement the centering procedure advocated by Nideffer (1985). Golfers also benefit from learning progressive muscle relaxation techniques. These techniques can be effective in helping the golfer get to sleep the night before an important round, and can also be used before and during the round to release muscle tension, particularly in the hands and fingers, and thus improve performance.

Thought Control

Like other athletes, golfers need to be aware of their arousal level, thoughts and feelings, and make appropriate adjustments to maintain an optimal performance state (Ravizza, 1998). Although it may be evident to their playing partners, golfers are sometimes unaware of the extent to which their self-talk is negative and adversely affecting their performance. Owens and Bunker (1989) used an interesting technique to convince a professional golfer that her self-talk was damaging her performance. She agreed to monitor her self-talk during a round and transfer a paper clip to her back pocket each time she had a negative thought. After a round of 84 shots she counted 87 paper clips in her back pocket!

Various techniques can be used to ensure that self-talk is positive (Zinsser, Bunker, & Williams, 1998). Thought stopping, substituting, countering, reframing and affirmation techniques can be very effective in developing thought control. However, Janelle (1999) warns that when cognitive load is high, the act of monitoring one's mental processes can have ironic effects that are detrimental to performance: "… by deliberately trying not to linger in an undesirable cognitive or emotional state, attention, thoughts, and actions are inadvertently drawn to the exact object that should be ignored" (p. 202).

Centering procedures can be adapted for effective thought control. Players can use cue words in combination with a deep centering breath to focus or refocus their thoughts, feelings and attention, thus creating a mental set for optimal performance. Jackson and Willson (1999) provide evidence that cue words are most effective when selected by the players themselves. Crace and Hardy (1989) suggested that players reflect on the time, place, and characteristics of their previous best performance in selecting their cue words. Nideffer (1992), on the other hand, suggested the cue words be selected from lists of physical and psychological feelings typically experienced by athletes in the zone of optimal performance. Such physical feelings include "smooth," "strong," "fluid," "light," and "relaxed." The list of psychological feelings includes being "focused," "powerful," "clear," "calm," and "in control."

Concentration

King et al. (1987) argued that "lapses in attention are the key to the stress-performance relationship" (p. 26). Systematic research on the influence of attentional patterns on golf performance confirms that consistent preshot behaviours, cognitions and psychophysiological patterns are associated with successful performance (Crews, 1994). Compared to less successful players, highly skilled tour players have longer, more consistent behavioural routines for the full swing and putt. Highly skilled players also use target and feel cues rather than biomechanical cues that attempt to consciously control the putting stroke. The best players display cardiac deceleration and consistent breathing patterns immediately prior to putting. Their EEG activity in the last second preceding the putt is characterised by less active information processing in the left hemisphere, but increased right brain activity representing a more relaxed state and increased readiness to respond. Such research highlights the importance of the preshot routine for attentional control and optimal performance, as is readily acknowledged by successful tour players (Beauchamp, 1999; McCaffrey & Orlick, 1989; Rotella, 1995).

Research also shows that preshot routine training increases adherence and improves golf performance (Cohn, 1990; Cohn, Rotella, & Lloyd, 1990; Crews, 1994). Nideffer (1985) suggested that athletes use the dimensions of attention to build preperformance routines. Figure 7 shows how these dimensions can be used to develop an effective preshot routine in golf. The process begins with a broad, external focus of attention in which all salient features are assessed. The focus shifts internally as information is analysed, an appropriate club is selected and the shot is visualised. The focus then narrows as the golfer prepares to play the shot. Arousal can be regulated through breathing techniques, and muscle tension reduced through contraction and relaxation. A performance cue can be verbalised to create an optimal mental set, and a practice swing or waggle can be used to develop the feel for the shot. The player is then fully prepared to act, adopting a narrow external focus on the target and ball when playing the shot.

Such a preshot routine creates the state of relaxed concentration needed for optimal performance (Gallwey, 1986, p. 96). It allows the golfer to

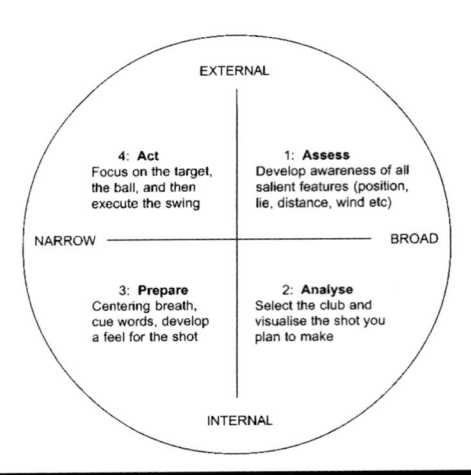

Figure 7
Building a preshot routine in golf based on shifts in the direction and width of attention.

switch on and off during a round, something that Jack Nicklaus and an overwhelming percentage of successful top-level golfers prefer to do (Coop, 1993). The use of cue words and relaxation techniques to regulate arousal levels prior to making the shot enables the golfer to play within the zone of optimal performance. Attention is focused on essential information, and that information is processed at the appropriate time to produce a clear picture of the shot and how it will be played. The preshot routine, particularly the narrow, external focus during the swing, ensures the golfer's attention is focused on the present moment rather than on earlier incidents or possible outcomes. It also prevents the intrusion of negative thoughts or emotions or other distractions. Having done the mental preparation for the shot, the golfer can swing the club or stroke the ball with confidence.

Other routines also assist the golfer to attain or maintain ideal performance states. Consistent precompetition routines bring top tour players to the first tee in a totally focused state characterised by positive imagery, a feel for the shot, and heightened awareness of the target. In contrast, club professionals often start their round thinking about how to execute the shot or what not to do (McCaffrey & Orlick, 1989). Time spent travelling to the course can be put to good use listening to music that creates the right state for optimal performance. Team competitions often involve early travel to the course and delayed tee-off times, placing a premium on the development of effective precompetition routines.

Many golfers benefit from developing posthole routines that enable them to quarantine their reaction to what happens on a particular hole and prevent the anger and frustration associated with mistakes or missed opportunities from carrying forward to subsequent holes. There is much that happens on the course that is beyond the golfers' control, but as indicated in Figure 5 they can control how they react or respond to what happens. Golfers are advised to implement the 3L routine — *look* at what they've done, *learn* from it, and *leave* it alone. To ensure they leave it behind them, golfers cease to think more about what has just happened once they turn their back on the green and move to the next tee. In helping players manage their thoughts and emotions during a round and attain ideal psychophysiological states, these cognitive-behavioural routines contribute significantly to optimising performance in golf.

Confidence

Confidence comes from being fully prepared, both physically and mentally. When learning new skills or refining existing skills, conscious control of movements is often necessary in their execution. However, once the golf swing is learned and well grooved through extensive practice, it can be performed automatically without conscious control (Moore & Stevenson, 1991, 1994). At this point, the golfer can let go of conscious control and trust automatic processes to execute the movement sequences successfully. The advantages of automatic processing of information during skilled performance have long been demonstrated in motor learning research (Schneider & Fisk, 1983; Schneider & Shiffrin, 1977; Shiffrin & Schneider, 1977). These advantages are also apparent in golf. Automaticity is characteristic of how PGA Tour golfers feel when they experience their best putting performance (Beauchamp, 1999). Elite amateur and professional golfers perceive the execution of skills during peak performance as effortless and automatic (Cohn, 1991). Our own research with amateur golfers showed that automaticity is significantly correlated with mental preparation, concentration, and the lack of negative thoughts and feelings (Thomas & Over, 1994b). All four factors significantly differentiate highly skilled players from other competitors, and the effect sizes are large particularly for automaticity.

Imagery plays an important role in the mental preparation associated with confident performance. Items comprising the Mental Preparation subscale of the GPS include references to mentally rehearsing each shot, visualising where the ball will finish, and visualising the putting stroke and the ball in the hole (Thomas & Over, 1994b). Imagery is also involved in the course management strategies defining this factor, such as working out how best to play each hole and where to place a shot. The factor structure associates these activities with a consistent preshot routine, confidence in playing to one's handicap, mental toughness in competition, and performing best under pressure.

In addition to using imagery in the preshot routine, golfers derive substantial benefits from imagining optimal performance in upcoming championships or competitions. The final session of our preparation program incorporates visual-motor behavioural rehearsal (VMBR) techniques originally developed by Suinn (1986). Players become deeply relaxed listening to scripts adapted from Nideffer (1992) and other sources. This relaxed state improves their concentration and their imagery is more vivid and controllable. They recall their own training objectives incorporated in their performance profile, focusing not on their initial weaknesses but on the gains made and their current strengths. They acknowledge that their commitment to training and practice has made them ready for competition. They imagine travelling to the course, implementing their preperformance routines, and arriving at the first tee "in control" and ready to perform at their best. Having familiarised themselves with the competition venue by playing practice rounds, studying videos, magazine articles and/or yardage charts, the players mentally rehearse playing the holes according to their game plan. They use both external and internal imagery perspectives to rehearse their preshot routines, seeing themselves playing the shots and developing the feel for those shots. As well as imagining ideal performance, players rehearse getting into trouble on the course, reacting appropriately and recovering successfully from those mistakes. These mental rehearsal techniques have a powerful effect on the players' confidence and have contributed significantly to many outstanding performances including six of the past eight national junior golf championships. Players in the program have also been successful in various international events including the last two World Junior Championships.

Conclusion

Our research has provided evidence of strong links between cognitions, emotions and golf performance. That research evidence is consistent with the views of players and coaches who readily acknowledge the importance of mental skills in golf. Most participants agree that mental skills account for at least 50% and probably more like 80% to 90% of performance, particularly at the higher levels of competition. Jack Nicklaus (1976) wrote that "hitting specific shots — playing the ball to a certain place in a certain way — is 50 percent mental picture, 40 percent setup, and 10 percent swing" (p. 77). He then proceeded to discuss how tension, concentration and confidence can affect setup and performance, further highlighting the importance of mental skills in golf.

Although the importance of these skills is widely recognised, players typically spend relatively little time deliberately practising them. Athletes competing in state and national amateur championships for three sports recently reported an average total training time of 11.25 hrs per week, of which 8 hrs were spent on physical skills, 2.3 hrs on technical skills, and only 0.9 hrs on psychological skills training (Jackson, Thomas, Marsh, & Smethurst, in press). Yet the evidence is clear — mental skills can be learned and must be deliberately practised like other skills to be used effectively. After extensive experience working with athletes, Loehr (1986) wrote, "Mental toughness is learned, not inherited" (p. 10). The place to start learning these skills is at practice. Elite golfers often set goals for competition, but neglect to do so for practice. Having clearly defined goals for physical, technical and mental skills at practice makes much more effective use of that time with consequent benefits for performance.

There is now a substantial body of research on psychological factors affecting performance in sport, with many studies focusing specifically on golf. Similarly, researchers in other disciplines including physiology, physiotherapy, sports medicine, biomechanics, kinetics and education have produced a wealth of relevant scientific information. Every four years, the World Scientific Congress of Golf (WSCG) focuses on The Golfer as one its main themes, and in so doing provides a valuable forum for researchers from these multidisciplinary perspectives to come together and share the results of their work. In this way, golf science research contributes significantly to our understanding of performance.

That same process is evident in this book which contains papers initially submitted for an interim conference of the Congress. New research findings are presented that advance our understanding of golf performance. In some cases the findings are consistent with earlier results, but in others the researchers have not found evidence to support their predictions or expectations. It is important to disseminate both types of results as they serve to confirm, clarify or challenge conventional wisdom — such is the nature of scientific enquiry.

Ultimately, however, these research findings need to be translated into practice if players are to optimise performance in golf. The task of translating theory into practice is often the responsibility of the coach, sport scientists and other professional practitioners who provide advice and assistance to players. Golf Science 2000 intended to bring all of these groups together to allow an interchange of ideas among those presenting work; to ensure that players could benefit from the work of researchers, practitioners and coaches; and to enable those working in the area to learn first-hand from the insights of prominent players. At least some of these objectives will be achieved by publishing the papers in this book. The WSCG Trust's publications such as *Golf Science International* serve a valuable role in bringing research findings to the attention of the wider golfing community. Some of the work presented in this book may well be included in future editions of such publications.

The process of optimising performance in golf is both challenging and rewarding. There is still much research to be done and those already engaged in this task have identified many of the issues needing further investigation. As in all fields of human endeavour, optimal performance in golf is highly rewarding, intrinsically and extrinsically, both for the players and for those involved in their preparation. Approximately 30 million people currently play golf in North America, and a total of 100 million rounds are played annually in Scotland and Japan (Price, 1999; Takeshita, Meshizuka, Kawashima, & Zaitsu, 1999; Theriault & Lachance, 1998). After walking, swimming and aerobics fitness activities, golf is the largest participation sport in Australia — 1.33 million (9.8%) adult Australians play golf of whom 589,000 participate in organised club sport (Australian Bureau of Statistics, 1999); and the national junior development program has introduced more than 275,000 children to golf since 1992. To the extent that the research findings presented in this book help players throughout the world to participate and improve their personal best, and in that sense achieve optimal performance in golf, they will derive substantial physical and mental benefits and rewards from their activities, and we will have made a valuable contribution through our work.

Acknowledgments

I wish to thank the Queensland Golf Union, members of the State representative teams, and the players and coaches from Gailes, McLeod, Pacific and Toowoomba Golf Clubs who participated in studies reported in this chapter.

References

Australian Bureau of Statistics. (1999). *Participation in sport and physical activities, 1998–1999* (No. 4177.0). Canberra, Australian Capital Territory: Author.

Beauchamp, P. (1999). Peak putting performance: Psychological skills and strategies utilized by PGA tour golfers. In M.R. Farrally & A.J.Cochran (Eds.), *Science and golf III: Proceedings of the 1998 World Scientific Congress of Golf* (pp. 181–189). Champaign, IL: Human Kinetics.

Butler, R.J., & Hardy, L. (1992). The performance profile: Theory and application. *The Sport Psychologist, 6*, 253–264.

Cohn, P.J. (1990). Preperformance routines in sport: Theoretical support and practical applications. *The Sport Psychologist, 4*, 301–312.

Cohn, P.J. (1991). An exploratory study on peak performance in golf. *The Sport Psychologist, 5*, 1–14.

Cohn, P.J., Rotella, R.J., & Lloyd, J.W. (1990). Effects of a cognitive-behavioural intervention on the preshot routine and performance in golf. *The Sport Psychologist, 4*, 33–47.

Coop, R.H. (1993). *Mind over golf.* New York: Macmillan.

Crace, R.K., & Hardy, C.J. (1989). Developing your mental pacemaker. *Sport Psychology Training Bulletin, 1(2)*, 1–6.

Crews, D.J. (1994). Research based golf: From the laboratory to the course. In A.J. Cochran & M.R. Farrally (Eds.), *Science and golf II: Proceedings of the 1994 World Scientific Congress of Golf* (pp. 127–137). London: E & FN Spon.

Csikszentmihalyi, M. (1990). *Flow: The psychology of optimal experience.* New York: Harper Perennial.

Feherty, D. (1993). In A. Fine, *Mind over golf.* [Videotape] London: BBC Enterprises.

Gallwey, W.T. (1986). *The inner game of golf.* London: Pan Books.

Greenspan, M.J., & Feltz, D.F. (1989). Psychological interventions with athletes in competitive situations: A review. *The Sport Psychologist, 3*, 219–236.

Hanin, Y.L. (Ed.). (2000). *Emotions in sport.* Champaign, IL: Human Kinetics.

Hardy, L. (1990). A catastrophe model of performance in sport. In G. Jones & L.Hardy (Eds.), *Stress and performance in sport* (pp. 81–106). Chichester: Wiley.

Jackson, R.C., & Willson, R.J. (1999). Using "swing thoughts" to prevent paradoxical performance effects in golf putting. In M.R. Farrally & A.J.Cochran (Eds.), *Science and golf III: Proceedings of the 1998 World Scientific Congress of Golf* (pp. 166–173). Champaign, IL: Human Kinetics.

Jackson, S.A., Thomas, P.R., Marsh, H.W., & Smethurst, C.J. (in press). Relationships between flow, self-concept, psychological skills, and performance. *Journal of Applied Sport Psychology.*

Janelle, C.M. (1999). Ironic mental processes in sport: Implications for sport psychologists. *The Sport Psychologist, 13*, 201–220.

King, M., Stanley, G., & Burrows, G. (1987). *Stress: Theory and practice.* Sydney: Grune & Stratton.

Kirschenbaum, D.S., Owens, D., & O'Connor, E.A. (1998). Smart golf: Preliminary evaluation of a simple, yet comprehensive, approach to improving and scoring the mental game. *The Sport Psychologist, 12*, 271–282.

Lazarus, R.S. (2000). How emotions influence performance in competitive sports. *The Sport Psychologist, 14*, 229–252.

Loehr, J.E. (1986). *Mental toughness training for sports.* Lexington, MA: Stephen Greene Press.

Martens, R. (1987). *Coaches guide to sport psychology.* Champaign, IL: Human Kinetics.

McCaffrey, N., & Orlick, T. (1989). Mental factors related to excellence among top professional golfers. *International Journal of Sport Psychology, 20*, 256–278.

Meichenbaum, D. (1977). *Cognitive behavior modification: An integrative approach.* New York: Plenum Press.

Meyers, A.W., Whelan, J.P., & Murphy, S.M. (1996). Cognitive behavioral strategies in athletic performance enhancement. In M. Hersen, R.M. Miller, & A.S. Belack (Eds.), *Handbook of behavior modification* (Vol. 30, pp. 137–164). Pacific Grove, CA: Brooks/Cole.

Moore, W.E., & Stevenson, J.R. (1991). Understanding trust in the performance of complex automatic sport skills. *The Sport Psychologist, 5*, 281–289.

Moore, W.E., & Stevenson, J.R. (1994). Training for trust in sport skills. *The Sport Psychologist, 8*, 1–12.

Morris, T., & Thomas, P.R. (1995). Approaches to applied sport psychology. In T. Morris & J. Summers (Eds.), *Sport psychology: Theory, applications and current issues* (pp. 215–258). Brisbane: Jacaranda Wiley.

Nicklaus, J. (1976). *Golf my way.* London: Pan Books.

Nideffer, R.M. (1985). *Athletes' guide to mental training.* Champaign, IL: Human Kinetics.

Nideffer, R.M. (1992). *Psyched to win.* Champaign, IL: Leisure Press.

Orlick, T. (1986). *Psyching for sport: Mental training for athletes.* Champaign, IL: Leisure Press.

Over, R., & Thomas, P.R. (1995). Age and skilled psychomotor performance: A comparison of younger and older golfers. *International Journal of Aging and Human Development, 41*, 1–12.

Owens, D., & Bunker, L.K. (1989). *Golf: Steps to success.* Champaign, IL: Human Kinetics.

Oxendine, J.B. (1970). Emotional arousal and motor performance. *Quest, 13*, 23–32.

Perna, F., Neyer, M., Murphy, S.M., Ogilvie, B.C., & Murphy, M. (1995). Consultations with sport organizations: A cognitive-behavioural model. In S.M. Murphy (Ed.), *Sport psychology interventions* (pp. 235–252). Champaign, IL: Human Kinetics.

Price, R.J. (1999). Golf course provision, usage, and revenues in Scotland. In M.R. Farrally & A.J. Cochran (Eds.), *Science and golf III: Proceedings of the 1998 World Scientific Congress of Golf* (pp. 594–599). Champaign, IL: Human Kinetics.

Ravizza, K. (1998). Increasing awareness for sport performance. In J.M. Williams (Ed.), *Applied sport psychology* (3rd ed., pp. 171–181). Palo Alto, CA: Mayfield.

Rotella, R.J. (1995). *Golf is not a game of perfect.* New York: Simon & Schuster.

Schneider, W., & Fisk, A.D. (1983). Attention theory and mechanisms for skilled performance. In R.A. Magill (Ed.), *Memory and control of action* (pp. 119–143). Amsterdam: North Holland.

Schneider, W., & Shiffrin, R.M. (1977). Controlled and automatic human information processing: Detection, search and attention. *Psychological Review, 84*, 1–66.

Shiffrin, R.M., & Schneider, W. (1977). Controlled and automatic human information processing: Perceptual learning, automatic attending and a general theory. *Psychological Review, 84*, 127–190.

Suinn, R.M. (1986). *Seven steps to peak performance: The mental training manual for athletes.* Toronto: Hans Huber.

Takeshita, S., Meshizuka, T., Kawashima, K., & Zaitsu, H. (1999). Golf course development in Japan II: Business in the period of depression. In M.R. Farrally & A.J.Cochran (Eds.), *Science and golf III: Proceedings of the 1998 World Scientific Congress of Golf* (pp. 609–616). Champaign, IL: Human Kinetics.

Theriault, G., & Lachance, P. (1998). Golf injuries: An overview. *Sports Medicine, 26,* 43–57.

Thomas, P.R. (1993). Psychological skills profiles of athletes: The effects of feedback. *European Journal for High Ability, 4,* 161–170.

Thomas, P.R. (in press). Professional practice in sport psychology: Developing programs with golfers and orienteers. In G. Tenenbaum (Ed.), *The practice of sport and exercise psychology: International perspectives.* Morgantown, WV: Fitness Information Technology.

Thomas, P.R., & Fogarty, G.J. (1997). Psychological skills training in golf: The role of individual differences in cognitive preferences. *The Sport Psychologist, 11,* 86–106.

Thomas, P.R., Hardy, L., & Murphy, S.M. (1999, November). *Cognitions, emotions and athletic performance.* Paper presented at the Fifth IOC World Congress on Sport Sciences, Sydney.

Thomas, P.R., Murphy, S.M., & Hardy, L. (1999). Test of Performance Strategies: Development and preliminary validation of a comprehensive measure of athletes' psychological skills. *Journal of Sports Sciences, 17,* 697–711.

Thomas, P.R., & Over, R. (1994a). Contributions of psychological, psychomotor, and shot-making skills to prowess at golf. In A.J. Cochran & M.R. Farrally (Eds.), *Science and golf II: Proceedings of the 1994 World Scientific Congress of Golf* (pp. 138–143). London: E & FN Spon.

Thomas, P.R., & Over, R. (1994b). Psychological and psychomotor skills associated with performance in golf. *The Sport Psychologist, 8,* 73–86.

Thomas, P.R., Schlinker, P.J., & Over, R. (1996). Psychological and psychomotor skills associated with prowess at ten-pin bowling. *Journal of Sports Sciences, 14,* 255–268.

Vealey, R.S. (1994). Current status and prominent issues in sport psychology interventions. *Medicine and Science in Sports and Exercise, 26,* 495–502.

Weinberg, R.S., & Comar, W. (1994). The effectiveness of psychological interventions in competitive sport. *Sports Medicine Journal, 18,* 406–418.

Williams, J.M., & Harris, D.V. (1998). Relaxation and energizing techniques for regulation of arousal. In J.M. Williams (Ed.), *Applied sport psychology* (3rd ed., pp. 219–236). Palo Alto, CA: Mayfield.

Yerkes, R.M., & Dodson, J.D. (1908). The relation of strength of stimulus to rapidity of habit formation. *Journal of Comparative and Neurological Psychology, 18,* 459–482.

Zinsser, N., Bunker, L., & Williams, J.M. (1998). Cognitive techniques for building confidence and enhancing performance. In J.M. Williams (Ed.), *Applied sport psychology* (3rd ed., pp. 270–295). Palo Alto, CA: Mayfield.

ABOUT THE EDITOR

The Editor with Greg Norman (Honorary Doctor of Griffith University).

Patrick R. Thomas is an Associate Professor and Director of the Centre for Movement Education and Research at Griffith University's Mt Gravatt Campus in Brisbane, Australia. CMER provides assessment and remediation programs for children with poorly developed motor skills, health and fitness programs for children and their parents, and psychological skills training programs for athletes and other performers. (See: www.gu.edu.au/centre/cmer/)

After completing a Teachers Certificate, Dr Thomas studied at the University of Queensland, graduating with first-class honours and a University medal in psychology. He subsequently completed research Masters and PhD degrees in organisational and cognitive psychology, and has taught psychology and research methods in the Faculty of Education for more than 25 years.

Dr Thomas was a foundation member of the College of Sport Psychologists of the Australian Psychological Society, and for the past 10 years has provided psychological services to athletes, particularly golfers. He is a member of the World Scientific Congress of Golf Steering Committee, and a member of the international panel of judges for GOLF Magazine's Science in Golf Prize. Pat has been a member of Pacific Golf Club in Brisbane since 1978. He got his handicap down to 9.8 on this tough course, so he still has one lifelong ambition to achieve now this book has been published.

LIST OF AUTHORS

Phil Ayres
Professional Golfers' Association of Australia
PO Box 1314
Crows Nest, NSW 2065
AUSTRALIA
E: payres@pga.org.au

Gi Broman
Medical Laboratory Science and Technology,
Karolinska Institute
Dept of Sport and Health Sciences
Stockholm University
College of Physical Education and Sports
Box 56 26, Stockholm, 114 86
SWEDEN
E: gi.broman@ihs.se

Jimmie Bullard
PGA Professional
Las Vegas, Nevada
U.S.A

John S. Carlson
Centre for Rehabilitation, Exercise
& Sports Science
Victoria University
PO Box 14428
Melbourne City MC, VIC 8001
AUSTRALIA
E: John.Carlson@vu.edu.au

Phillip J. Cheetham
3DGolfWorld Inc
1202 E. Maryland Ave. Suite 1G
Phoenix, AZ 85014
U.S.A
E: phil@3dgolfworld.com

David Chettle
Under Construction Pty Ltd
PO Box 2344
Fortitude Valley BC, QLD 4006
AUSTRALIA
E: chirpy@uq.net.au

Richard L. Cox
Dept of Physical Education, Sport
& Leisure Studies
Faculty of Education
University of Edinburgh
Edinburgh, EH4 6JD
SCOTLAND
E: Richard.Cox@ed.ac.uk

Michael J. Dalgleish
The Golf Athlete Pty Ltd
PO Box 1014
Milton, QLD 4064
AUSTRALIA
E: mikedalg@nwi.com.au

Steve Danish
Life Skills Center
Virginia Commonwealth University
PO Box 842018
Richmond, VA 23284-2018
U.S.A
E: sdanish@saturn.vcu.edu

Vicki A. de Prazer
Sport Psychology Unit
Australian Institute of Sport
P.O Box 176
Belconnen, ACT 2616
AUSTRALIA
E: vdePrazer@ausport.gov.au

David Else
Faculty of Sciences
University of Southern Queensland
Toowoomba, QLD 4350
AUSTRALIA
E: else@usq.edu.au

K. Anders Ericsson
Department of Psychology
Florida State University
Tallahassee, FL 32306-1270
U.S.A
E: ERICSSON@PSY.FSU.EDU

Gerard J. Fogarty
Faculty of Sciences
University of Southern Queensland
Toowoomba, QLD 4350
AUSTRALIA
E: fogarty@usq.edu.au

Chris Graham
Faculty of Sciences
University of Southern Queensland
Toowoomba, QLD 4350
AUSTRALIA
E: grahamc@usq.edu.au

J. Robert Grove
Dept Human Movement & Exercise Science
The University of Western Australia
Crawley, Perth, WA 6009
AUSTRALIA
E: Bob.Grove@uwa.edu.au

Mark A. Guadagnoli
Department of Kinesiology
University of Nevada, Las Vegas
4505 Maryland Parkway
Las Vegas, NV 89154-3034
U.S.A
E: mark@nevada.edu

Lew Hardy
School of Sport, Health and Physical Education Sciences
University of Wales, Bangor
Gwynedd LL57 2DG
UNITED KINGDOM
E: l.hardy@bangor.ac.uk

William R. Holcomb
SIM Program Director
Department of Kinesiology
University of Nevada
Las Vegas, NV 89154-3034
U.S.A

Robin C. Jackson
Department of Sport Sciences
Brunel University, Osterley Campus
Borough Road
Isleworth, Middlesex TW7 5DU
UNITED KINGDOM
E: Robin.Jackson@brunel.ac.uk

Sandy Jamieson
PGA Golf Professional
La Trobe Driving Range
Melbourne, VIC
AUSTRALIA
E: jamo@golf.com.au

Kieran M. Kingston
School of Sport, P.E. & Recreation
University of Wales Institute, Cardiff
Cyncoed Campus
Cardiff, CF23 6XD
UNITED KINGDOM
E: KKingston@uwic.ac.uk

Peter W. Knight
NSW Golf Association
PO Box 704
Darlinghurst, NSW 1300
AUSTRALIA
E: pknight@nswga.com.au

Raymond J. Leigh
University College Chichester
Bishop Otter Campus
College Lane
Chichester, West Sussex PO19 4PE
ENGLAND
E: R.Leigh@chihe.ac.uk

LIST OF AUTHORS

Philip Martin
Exercise Science and Physical Education
Arizona State University
Tempe, AZ 85287
U.S.A
E: philip.martin@asu.edu

John F. Mathers
Department of Sports Studies
University of Stirling
Stirling, FK9 4LA
SCOTLAND
E: j.f.mathers@stir.ac.uk

Al McDaniels
College of Extended Studies
University of Nevada, Las Vegas
4505 Maryland Parkway
Las Vegas, NV 89154
U.S.A
E: mcdania1@nevada.edu

Jennifer M. McKay
Victoria University
PO Box 14428
Melbourne City MC, VIC 8001
AUSTRALIA

Tom M. McLellan
Defence and Civil Institute of Environmental Medicine
Environmental and Applied Ergonomics Section
Toronto, Ontario M3M 3B9
CANADA
E: tmclella@dciem.dnd.ca

Ramsay McMaster
The Melbourne Golf Injury Clinic
1100 Dandenong Road
Carnegie, VIC 3163
AUSTRALIA
E: ramsay@iaa.com.au

Kevin Morris
Times Mirror Magazines
Two Park Avenue, 10th Floor
New York, NY 10016
U.S.A
E: Kevin.Morris@tmm.com

Tony Morris
Centre for Rehabilitation, Exercise
& Sports Science
Victoria University
PO Box 14428
Melbourne City MC, VIC 8001
AUSTRALIA
E: Tony.Morris@vu.edu.au

Robert E. Mottram
The Golf Health and Performance Center
544 3rd Street
Encinitas, CA 92024
U.S.A
E: GolfPT@aol.com

Richard Mullen
School of Sport
University of Wales Institute, Cardiff
Cyncoed Road
Cardiff, CF2 6XD
UNITED KINGDOM
E: RHMullen@uwic.ac.uk

Robert J. Neal
Golf BioDynamics Pty Ltd
PO Box 365
Indooroopilly, QLD 4068
AUSTRALIA
E: gbd@nwi.com.au

Russell Pitcher
c/- Sport Psychology Laboratory
Dept Human Movement & Exercise Science
The University of Western Australia
Crawley, Perth, WA 6009
AUSTRALIA

Albert D. Potts
School of Education
University of Durham
Leazes Road
Durham, DH1 1TA
UNITED KINGDOM
E: a.d.potts@durham.ac.uk

Neil K. Roach
Dept of Exercise and Sport Science
Manchester Metropolitan University
Alsager
Stoke-on-Trent, ST7 2HL
UNITED KINGDOM
E: n.roach@mmu.ac.uk

Steve E. Selig
Centre for Rehabilitation, Exercise
& Sports Science
Victoria University
PO Box 14428
Melbourne City MC, VIC 8001
AUSTRALIA
E: Steve.Selig@vu.edu.au

Eric J. Sprigings
College of Kinesiology
University of Saskatchewan
Saskatoon, S7N 1M3
CANADA
E: sprigings@sask.usask.ca

Bryan F. St. Laurent
Skill Technologies Inc
1202 E. Maryland Ave. Suite 1G
Phoenix, AZ 85014
U.S.A
E: skill@skilltechnologies.com

Richard D. Tandy
College of Health Sciences
University of Nevada
4505 Maryland Parkway
Las Vegas, NV 89154-3034
U.S.A
E: dtandy@nevada.edu

Patrick R. Thomas
Centre for Movement Education and Research
Mt Gravatt Campus
Griffith University, QLD 4111
AUSTRALIA
E: P.Thomas@mailbox.gu.edu.au

Bill Vicenzino
Musculoskeletal Pain and Injury Research Unit
Department of Physiotherapy
The University of Queensland, QLD 4072
AUSTRALIA
E: vicenzino@physio.therapies.uq.edu.au

Dominic Wall
Australian Golf Union
Golf Australia House
153-155 Cecil Street
South Melbourne, VIC 3205
AUSTRALIA
E: dominicw@agu.org.au

Robert Weinberg
Dept Physical Education Health & Sport Studies
Miami University
Oxford, OH 45056
U.S.A
E: Weinber@muohio.edu

Leonard Zaichkowsky
Developmental Studies and Counseling
Boston University
605 Commonwealth Avenue
Boston, MA 02215
U.S.A
E: sport@bu.edu

INDEX

For frequently used terms, first page numbers of relevant chapters are in **boldface**.

10-year rule, 5, 9–11, 60, 64
3L routine, 347
54 vision, 71

A
abdominal
   breathing, 313
   control, 217
   muscles, 209, 211, 217, 220, 236
   strength, 211, 236
ability, **1**, 63, 72, 87, 101–102, 105, 114, 127, 134, 164, 172–173, 183,185–187, 207, 254, 259, 266, 275, **289**, **300**, **311**, 327–328, 344
academy, 13, 72, 86, 90–91
access, 11–12, 40, 42, 62, 64, 67–68, 73, 81, 84, 89, 91, 93, 127, 208, 240–241
accuracy, 6, 20, 29–31, 97–100, 104, 177–178, 185, 189, 217, 282–283, 302, 306, 313
achievement, 1, 5–6, 10, 60, 87, 90, 289–291, 298–299
activation, 26, 180–183, 211, 217, 219–220, 256, 265, 343–344
adaptation, 3, 17–18, 40, 43, 45, 54, 65, 131, 136, 211
address position, 34, 36, 196, 202, 204, 209, 211, 217, 234–236, 239, 265, 275, 322
adherence, 215, 219, 266, 276, 282, 318, 346
adolescence, 41, 63, 204
adolescent, 10–11, 38, 50, 70, 74, 75, 299
adrenocorticotropin (ACTH), 171
aerobic
   capacity, 149, 152, 157–158, 166, 168, 171
   fitness, 42, 56, **127**, **149**, **164**, 213
   power, 136, 158, 162, 165, 171
affirmation, 322, 345
afternoon, 15, 131–132, 140–141, 175
age, 1, **58**, 69, 71, 127–128, 141, **149**, 209, 227, 239, 241, 285, 303, 338
aging, 10, 43–44, 141, 215
aim, 8, 9, 19, 23–24, 28–30, 80, 105, 108
alcohol, 133, 142
alignment, 16, 47, 51, 54, **104**, 212, 220
amateur, 80
   bodies, 83–84
   coach, 75, 85, 87, 89
anaerobic fitness, 5
anatomy, 2, 80, 233, 239
anger, 328, 329–331, 333, 338, 347
annual plan, 112–115
anthropometric measures, 136, 138, 145
anticipate, 22, 29
anticipatory processing, 46
anxiety, 27, 50, 61, 80, 116, **164**, 231, 245, 266–267, 292, 312, 332, 343–344
   and performance, 245, 343–344
   cognitive, 169, 246–249, 254, 258, 343
   somatic, 167–170, 172, 246–250, 261
   state, 165, 167–168, 171–174, 252, 261–262
   trait, 174, 299
apprentice, 83
approach shot, 30–31, 36, 269–274
arm swinging, 226
Armour, Tommy 300, 309
arousal, 246–248, 250, 258, 264–266, 319, 332, 342–344, 346–347
assessment, 48
   coaching, 77, 79
   imagery ability, 312, 314, 318, 320
   mood, 333–334
   performance, 268, 270, 273–274, 282
   physical, 202, 208, 210, 215–216, 233–235, 239, 241
   program, 68, 72
   psychological, 268, 339
   skill, 116–117
   stress, 165
   tools, 290
associative phase, 19
asymmetry factor, 246–247, 250
atherosclerosis, 159
athleticism, 163, 178, 207
attention, 33, 36, 165, 250, 256, 259, 265–266, 276, **279**, 319, 345–347

attentional
    capacity, 249, 253
    control, 280, 284, 338, 342, 346
    deficit, 253
    focus, 264, 274, 280, 285, 287, 319, 344
    narrowing, 259, 346
    strategy, 285
    threshold, 253, 255
attitude, 39, 61–63, 70, 72
attribution, 269, 292
audiotape, 321, 323
Augusta National, 67, 121, 126
Australian Institute of Sport (AIS), 165, 231, 239, 241
autogenic training, 319
automatic control, 251, 348
automaticity, 1–2, 12, 17–19, 27–28, 31–32, 34, 36–38, 73, 224, 231, 251, 260, 264, 266–267, 269, 274–275, 285, 320, 322, 338, 348
autonomous phase, 19, 279

B
back pain, 225, 230, 234, 243–244
backswing, 23, 32, 34, 96, 101, 187–189, **192**, 202, 209, 235–237, 268, 279
balance, 25, 33, 35, 114, 211, 213–214, 220, 232, 235
ball, 125
    trajectory, 9, 23, 27–28, 46, 49, 282, 311
Ballesteros, Severiano 123–124
biomechanics, 26, **175**, 199, 205, 216, 219, 223, 230, 233, 349
birth dates, 41–42
blood
    lipid, 149–150, 154, 157, 159–161
    pressure, 138, 150, 154–155, 160–162
body
    composition, 128, 140, 151, 163
    fat, 153–154, 157, 159, 161
    rotation, 235
boredom, 61, 344
breathing, 4, 116, 255, 313, 319, 344–346
Burke, Jackie 21, 124
burnout, 15, 40
butterflies in the stomach, 246

C
caddie, 105, 109–110

caffeine, 133
calibration, 27, 302–310
cancer, 144, 158, 231
carbohydrate, 135
carbon-fibre, 177
cardiac deceleration, 277, 285, 287, 323, 345
cardiovascular, **127**, **149**, **164**, 255, 262
    disease, 150, 157–158
    fitness, 208, 213–214, 217, 232
career, 15–16, 35, 44, 63–64, 71, 86, 240–241
carry distance, 117
catastrophe models, 245–251, 343
centering, 116, 344–345
cerebral activity, 285
certification, 68, 70, 87
challenge, 22, 26, 58, 71, 128, 265, 322–323
champion, 58–59, 122, 124, 184, 193, 335
chance factors, 20–23, 38, 45–46, 172
character, 73
child, 9, 12, 14, 16, 40–41, 58, 60, 62–65, 74
    prodigies, 9
childhood, 41, 60, 62
children, 10, 16, 24, 33, 40–42, 50, **58**, **67**, 76, 80, 85, **224**, 260, 298, 351
chipping, 16, 26, 80, 117, 187, 269–274, **300**
chiropractor, 201
choking, 252, 254, 260, 262, 300, 338
cholesterol, 151, 154–155, 159–162
circadian rhythm, 128, 140, 167
closed skills, 260, 264–5, 277, 280, 284, 287, 319
clothing, 128–134, 136, 141–147
club
    design, 187
    fitting, 187, 190
    swinging, 180, 226
clubhead, 22, 23, **175**, 257
    speed, **175**, 192, 197, 209, 216, 232
coach, 1, 60, 64, 71, 75, **82**, **94**, **112**, 168, 173, 175, 179, 184, 190, 203–205, 215, 217, 225, **231**, 252, 275, 297, 309, 311–312, 337, 340, 349–351
    education, 75, **82**
    female, 78
coaching, **1**, 64, 75, **82**, 116, 176–177, 189, 216, 225, 241–242, 252, 302
    accreditation, 75, **82**
    updating program, 77, 85, 89

cognitions, 22, 166, 264, 275, 289–290, 297, 302, 332, **337**
cognitive
  abilities, 8
  activities, 33
  approach, 259, 289
  cues, 280
  effort, 266
  factors, 8
  imagery, 319
  involvement, 279
  mechanisms, 6, 18
  patterns, 273
  phase, 19
  preferences, 56
  processes, 51, 265, 275, 287, 302
  psychology, 3, 53, 303
  resources, 275
  restructuring, 342
  skills, 18, 50, 69, 318
  state, 345
  styles, 318, 325
  systems, 33
cognitive-behaviour theory, 341–342
cognitive-behavioural
  interventions, 284–286
  routines, 347
  skills, 277, 280, 284
  strategies, 264–267
  techniques, 264
commitment, 11, 60, 143, 282, 348
competencies, 87, 89
competing, 40, 63, 70–71, 80, 112, 115, 117, 121–123, 165, 205, 293, 349
competition pressure, 55, 164, 168, **245**
composure, 319
concentration, 13–17, 21, 35, 61, 116, 213, 215, 242, 283–288, 338, 345–349
confidence, 21, 92, 118–119, 231, 287, 292, **300**, 319, 321–323, 329, 347–349, 353
confusion, 42, 328–331
conscious, 34, 37, 63, 347–348
  attention, 36, 279, 285
  control, 2, 28, 36, **245**, **264**, 285–286, 345, 347–348
  processing, 251–256, 260, 262, 267, 275
consequence analysis thinking, 69

consistency, 25, 27–28, 31–32, 38, 45–46, 49–51, 53, 185, 189, 213, 215–217, **264**, 279, 320
consultancy approach, 268
contextual factors, 320
contraceptive, 139, 144, 147
control, 1, 175, **207**, **245**, **264**, 279
  ball, 18–19, 31, 49
  body, 26, 35, 49, 215, 217–218, 220, 234–235
  conditions, 6–7, 22, 171–172, 253
  confidence, 118
  destiny, 60
  direction, 29
  distance, 29, 186
  goals, 70, 297
  hypertension, 141
  motor system, 24, 26, 33–34, 49
  movement, 46, 208, 251, 256, 260, 312, 333, 347–348
  paradox, 36, 61, 267, 275, 279, 348
  processes, 22, 245
  shots, 8, 19, 22, 28, 31, 34, 36, 45, 49, 109, 215, 345
  swing, 25–27, 32, 33, 36, 46, 234, 256
controllability, 318
conversion rate, 186
coordinated
  action, 43
  movement, 269
coordination, 43, 63, **207**, 211, 213, 232
coping, 343
  strategies, 60
core temperature, 128, 130, 134, 136–140, 145–146
coronary artery disease, 159
cortisol, 165–169, 171–174
course management, 30, 213, 219, 259, 334, 339, 348
credentials, 84–85, 236
Crenshaw, Ben 20, 124
criteria for success, 295–298
cross-training, 213
crucifix position, 237
CSAI-2, 166–170, 172–173
cue, 48, 95, 105, 252–253, 265, 268–270, 274, 280, 284, 286, 345–347
culture, 62
curriculum, 69, 86, **224**

D

decision making, 11, 50, 69, 213, 264
dehydration, 133–135
deliberate practice, 1–2, 5–6, 13–19, 23, 31, 39–41, 44–45, 49–50, 60–61, 64–65, 339
depression, 328–332, 353
desire, 63, 65, 200, 225
developmental, 66, 69, 74, 113, 303
diabetes, 158
diary, 34, 66, 118
diet, 158, 339
dietitian, 233
direction, 23, 29, 31, 98, 106, 197, 267, 282, 320, 346
distance, 6, 19–20, 26, 29, 31, 38, **94**, 106, 108, 117, 152, 157, **175**, 217, 232, 240, 246, 282–283, 303–304, 308, 313–315, 317
distraction, 165, 279, 319
diuretics, 133, 141
doctor, 233
doubt, 10, 282, 329, 333, 343
downswing, 22, 26, 32–34, 36, 46, 183, 188–190, **192**, 203, 236, 243, 257, 268
draw, 23, 34, 117
dream, 70
drills, 80, 109, 118–119, 204, 211, 213, 234–235, 238–239, 318, 322
drive, 6, 19, 21–23, 28, 31–32, 38, 51, 70, 177, **192**, 270–274, 322, 343
driving
    accuracy, 6, 22, 31, 177, 184–185, 189
    consistency, 23, 26, 35, 38, 45
    control, 19, 21
    distance, 6, 22, 31, 32, 38, 117, 177–178, 185, 188–189, 192–192
    performance, 10, 189, 248, 271, 274
    range, 16, 27, 68, 320, 322
    results, 24, 322
    trajectory, 28
drugs, 80, 339
dynamic
    postural control, 208, 212–213
    systems theory, 256
dynamics of the golf swing, 194

E

early
    experience, 10
    intervention, 239

education program, 284
educational psychology, 61, 261–262, 298
Edwards, David 21
EEG, 346
effort, 19, 31, 34–38, 49–50, 175, 202, 215, 249–250, 254–255, 258–259, 266
effortless, 22, 31, 348
ego orientation, 290–297
ego-involved perspective, 290, 297
elastic energy, 191, 197
elite
    athlete, 2, 10, 20, 224, 240, 242, 290, 327–328
    competition, 293, 334
    golfer, 10–11, 21–22, 28, 31, 33–36, 39, 44, 62, 112, 114, 165, 169, 171–173, 200, 207, 216, 232, 236, 238, 241–242, 266, 280, 328–329, 333, 342, 348–349
    level, 40, 242, 279
    performance, 2, 10, 12, 16, 18, 40, 44, 49, 327, 331
    performer, 10–13, 15, 50, 279, 291
    player, 24, 61, 116, 333, 337
    programs, 84, 239–241
EMG, 27
emotions, 22–23, 71, 164, 275, 290, **327**, **337**
emotional
    control, 23, 337–338, 341–342
    effects, 22
    intelligence, 72
    state, 317, 327, 345
empathy, 72
empower, 233, 339
encouragement, 60, 63–65
endurance, 42, 145, 151, 157, 160–162, 215, 232
energisation, 116, 118–119, 329
engagement, 9, 11, 13
enjoy, 11, 37, 61, 63–64, 328
enjoyment, 16, 96, 102, 297
enthusiasm, 61
equation, 130–131, 181, 185, 330
equipment, 11–12, 61, 68, 77, 126, **175**, **207**
etiquette, 68, 76–77, 80
evaluation of progress, 322
excellence, 7, 39, 58–60, 63, 65, 82, 87, 93
execution, 8, 22, 24–27, 35–36, 41, 210, 231, 264–265, 267, 269–270, 285–286, 347–348

exercise, 42, 127, **149**, **164**, 205, **207**, **224**, **231**, 247, 290, 313, 319, 334
   intensity, 134–135, 146, 149, 157–159, 171–172
exhaustion, 127, **138**, 140, 165
experience, 1, **58**, 69, 72, 77, 87, 95, **104**, 215, 225, 252, 259, 276, 281–282, 297, 301, **311**, 342, 345, 349
expert, 1, **58**, 102, 104, 128, 214, 257, 266, 268, 285, 303
   golf instruction, 87, 89, 93
   performance, 1, **58**
expertise, 1, **58**, 78, 303
explicit
   focus, 267–268, 275
   knowledge, 251–254, 286
   learning, 251–252
   rules, 251–252, 267
eyes closed, 23, 313, 322

F

fade, 23, 34, 47, 117
failure, 65, 116, 162, 246, 262, 269, 290, 297
Faldo, Nick 105, 124
family influences, 61–62
father, 29, 58, 61–65
fatigue, 16, 114, 117, 151, 157, 165, 172, 213, 215–217, 328, 330–332
feedback, 12, 45, 49, 61, 70, 72, **94**, 106, 166, 307, 309, 353
feel, 21, 33–35, 39, 42, 119, 265, 268, 270, 318, 321–322, 345–349
feeling image, 319
feelings, 1, 264, 267, 301, 321–322, 329, 342–345, 348
Feherty, David 344, 351
fine motor skill, 10, 15–16, 165, 333
first tee, **67**, 231, 234, 347–348
fitness, 5, 42, 80, **112**, 127, **149**, **164**, **207**, **231**, 339, 350
flexibility, 116, 119, 178, **207**, **231**
   training, 216, 223, 232, 243
flow, 61, 129, 135, 139, 144, 335, 344, 351
Floyd, Ray 10, 37, 39, 49, 53, 124
fluid
   balance, 131, 135, 141–142, 146
   replacement, 133–135, 141–142, 144, 146
freedom, 63
free-weight training, 214

fun, 16, 37, 60–61, 63–64, 76–77
further research, 44, 65, 110, 161, 173, 189, 216, 219, 245, 259, 272, 275–276, 296, 332–334, 350

G

game plan, 30, 349
gender, 127–128, 138, 140, 145, 303
generalise, 7, 9, 283, 320
genetic, 5, 60
Get Fit for Golf, 120, 237–239, 241–242
goal, 12–13, 19, 32, 34, 45–47, 50, 61, 64, **67**, 113, 119, 203, **207**, 254, 256, **264**, **289**, 322, 340, 349
   ladder, 70
   orientation, **289**
   perspectives, 289–291, 296, 298, 335
goal-kicking, 283
Go-Go Golf, 75–76
Going for the Goal Program, 71
golf
   conditioning, 211, 214
   instruction, 32, 68–70, 72, 75, 84, 87, 89, 93, 300
   professional, 38, 44, 49, 71, 76, **82**, 96, 225, 228–229
governance, 84
GPS, 337–339, 348
graphite, 177
greens in regulation, 10, 184
grip, 16, 25, 32–33, 38, 77, 80, 98, 106, 179, 202, 232

H

handgrip strength, 151, 156–157, 160–161
HDL, 154–155, 159–160
health, 73, **149**, 164, 202, 205, 213, **231**, 327–328, 339
heart
   disease, 158–160
   rate, 133–136, 165–166, 168–173, 247, 255, 285, 319
heat, **127**, 190
   acclimation, 131–147
   acclimatisation, 128–143
   adaptation, 137
   capacity, 140
   dissipation, 130
   exchange, 127–132, 138

exhaustion, 127
injury, 128, 140–142
loss, 129–134, 136, 138–139, 141
storage, 129–130, 134, 136, 138, 140
stress, 130–132, 134, 136–137, 139–142, 144–148
stroke, 127
tolerance, 134, 138–140, 142–143, 145–147
transfer, 129–132, 143, 145
highlights tape, 321
hip rotation, 209, 232
Hogan, Ben 16, 21, 25–27, 34, 53, 124, 175, 190
holistic
  approach, 241–242
  process goal, **264**
  swing thought, 257, 260
hooking, 22
horizontal alignment, 105, 107–110
hormone replacement therapy, 140, 143
hot streaks, 20
HPA activity, 167
humidity, 128, 131–132, 142
hydration, **127**
hypermobility, 235–236
hypertension, 141, 158, 160
hypohydration, 133–135, 144, 146–147
hysteresis, 247–248, 250–251

I
ideal model, 321
image, 29, 46, 48, 118, 265, **311**, 325, 342
  generation, 317
  rotation, 317
imagery, 48, 164, 264–266, **311**, 340, 347–349
  ability, **311**
  control, 315
  external perspective, 320, 349
  internal perspective, 320, 349
  script, 321, 348
  techniques, 242, **311**
  training, 277, 317–321, 324–325
  vividness, 315
imagination, 21, 259, 324
impact position, 202–203
implicit learning, 252, 277
individual differences, 1, 16–17, 69, 266, 275, 301, 306, 343

individualised program, 214
injury, 3, 15, 43–44, 80, 98, 114, 116, 128, 140–142, 176, 187–188, **200**, **207**, **224**, **231**, 353
  prevention, 80, 205, 209, 211, 216, 233, 239–242
  risk factors, 241
  treatment, **200**, 233, 241
innate talent, 1, 17, 40, 50, 53, 66
inspirational music, 321
institute, 84, 165, 199, 223, 231, 239–241
instruction, 32, 39, 63–65, **67**, 75, **82**, 226, 251, 284, 300, 317
instructional video, 38–39, 98
instructor, 71, 72, 75–76, 84, 96, 102, 193
  antecedents of expertise, 87, 89, 93
integrated approach, 75, **231**, 287
intensity
  exercise, 133–135, 137, 149, 157–160, 171–172, 208, 213
  practice, 43–45, 119, 236
  pain, 204
intentional control, 33
internalising, 267
international golfers, **121**
interpersonal
  communication, 70
  skills, 72, 339
introspection, 266
invitation to the US Masters, 122
involvement, 5, 9–11, 42, 45, 61, **82**, 176, 180, 183, 208, 279, 291–292, 338
ironic
  control processes, 22
  effects, 259, 262, 345

J
Janzen, Lee 64
jet lag, 233
joint stretches, 210
Jones, Bobby 34–35, 48, 53, 121, 125–126
junior golf, **67**, 76–77, 84, 89, 201, 215, **224**, 232, 240, 340, 349
  development programs, 89, 350

K
key thoughts, 322
kinematic
  analysis, 254–255, 259

variation, 176
kinesthesis, 321
kinesthetic imagery, 317–318
kinetic link principle, 193
Kite, Tom 35, 53
knee extensor strength, 150, 156, 160
knowledge, 1, 245
    acquisition, 4, 35, 39, 45, 70, 77, 229, 239, 241
    applied, 39, 117, 184, 350
    expert, 6, 18, 20, 31, 46, 49, 205, 268
    explicit, 251–254, 286
    of results, 94, 107
    of rules, 68, 76–77, 80, 305, 309
    research, 6, 39, 46, 59, 149, 203, 210, 225, 349–350
    tacit, 277
kyphosis, 235, 237

L
laboratory, 6–8, 10, 12, 22, 27, 36, 94, 97, 150, 171–172, 309, 313
laser, 104
LDL, 154–155, 159–160
leadership, 72–73
learning
    environment, 12, 62
    explicit, 251–252
    implicit, 251–252, 277
    initial, 40, 61, 95, 314, 319–320
    outcome, 50, 67–68, 225
    phase, 279, 285
    schedule, 41
    skills, 18, 69–70, 94, 285, 311, 344, 347–348
    stage, 256, 285, 319, 321
    swing, 26, 94
    task, 290, 295, 297
    theory, 94, 281, 290
    transfer, 25, 40, 73
lie, 23, 30, 36, 187, 304, 346
life
    skill, 61, 67, 339
    span, 6, 40, 66, 51, 288
    trajectory, 69
lifestyle, 142–143, 158–160, 162–163, 234
lifetime, 61, 69, 122
logbook, 322

longevity, 149, 200, 215, 334
losing, 16, 172
low-income families, 67
LPGA, 57, 67–68, 265, 280, 282
luck, 38

M
machine-weight training, 214
making the cut, 123, 142
management skills, 89
massage, 235
massed practice, 316
masseur, 233
master, 1, 69, 90, 121, 210–211, 231, 290, 295, 297
maximal oxygen uptake, 149, 152–153, 158
McLean, Jim 16, 21, 25, 54, 188, 190, 192–193, 199
medical
    diagnosis, 11
    science, 239–242
medication, 141, 201
meditation, 319
melanoma, 131, 143
memory, 3–5, 17, 39, 48–49, 253
menopause, 140
menstrual cycle, 128, 139, 144–145, 147
mental
    games, 117
    health, 327–328, 335
    imagery, 313, 315, 320, 324–326
    practice, 15, 49, 323–324
    preparation, 277, 302, 334, 338, 347–348
    rehearsal, 242, 284, 311–313, 318–323, 325–326, 349
    representation, 54, 95–96, 101
    set, 345–346
    skills, 70, 73, 114, 116–117, 119, 207, 219, 231, 242, 284, 339, 349
    toughness, 232, 324, 348–349, 352
mentor, 71
meta-analysis, 174, 323–324, 335
metabolic rate, 130–132, 135–136, 146
metacognition, 302–303
metal woods, 177
meta-strategy, 322
minorities, 67
MIQ, 318

modelling, 177, 180, 184, 189, 260, 313, 321, 324
moment of inertia, 177, 179
monitoring, 18, 33, 45, 49, 117, 300, 345
Montgomerie, Colin 64
mood, 318, **327**, 342
moral factors, 60
morning, 14–15, 21, 131–132, 140–141, 150
motivation, 42, 44, 50, 61, 116, 149, 157, 175, 266, 268, 275–276, 284, 289–291, 297, 300, 319, 339
motor control, 24, 34, 103, 333
movement patterns, 26, 175–176, 184, 189, 211, 235, 312, 321
multidisciplinary, 233, 350
muscle, 3, 26–27, 33–34, 39, 50–51, 60, 151, 157, 160–163, 176, 179–181, 184, 188–191, 197–199, 202–203, **207**, 224, 226, 228, **231**, 344, 346
   groups, 43, 211, 234–236
   inflexibility, 209
   recruitment patterns, 210, 219
   stiffness, 224
   stretches, 210, 226
   tension, 27, 210, 231, 319, 344, 346
muscular
   awareness, 313
   balance, 114
   control, 178
   endurance, 151, 157, 161, 232
musculoskeletal screening, 113–114, 234–236, 238–241
music, 2, 7–9, 11–13, 15–17, 40–43, 46–48, 50–52, 54, 321, 325, 347

N

nature versus nurture, 58–59, 65
needs, 208, 210–211, 214–217, 239–240, 318, 339, 342
negative, 300, 343
   emotions, 22, 332, 338
   experience, 62
   images, 319
   thoughts, 246, 266, 345, 347–348
neural
   links, 319
   stretches, 210
Nicklaus, Jack iii, 2, 15–16, 28, 33–35, 37, 46, 48, 55, 124, 311, 347, 349

novice, 7, 22, 26, 29–31, 37, 46, 48, **94**, **104**, 171, 251, 259, 262, 274, 284–287, 316, 319
nutrition, 80, 145, 339

O

obesity, 158
objectives, 16, 113, 119, 123, 236–237, 268, 273, 289, 295, 297, 348, 350
operant learning, 281
opportunity, 6, 40, 47, 63, 70, 73, 84, 110, 239, 273, 275, 297, 305–307, 320
optimal
   arousal, 265, 343
   experience, 61, 351
   feedback, **94**
   mood, 327
   performance, 127, 200, 231–232, 266, 333, 339, 343–351
   swing, 26, 182, 203, 205
Ouimet, Francis 37, 55
outcome, 23, 29, 31, 70, 94, 104, 118, 181, 225, 265, 305, 309, 311, 313, 320, 322, 333–334, 347
overtraining injuries, 15
overuse injuries, 203, 232
oxygen uptake, 149, 151–153, 158

P

pain, **200**, 225, 234
Palmer, Arnold 64, 124
paralysis by analysis, 242
parenting attitudes, 61, 63
parents, 10–11, **58**, 76, 299, 337
peak, 112–113
   career, 44
   experience, 285
   performance, 10, 36, 42, 322, 334, 343, 348
perceived
   ability, 290, 296, 320, 344
   competence, 297
   effort, 250
   exertion, 135
   influence, 62
   talent, 42
Percent Error Index (PEI), 185
perception, 33, 62, 123, 246, 250, 266, 273, 290, 301, 328, 344
perceptual experience, 318
perceptual-motor, 8, 10, 36, 40, 45

perfect, 15, 20–22, 33, 41, 61, 210, 262, 320, 352
performance
  acquisition, 3, 7, 11, 14, 17–18, 24, 37, 39–40, 44–45, 49, 311, 318–319, 322
  characteristics, 176
  enhancement, 110, 120, 164, 214, 216, 250, 260, 277, 287, 302, 324, 335, 352
  improvement, 12, 17
  profile, 339–341, 348, 351
  statistics, 57, 114, 184
periodisation, **112**
personal
  par, 69–71
  trainer, 236
personality, 61
PGA, 10, 20, 44, 50, **58**, 67–68, 78–80, **82**, 94–95, 99, 114, 120, 122, 178, 184, 188, **192**, 200–201, 241, 348
physical
  adaptation, 210
  condition, 23, 208
  conditioning, **207**, 232, 334
  development, **231**
  education, 4, 97, **224**, 299
  factors, 60, 128
  feelings, 345
  practice, 242, 319–320, 322
  skills, 69, 114–116, 232, 318, 339, 349
  stress, 200
  therapist, 208
  training, 113–115, 131, 137, 171, 216, 219, 223
physician, 163, 202, 205, 223, 243
physiological
  adaptation, 17, 41, 137, 150, 161
  arousal, 246–248, 250, 258, 343
physiology, **127**, 233, 239, 349
physiotherapist, 202, 211, 215–217, 219, 234–236, 239–240
physiotherapy treatment, 201, 205, 216
physique, 147, 210
pitching, 80, 117
plan, 30, 46–47, 70, 72–73, **112**, 216, 349
planning, 24, 30–31, 45, 48, 71, 77, 116, 119–120
Player, Gary 11, 26, 35, 55, 123–124
podiatrist, 233
POMS, 327

postural
  alignments, 212
  awareness, 235
  control, 208, 211–213
  deviations, 212, 235
  imbalances, 211, 215
posture, 25, 32–33, 36, 202, 204, 211–212, 214, 217, 220, 234, 240
  exercises, 204
power, 25–26, 136, 158, 165, 171, 197–198, 207, 209, 211
practice, 1, **112**
  amount, 2, 4, 10, 14–17, 39–42, 45, 62, 64, 203, 213, 215, 241, 297, 347
  daily, 15, 17, 42–45, 118, 203–204
  deliberate, 1–2, 5–6, 13–19, 23, 31, 39–41, 44–45, 49–50, 60–61, 64–65, 339
  drills, 80, 109, 119, 204, 242, 320, 322
  goals, 292, 349
  habits, 59
  intensity, 3, 10, 43–44, 60, 117, 236, 239
  mental, 15, 49, 117, 318, 349
  methods, 35, 50, 225
  on-course, 36
  plan, 112, 118–119, 187, 189, 339
  protocols, 94
  quality, 16–17, 44, 60–62, 64, 239–240, 242, 312
  range, 95, 240, 322
  regime, 41, 175, 234–235, 239, 259
  round, 30, 269, 320, 348
  specialised, 43, 50
  structure, 15, 259, 318
  swing, 98, 280, 282, 322, 346
  systematic, 37, 175, 322
precompetition, 112–113, 117, 240, 293–296, 327–334, 347
pregnancy, 139, 145, 148
preparation, **112**, 350
  mental, 113, 302, 334, 338, 347–348
  phase, 112
  physical, 113, 116, 241, 283–284
  precompetition, 117, 333
  prepractice, 225
  psychological, 126
  shot, 9, 24, 28–29, 46, 269
  specialised, 40, 112–113, 117
  tournament, 168
preperformance routine, *see* routine

preshot routine, *see* routine
pressure, **245**
    blood, 138, 150, 154–157, 160–161
    choking, 254, 260, 338
    competition, 55, 164
    performance, 259, 285–287, 340, 344, 348
Price, Nick 25, 31, 34–35, 55
pride, 322
proactive programs, 239
process
    automated, 33, 348
    and outcome, 320
    goals, 70, 254, 256, **264**
    information, 102, 251, 346–348
    of performing, 251, 256
processing efficiency theory, 249–250, 254, 259, 261
professional
    coach, 79
    development, 82–85, 87, 89–93, 241
    golfer, 10, 16, 20, 23, 36, 61, 75, 178, 184, 194, 216, 233, 259, 265, 268, 283, 313, 345, 348
    practice, 337, 339, 342, 353
progressive muscle relaxation, 344
proprioception, 232
proximal to distal sequencing, 176, 183
psychological
    factors, 60, 349
    feelings, 345
    profile, 327
    skills, 265, 284, 311, **337**
    stress, 164, 172, 247
psychologist, 72, 233, 289, 297, 311, 339, 341
psychomotor skills, 37–38, 281, 334, 338
psychophysiological
    patterns, 285, 345
    responses, **164**
    state, 164, 273
putting
    alignment, **104**
    conditions, 29, 35, 251, 255, 259
    confidence, **300**
    consistency, 25–26, 265, 270, 280, 282
    control, 19–22, 28, 45–46, 109, 258, 345
    conversion rate, 186
    drills, 235
    green, 27, 320

    imagery, 29, **311**, 348
    line, 29, 105–110, 269–270
    performance, 19–20, 71, 104, 109–110, 184, 231, **245**, 266, 282, 285, **300**, 315, 338, 348
    probability, 20, 186
    representations, 29, 48
    reproducibility, 6, 8, 18, 21, 23, 39, 207
    routine, **264**, 279, 345
    skills, 38, 77, 80, 95, 104, 165, 285, **300**, 316, 338
    style, 37, 187

Q
QMI, 315, 323

R
range of motion, 41, 187, 208, 215, 220, 232
reading the green, 105, 109
realistic, 30, 36, 45, 111, 113, 117, 158, 176, 180, 269, 275, 304, 308, 320, 340
recovery, 116, 142, 213, 219, 269
recuperating, 15
refinement, 91, 116, 255, 267, 269, 275, 319–320, 347, 353
re-freezing, 256, 259
registration, 84–85, 87, 89
regression, 152, 159, 256–257, 259, 268, 330, 332, 338
rehabilitation, 158
reinvest, 256, 286
relative
    age, 42, 51, 53
    humidity, 128, 131–132
    rotation, 188, 192
    task difficulty, 95
relaxation, 80, 116, 164, 255, 260, 264, 313, 319, 341–342, 344, 346–347
relaxed concentration, 346
repetition, 13–14, 25, 49, 204, 210, 220, 248
representations, 17–19, 29–30, 34–37, 45–49, 95–96, 101, 268, 312, 317
reproducibility, 23–24, 26, 31, 33
resistance training, 116, 212
respiration, 130, 319
respiratory
    exchange ratio, 165
    movements, 27

rest, 14–15, 131–132, 135, 138–140, 150–160, 201–203, 211–212, 315–316
retail services, 85, 93
reverse pivot, 236–237
riding, 131–132, 134, 141
rotation
  axis, 179, 188, 190
  control, 219
  distal, 184, 193
  speed, 187
  strength, 210–211, 219
rotational
  muscles, 197, 220
  position, 194, 232, 235–237, 242
round analysis, 113, 117, 119
routine, 80
  cognitive-behavioural, 347
  competition, 17, 252
  consistency, 266–267, 273, **279**
  posthole, 347
  practice, 318, 320
  precompetition, 117, 240, 347
  preperformance, **264**, **279**, 346, 348
  preshot, 27, 117, 260, **264**, **279**, 319, 322, 345–349
  putting, **264**, **279**, 345
  rehearsal, 322, 349
  stretching, 208, 217, 225
  warm-up, 166, 226, 232
rub of the green, 334
running, 118, 135, 138, 166, 312
rushed, 269
Ryder Cup, 123, 126

S
saliva, 166–168, 174
sand shots, 16, 80, 117, 339
school, 11, 68–69, 73, 76, 80–81, 86, 89, 186, 201, 204, 224, 226, 228–229, 241
screening, 113, 208, 216, 234–236, 238–242
SC-state, 301
SC-trait, 301
segmental control, 208
self-
  awareness, 71, 252
  concept, 353
  confidence, 71, 116, 167–172, 247–249, 257–259, 269, 276, **300**, 312, 342

conscious, 61, 260
discipline, 61
efficacy, 260, **300**, 323–324
esteem, 61
management, 240, 242
monitoring, 300, 345
paced, 264–265, 278–285
referenced, 290, 295, 297
regulation, 174, 234, 260
report, 167, 171, 204, 254–255, 301–303, 308–310, 326
talk, 71, 116, 118–119, 264, 266, 321–322, 338, 340, 342, 345
testing, 234, 238–239, 340
selection
  club, 31, 260, 346
  shot, 28, 260
semantic differential, 328–329, 334
senior golf, 10, 44, 50, **58**, 64–65, 83, 188, 192, 209
sequencing, 176, 183–184, 193, 199, 208
set-up, 25, 28–29, 33–34, 36, 46, 77, 80, 232, 236–237, 254, 265, 281, 285–286
shaft, 106, 177–179, 187
short game, 36, 64, 77, 80, 117, 186, 191, 259
shoulder
  mobilising, 226
  rotation, 188, 242
simulation, 29, 179–183, 320, 324, 348
situational factors, 173, 289, 292, 298, 301
skill
  acquisition, 4–5, 18, 23, 27, 31–35, 37, 40, 69, 76, 94, 116, 210, 251, 284–285, 324–316, 319–320, 347
  automatisation, 18, 266–267, 274, 279, 348
  deterioration, 213
  execution, 36, 264–265, 267, 348
  fine motor, 10, 15–16, 165, 333
  improvement, 10, 12, 15, 26, 61–65, 84, 110, 176, 213, 286, 317, 349
  level, 7–8, 22, 26–27, 31, 33, 58–59, 65, 108, 176, 186, 188, 193, 195, 254, 265–266, 274–275, 279, 282, 285, 294, 297, 313, 338, 344–345, 348
  profile, 231, 291, 339–341
  rehearsal, 225, 319–320
  testing, 113, 117, 308
  transfer, 40, 69
skin cancer, 131, 143–144

sleep, 15, 339, 344
slicing, 22
slopes, 28
smoking, 159
Snead, Sam 16, 36, 42–43, 56, 124
social
    comparison, 295–296
    relationships, 60
social-cognitive approach, 290, 298, 309
soft tissue, 188, 204, 209, 213
soreness, 201, 224
sound, 14, 43, 46–47, 313, 321
spectators, 173
spine, 181, 187, 190, 211–212, 217, 220, 232–237
splitting factor, 246
sport drinks, 135
sports medicine, 127, 215, 241–242, 349
spring effect, 177
SSCI, 301–303
stability, 26, 127, 207, 212–213, 215, 219–220, 235
    performance, 11, 44, 246
    routine, 266–267, 270–271, 273, 275
stage, 12, 24–25, 32, 64–65, 196, 210, 267, 275, 307
    of development, 41, 60
    of learning, 256, 285, 319, 321
stance, 16, 25–26, 32–33, 36, 47, 98
starting age, 10, 11, 13, 17, 40–41, 62, 64
state of mind, 27, 118
static posture, 211–212
statistics, 51, 55, 57, 113, 126, 178, 184
stochastic modelling, 184
strategic processes, 30
strategies
    alignment, 104
    attentional, 254, 280, 285
    cognitive-behavioural, 264–267, 342
    control, 268, 286
    coping, 60
    five-step, 286
    fluid replacement, 133, 141–143
    implementation, 68, 323
    intervention, 204, 233
    performance, 338
    planning, 45, 348
    practice, 315

psych-up, 164
rehearsal, 311–312, 318–319, 323
relaxation, 255, 319
strength, 5, 42, 113–116, **149**, 161, 177–178, 201–202, **207**, **231**, 320, 338
    and conditioning, **207**, 236, 239–241
    training, 160, 162, 201–203, 210, 214, 219
stress
    heat, 127–143
    management, 159, 284, 339, 342
    performance, **245**, 268, 276, 286, 343–345
    physical, **200**, 233, 239
    psychological, 164, **245**
    psychophysiological, **164**
    test, 202, 251–252
stretch
    80, 118, 187–189, **192**, 204, **207**, **224**, **231**
structure
    performance, 2, 7, 18
    program, 73, 84, 87, 89, 186, 240, 318–319
success, 3, 6, 11–12, 16–17, 36, 40, 67, 69, 73, 84, 104, 107–110, 123, 175, 184, 212, 229, 241, 249–250, 258, **279**, **289**, 301, 319, 325, **327**, 340, 345–349
sunscreen, 141
SUPER Program, 71
superstition, 21, 51, 288
support, 42, 49, 62–64, 71, 268
sway-back, 236
sweat, **127**
sweet spot, 22
swing
    changes, 187, **200**, 231–232, 242, 322
    computer, 116, 118, 180, 192–194, 216
    consistency, 23, 25–27, 31, 38, 176, 213, 215–216
    dynamics, 194
    faults, 118, 175
    feel, 34, 119
    improvement, 15–16, 26, 35, **94**, 116, 215
    mechanics, 25–26, **175**, **192**, **200**, **207**, 232, 242, 317
    model, 176, 180, 194, 214
    path, 36, 202–204, 208
    plane, 94, 235
    position, 195–196, 239
    rehearsal, **311**
    style, 25, 176, 214

technique, 119, 178, 186, **200**, **207**, 232–235
thoughts, 34, 254–260, 265, 287, 345–346
weights, 177, 187
Swiss ball, 116, 213, 217, 219–220, 222, 235–237, 240
synovitis, 202, 204

T

tactical skills, 113–114, 117, 339
tactics, 117, 338
tactile, 318
talent, 1, 2, 17, 40–42, 50, 60–61, 64–65, 84
 development, 40, 60
talented, 2, 10, 15, 25, 39–42, 58, 60, 64–65
target, 9, 16, 31, 40, 97–99, 105–110, 117, 119, 185, 196, 202, 205, 232, 236–237, 267, 269, 280, 284, 304, 317, 322, 340, 345–347
task orientation, 290–291, 294–297
task-involved perspective, 290
teacher, 7, 11–13, 15–16, 40, 49–50, 60, 64, 71, 80, 94, **224**, 282
teaching, 61, 65, **67**, 80, 83, 85–87, 90, 95, **175**, 213, 215, **224**, 284
 process, 186
 professionals, 83, 186, 213, 215, 226–229
technical
 development, 15, 50, 76, 116, 203, 207, 215, 219, **231**
 errors, 118
 fault, 208–209, 232
 problems, 208, 212, 215, 217
 skills, 113, 114, 116, 126, 234, 242, 339, 349
technique
 change, 113, **200**
 flaws, 200
technology, 92, 95, 125, 178
teenage, 38, 64–65
temperature, **127**, 167
 regulation, 131, 139, 141
tempo, 47, 257, 265, 267, 313, 322
tension, 21, 27, 141, 158, 160, 210, 231, 319, 328–333, 344, 346, 349
TEOSQ, 290–294, 296
testing, 34, 113–114, 117–118, 166–167, 172, 179, 202, 234, 252, 238–239, 305
thermoregulation, 134–147

thought control, 284, 342, 344–345
timing, 95, 113, 181–183, 208, 217, 266–267, 269–271, 275, 322
titanium drivers, 177–178
TOPS, 338–339
torque, 162, 179–183
tournament, 7, 23–24, 35–37, 47, 49, 70, 114, 117, **121**, 128, 141–142, 165, 168, 173, 201, 213, 225, 280, 330, 337, 343
tour professionals, 10, 20, 44, 51, 57, **58**, 67, 83–84, 114, 118, 122, 141–142, 176, 178, 184–185, 188, **192**, **200**, 207–208, 225, 232–233, 240–241, 277, 280, 285, 323, 345–348
trainee, 83, 86–87, 92, 241
training
 activities, 4, 15, 18, 49, 322
 extent, 2, 11–12, 17, 40, 84, 349
 facilities, 11–12, 40, 42, 64
 fitness, 114, 134, 136, 165
 frequency, 17, 42, 137, 318
 intensity, 41, 60
 interventions, **94**, **104**, **149**, **164**, 216, **264**, **311**, 339
 methods, 12–13, 186
 objectives, 50, 114, 348
 outcomes, 2, 4, 11, 31, 41, 49, 65, 149, 317, 320, 340
 pattern, 59, 61
 phase, 12, 40, 41, 85, 112, 116, 321
 physical, 113, 131, 137, 171, **207**
 program, 71–72, 80, **82**, 116, 137, 166, 186, 216, 232, 241, 268, 280, 311, 317, 339
 psychological, 116, 207, 219, 276, **311**, 334, **337**
 resources, 12
 structure, 318–319
trait, 61, 174, 299, 301
trajectory, 9, 23, 27–28, 46, 69, 282, 311
trampoline effect, 177
transfer
 energy, 189
 heat, 129–132, 143
 learning, 40, 69, 73, 317, 319
 weight, 217, 236
travel, 15, 80, 128, 142, 213, 233, 236, 240, 347–348
treadmill, 135, 138, 151, 165–166, 172
trunk
 control, 234

muscles, 189, 197, 209, 211
  rotation, 187, 204–205, 209, 217, 232, 236
  stability, 219–220
  twisting, 226
trust, 258–259, 267, 269, 322, 348
TSCI, 301
turf, 97, 203, 320
TVIC, 315, 323

U

updating, 77, 84–85, 89, 236
US Masters Champions, 124

V

values, 69–73
Vardon, Harry 24, 55–56
velocity, 151, 177–184, 188, 192, 197
verbal
  cue, 95, 286, 346
  feedback, **94**
  instruction, 317, 321
  persuasion, 301
verbalisation, 317–318
verbal-motor stage, 285
video
  analysis, 97, 116, 118–119
  feedback, **94**
  recordings, 48–49, 202, 320–321, 348
videotape, 38–39, 98, 106–107, 179, 219, 313, 321, 351
vigour, 10, 42–43, 328–332
violin, 13–16, 31–32, 42–43, 48
vision, 67–68, 71, 97, 101, 118–119, 312, 321, 325
visual
  cues, 286
  image, 48, 315, 318
visualisation, 80, 116, 321, 346
visual-motor behavioural rehearsal (VMBR), 348
VMIQ, 312–313, 324
VO_2 max, 135–137, 140, 165–166, 168, 171–172
vocational training, 86
Von Nida, Norman 84, 93
VVIQ, 315

W

waggle, 265, 346

walking, 16, 26, 37, 131–135, 138, 141, **149**, 165–166, 171, 214, 334, 350
wall thickness, 177–178
warm-up, 27, 76, 98, 150, 166, 203, **224**, 232, 234, 239, 322
water, 2, 127–130, 132–133, 136, 142, 151
Watson, Tom 20–21, 30, 57, 124
weather, 28, 30, 46, 125, 127–128, 293, 320
weight, 133–134, 140, 142, **149**, 165, 168, 210, 213, 217, 232, 236, 321
  control, 158–159, 213
  training, 115–116, 210, 214, 216–217
  transfer, 217, 236
well-being, 119, 164, 239
win, iii, 43, 64, 123, 168, 297
wind, 4, 23, 28, 128, 320
winner, iii, 12, **121**, 66, 168, 184
winning, 70, 172, 186, 296
Woods, Tiger 29, 40, 57, 59, 61, 64, 66, 124
workload, 158, 165, 171, 210, 216
worry, 35, 64, 167, 246, 249–250, 267, 304, 343
wrist, 179–184, 187, 191, **200**, 220, 232–233, 256–257
  break, 256
  injury, **200**, 232
  pain, **200**
  torque, 179–183

X

X-Factor, 187–190, **192**, 243

Y

yips, 256, 338
young players, 10, 13, 16, 39–44, 49, 60–65, 67, 86, **224**, 241, 285, 337–338, 340–341
youth participation, 67

Z

zone
  of optimal functioning, 263, 335, 344
  of optimal performance, 343–345, 347